Issue | 126

RADICAL HISTORY *Review*

Reconsidering Gender, Violence, and the State

Editors' Introduction

Reconsidering Gender, Violence, and the State

As emerging feminist scholarship and queer-of-color critique make clear, archives contain surprising histories about gender, sexuality, and violence, stories that challenge axiomatic, gendered oppositions of power and vulnerability. More than simply repositories of untold stories, archives reproduce, obscure, engender, and distort histories of violent subjugation, conditional accommodation, and creative resistance. This issue of *Radical History Review* unearths and deconstructs such bodies of knowledge in order to reassess conflicting narratives of victimization, subjection, retaliation, and self-defense that arise under, coincide with, and partially constitute forms of state authority.

Events and developments over the last two centuries reveal complex histories of race, gender, and violence. Long-term trends, such as the expansion and dissolution of empires, the growth and subsequent mitigation of racial slavery, the rise of the carceral state, and the emergence of decolonization movements, as well as more contemporary issues, such as the torture and abuse at Abu Ghraib and the recent mass kidnapping of girls in Chibok, Nigeria, reveal the state's complex, evolving role as enforcer, perpetrator, and/or protector. These histories remind us that gendered violence and gendered understandings of violence are political and intersectional topics of lasting significance. Indeed, during the months that this issue of *Radical History Review* was in production, activist scholars in the United States created the African American Policy Forum and launched the "Say Her Name" campaign to incorporate black women's historical and contemporary experiences into the growing movement against the nation's militarized police forces and their concomitant forms of brutality. The intervention represented by this project represents a complex admixture of historical longevity and politicized evolution characteristic of all of these stories of gender, violence, and the state.

Radical History Review
Issue 126 (October 2016)   DOI 10.1215/01636545-3594359
© 2016 by MARHO: The Radical Historians' Organization, Inc.

We came to this issue of *Radical History Review* with a number of interrelated questions: How have historically shifting conceptions of masculinity and femininity informed the persistence of and punishments for gendered violence? What do the archives reveal about the larger structural factors that perpetuate and engender violence? How have feminist and queer organizing efforts to protect and/or avenge victims further complicated legal, penal, and legislative efforts to address gendered violence?

The questions owe an enormous debt to earlier scholarship about gender, violence, and the state. Judith Walkowitz's path-breaking analysis of the Contagious Diseases Acts in 1860s England, *Prostitution and Victorian Society* (1982), alerted scholars to the unintended consequences of state action and regulation of female sexuality, showcasing the state's penchant for overreach, the resulting incarceration of suspected prostitutes, and the license such laws gave to harassment of women in the public sphere. In the United States, efforts to curb domestic violence foundered on stereotypes of the inherent "brutishness" of working-class men in the late nineteenth century and focused disproportionately on bourgeois interventions of "uplift," to a large extent sidestepping the social and economic roots of violence. Simultaneously, African American women developed a powerful critique of white rape of black women, and of its counterpoint, the rape-lynching narrative that posited all black men as rapists. A growing body of scholarship on the history of the US carceral state makes clear that more complicated readings of gender, violence, and the state are critical to any reconsideration of the state's power to coerce and control through gendered violence and the proposed abolition of the prison-industrial complex.[1]

Meanwhile, scholars of empire, ethnicity, and postcolonial studies have generated new understandings of the ways in which gender, violence, and the state interact. Scholars engaging in queer-of-color critique have laid bare the connections between the expansive western (neo)liberal state and the concurrent acceptance of violent suppression of "others" as suspected terrorists, as noncitizens, as postcolonial subjects.[2] Building on the longer history and contemporary debates and conversations about feminism, its evolving critique of violence, and some of its blind spots, the goal of this issue is to reanimate conversations about gender, violence, resistance, victimization, and the role of the state as arbiter among these categories.

Five separate but complementary sections explore these questions from different angles. Three feature essays dig deep into the historical intertwining of gender, violence, and the state in three discrete time periods and settings. Three interventions on antiviolence activism and the state explore the sometimes conflicting individual, state, and community approaches to antiviolence work. The five compact articles in "Ways of Seeing and Knowing Violence" offer new findings and new interpretive insights into existing and future archives of violence. A visual essay questions the validity of photographic documentary "evidence" of state violence against its own citizens. Finally, the issue's Curated Spaces contribution showcases a creative new approach to the project of antiviolence documentation. Together, these varied perspectives, approaches, and methodologies sketch out new lines of inquiry and sites of intervention. They demonstrate what can be gained by approaching the archives with new eyes and probing previous assumptions in ways that challenge received wisdom and familiar historiographies. While in some cases the authors push the limits of what the archives reveal, they nevertheless insist that we reconsider the vexing intersections between gendered violence and state power.

The three feature articles collected here introduce the key themes explored throughout this issue. The articles in this section uncover the role of violence in the carceral and militarized state, and they examine moments when women enact violence upon others, placing these actions in the service of political or personal agendas. They also raise critical questions about the ways in which some forms of media have employed narratives about violence to create and shore up ideals of femininity, masculinity, family, and heteronormativity. Together they investigate the mutual constitution and/or imbrication of gender, violence, and the state, with an awareness of intersectional factors that connect the three categories. Further, each provides detailed analysis of a place in time and a highly specific context, while reconsidering broader themes about the interrelationships among gender, violence, and the state.

The violent treatment of female prisoners was both inherent and invisible to the early development of the penitentiary system in New York State, as Jen Manion reveals through a close reading of two notorious incidents of violence used against female prisoners in the early 1800s. During this time, the idea of a penitentiary was in transition from one of a nonviolent, reflective space designed to promote redemption through reflection and prayer to that of the more familiar and punitive model that infused the modern prison system. Protestant reformers, imbibing romanticism and the Second Great Awakening's emphasis on individual redemption through self-improvement and good works, advocated "punishment without violence," a regime that included solitude (at the time deemed a nonviolent treatment), silence, and prayer as a means of "humane" correction of criminals, particularly female ones. Very soon, however, both male guards and female wardens found rationales, in the "masculine" or nonsubmissive behaviors of their Irish and African American prisoners, for the imposition of violence as an essential tool for prison control. Sentimental notions of female delicacy, in other words, gave way to the infliction of ever-harsher punishments, even for women, at times meted out by (female) authorities who banded together to protect their professional standing and authority and prevent legal oversight for their actions. In this case, the state eschewed its own highly gendered regulations governing the administration of violent punishments for and by women.

In a very different setting, Tomoko Seto shows how, nearly a century later, police authorities used violent means to contain Japanese anarchist and socialist women protesting during the 1908 Red Flag Incident in late Meiji Japan. Dubbed "anarchist beauties" by the Japanese press, a few radical, nonconformist women dramatized their defiance of conventional feminine gender roles with unconventional clothing and hairstyles and with unfeminine speech and behavior on the street, asserting their visibility within the socialist/anarchist movement. Their accounts of violent abuse by the police, evident at the time and further detailed in court testimony months later, exposed numerous contradictions in popular and media perceptions (and prescriptions) about legitimate gender roles, specifically relating to political power, visibility in public, and/or legitimacy as mouthpieces of a radical ideology and socioeconomic critique. Ironically, state overreach in punishing (i.e., jailing) the radical women generated lively media commentary that—at least in the short term—expanded the reach and inflated the importance of the anarchist critique, in the process attracting young (male) students intrigued by the activities and descriptions of female radicals. The enthusiasm proved short-lived, however; in 1910, the state cracked down on political radicals after the High Treason Incident and imposed a traditional gender order that effectively suppressed the women's expressions of political radicalism.

Josh Cerretti's article on domestic militarism examines the engendering of violence from a late twentieth-century US perspective, tracing the US government's rationales for military intervention abroad and military-style suppression at home. Through strategic invocation of threats to women and children, he argues, the government introduced something akin to a "civic family," enforced by masculine warriors and sanctioned by the state. To document this "militarization of heterosexuality," Cerretti juxtaposes four geographically diverse events: the Gulf War in Iraq (1990–94); the Los Angeles riots (1992); the siege in Waco, Texas (1993); and the bombing of the federal building in Oklahoma City (1995). In each case, Cerretti tests how well the idea of state "protection" of the innocent and vulnerable offered political cover for military or quasi-military responses to threats foreign and domestic. So, US intervention to prevent Iraq's invasion of US ally Kuwait was framed as a necessary response to the sensational (but later discredited) news accounts of the "slaughter" of infants in a hospital ward in Kuwait, rather than as a strategic deployment to secure access to oil-rich territory in the Gulf. Similarly, military-style crackdowns against unrest in Los Angeles following the acquittal of police officers involved the Rodney King beating invoked protection of communities and restoration of order from lawless rioters rather than suppressing legitimate outrage against a questionable verdict. Likewise, the FBI justified its siege and attack on the Waco Branch Davidian compound with (later discredited) stories of child abuse. Cerretti reads these disparate cases together as evidence that the US state frequently employs the protection of women and children to deflect criticism of a variety of militaristic responses to complex conflicts both abroad and at home. The twin ideas—the warrior as protector, the "womenandchildren" as victims—he suggests, have disguised the rise of domestic militarism in the United States.

The three essays in the "Antiviolence Activism and the State" section ask us to reconsider the efficacy and/or legitimacy of state solutions to gendered violence in the US context. They differ in approach, analysis, and range of solutions posited over recent decades: self-protection, community organizing, and reexamination of opportunities lost in the state takeover of antiviolence intervention through punishment. For example, Catherine O. Jacquet explores a period in the early 1970s when some activist women, inspired by the militancy of the Black Panthers and other radical organizations of the time, embraced a philosophy of self-defense as a means to female empowerment. Frustrated by the lack of organized protest against sexual violence and rape, and disgusted by the state's well-documented failure to win prosecutions in individual cases, a few women's organizations advocated female self-defense as an alternative to state legislation or prosecution. They believed that, through acquisition of personal skills (e.g., martial arts training, marksmanship), women could develop autonomy and reject governing cultural logics that conflated female subjectivity and victimhood. Rhetorically, these movements posited personal militancy as one possible route to political and social equality.

The personal approach emerged, in part, as a reaction to failed state efforts to tackle gendered violence during the same period. As Raphael Ginsberg demonstrates, anti-domestic violence initiatives since the mid-1970s abandoned the original community-based, structural critique for a law-and-order approach of state punishment. A 1978 consultation of the US Civil Rights Commission, influenced by feminists and antibattering activists, identified the root cause of domestic violence firmly within the traditional, patriarchal family structure and the dearth of economic opportunities and support structures for women outside the home. Conservatives quickly rejected the report's recommendations for federal, state, and local funding for services (safe houses, job training, and housing support for domestic violence survivors), however, as antithetical to traditional family. They pushed instead for a criminal justice approach that focused on punishment of offenders, without consideration of the ability of survivors (typically women and children) to survive outside of marriage, creating an inherent conflict between the need for protection from physical violence and the need for economic survival. Recently, activists have challenged both the state interventions and punishment ethos that took root in the 1994 Violence Against Women Act, instead advocating for renewed attention to a societal, structural approach to domestic violence.

Other recent efforts to address structural inequality, however, threaten to resuscitate rather than avoid the heteronormative patriarchal ideal. Xhercis Méndez explores community activism as an alternative to state-sanctioned efforts to bolster the patriarchal family structure, this time with a primary focus on the African American community. President Barack Obama's My Brother's Keeper initiative, designed to provide training, counseling, and other support services for young African American men at risk, she notes, ironically revives the largely discredited patriarchal bias of the 1965 Moynihan Report. Critics at the time, and since, have questioned Daniel Patrick Moynihan's assumption of a "pathological" black family structure as a cause for poverty, low educational status, and crime. My Brother's Keeper's embrace of Moynihan's approach, its espousal of a version of individual "uplift" for African American men, does little to challenge the structural causes of inequality. Community-based organizations such as Black Lives Matter and social critics like Julieta Paredes, by contrast, see addressing these root causes—high rates of incarceration for African American men, underfunded and/or highly segregated public education, limited training and job opportunities, a lack of affordable housing, and so forth—as central to efforts to address poverty and unequal justice. Again, it is clear that the state's primary investment in the patriarchal family, and a simultaneous commitment to punishment—the carceral-industrial complex—diverts precious resources from positive infrastructure alternatives and contributes to the failures of modern US antiviolence policies.

The five case studies in the "Ways of Seeing and Knowing Violence" section explore surprising new findings and/or critical reinterpretations of older materials in the archive of violence and antiviolence work. By focusing on the archive as a site of knowledge production, these articles recognize its role in shaping current understandings of gender, violence, and the state and its lasting imprint on future quests for restitution or reconciliation. These authors highlight the importance of critical (re)evaluation of archives and archive building, demanding a full reconsideration of what rightfully belongs in the archive, what has been excluded or overlooked, and/or what can be read in a more critical light. In the process, they caution scholars of the inherent unreliability and instability of existing documentation of violence and the need for greater attention to and intentionality in their compilation.

Reading case files from colonial South Africa's Cape Colony in the early 1800s, for example, Carla Tsampiras brings to light stories of enslaved women resisting and/or "provoking" unsanctioned violence at the hands of their purportedly feminine women slave owners. In the 1820s and 1830s, a series of measures designed to "ameliorate" the Cape Colony's slavery system, emerging from London, officially lessened and finally outlawed violence against female slaves. The measures rested on a highly sentimentalized rationale of domesticity and femininity emerging in England and throughout the empire during this period. In the remote frontier town of Graaff-Reinet, however, such restrictions collided with more ambiguous gender norms. Local officials charged with upholding the new rules lamented the newly empowered slaves (the "stubborn, masculine women") who resisted slavery's subjection. Far from embracing the prescriptions of feminine docility emanating from the metropole, mistress and slave alike fought hard, both physically and in court, to exercise and/or resist slavery's violent control. Enslaved women took their mistresses to court under the new measures, often at great personal risk or hardship, so as to highlight the violence administered by female owners in violation of colonial regulations. Read alongside the new regulations, these cases suggest that, in this remote stock-raising region at least, there was a profound gulf between expected and actual behaviors relating to gender and violence.

Likewise, Deana Heath explores the disconnect in twentieth-century colonial India between prescribed and actual practices of gendered violence, through her discovery of an anomalous presence in the archive: the sexual assault of an Indian man documented in legal records that otherwise avoided explicit mention of male rape. In 1915, the rape (and subsequent death) of Rahmat Musalli, tortured at the hands of minor local officials, was downplayed and ignored by the British magistrate and again on appeal, and it entered the legal archive on second appeal only because the Punjab Chief Court questioned the ruling, thus preserving details of the torture for the historical record. Sexual violence against men was neither uncommon nor unknown (if unnamed) in the colonial setting; it was not imported from Britain, Heath argues, but rather emerged in the process of colonization and assertion of imperial control over India, mirroring the gendered violence in comparable colonial settings designed to turn colonized men and women into obedient colonial subjects. The logic of colonial gendered power relations made it virtually impossible to admit that sexual assault of Indian men occurred because, in the hierarchy of authority, male rape called into question the masculinity and virility of the British imperialist and thus could not be named. As desire was transformed into discipline, however, so acts of sexual violation could be dismissed as torture. Only an oppositional reading of the details of that torture at the time allowed this particular case of rape to be preserved for later discovery in the archive.

In their study of twentieth-century Ireland, Jennifer Yeager and Jonathan Culleton provide another way to challenge the distortions imposed by a partial and/or incomplete archive. The erasure from the national archives of the Irish "Magdalenes," or women confined in religious Magdalene Laundries for pregnancy or other sexual transgressions, they argue, fosters a kind of cultural amnesia about the violence the women endured. Testimonies from oral histories gathered in the Waterford Memories Project and elsewhere do more than challenge the official suppression of the laundries from official Irish histories. More important, the oral histories make evident how laundry survivors themselves have begun to insist on their inclusion in the archive; their importance to the process of national remembering, acknowledgment, and healing; and the value of undoing the silence around their economic exploitation and incarceration in the name of Irish family values. The women's oral histories detail and corroborate years of coercive violence against women, but also they demand that scholars handle official archival materials with caution; only a full accounting and recognition of the "work" done by the laundries will allow the nation to come to terms with its own history of oppression of women.

Jessie Kindig also proposes a more critical approach to the imperial archive, in this case through a close, contextualized visual analysis of souvenir snapshots taken by US servicemen in post–World War II Japan and Korea. Using a single collection of more than 120 Kodak instant snapshots, she analyzes their exposure of the "violent embrace" of the two occupied nations by US military power in general and US servicemen in particular. The images appear to show men with Asian "girl-friends," but attention to the wider context reveals "what is outside the snapshots' frame," thus enabling the viewer to see beyond the camera's coercive lens. Read against the high incidence of rape, the photos, and their hand-written captions about "good pieces," force a clearer understanding of the role of the US military in promoting and defending servicemen's (transactional and/or violent) access to Asian women and the efforts of Korean and Japanese women to resist violent sexual subjugation. This kind of reexamination of seemingly benign memorabilia in the archives makes it possible to retrieve the unstated and unmentioned sexual violence underlying the banal and chilling phrases like "rest and relaxation" or "rape and restitution." Further, it demands that scholars remain vigilant in decoding gendered power relationships during wartime, particularly when the archives contain such partial evidence.

The need for care in extracting evidence of gendered violence from the archive is also vividly evident in Benjamin N. Lawrance's analysis of contemporary African asylum narratives and claims. Writing as an expert witness and legal historian, he reflects on the power of mimesis as a narrative strategy, allowing asylum seekers to invoke a current threat—Boko Haram—to bolster their claims of past abuse and/or future jeopardy. Perusal of a personal collection of letters from asylum seekers and their lawyers reveals the growing insertion of Boko Haram into asylum cases, even those coming from regions lacking Boko Haram activity, or citing past harms that predate the organization's existence. Asylum seekers' use of mimetic devices to strengthen their claims portrays Africa in ways that conform seamlessly to western stereotypes about Africa. Meanwhile, media accounts of dramatic (and typically unsuccessful) asylum claims constitute a parallel popular archive in process of formation, one that further reproduces and embeds the Boko Haram mimesis within the context of other, unconnected fears (e.g., genital cutting). The very present reality of the Boko Haram threat becomes obscured, as it comes to stand in for a host of other, unrelated potential harms, even as claimants insert "evidence" of gendered violence into the archive in ways that pander to western fears.

The collection's visual essay deepens this questioning and reexamination of the archive of violence through the refabrication of discredited photographs of "false positives" that the military in Colombia used to document alleged rebel militancy. By questioning the reliability of photographic documentation, the drawings make visible a scandal in which young men were killed, put into uniform, and left in public spaces for civilians to "document" (for reward money) the military's successful campaign against rebels. As Claudia Salamanca points out, the hand-drawn reproductions (by artist Luis Morán) highlight the photographs' illegitimacy—their demonstrable falsity, in other words—thus establishing an alternative archive to a body of photographic "evidence" that may yet be redeployed to validate future military brutality. If the photographs transformed the typically marginal and often developmentally disabled boys and young men, enticed away from distant homes with promises of jobs and other enticements, into hypermasculine "warriors" replete with the gear and costumes of war, Morán's new, more obviously fictive archive of drawings allows future historians to displace the discredited photos, together with the military brutality they were meant to legitimate. By highlighting the staged quality of the photographed bodies, as well as the discrepancies, or "anomalies," within each image, both artist and author insist on a more capacious archive, one that inspires reflection and critique of unchecked state power.

The significant role of the visual in antiviolence work is evident in Efeoghene Igor's Curated Spaces essay, a powerful conception of what an alternative to the archive of violence might look like. In an exploration of a series of photographs by South African photographer Zanele Muholi, titled *Phases and Faces* (2006–14), Igor reveals the artistic, expressive, and political value of establishing a new archive of violence, resistance, and subjectivity, one that both problematizes and resists oppressive readings and suppressive "disappearing" of antilesbian violence in post-apartheid South Africa. The photographs attest to the presence of lesbian women in South Africa, while hinting at a history of sexual violence largely ignored or unprosecuted by the state. Rather than reproducing pain, violence, and suffering, the photos detach the subjects from the national and local context, focusing instead on the faces, the subtle nuances of gaze and expression, as mute interrogators of viewers' failure to act, intervene, and/or protest. The portraits constitute a wholly new archive, one that emphasizes the subjectivity of the faces in the frame. Muholi's images and Igor's commentary remind us of the crucial importance of tending to the archive in process, building of bodies of evidence that truly acknowledge past injustices while gesturing toward a future of restitution and reconciliation.

Together, the histories, reflections, interventions, and imagery collected in this issue of *Radical History Review* reveal how gender and violence are mutually constituted categories of personal, political, cultural, and legal subjectivity. They further demonstrate how violence—and narratives of violence—have been used (and misused) to uphold, resist, or reshape the ordering structures of the state in a variety of national, geopolitical, and socioeconomic contexts. Finally, the pieces here challenge readers, viewers, and scholars to interrogate the archive as a site of knowledge and a body of sources, in order to construct a more accurate, and usable, past.

—Lisa Arellano, Erica L. Ball, and Amanda Frisken

Notes

1. See, for example, Judith Walkowitz, *Prostitution and Victorian Society: Women, Class, and the State* (New York: Cambridge University Press, 1982). On US antiviolence legislation, see Linda Gordon, *Heroes of Their Own Lives: The Politics and History of Family Violence—Boston, 1880–1960* (Champaign: University of Illinois Press, 2002); and Elizabeth Pleck, *Domestic Tyranny: The Making of American Social Policy against Family Violence from Colonial Times to the Present* (Champaign: University of Illinois Press, 2004). On antirape efforts of African American women from the 1890s, see, for example, Mia Bay, *To Tell the Truth Freely: The Life of Ida B. Wells* (New York: Hill and Wang, 2010); Gail Bederman, *Manliness and Civilization: A Cultural History of Gender and Race in the United States, 1880–1917* (Chicago: University of Chicago Press, 1996); Lisa Duggan, *Sapphic Slashers: Sex, Violence, and American Modernity* (Durham, NC: Duke University Press, 2000); and Rebecca M. McLennan, *The Crisis of Imprisonment: Protest, Politics, and the Making of the American Penal State, 1770–1941* (New York: Cambridge University Press, 2008). There is an abundant literature on the rise of the carceral state; for a few recent examples, see Michelle Alexander, *The New Jim Crow: Mass Incarceration in the Age of Colorblindness* (New York: New Press, 2012); and Talitha LeFlouria, *Chained in Silence: Black Women and Convict Labor in the New South* (Chapel Hill: University of North Carolina Press, 2015). On the new abolition movement, see Angela Y. Davis, *Abolition Democracy: Beyond Empire, Prisons, and Torture* (New York: Seven Stories, 2005).

2. See, for example, Chandan Reddy, *Freedom with Violence: Race, Sexuality, and the US State* (Durham, NC: Duke University Press, 2011); Jasbir Puar, *Terrorist Assemblages: Homonationalism in Queer Times* (Durham, NC: Duke University Press, 2007); and Christina B. Hanhardt, *Safe Space: Gay Neighborhood History and the Politics of Violence* (Durham, NC: Duke University Press, 2013).

Gendered Ideologies of Violence, Authority, and Racial Difference in New York State Penitentiaries, 1796–1844

Jen Manion

In January 1826 an Irish woman named Rachel Welch died in Auburn State Penitentiary, just one year into her three-year prison sentence for petty larceny.[1] Her death led to an investigation that exposed the chaos and violence characteristic of the early penitentiary. She became pregnant while serving time in what was supposed to be solitary confinement, and she was whipped by guards despite a legal prohibition on the flogging of women in prison.[2] The ordeal put the penitentiary on trial at a crucial moment in its history. Despite substantial evidence of abuse and mismanagement, investigators refused to conclude that Welch was a victim of wrongdoing. Rather, they relieved guards of responsibility and blamed Welch for disrupting the gendered and sexual order of the penitentiary.

A generation of reformers in the postrevolutionary period called for sympathy and reform for suffering and destitute prisoners. Thirty years into the great experiment in enlightened justice, there was a new subject in need of compassion: the white male prison keepers and guards who ran the penitentiaries.[3] One keeper reported that four women in prison made "more trouble" than the ninety-three men also under his charge. The same account also quoted the superintendent of New York's Auburn Prison, suggesting his predicament was even worse: "I have (says he) under my care, about four hundred and fifty male prisoners, and *nine* females; and I

Radical History Review
Issue 126 (October 2016)   DOI 10.1215/01636545-3594321
© 2016 by MARHO: The Radical Historians' Organization, Inc.

could cheerfully undertake the care of an *additional four hundred and fifty men* to be rid of the nine women."[4] These accounts circulated amid growing public debate over the purpose of punishment and harsh conditions faced by women in prison. The importance of addressing women's needs and rights in an institution chiefly designed for men was publicly mocked, while the white male guards gained public support and sympathy.

This essay examines the roots and legacy of violence against women in prison at the hands of guards and matrons during the first fifty years of the penitentiary in New York State. Though officially prohibited by law, whipping female inmates was practiced by numerous matrons and guards who were subject to formal investigations. While immigrant and black women were disproportionately victims of institutional violence, US-born white men and women dominated the staff.[5] News of violent encounters involving women generated voluminous and sensational headlines that outpaced coverage of the more pervasive and widespread violence against men. Coverage also raised questions about the merits of flogging, the discretion of guards, the competency of supervisors, and the rights of inmates. Two major incidents—one in 1826 and one in 1839—threatened to bring the system to its knees. Instead, investigators privileged guard discretion over law and authorized the expansion of the system. None of this happened without great conflict—internal to the prison and within the community at large—when inmates, guards, inspectors, reformers, and state officials squared off. The public debates over these two scandals helped establish broad support for state-sanctioned violence against prisoners—especially black and immigrant women and men, the central targets of the carceral state from the beginning.

In much of the voluminous scholarship on the origins of the penitentiary system, the particulars of racial hierarchies, gender roles, and sexual norms are deemed negligible in the quest to understand the expansion of state power. Important scholarship that establishes labor and profit as cornerstones of punishment in New York State, for instance, neglects the vital role of race and gender in shaping the institution.[6] Prisoners were compelled to work diligently and silently through force, coercion, and violence. Authority was asserted in a highly racialized and gendered way that reinforced white patriarchal supremacy, especially on the bodies of black women.

This essay contributes to a growing body of work by historians of race, gender, and sexuality who are rewriting this narrative. Estelle Freedman and Nicole Hahn Rafter first showed that women were subject to terrible neglect and abuse as tenants of the nation's first jails and penitentiaries. Many have looked to the work of female reformers and matrons who experimented with hard labor, redemptive suffering, phrenology, and domesticity in managing women in prison.[7] An imagined sisterhood among female inmates, matrons, and reformers, however, was never meant to be, as studies of African American women in prison reveal the persistence of racism in punishment. Racist ideologies defined to justify enslavement were later used to criminalize free blacks.[8] From early republican Pennsylvania through postbellum Georgia to Progressive Era New York, Chicago, and Philadelphia, black girls and women were disproportionately incarcerated and more harshly treated.[9] Research in the new fields of sexology and criminology were anchored in and also further promoted negative associations between African American women and masculinity, female masculinity and sexual deviance, and sexual deviance and criminality.[10] By examining the racial dimensions of the use of violence against women in prison during this formative period, we can better understand how racialized gender norms of patriarchal white supremacy structured the penitentiary, making the promise of American justice so elusive for black and immigrant women.

. . . . .

In the final decade of the eighteenth century and early years of the nineteenth, penitentiaries opened throughout the United States with a mission to reform criminals, abandon corporal punishment, and reduce reliance on capital punishment.[11] When statesmen, lawyers, judges, and reformers came together to devise a distinctly American form of punishment in the postrevolutionary period, the whole point was to eschew violence. Inspired by similar developments in neighboring Pennsylvania, New York revised its criminal law in 1796, called for the establishment of two state penitentiaries, and aspired to make punishment "proportioned to the different degrees of guilt."[12] This work was led by Quaker Thomas Eddy, who helped design and oversee Newgate Prison, opened in 1797 in Greenwich Village. Auburn Prison was later opened in 1818, organized around a system of congregate labor in silence by day and separate confinement by night. By 1823, the "Auburn Plan" was heralded as a model and adopted in numerous states throughout the country. This "success" inspired state officials to authorize construction of yet another prison. This new prison, opened at Mt. Pleasant in the town of Ossining in 1828, was built by prisoners themselves under strict supervision and threat of violence.[13]

Eddy, New York's leading prison reformer, was deeply engaged in the international debates among reformers and statesmen from across the United States and England. For Eddy, the key was to "govern" offenders through "kind treatment" and humanity while inculcating them with "industrious habits and moral sentiments."[14] The law stipulated that keepers were authorized to punish convicts only by putting them in solitary confinement—assumed to be a nonviolent punishment—and restricting their diet to bread and water. Even this punishment needed to be approved by two inspectors so as to prevent abuse and ensure that numerous reasonable people agreed to the proper length of the punishment.[15] The policy also stated explicitly, "No keeper or assistant-keeper is permitted to strike a prisoner." Punishment without violence would be the hallmark of democracy.

Eddy also served as Newgate's first agent and expected the keeper and his assistants to embrace their work "with a heart warmed by the feelings of benevolence" combined with an ability to be firm, resolute, dignified, and commanding.[16] Eddy offered an elaborate explanation of the particular way he wanted the keeper to punish inmates who broke the rules: "In the infliction of punishment, he should be calm and inflexible, without anger, so that he may convince the offender that he acts not from passion or vengeance, but from justice."[17] In fact, keepers and assistants were held to the highest standards of conduct, including refraining from "impropriety of speech and conduct" so they might serve as role models for inmates.[18] A special kind of person was needed to work in the prison, as the weight of the entire project of penal reform—and potentially the stability and order of the nation—would rest on the shoulders of the poorly paid white men (and later women) who would staff the prison. It was no secret that early reformers believed that "hard-hearted" keepers needed to be replaced with men of feeling who understood the sentimental project of prison reform.[19]

Even though guards were specifically prohibited from whipping inmates in the early decades, the system of oversight was still anchored in violence. One inmate was chosen to whip others into obedience—a disciplinary strategy commonly used against enslaved people. This "captain" served as the eyes and ears of the jailer. Elizabeth Munro Fisher, imprisoned for forgery and sentenced to five years in 1801, recounted that inspectors Thomas Eddy and John Murray "put the women prisoners under my command" during one of their visits.[20] Eddy confirmed this, stating, "One woman is appointed by the keeper to preserve order, and is styled the captain, and she exercised the whip on her fellow-prisoners at discretion."[21] Elizabeth, a white woman, would have overseen the thirty-five other women in prison at that time, including fifteen African American women.[22]

The formal ban on corporal punishment was overturned by a law passed on April 2, 1819, authorizing keepers to whip any prisoners who "shall refuse to comply with the rules of the institutions, or refuse to perform their daily task, or shall resist any of the officers of either of the prisons in their lawful authority, or shall willfully destroy any of the property." There were two conditions to the use of force: it was to be applied only to men and required the approval and presence of two inspectors.[23] This policy change coincided with a leadership change at Auburn. The new principal keeper was Elam Lynd, a military man who introduced stricter discipline. In June 1818 inmates rebelled against his changes, causing an uproar that required the military to quell. Over one hundred men were put in solitary confinement—an untenable situation.[24] Prison officials used the rebellion as evidence that greater use of force was needed to maintain control of the prison. Governor DeWitt Clinton wanted to build yet another prison more suitable for a "mild system of criminal jurisprudence," but the inspectors defended the wishes of their new keeper and prevailed in advocating for "a more *energetic* discipline."[25] The law granted considerable latitude for state-sanctioned violence against prisoners but left several questions unanswered, including how strictly the policy would be enforced and what consequences there would be for violations.[26]

. . . . .

The public responded to rumors of excessive flogging of inmates at Auburn Prison because it contradicted the promise of the penitential ideal: that punishment would be predictable, controlled, and rational—a counter to barbaric punishments of old Europe.[27] News that a woman had been flogged evoked even greater anger because it undermined the paternalistic vision of punishment. Anchored in Anglo-American republican family values, this view promised the largely immigrant, black, and poor white women prisoners protection from the white male state in exchange for embracing female domesticity, submission, and dependency.[28] Inspectors George Tibbits and Samuel M. Hopkins were ordered to lead the investigation of alleged prisoner abuse in 1826. In an investigation of unprecedented scope, they interviewed nearly seventy witnesses.[29] They found evidence of twenty-one instances of punishment "of a character to deserve investigation" in a nine-month span defined by the tenure of Mr. Goodell as chief agent of the prison. They concluded that eight of the cases were "justifiable and proper," while fourteen of the total were "severe," and four were "abusive and unjustifiable" (30). Even this degree of accountability was remarkable given the parameters of the investigation, as the investigators refused to hear the testimony of any convicts, stating, "We inflexibly overruled every attempt, to make use of the testimony of convicts; whether urged as testimony on oath, or as hearsay" (2). So even though the aggrieved victims were denied a voice, the violence committed against them was so great that other witnesses—chiefly prison staff with great incentive to protect each other and the state—testified on behalf of inmates.

Inspectors argued that it was for the public's own safety that the keepers resorted to violent means on so many different occasions. When an inmate named Rosenburgh "called out for liberty" in the dining hall, he was "struck down by a keeper." The inspectors chastised the citizens of Auburn who complained, and warned them that "if the prison had been broken, their houses, families and property" would have been destroyed (13). With each incident reported, the inspectors justified the actions of the guards in their report. After recounting horrific treatment of a man named Mastison, they suggested that people were naive to the real evil of prisoners who were cunning, manipulative, passionate, and the embodiment of "giant strength and demoniac fury" that must be properly disciplined and channeled (14–15). In this damning statement, the inspectors undermined the very principles of reformative incarceration that stood at the heart of the penitentiary project.

Only one of the twenty-one instances of abuse reported concerned violence against a woman, but the outstanding circumstances of the situation compelled the inspectors to dedicate twelve pages to recounting the details (19–30). In the middle of a vast report about a long line of abuses against men, they noted that the singular account of violence against a woman was "by far the most important" because it had considerable "influence upon the public feeling." Even without her direct testimony, reports of the treatment of Rachel Welch were indisputably terrible. Welch was born in Ireland. She sailed to Quebec in 1824. At some point she traveled to Rochester, New York, where she was convicted of larceny and sent to Auburn Prison on January 5, 1825, to serve her term. Welch was sentenced to a term of solitary confinement and became pregnant while living in isolation. Later, after she returned to the cell with other women, a turnkey punished her by "beating or whipping" her during her sixth or seventh month of pregnancy. She gave birth December 5, 1825, and died shortly after. Nothing is said about the fate of her child (4, 19).

Inspectors reported that the extraordinary circumstances of Welch's confinement were a result of the challenge faced by guards to find a proper space inside the prison for her term of solitary confinement. One testified, "For she must be kept in a room constantly warm, and yet without access to fire; and it is obvious that she must receive her food, and that some necessary offices about her room must be performed by men, or else women must be brought from a remote part of the prison to perform them" (19). Because women made up a minority of inmates, their presence challenged penal authorities, who could not figure out where to house them or how to treat them. Unable to enforce both the total isolation of Welch (per her sentence) and complete segregation from male inmates (per prison policy) they settled on cell 15, "a large room over keeper's hall" that also served as a storage space for "tools, cordate, lead," and other materials. According to testimony of the master carpenter, Samuel C. Dunham, this space was far from solitary but in fact functioned as a thoroughfare for keepers, turnkeys, and workers. He stated, "The turnkeys resorted to it often, for articles wanted; the deputy keeper passed through it often, to put away and take out convicts' clothes. I passed through it often for tools and other articles, and to repair the roof of the building." Despite this long list of workers who had unregulated access to the room, responsibility for getting Welch pregnant was laid on an inmate (137).

One of the inmates who worked as a cook was an Irish immigrant named John White who most commonly delivered Welch her meals. Several reports suggest that the guard charged with White's speedy entry and exit into Welch's quarters was not particularly vigilant, leaving ample time for the two to develop a relationship and also potentially have sex. Evidence that Rachel gave John a gift (a pair of knit suspenders with needlework that said "a gift of love from R.W. to J.W.") was used as proof that the two were intimate. The monogrammed suspenders carried tremendous weight in the testimony by suggesting that Rachel loved John. If this was the case, it was easier for authorities to assume that she consented to sexual intimacies with John rather than accept she may have been the victim of sexual assault by him, another inmate, or a guard. The interrogation into who had access to her room and why revealed numerous weaknesses in internal security and inconsistencies in prison policy (20).

Once the likely circumstances for Welch's pregnancy were established, questions turned to her beating and death. Accounts of Welch's aggressive behavior were recalled again and again to justify the actions of the keeper who beat her, Ebenezer B. Cobb. Welch was said to behave in a way of "outrageous passion, insult, and abuse, towards her keeper, accompanied with language in the highest degree provoking, profane, and indecent" (21). Cobb reported that others encouraged him to whip Welch, including Mr. Parks, the deputy keeper, as well as Dr. Tuttle and Dr. Bigelow. As Cobb's supervisor, Parks very well may have ordered him to whip her. His testimony showed he was unsympathetic toward Welch and actually held another woman responsible for the entire episode: Mrs. Goodell, wife of chief keeper Goodell. Hughes McCallen, a thirty-five-year-old contractor who worked at the prison for two years, testified to overhearing Mr. Parks complain, "Mrs. Goodell and her adopted daughter had been fussing about Rachel, bringing her tea and good things, which made her take airs, and caused all the difficulty" (115). Cobb had other excuses as well. Dr. Tuttle encouraged him to discipline her, stating, "Damn her, whip her, she is a troublesome, outrageous hussey; whip her," while Dr. Bigelow reported that Cobb asked him if "flogging would do her more good than medicine," to which he replied "in reality it might" (22). As if he needed another excuse, Cobb also contended that he did not know whipping women was prohibited by law (101).

There is no disputing that Cobb whipped Welch, only questions about the circumstances in which he did so, including which parts of her body he flogged, how hard he hit her, whether or not he drew blood, and if two black male prisoners pinned her down (she claimed they did; he claimed they did not) (23). Cobb reported that he used the two men as bodyguards for fear she might attack him. Welch's account of the encounter is recorded in the testimony of Dr. Tuttle, who reported, "She said she was held down by two big negroes, and whipped almost to death." Tuttle claimed this account was corroborated by Cobb himself, who confessed to that fact (24). This seemingly trivial point took on greater significance because the idea that a woman of European descent—even a poor unruly Irish immigrant—would be restrained by two black men signaled even further violation of the norms of racialized gender hierarchy that organized society.

Accounts from various keepers and doctors disputed the extent of Welch's injuries. The chaplain noticed that Welch seemed very sick and shortly decided "it proper to address her in some serious conversations" despite the fact that she generally laughed at him and lacked "female delicacy" (93–94). Her room was informally divided by "hanging up blankets" and shared by several other women, including an English girl named Betsy, an old Welsh woman named Elizabeth, and an old woman named Sarah who enjoyed talking with the chaplain. Dr. Tuttle reported her skin was broken in some places and "from her neck to below her shoulders, or towards the small of her back" was black and blue (25). Dr. Tuttle, the only one who seemed to support Welch and communicate her voice, was fired for his drinking shortly before the investigation. This fact was used to discredit his testimony (27). Dr. Bigelow blamed Welch herself for the injuries, stating, "I have no doubt she hurt herself as much or more by her struggles at the time, and raving and agitation afterwards, than the punishment hurt her" (26). He reported markings that were more contained and less dramatic. The inspectors concluded that the whipping did not cause her death.

Reports of Welch's flogging forced the public to reconsider violence against women by the state. The press was divided: some spoke of Welch's plight with passionate outrage and called for the firing of everyone involved, while others defended the right of guards to use violence in maintaining order. Use of corporal punishment for a whole host of subjects, from children and wives to those imprisoned or enslaved, was up for debate during the period.[30] Concern for the imprisoned and enslaved was part of a broader cultural shift in attitudes toward pain, including an awareness of the power of violence to elicit both excitement and revulsion.[31] Flogging was so tainted by its association with the brutality of slavery that prison officials increasingly felt the need to explain how judiciously and carefully it was administered. For those whose imaginations conjured up visions of bloody lacerations, the reports qualified that flogging was "never [administered] with such severity as to draw blood."[32] If slave floggings were brutal, irrational, and deadly, penal floggings would be fair, reasoned, and nondeadly. Just as abolitionists selected images of brutal violence for their antislavery tracts, those concerned about the excessive use of force in punishment turned to incidents of flogging to draw attention to prison management and state violence.

Men deeply invested in humanitarian reform efforts fiercely debated the ethics, utility, and consequences of corporal punishment inside the penitentiary. This was captured in numerous public exchanges between British and American reformers. Phrenologist Charles Cardwell entered into a debate between Philadelphia's Roberts Vaux and England's Edward Livingston to argue against lashing because of the effects that flogging had on the flogger, rather than the victim. Cardwell was unflinching in his view that this practice was terrible not only for penal authority but also for society at large. He wrote that flogging "tends to the extinguishment of all high, amiable, and honorable feelings in the hirelings who pursue it, almost as inevitably as in the convicts who are the subjects of it." To Cardwell, flogging represented humanity's basest animal instincts and pushed men farther away from the desired ideals of morality, virtue, and feeling.[33] While both state officials and reformers in Pennsylvania agreed with Cardwell's assertions, New York prison officials were not convinced that whipping inmates was the worst thing or that the cultivation of sentiment was a valued part of punishment.[34]

In concluding the investigation into Rachel Welch's death, the inspectors blamed neither the inmates nor the keepers but the project of reformative incarceration itself. This was a startling conclusion to a deeply disturbing investigation that was regularly reported in the press over a number of months. The inspectors decided that the attempt to make punishment less violent and more humane—and more appropriate for a modern democracy—was foolhardy. They blamed the chief keeper Mr. Goodell for being "too far infected by the feelings of those well meaning men in Europe and America, who, without actual acquaintance with the character of criminals, have framed theories grounded upon the good qualities of convicted felons." They chastised Goodell and Cobb not for breaking the law but for being too soft and naive.[35] Their inability to manage women prisoners was held up as even greater evidence of the failure of humane punishment. The idea that women were too much to handle and invited abuse, something widely promoted by inspectors, keepers, and doctors in Welch's case, prevailed.[36] This discrepancy between ideals of womanhood anchored in white middle class values—such as submission—and the behavior of actual women imprisoned created great anxiety and conflict for keepers and inspectors. It pushed Cobb to the brink, for if only Welch had obeyed him and submitted to his wishes, he would not have beaten her. Too many white men in authority believed in the unrestricted right of white men to expect total submission from women. Here we see an abandonment of the principles of reformative incarceration just as the movement began.[37]

In this single case, the optimism and hope that had defined prison management just a generation earlier was now replaced by a defensive cynicism that privileged the rights of keepers over other ideals such as humanitarianism. Though some states actively questioned the efficacy of corporal punishment, especially Pennsylvania, New York State commissioners reasserted "the power to administer prompt correction with the rod" was central to maintaining order.[38] But social order was violated by the very fact of imprisonment. Everyone understood that the idea of captivity as punishment was compelling only because of humanity's great desire for freedom.[39] The structure of carceral punishment was so unnatural and dehumanizing that it compelled human resistance. Enforcement of penal order required even greater violence to command total submission and obedience of its subjects. The belief that violence was the only way to maintain order in the penitentiary of the antebellum period was embraced to devastating and deadly ends.

. . . . .

Despite this turn, a group of reformers refused to abandon their effort to improve women's conditions in prison. They reported that the women in Auburn Prison were kept "in a large single room in the attic" with no ventilation. Over twenty women were crowded together in this room, "of all ages, colours, and crimes, without the means of discipline or useful employment." They recommended to Governor Clinton the establishment of a distinct institution for women.[40] White female reform-ers, inspired by the famed Dorothea Dix, also joined the movement and argued that matrons should oversee women instead of male guards. This idea was part of a larger movement to embrace "separate spheres" for men and women, an ideology that was anchored in distinctly racialized gender norms that marked white middle-class women as fundamentally peaceful, virtuous, and maternal.[41]

Officials relented and invited women into prison management, with mixed results. Reports of daily living conditions in the women's section were contradictory. The chaplain from 1836 to 1839 claimed women did not have access to religious services or reading lessons, while the matron claimed they received both.[42] Women were fed a diet of bread and meat for breakfast and dinner that was sometimes sup-plemented by potatoes, pea soup, or bean soup. Supper consisted of mush or bread and tea.[43] The women were definitely put to work more consistently and rigorously than previously. In 1839, of the forty-six women inmates, thirty-two labored on con-tract "binding and trimming hats" or "stitching, closing, and binding boots," while the others took up the domestic tasks of the prison, such as washing, hall work, and making all of garments for both male and female inmates.[44] None of this did any-thing to stop the expansion of violence in punishment. The system of discipline and authority ordered by the penal state would prove too great, violent, and debased for even the most virtuous of matrons.

In January 1839, the state legislature debated whether they should inquire about the accusations that prison punishments were cruel and unusual.[45] Alexan-der H. Wells, publisher of the *Hudson River Chronicle*, submitted a petition for a committee "to inquire into the management of the Mount Pleasant State Prison."[46] Numerous former male inmates who published pamphlets detailing their time in New York's state penitentiaries cited many abuses throughout the 1830s.[47] The press published rumors of abuses, including accusations that the agent profited from pris-oners' labor, prisoners were starved, prisoner deaths were swept under the rug, and vicious means of corporal punishment were used by the guards from "the scourging of men with hot irons" to "the laying open of heads with three foot rules."[48] A law passed in 1834 allowed for wider latitude on the part of keepers in punishment by "stripes upon their naked back with the cat" for any convicts who "willfully or obsti-nately" violated the rules of the prison. Certain parts of the body were off limits, including "the head, face, or eyes," along with special consideration to general health and limbs.[49] Articles calling for an investigation never challenged the need for pris-ons or punishment itself but emphasized the importance of consistency—that pun-ishments be "fixed by law" and not left to the discretion of a keeper.[50] The investiga-tion of Mount Pleasant began February 28, 1839.[51]

Once again, violence against women was a small fraction of the terrible abuses levied against prisoners, but it merits particular attention because it was committed chiefly by the female matron and her assistants—people hired explicitly to protect women from abuse. Numerous male guards were questioned about the behavior of the matron and the whipping of female inmates. Barton W. Powell, assistant keeper from December 1834 until May 1839, testified that he asked matron Isabella Bard how she kept order without flogging. He claimed she replied, "She could not get along without" the flog and that she did the flogging herself with either a rawhide or rattan.[52] Upon cross-examination, the counsel for the prison aimed to justify Bard's illegal action by establishing that she acted in self-defense of a black woman who was large, strong, and frightening. The prison counsel asked Powell, "Did she not tell you that the convict came at her with great violence to take hold of her, and that she caught up the instrument she used, and struck the convict in her defense?" and "Did she not say that the black woman was a large and strong person?"[53] Powell confirmed none of these things, leaving open the possibility that Mrs. Bard was lying. Most of the women incarcerated were convicted of larceny and were without histories of violence or violent tendencies. If they posed a threat to the matrons, it was likely their time in prison made them violent or threatening.[54]

Bard was no middle-class Protestant reformer. Born Isabella McNichol in Nova Scotia, Canada, in 1790, she married James Bard of Dublin, Ireland, in New York City in 1808.[55] Her husband died in 1828 at the age of thirty-seven, leaving her alone with seven children ranging in ages from three to nineteen. She kept a lodging house for "gentlemen" that served breakfast and tea for a number of years in New York City. Bard brought a libel case against a former tenant and ex-sheriff of London, who gave "her house and establishment a bad name" and declared her "a more worthless character." She won the case along with $6,500 in damages, no small sum.[56] The publicity also established Bard as a hardworking, astute, and respectable woman who was described in one account as "a widow lady of irreproachable character, and the mother of a large family."[57] She was hired as the matron because her son-in-law, Robert Wiltse, was the principal keeper at Sing Sing from 1830 to 1840, but she had proved herself more than capable. By the time scandal rocked the prison in 1839, it was no secret that management of the prison was a family affair. Wiltse married Bard's middle daughter Mary Romeyn Bard, and together they named their baby girl Isabella after her grandmother.[58] When the baby died at just fourteen months of age, a notice went out in the local paper inviting friends of the family to attend the funeral—at the prison.[59]

Robert Lent had worked at Sing Sing for nine years in various capacities, first as a carpenter and then as an assistant keeper in the stone shop, when he was called to testify before the committee.[60] He gave a detailed account of the violent abuse toward Jane Coffin, a black inmate, at the hands of assistant keeper Miss Green. Lent stated, "I saw a black female convict, tied up by her wrists to the gallery floor," at which point he went outside within earshot. He heard about a half dozen whips and returned to see "one of the female keepers standing by her, about a good striking distance from the convict, with a rattan in her hand, and I saw blood on the clothes of the convict on her back in two spots."[61] Not only did Lent provide a crucial eye-witness testimony for this graphic scene involving Miss Green, but he also verified the worst of it: Mrs. Bard, the head matron, not only authorized and witnessed Green's actions but also abused other women herself.[62]

If the testimony of the male keepers offered legitimacy to the complaints, the testimony of the women themselves, matron Isabella Bard and assistant matron Harriett Clark, provided powerful insights into the justification for violence.[63] Clark had worked at the prison since 1837 in several capacities, both as assistant matron and as instructor of women's work "in stitching and binding boots." When Mr. Wells questioned Clark, she admitted that she, Miss Green, and Mrs. Bard all punished female convicts by "tying them up merely." It should be noted that when women were tied up, it was often "in such a manner that their toes barely touched the floor."[64] When asked directly, "Did you ever see blows inflicted upon a female convict; and if so, by whom?" she replied, "I have, by Mrs. Bard and Miss Green, and I have myself." The questioning turned to the role of a male keeper, Courtland Lawrence, in punishing female convicts. Clark said he didn't really punish women but that the matrons called him to assist them in subduing another black woman named Sarah Rose Harris. Clark declared that Harris "rose upon us and declared she would kill us, and called for a large pair of scissors and declared she would stab us, both Mrs. Bard and myself" and that this is what occasioned them to reach out to Lawrence. Clark again contradicted herself when asked about the extent of Lawrence's violence against women. She said she never saw him kick or strike a woman but then detailed the violent encounter between him and Harris, stating, "I saw him strike at the same one I have mentioned, with a rattan he happened to have in his hand about a foot long." While the investigators sought to expose instances of violence against women, prison council used their cross-examination to justify use of violence, asking, "Was not Sarah Harris a strong, powerful woman?"

Isabella Bard was the matron of the women's prison for two years and was interviewed last. Bard testified to overseeing forty-six inmates, twenty of whom were African American. When asked, "What is the method of punishing the female convicts?" she replied, "I confine them in a dark cell, and sometimes tie them up." She stated whipping was only used for a three-month period of her tenure, at which point she "occasionally used a small rattan over all their clothes." Here Bard invoked a sense of maternal authority and feeling, suggesting she viewed inmates as part of her family in that she did not punish them any more severely than she did her own children. She maintained an exception, however, for black women, two of whom she said "now appear to be so refractory as to require punishment."[65] Maternal feelings had limits when the matrons were unable to pity or sympathize with their charges but rather retained a cold, fearful distance, as Bard did with the black women in her care.

Bard was asked about the beating of Jane Coffin by Miss Green that Robert

Lent described. She denied the beating and the blood but also sought to justify Coffin's punishment, saying "this black woman had been very abusive and insulting to her, and Miss Green reported her conduct to me." As days passed and Miss Green reported "she could stand it no longer," Bard claimed she "ordered Miss Green to tie her up, or have her tied up." Bard took the unusual position of claiming that even though she was very sure Green did not whip Coffin, even if she had, Bard was certain there would not have been blood.[66] Bard's denial saved her own career and showed that white women could rely on racist ideologies about black women as threatening to justify their own incompetence and violent behavior. Even though Bard tried to protect Miss Green with her testimony, Green was immediately fired. Rumors suggested Green was "too talkative" and shared secrets from behind the prison's walls too freely.[67]

The governor addressed the state senate about the contents of the report on April 16, 1839. He cited a long list of the most egregious abuses and condemned the entire situation. "If our system of imprisonment, with solitary dormitories and social labor, cannot be maintained without the constant infliction of such punishments as are disclosed by this report, it was established in error, and ought to be immediately abandoned."[68] Never were truer words spoken, had he stopped there. But the governor could not imagine an alternative and so proceeded to justify the extension and expansion of this disaster, concluding, "But such is not the case. . . . Equality and justice, kindness and gentleness, combined with firmness of temper, would, with very few exceptions, assure the cheerful obedience even of the tenants of our State Prisons." With this statement, the governor reasserted what Michel Foucault referred to as the "techno-politics of punishment"—the imperative that law must treat in a "humane" way the outlaw—the person who is "outside nature." This was not based on an idea of humanity that the law concedes in the outlaw but, rather, "a necessary regulation of the effects of power"—a power, in this case, strengthened by softening its public face and its enforcement.[69]

Coincidentally, just months after the findings were reported, New York opened the first women's prison in the country in June 1839. The new facility was first authorized in 1828 by Governor Clinton in the aftermath of the 1826 scandal that killed Rachel Welch. Women were ordered removed from the main jail and relocated to the women's prison, which would focus on the "softening and subduing" of the female inmates in a new, special environment.[70] Despite damning testimony aired during the interrogation, Isabella Bard was put in charge, creating a divided response. One news story declared Bard to be "a lady whose assiduous attention to the duties of her station, and successful employment and control of the wretched beings committed to her care, have elicited the most unqualified expressions of approbation and pleasure from all who have known them."[71] Her whiteness, along with her defense of the state, played an important role in her own promotion.[72] Other reports expressed outrage and disbelief that she remained in her position, stating, "It was proved that Mrs. Bard inflicted not only *cattings*, but *cainings*, upon female convicts, although the law expressly declares that female convicts shall not be struck or scourged."[73] They felt the inspectors went against public opinion in keeping her on.[74] In the grand scheme of the controversy, Bard was low-hanging fruit as the matron of the women's ward. The original investigation into prisoner abuse was stoked in 1838 by the Whig press in an attempt to overthrow the Democratic administration. The dismissal of Robert Wiltse satisfied most critics, as Wiltse would have been Bard's superior whose example she followed.[75]

It was also becoming clear that any system of imprisonment was too harsh and violent to be tamed. While Miss Green was dismissed, the justification of the future of punishment required the defense, protection, and ultimately promotion of Mrs. Bard, who was making $650 a year in 1841.[76] White women were increasingly hired as matrons in prison to care for the predominantly black and immigrant women imprisoned. The fact that they turned to violence themselves signaled betrayal for those who believed esteemed female matrons would provide council and a positive example for prisoners to emulate. The cult of white womanhood proved no match for the violent system of punishment that brought out the worst in everyone.[77] This dynamic was greatly shaped by slavery's legacy—a view that black women were strong, masculine, and a threat to white women. This legacy justified a great many abuses against black women in prison by white keepers, male and female.[78] The weight of this racist logic was so great that the newspaper trying to demand state accountability even neglected to report that one of the female victims was black in an attempt to gain more sympathy from a readership who might not see black women as vulnerable or innocent.[79]

Years later, a young assistant matron named Georgina Kirby captured some of the contradiction in white attitudes toward the plight of African Americans and the justice system in America. In one breath, she expressed outrage that black women were generally convicted to long sentences "on the flimsiest testimony," while in the next breath she described the black women inmates she worked with in overtly racist, animalistic, and even satanic terms: "They had the air of Amazons, with their dilated eyes and distended nostrils. When they threw their heads back with an impatient gesture, one almost expected them to paw the ground with their hoofs. Their eyes had the unreflecting character of the animal, indicating neither reason nor memory."[80] And so white women continued to dehumanize, vilify, and violate black women while boasting of their own benevolence in working as prison matrons.

The violence against black women that occurred under Bard's care and at the hands of her assistants, Clark and Green, was preserved in the historic record of the state senate but completely overlooked (or ignored) by white female reformers. The popular myth that women in New York prisons were never whipped was reasserted just a few years later and became etched in popular memory through the widely circulated words of the famed prison reformer Dorothea Dix. In her account of the treatment of women in Mount Pleasant, Dix celebrated the fact that "the lash is never used."[81] With the scandal erased from popular narrative, Dix and others like her could reassert white women as saviors of black and immigrant women in prison.

The plight of African American women in America's jails has been inhumane for a very long time.[82] Prisons in the postbellum South notoriously enacted multiple violences on their disproportionately black female inmates, much of this ill treatment justified using "preconceived ideas about black female promiscuity" that enabled abusers to blame the women themselves.[83] Violence is so common inside women's prisons in the United States that Amnesty International issued a report in 1999 citing a long list of human rights violations, from the denial of reproductive medical care and excessive use of restraints to sexual exploitation and humiliation in the name of security.[84] As we look back on an institution over two hundred years old, we can see a cycle of violence, outrage, and investigation repeat countless times, often resulting in a reassertion of punitive authority and an expansion of carceral reach. We wonder how a system named "justice" could continue to function as a source of injustice for so long. Prison abolitionists are challenging everyone to wake up—to see the fact that the system is *not* broken but, rather, is doing *exactly* what it was intended to do.[85]

Notes

Parts of this essay were first presented as a paper at the Organization of American Historians annual meeting in 2011. I am grateful for the remarks of the panel chair, Cornelia Dayton, as well as the comments made by those present, and the constructive feedback from the peer reviewers for the *Radical History Review*.

1. "(No. 1) List of Convicts Discharged from the State Prison, Auburn, by Expiration of Sentence, Death and Escape, from 1st January to 31st December, 1826," *Annual Report of the Inspectors of the State Prison at Auburn* (Albany, 1827).

2. "Appendix A, Report of the Commissioners, Directed by the Act of 17th April, 1826, to Visit the State Prison at Auburn. Made to the Senate, January 13, 1827," *Journal of the Senate of the State of New York at Their Fiftieth Session* (Albany, 1827), 19.

3. On suffering and redemption, see Karen Halttunen, "Humanitarianism and the Pornography of Pain in Anglo-American Culture," *American Historical Review* 100, no. 2 (1995): 303–34; and Jennifer Graber, *The Furnace of Affliction: Prison and Religion in Antebellum America* (Chapel Hill: University of North Carolina Press, 2011).

4. "Anecdote for the Ladies," *Bachelors' Journal*, July 3, 1828; *Socialist*, July 18, 1828.

5. For example, in 1827, fifteen of seventeen guards employed by Auburn State Penitentiary were described as "American born." "Appendix A," *Journal of the Senate*, 31.

6. Rebecca M. McLennan, *The Crisis of Imprisonment: Protest, Politics, and the Making of the American Penal State, 1770–1941* (New York: Cambridge University Press, 2008). McLennan challenges long-standing arguments that the prisons were not profitable, especially prior to the Civil War, but largely neglects race. Pennsylvania prisons were not profitable; see Mary Ellen Curtin, "State of the Art: The New Prison History," *Labor: Studies in Working-Class History of the Americas* 8, no. 3 (2011): 106–7. See also Michael

Meranze, *Laboratories of Virtue: Punishment, Revolution, and Authority in Philadelphia, 1760–1835* (Chapel Hill: University of North Carolina Press, 1996), 226–27; and Jen Manion, *Liberty's Prisoners: Carceral Culture in Early America* (Philadelphia: University of Pennsylvania Press, 2015), 33–47.

7. Estelle Freedman, *Their Sisters' Keepers: Women's Prison Reform in America, 1830–1930* (Ann Arbor: University of Michigan Press, 1984); Nicole Rafter, *Partial Justice: Women, Prisons, and Social Control* (Boston: Northeastern University Press, 1985); Estelle Freedman, *Maternal Justice: Miriam Van Waters and the Female Reform Tradition* (Chicago: University of Chicago Press, 1996); Anne Butler, *Gendered Justice in the American West: Women Prisoners in Men's Penitentiaries* (Champaign: University of Illinois Press, 1997); L. Mara Dodge, *"Whores and Thieves of the Worst Kind": A Study of Women, Crime, and Prisons, 1835–2000* (DeKalb: Northern Illinois University Press, 2006); Susan Branson, *Dangerous to Know: Women, Crime, and Notoriety in the Early Republic* (Philadelphia: University of Pennsylvania Press, 2008).

8. See Jeannine Marie DeLombard, *In the Shadow of the Gallows: Race, Crime, and American Civic Identity* (Philadelphia: University of Pennsylvania Press, 2012).

9. Leslie Patrick-Stamp, "Numbers That Are Not New: African Americans in the Country's First Prison, 1790–1835," *Pennsylvania Magazine of History and Biography* 119, no. 1/2 (1995): 95–128; Kali Gross, *Colored Amazons: Crime, Violence, and Black Women in the City of Brotherly Love, 1880–1910* (Durham, NC: Duke University Press, 2006); Cheryl D. Hicks, *Talk with You Like a Woman: African American Women, Justice, and Reform in New York, 1890–1935* (Chapel Hill: University of North Carolina Press, 2010); Tera Agyepong, "Aberrant Sexualities and Racialised Masculinisation: Race, Gender and the Criminalisation of African American Girls at the Illinois Training School for Girls at Geneva, 1893–1945," *Gender and History* 25, no. 2 (2013): 270–93; Talitha LeFlouria, *Chained in Silence: Black Women and Convict Labor in the New South* (Chapel Hill: University of North Carolina Press, 2015).

10. Lisa Duggan, *Sapphic Slashers: Sex, Violence, and American Modernity* (Durham, NC: Duke University Press, 2000); Cesare Lombroso, Geglielmo Ferrero, Nicole Hahn Rafter, and Mary Gibson, *Criminal Woman, the Prostitute, and the Normal Woman* (Durham, NC: Duke University Press, 2004); Regina Kunzel, *Criminal Intimacy: Prison and the Uneven History of Modern American Sexuality* (Chicago: University of Chicago Press, 2008); Kali Gross, "African American Women, Mass Incarceration, and the Politics of Reform," *Journal of American History* 102, no. 1 (2015): 25–33. Also see Kali N. Gross and Cheryl D. Hicks, eds., "Gendering the Carceral State: African American Women, History, and the Criminal Justice System," special issue, *Journal of African American History* 100, no. 3 (2015).

11. There is an extensive literature on the transformation of punishment in early America. See David Rothman, *Discovery of the Asylum: Social Order and Disorder in the New Republic* (Boston: Little, Brown, 1971); Michael Ignatieff, *A Just Measure of Pain: The Penitentiary in the Industrial Revolution, 1750–1850* (New York: Pantheon, 1978); Michael S. Hindus, *Prison and Plantation: Crime, Justice, and Authority in Massachusetts and South Carolina, 1767–1878* (Chapel Hill: University of North Carolina Press, 1980); Meranze, *Laboratories of Virtue*; Mark Kann, *Punishment, Prisons, and Patriarchy: Liberty and Power in the Early American Republic* (New York: New York University Press, 2005); McLennan, *Crisis of Imprisonment*; and Michele Lise Tarter and Richard Bell, eds., *Buried Lives: Incarcerated in Early America* (Athens: University of Georgia Press, 2012).

12. New York State, *Collection of Penal Laws and Laws Concerning the State Prison* (New York, 1799), 3.

13. Orlando F. Lewis, *The Development of American Prisons and Prison Customs 1776–1845* (Albany, NY, 1922), 109.

14. *A View of the New York State Prison in the City of New-York by a Member of the Institution* (New York, 1815), 15.

15. New York State, *Collection of Penal Laws*, 17.

16. Thomas Eddy, *An Account of the State Prison or Penitentiary House in the City of New York* (New York, 1801), 25–26.

17. Ibid., 26–27.

18. Ibid., 28.

19. In Philadelphia, inmates tried to exploit the gap between keepers and inspectors by instigating conflict between the two. See Jennifer Lawrence Janofsky, "'Hopelessly Hardened': The Complexities of Penitentiary Discipline at Pennsylvania's Eastern State Penitentiary," in Tarter and Bell, *Buried Lives*, 106–23. For more on class struggle, see Heather Ann Thompson, "Rethinking Working-Class Struggle through the Lens of the Carceral State: Toward a Labor History of Inmates and Guards," *Labor Studies in Working-Class History of the Americas* 8, no. 3 (2011): 26.

20. Elizabeth Munro Fisher, *Memoirs* (New York, 1810), 40–41.

21. Thomas Eddy, Peter Augustus Jay, John H. Hobart, and J Morton, "Report, December 26, 1809," *Theophilanthropist*, February 1, 1810.

22. "New York, March 9. Abstract of the Annual Account of Prisoners in the State Prison," *Gazette of the United States*, March 12, 1802. By 1817, there were nineteen white women and twenty-nine black women. "Annual Census," *Commercial Advertiser*, May 14, 1817.

23. "Appendix A," *Journal of the Senate*, 5.

24. Scott Christianson, *With Liberty for Some: Five Hundred Years of Imprisonment in America* (Boston: Northeastern University Press, 1998), 111–12.

25. "No. 120 in Senate, April 11, 1846, Report of the committee on State prisons, on petitions praying for a law abolishing the sue of the whip in our penitentiaries," *Documents of the Senate of the State of New York, Sixty-Ninth Session, 1846* 4 (Albany, 1846): 4–5.

26. "Appendix A," *Journal of the Senate*, 6–7.

27. Michael Meranze, "Penitential Ideal in Eighteenth-Century Philadelphia," *Pennsylvania Magazine of History and Biography* 108, no. 4 (1984): 419–50.

28. Manion, *Liberty's Prisoners*, chap. 2; Kann, *Punishment, Prisons, and Patriarchy*.

29. "Appendix A," *Journal of the Senate*, 4. Further cites to this work in this section appear in parentheses in text.

30. Myra C. Glenn, "Wife-Beating: The Darker Side of Victorian Domesticity," *Canadian Review of American Studies* 15, no. 1 (1984): 17–33; Kelly Birch and Thomas C. Buchanan, "The Penalty of a Tyrant's Law: Landscapes of Incarceration during the Second Slavery," *Slavery and Abolition* 34, no. 1 (2013): 22–38.

31. Halttunen, "Humanitarianism."

32. "Auburn State Prison," *Ohio Monitor*, June 2, 1830.

33. Charles Caldwell, *New Views of Penitentiary Discipline, and Moral Education and Reform* (Philadelphia, 1829), 4.

34. Graber, *Furnace of Affliction*, 107.

35. "Appendix A," *Journal of the Senate*, 30.

36. One way to deflect accountability among men is to hold "female victims responsible for their role in their own victimization"; see Nancy Berns, "Degendering the Problem and Gendering the Blame: Political Discourse on Women and Violence," *Gender and Society* 15, no. 2 (2001): 269.

37. In Rothman's *Discovery of the Asylum*, this movement had just begun. Michael Meranze shows the movement's origins in the revolutionary period in *Laboratories of Virtue*. Most studies look to the origins and expansion of reformative justice throughout the nineteenth century and consider its failings in the twentieth.

38. Pennsylvania reformers published extensively on the use of whipping and flogging. See *Pennsylvania Journal of Prison Discipline* 1 and 2 (1845 and 1846); and "Appendix A," *Journal of the Senate*, 8.

39. Benjamin Rush, *An Enquiry into the Effects of Public Punishments upon Criminals and upon Society. Read in the Society for Promoting Political Enquiries* (Philadelphia, 1787).

40. *Annual Report of the Inspectors of the Auburn State Prison: Made to the Senate, January 26, 1829* (Albany, 1829), 7.

41. "Separate spheres" ideology was highly raced and classed; see Carroll Smith-Rosenberg, "Female World of Love and Ritual," *Signs: Journal of Women in Culture and Society* 1, no. 1 (1975): 1–29; Nancy Cott, *Bonds of Womanhood: "Woman's Sphere" in New England, 1780–1835* (New Haven, CT: Yale University Press, 1977); and Jacqueline Jones, *Labor of Love, Labor of Sorrow: Black Women, Work, and the Family from Slavery to the Present* (New York: Basic Books, 1985).

42. "Testimony Taken by the Committee Appointed by the Senate to Investigate the Affairs of the Auburn and Mount Pleasant State Prison," *Documents of the Senate of the State of New York, Sixty-Third Session* 2, no. 48 (1840): 297.

43. Ibid., 296.

44. Ibid., 300.

45. "Legislature of New-York. In Senate–Thursday, Jan. 24," *Commercial Advertiser*, January 26, 1839.

46. "In Assembly—Jan 24," *Hudson River Chronicle*, February 5, 1839.

47. Graber, *Furnace of Affliction*, 113.

48. "Sing Sing, Feb 7, 1839," *Hudson River Chronicle*, February 12, 1839.

49. "Testimony," *Documents of the Senate*, 104.

50. "Sing-Sing State Prison."

51. "State Prison Investigation," *New York Spectator*, March 21, 1839.

52. "Testimony," *Documents of the Senate*, 148, 150.

53. Ibid., 152.

54. Nicole Hahn Rafter, "Prisons for Women, 1790–1980," *Crime and Justice* 5 (1983): 143.

55. Isabella Bard, 1860 and 1870 United States Federal Census, Village of Sing Sing, Town of Ossining, Westchester County, New York, Ancestry.com (December 8, 2015).

56. "United States Circuit Court New York Isabella Bard vs. Joseph W. Parkins," *Daily National Intelligencer*, April 16, 1833; "Slander," *Boston Commercial Gazette*, April 15, 1833.

57. "Slander," *Alexandria Gazette*, April 16, 1833.

58. George Hill Bottome, *An Unvested Sister: Recollections of Mary Wiltse* (New York, 1891).

59. "Died," *Hudson River Chronicle*, August 28, 1838.

60. "Testimony," *Documents of the Senate*, 176.

61. Ibid., 179.

62. Ibid., 181.

63. Ibid., 173–74.

64. W. David Lewis, "The Female Criminal and the Prisons of New York, 1825–1845," *New York History* 42, no. 3 (1961): 231.

65. "Testimony," *Documents of the Senate*, 299–301.

66. Ibid., 300.

67. "How Is This?," *Hudson River Chronicle*, March 19, 1839, and *Eason Gazette*, April 20, 1839.

68. "Sing-Sing State Prison. The Governor's Message to the Senate," *Albany Evening Journal*, April 26, 1839.

69. Michel Foucault, *Discipline and Punish: The Birth of the Prison* (New York: Vintage, 1995), 92.

70. "Female State Prison," *Commercial Advertiser*, June 24, 1839.

71. "Female State Prison," *New York Spectator*, June 27, 1839.

72. Black women with claims to respectability through marriage, employment, or faith often struggled to be seen as sympathetic figures in the face of state violence. See Hicks, *Talk with You like a Woman*, 73–80.

73. "We have received a long and well written communication," *Hudson River Chronicle*, November 17, 1840.

74. "Hon. Frederick A. Tallmadge," *Hudson River Chronicle*, February 16, 1841.

75. W. David Lewis, *From Newgate to Dannemore: The Rise of the Penitentiary in New York, 1796–1848* (Ithaca, NY: Cornell University Press, 1965), 204–9.

76. "Hon. Frederick A. Tallmadge."

77. Carroll Smith Rosenberg, "Beauty, the Beast, and the Militant Woman: A Case Study of Sex Roles and Social Stress in Jacksonian America," *American Quarterly* 23, no. 4 (1971): 562–84; Nancy A. Hewitt, "Taking the True Woman Hostage," *Journal of Women's History* 14, no. 1 (2002): 156–62; Stephanie Camp, "'Ar'n't I a Woman?': In the Vanguard of the History of Race and Sex in the United States," *Journal of Women's History* 19, no. 2 (2007): 146–50.

78. Hicks, *Talk with You like a Woman*, 66, 125–27.

79. "How Is This?," *Easton Gazette*, April 20, 1839.

80. Georgiana Bruce Kirby, *Years of Experience: An Autobiographical Narrative* (New York, 1887), 200–202.

81. Rafter, "Prisons for Women," 140.

82. See Angela Y. Davis, *The Meaning of Freedom and Other Difficult Dialogues* (San Francisco: City Lights Books, 2012); Beth Ritchie, *Arrested Justice: Black Women, Violence, and America's Prison Nation* (New York: New York University Press, 2012); and Jill A. McCorkel, *Breaking Women: Gender, Race, and the New Politics of Imprisonment* (New York: New York University Press, 2013).

83. Talitha LeFlouria, "'The Hand That Rocks the Cradle Cuts Cordwood': Exploring Black Women's Lives and Labor in Georgia's Convict Camps, 1865–1917," *Labor: Studies in Working-Class History of the Americas* 8, no. 3 (2011): 61; LeFlouria, *Chained in Silence*.

84. "'Not Part of My Sentence': Violations of the Human Rights of Women in Custody," Amnesty International, February 28, 1999, www.amnestyusa.org/node/57783; Michelle VanNatta, "Conceptualizing and Stopping State Sexual Violence against Incarcerated Women," *Social Justice* 37, no. 1 (2010–11): 27–52; Angela Y. Davis and Cassandra Shaylor, "Race, Gender, and the Prison Industrial Complex California and Beyond," *Meridians: Feminism, Race, Transnationalism* 2, no. 1 (2001): 1–25.

85. This argument has been popularized by the organization *Critical Resistance* (criticalresistance.org).

"Anarchist Beauties" in Late Meiji Japan

Media Narratives of Police Violence
in the Red Flag Incident

Tomoko Seto

On June 22, 1908, in Tokyo's Kanda area, fourteen socialists were arrested for carrying red flags with anarchist slogans and fighting with police officers in the street outside the Kinkikan meeting hall, where a socialist gathering had been held immediately prior to the arrests.[1] This, the so-called Red Flag Incident, is known today as the beginning of the severe persecution of radicals that later escalated into the 1910 High Treason Incident—the nationwide mass arrest of socialists and anarchists and the subsequent execution of twelve individuals for allegedly plotting to assassinate the Meiji emperor.[2] Immediately after the Red Flag Incident, however, a few major newspapers focused on four young female socialists among those arrested, dramatizing them as "anarchist beauties" who daringly brawled with policemen in the street.[3] Two months later, one article on their trial, titled "Full House, Sold-Out Trial," reported that four hundred spectators had filled the courtroom while another hundred had loitered in the hallway outside the door.[4] During the trial, new reports of their testimony about the severe police brutality highlighted both the women's own physical frailty and their righteous devotion to their political cause. Images of women fighting policemen in the street and dramatic accounts of police violence in the courtroom marked the Red Flag Incident as an unprecedented event, one that caught the attention of bystanders and the media and blurred the boundary between entertainment and politics.

Radical History Review

Issue 126 (October 2016)   DOI 10.1215/01636545-3594333

© 2016 by MARHO: The Radical Historians' Organization, Inc.

This article examines the Red Flag Incident as represented in popular news-papers, with a particular focus on the media's narrative appropriation of police vio-lence inflicted on the female activists. Though the newspapers generally treated these women as criminals, the gendered popular media portrayal of the fight and the subsequent court trials at once helped disseminate these activists' dissident mes-sages and advertise their political activities to a broad range of readers. These media narratives emerged as the result of an accidental entanglement of different assump-tions and intentions unwittingly forged by journalists, male and female activists, state authorities, and spectators; no single agent can be identified as the sole instiga-tor of the emergence of such ambiguous representations. By describing the battle between the police and the female socialists with curiosity and amazement, the newspapers became an accomplice to the broad dissemination of socialism. These narratives of police violence also eventually inspired the intensified state persecu-tion of radicals and spurred the political engagement of women with the news media that began in the 1910s.

Historians of modern nation-states have studied the homogenizing functions inherent in newspaper media as one vital force reiterating norms regarding variables such as gender, class, and nationalism. As Lisa Duggan points out, modern cultural narratives, in particular popular newspapers, can profoundly devalue the political meaning of women's struggles and demands for change.[5] In the context of the late Meiji period (1868–1912), scholars of cultural studies in Japan have also discussed the print media's discriminatory nature, which reiterated the norms and boundar-ies of the imperial nation-state.[6] Indeed, the turbulent years following the media fever of the Russo-Japanese War (1904–5) against the background of the spread of literacy through compulsory education saw a flood of sensational news and scandals in newspapers, simultaneously entertaining and disciplining readers of all classes.[7] In this context, it is indeed possible to view the portrayal of these female socialists as an example of dominant narratives reducing their appearance to a joke and reinforc-ing gender ideology. As I will demonstrate, however, the end of the war with Russia also inspired the popular media to accuse the government of incompetence in deal-ing with the social inequalities caused by loss of family members and high taxes for war contributions. The advent of modern media gave rise to not simply a unidirec-tional dominance between those in power and those subject to power but a constant and contingent series of interactions and ideas involving different actors. Just as the American sporting press helped Victoria Woodhull bring "the idea of sexual hygiene activists into the commercial public sphere" in the late nineteenth century, media coverage of the arrested female anarchists made overtly dissident activists visible in the eyes of the public.[8]

Historians of modern Japan generally examine the Red Flag Incident and police violence within the history of Japanese socialism using police sources and male activists' own accounts. Such studies have often ignored the female activists and have instead stressed police persecution and the unusually harsh sentences given to male leaders.[9] Scholars of women's history in Japan have traced the socialist women's activities and writings to identify them as the "pioneering" feminists but have also overlooked their media portrayal in the Red Flag Incident, presumably judging that it was mere gossip constructed by male writers.[10] Assuming that the movement was mostly limited to a circle of elite activists and their sympathizers, these studies have paid little attention to the popular media narratives in the context of largely shared resentment toward the police, which greatly affected the tone of the news reports. In sum, in treating the popular media as either a disciplining apparatus or gossip entertainment, scholars of both cultural studies and activist history in modern Japan have failed readers.

Popular newspaper depictions of the Red Flag Incident demonstrate that the media did not merely depoliticize the female activists but in fact simultaneously dramatized them and spread their politics, regardless of reporters' intentions. These representations also help us understand perceptions of activism in general—activism that provided one option for late Meiji people to protest against violent authority. By studying the political potential of these seemingly apolitical popular media portrayals, I also challenge the general hierarchical assumption of what counts as "political" content—empirical facts primarily involving famous male activists and "serious" essays written by activists themselves. When assessing the significance of activism, popular media representations of female activists have rarely been included in the realm of the political. But the media plays a role beyond that of a disciplining apparatus, and its widespread influence might inspire collective action. In what follows, I first discuss media depictions of the incident focusing on the female socialists, then analyze the socialists' responses in their own publications, and finally explore the popular media reports on police brutality described in the testimony of the female activists during their trials.

The "Anarchist Beauties" versus Policemen

The Red Flag Incident took place immediately after an "out-of-jail" celebration party at the Kinkikan meeting hall for the socialist activist Yamaguchi Koken (1883–1920).[11] During Yamaguchi's jail term in 1907, an internal conflict had divided leading socialists into the "law-abiding" faction and the "direct-action" faction, led by the radical intellectual Kōtoku Shūsui (1871–1911), which favored syndicalism. From that point on, the debates between the two factions intensified, and police persecution of the direct-action activists became severe. Because Yamaguchi had missed the internal conflict while serving his sentence, his return from jail brought both factions together and resulted in a relatively large socialist gathering. When the attendees dispersed in the late afternoon, some of the direct-action activists left the venue singing revolutionary songs and raising red flags that read "Anarcho-Communism" and "Communism." Policemen at once rushed to stop them, causing a large-scale fight and instantly attracting a crowd of bystanders along the bustling street of Kanda.

Most of the activists who were arrested in the incident had been involved with the socialist press Heiminsha (Commoners' Society, 1903–5), including one of its cofounders, Sakai Toshihiko (1871–1933). Today, the Heiminsha is widely known as the most notable pacifist group opposing the Russo-Japanese War and as Japan's first large-scale nationwide network of socialists advocating equality, socialism, and pacifism.[12] Though the government forced the group's dissolution in 1905 before the end of the war, leading Heiminsha personnel organized the Japan Socialist Party (1906–7) and continued to engage in political activities.

Since their introduction from the West to Japan in the 1890s, the ideas that contemporaries referred to as socialism included various theories, such as Marxism, so-called utopian socialisms, Christian pacifism, syndicalism, and Russian anarchist-style terrorism. Because those who openly identified themselves as socialists like-wise held eclectic visions from which they critiqued capitalism and imperialism, socialism in the period can better be described with reference to "socialistic activi-ties and thoughts." Though the term requires detailed contextualization, the media and the police alike at the time of the Red Flag incident usually used *socialist* to refer to an activist involved with the Heiminsha and its successor organizations, and *anarchist* for a member of the direct-action faction. Hereafter I will use the term *socialists* and *anarchists* as the media depicted these activists and as they called themselves.

Initially, journalists' reactions to the Red Flag Incident differed greatly; some depicted those involved as insane and immoral criminals, while others represented them as eccentric yet innocent activists miserably taken into custody by the police. Most notably, newspapers reported on the presence of female socialists, mainly because these women had directly fought the policemen while agitating their male counterparts and the surrounding crowd.[13] Earlier, newspapers had frequently cov-ered street battles between male socialists and policemen due to the proliferation of their activities, ultimately challenging imperialism. Since male socialist leaders had also worked as writers for the major press and published books on political theories and social criticism, they had often appeared in the media as intellectual critics, at times supporting the reformist opinions of major newspapers' editorial writers. In the Red Flag Incident, however, the female socialists unexpectedly entered a scene hitherto dominated by men. Still, these women emerged in the media not as intel-lectual activists but as astonishing agitators. Images of women's active participation in the street fight were, regardless of their accuracy, newsworthy, and the press used such stories to attract readers.

The most notable initial coverage of the female socialists appeared in the widely circulated *Kokumin shimbun* (*National News*), a newspaper that had been pro-government until the end of the war with Russia but had increasingly turned "vulgar" afterward.[14] Under the headline "A Beauty's Anarchist Speech," *Kokumin* reported the incident using almost one-third of a page in the gossip section.[15] From the tumultuous crowd, according to the article, there emerged

> [a] beauty in a purple *hakama* skirt with slight makeup and *hisashi gami* hairdo [a low pompadour style typical for female students], screaming out loud, "Everyone, what a tyranny by policemen!" She grabbed the red flag of anarchism from a man next to her, raised it high, and attempted to attack the policemen while vigorously inculcating anarchism. As she cried out, "True faith," "Revolution," and "Coup d'état," the already excited crowd increasingly behaved suspiciously. . . .
>
> The big brawl between the socialists and the police lasted about one hour. The beauty with *hisashi gami* hair and three other women resisted most strongly, with their sleeves rolled up unlike women.[16]

The article dramatically depicted the initial appearance of the "beauty," whose out-fit implies a female student of higher education. Beginning in the mid-1900s, media images of promiscuous female students were pervasive as objects of erotic curiosity and scorn. Newspapers frequently reported about female students seducing their male counterparts, and novels portrayed female students with mysteriousness or silence in emergent public spaces such as commuter trains and parks in their distinctive clothes and hairstyle.[17] In print media, their appearance acted as a social marker that depicted female students as an anonymous collective without individuality, linking the icon of "anarchist beauty" with the more familiar image of the female student.

At first glance, the "beauty" implies a temptress quality because she dramatically emerged from a crowd of male socialists. In the *Kokumin* article, however, she confounded readers' expectations by being far more articulate and active than the stereotypical female students in the media. In contradiction to the conventional view of women as bystanders or followers of men, the "beauty" was the one who instigated the quarrel that ended in a fight with the police. Because the 1900 Public Peace Police Law prohibited women's participation in any political event or group, the presence of women in such an overtly political scene likely seemed unprecedented.[18] By contrast, the press generally depicted their male counterparts as rogues fighting against the police and Sakai as an older leader attempting to stop them. In this and other articles describing the Red Flag Incident, it was the "beauties" who engaged in agitating speech and dramatically played a heroic role.

Popular media depictions of women in the Red Flag Incident stressed both the fear and exotic allure of revolution brought by the "beauties," which could help recruit ordinary men. *Tokyo Asahi shimbun*, another major newspaper, sensationalized the story with a headline reading, "Russification of Japan: Big Fight in Front of Kinkikan; Anarchists Were Arrested; . . . Among Them Were Young Beauties."[19] The report highlighted both the active participation and danger of the "beauty":

Future Dangerous Figure: . . . one of these young beauties is Sugawara Tomoko (age 18), who is currently staying at Mr. Sakai Toshihiko's. She has considered Joan of Arc as her ideal figure and been determined to cause a commotion once there is an opportunity. Needless to say, she is a dangerous figure of the future but astonished gawkers by her unflinching courage based on her self-confidence. One student said, "Japan is gradually becoming like Russia. There will be trouble if more women like her come out." From the rooftop of the nearby schools, [male] students with a twinkle in their eyes saw them [the activists] off to the police station.[20]

The reporter piqued readers' curiosity by indicating the mysteriousness and delinquency of the "beauty" Sugawara, who was likely being confused with Kogure Reiko (1890–1977), Sakai's live-in protégée.[21] This article is one piece of evidence briefly analyzed in literary scholar Naitō Chizuko's study of the media depictions of female activists as a "danger" to the nation-state.[22] As shown by the mention of Sugawara's "unflinching courage" and the students "with a twinkle in their eyes" (Naitō omits these sentences), this report showcased both the woman's serious engagement in the dissident cause and its impression on the male students. The article sensed the "future danger" not simply against the state and gender propriety but also as a means to spread the dissident movement among young men inspired by the valiant "beauty."

The article's reference to Russia also suggests both the perceived danger and heroism of anarchist activity. Since the Freedom and Popular Rights Movement in the 1880s, which had demanded the promulgation of the constitution and the opening of a parliament, political novels and newspapers had typically associated Russian anarchism with assassinations by bombing, particularly at the hands of heroic female anarchists such as Sophia Perovskaya (1853–81).[23] News of the 1905 Russian Revolution and the Bloody Sunday Massacre had not completely faded away by this time, either. Images of anarchists as mysterious figures had reached the realm of popular imagination, as evidenced by an adventure novel published in 1908 that featured an anarchist youth as a righteous outlaw.[24] Linked in popular imagination to their Russian counterparts, the female anarchists' involvement with this event magnified the fear of possible terrorist actions, which could attract the public. The message in this article invoked multiple interpretations: for some readers it was part of the ideological apparatus showing a counterexample, while for others, like the students depicted in the report, it was a spectacular inspiration to be enjoyed and potentially joined as a protest against police violence. It is the latter possibility that the reporter feared as a "danger," because it was not too unrealistic for contemporaries; many male Tokyoites had participated in street fights with policemen during popular protests that had become increasingly common in the city since the 1905 Hibiya Riot.

When covering the Hibiya Riot, many journalists in Tokyo had been particularly critical of police violence. The riot started as a "national rally" on September 5 organized by dissident journalists and politicians, who demanded that the foreign minister more firmly negotiate for the war indemnities from Russia at the conclusion of the Portsmouth Peace Treaty of 1905. The massive crowd at the rally against the treaty took to the streets and rioted throughout the city for three days. During the riot, policemen thrashed rioters with swords, killing seventeen and injuring an additional 528 people.[25] Because the leading opponents of the peace treaty included reporters from major newspapers, the media coverage of police violence against rioting citizens was particularly gruesome and furious.[26] The subsequent government orders temporarily banning the publication of various Tokyo newspapers, including the ones discussed here, further enraged journalists. Immediately after resuming publication, reporters harshly criticized police brutality, and some even organized themselves along with like-minded politicians to propose abolition of the Tokyo Metropolitan Police Department to the Lower House.[27] Against this background of the lingering tension between police and journalists, the Red Flag Incident provided many reporters with another opportunity to use police brutality as a means to criticize the police and, by extension, the Meiji government.

In contrast to the ambivalence expressed in *Kokumin* and *Asahi*, coverage of the Red Flag Incident in *Tokyo Niroku shimbun* sympathized with the male and female socialists as victims of police persecution. Its overt support is perhaps due to the fact that *Niroku* presented itself as a worker- and union-friendly newspaper and employed a Heiminsha socialist as a reporter. As in the other newspapers, its report highlighted the appearance of the female socialists with the headline "Brave Fight of Beauties," stating that they attracted bystanders and implying that it was their alluring beauty that gained their sympathy.[28] Still, these gendered expressions also highlighted the female activists' passionate devotion to their cause. The report continued:

Kicking down a woman: [During the fight] policemen cruelly molested the two women. One of them, some Sugawara, had attended the party despite her illness. [From Kinkikan] she walked toward the nearby Foreign Language College with her comrade and encountered the commotion. As she watched with sympathy, a policeman said, "How dare you, you are just a women. You must be one of them." Immediately, a few policemen sought to capture her. As she resisted, one of them suddenly kicked her down with his shoes.[29]

Similar to those in other newspapers, this report described the woman as resisting the violent policemen. *Niroku*'s clear emphasis on police brutality is evident in its reference to "some" Sugawara, likely referring to Kanno Sugako (1881–1911), who was ultimately shown as a frail and innocent activist. By contrast, the report described male activists with concrete names and titles while still provoking the readers' sympathy: Ōsugi Sakae (1885–1923), an "anarchist who is famous as a French scholar and Esperantist . . . repeatedly screamed, 'Long live anarchism,' even as he was being dragged [by the police]."[30]

Niroku also highlighted spectators' participation in the event:

The anarchists firmly held the red flags, but the mighty several dozen policemen with all their strength forcefully tried to grab the flags. . . . As they fought, gawkers . . . crowded around like an army of ants and cheered the anarchists by screaming, "Beat 'em down," "Punch them," and "Don't let the flags go." As the situation was about to turn into a big event, the policemen who had grabbed the flags dragged the anarchists in the middle of the grand street toward the police station. From the crowd, there were many who rushed like a landslide to help the anarchists.[31]

Unlike the other examples, in this account the spectators emerged as active partici-pants who verbalized their support for the unfairly abused anarchists. The article also mentioned that a few among the crowd assaulted the policemen in an attempt to rescue the activists. According to this report, the socialists themselves were far from belligerent, justifying the spectators' participation in attacking the police to protect them. This participation by the spectators encouraged readers to imagine the event as if it were a theatrical drama. Audience participation in theater and other public events was common among local *shitamachi* ("Low City") residents in Tokyo, or at least the *Niroku* reporter likely imagined this to be so.[32] The reporter's perception of engaged spectators was likely based on the neighborhood of his office in Kanda, one of the central towns of the Shitamachi area of Tokyo typically imag-ined as the birthplace of "Edo natives" (Edokko), who enjoyed "fires and fights," in commonly used expressions.

Most of the arrested male and female socialists had previously engaged in street demonstrations accompanied by musical instruments and street fights with policemen, particularly in the neighborhood of the socialist headquarters in Shitamachi. On such occasions, a large part of the audience were their immedi-ate neighbors, whose daily lives had been associated with the performing arts and audience participation. The socialists themselves were also aware of the advertising effect of a brawl with the police, as indicated by a 1904 report in the Heiminsha's organ alluding to a speech meeting that was violently terminated by the police, which "turned out to advertise" the next speech meeting, which drew even more spectators.[33] The severity of the police persecution from which the activists suffered cannot be denied, but we also should not ignore the local cultural practices that led to an appreciation of theatrical violence against authority. Likewise, the media's emphasis on the devotion of the "anarchist beauties" to their political cause and their struggle against the police helped maintain the political nature of the incident, potentially fascinating and inspiring readers.

Responses from Socialists

The two socialist factions reacted differently in response to media depictions of the incident. The law-abiding faction defended the arrested men and women of the direct-action faction. By then, the two factions had often quarreled between themselves. However, the law-abiding faction's magazine, *Tokyo Shakai shimbun* (*Tokyo Social News*), was one of the only surviving socialist magazines based in Tokyo due to increased state censorship following the 1907 miners' riots in the Ashio Copper Mine, after which the sympathetic *Nikkan (Daily) Heimin shimbun*, the successor of *Shūkan (Weekly) Heimin shimbun*, had been banned. Thus, accounts of the Red Flag Incident in *Social News* did not demonstrate outright hostility toward the arrested activists but rather called for support from their comrades. Claiming "ordinary newspapers' reports [on the Incident] are inaccurate in many cases," *Social News* provided a purportedly accurate report of the incident, which was considerably less dramatic than the newspapers had reported.[34]

By contrast, in *Kumamoto Hyōron* (*Kumamoto Review*), in a Kyūshū-based socialist magazine close to the direct-action faction, Takeuchi Zensaku reported that the incident had erupted like a flare-up of urban warfare against the state.[35] The report emphasized the spread of street battle and the courage of the activists, saying, "[The] bourgeoisie was astonished, and the capitalist government was frightened."[36] It also praised the newspapers' accuracy and extensive coverage. Further, in the same issue, Sakamoto Kassui emotionally recounted, "I was surprised and shed tears. But my eyes are filled with the light of hope. This is 'the rebellion of [June] 22nd,' the 'first step toward the revolution.'"[37] Neither Takeuchi nor Sakamoto, however, discussed the female activists besides their names. These sympathetic writers highlighted the male anarchists' "revolutionary" fight as the primary feature of the incident, without detailing the involvement of their female counterparts.

Kumamoto Review further suggested the gendered division within the anarchist faction by emphasizing the anarchist "rebellion" as a masculine act. It also featured comments by Sakai Tameko (1872–1959) and Ōsugi Yasuko (1883–1924), the wives of arrested Sakai Toshihiko and Ōsugi Sakae, respectively. In these comments, Sakai Tameko was presented as a responsible and supportive wife, and Ōsugi Yasuko showed her concern for Kanno Sugako, who was incarcerated in a ward for the sick.[38] The voices of these wives as caretakers and kind comrades reinforced the image of a masculine revolution, emphasizing the virtuousness of female socialists in contrast to the publicized militancy of their male counterparts while reducing the women's role in activism to that of subordination.

Presumably drawing from these and other depictions in socialist publications, historian Vera Mackie assumes that female socialists at this point were primarily limited to roles as "supporters of male activists."[39] After the war with Russia, however, some female activists drew upon socialism as a source of inspiration for their own political engagement. For example, one of the women arrested in the Red Flag Incident, Kamikawa Matsuko (1885–1936), stated her enthusiasm about active engagement with the revolutionary cause, at least at a figurative level. In the issue of *Kumamoto Review* published immediately before the incident, she wrote, "Be loyal to revolution even if you have no friend. Be enthusiastic about revolution even if you have no comrade. Be devout for revolution even if you have no mentor."[40] A student of Russian literature, Kamikawa frequently contributed her poems and essays to socialist magazines.[41] The other arrested women, in particular Kanno, had also written for socialist magazines to express their opinions about activism.

By the time of the Red Flag Incident, female socialists had engaged in a variety of political activities using their own skills and creating their own networks. They had attended and organized women's meetings at the Heiminsha headquarters, taken part in the protest against Tokyo's streetcar fare hike in 1906, and edited socialist magazines catering to women, such as *Sekai Fujin* (*Women of the World*) and *Katei Zasshi* (*Home Magazine*). They engaged in the movement along with their male counterparts while articulating problems relevant to women through writing, public speaking, and networking. Still, the number of female activists was small, and precisely because of their minority status in the socialist movement, their involvement in the Red Flag Incident was novel and notable in the eyes of many newspaper reporters.

Trials of the Red Flag Incident

In August 1908, two months after the Red Flag Incident, newspapers heatedly reported on the court trials of those who had been arrested and relayed the female activists' testimonies of police violence as a form of entertainment. Here, the courtroom emerged as a theater in which socialists performed dramatic roles supported by the policemen and judges, surrounded by curious audience members, including the reporters themselves. The female activists' speeches and actions clearly enlisted the curiosity of some journalists, and the women used these opportunities to further their political agendas, specifically regarding the legitimacy of their actions for gender equality. Journalists' coverage revealed multiple meanings and usages of the symbolic "woman," reflecting different intentions and interpretations. In her study of gendered media, Naitō Chizuko discusses newspaper reports of the Red Flag Incident and the negative depictions of the arrested women as infused with discriminatory language and suggestions of illness, promiscuity, and assassination.[42] Naitō, however, fails to fully examine the dynamics of these contradictions and their meanings. In the newspapers covering the incident, she claims, the "'dangerous' narratives pertaining to 'anarchists' were marked by the sign, 'woman.'"[43] This "symbolic woman," however, did not always carry the same meaning for contemporaries. In what follows, I seek to identify the possible effects of the symbolized women's narrative of police violence that was constructed by newspaper reporters and the female socialists themselves, who were appearing and acting to provoke several audiences, including spectators, reporters, and, by extension, readers.

Newspapers generally captured the theatrical air of the courtroom and particularly highlighted the police brutality in the female socialists' dramatic narratives. Though the contemporary meaning of courtroom spectatorship calls for further study, we can say that media sensationalism of the time had motivated many people to watch trials involving controversial incidents. For example, in June 1908, a famous trial of the so-called Debakame Incident, which involved a purportedly sexually deviant murderer, also attracted a packed courtroom. In that case, according to a *Niroku* report, spectators who could not enter loitered outside expectantly waiting for someone to exit the courtroom, and once it happened, "the crowd rushed into the courtroom ignoring policemen's repression."[44] This article also noted that the spectators later complained about the chief judge, who suddenly closed the trial to the public due to the possible obscene content of testimonies. Frustrated spectators criticized the judge by comparing him with the chief judge who had presided over the case of Noguchi Osaburō, another controversial murder case, evaluating the latter's rank as higher.[45] The spectators reportedly resembled the amateur critics of Kabuki theater and other performing arts. As such cases suggest, courtrooms at this time were considered, or at least depicted, as potential sources of entertainment in the same light as the theater.

Newspaper coverage of the first trial of the Red Flag Incident on August 15, 1908, emphasized the female socialists, and specifically their complaints about inaccurate interrogation documents and inhumane treatment in the police station. Trial coverage was decorated with references to the women as both "eloquent" and "audacious." According to *Yomiuri shimbun*:

To the [judge's] question to each [of the defendants], "Is your objective anarchism?" most men replied, "The ultimate objective of socialism is anarchism, but we have not publicly mentioned it yet." But Kanno Sugako said, "I am an anarchist rather than a socialist. I feel more strongly so as my thoughts have progressed nowadays." With her stylish (*iki*) outfit of arrow-patterned silk kimono and loosely tied satin purple sash, she said such an audacious thing. Hearing this, even the chief judge was astonished.[46]

Iki refers to a sense of refinement or stylishness, typically appreciated in Shitamachi society. Identifying Kanno's outfit as *iki* stresses the gap between her appearance and the content of her speech. This gap must have provoked some readers to imagine her as dangerous, yet interesting; in order to appear as *iki*, one needs an acquired sense that cannot be easily learned. In other words, she could not be labeled as a mere ignorant woman with no understanding of stylishness or intellect who had simply been dragged along by male activists.

Other newspapers described the same event using different terms while recounting Kanno's claims. *Kokumin* emphasized Kanno's identification with anarchism by noting her characteristic eloquence. At the same time, the description of her eloquence referenced Kanno's own message—that is, the defendants were unjustly subjected to police brutality. The report said, "[After surprising the court officials with her self-identification as an anarchist] she fluently accused the policemen of unlawfulness."[47] It should be noted that the arrested female socialists had experience with public speech from women's high schools and socialist meetings. Christine L. Marran points out that the early Meiji phenomenon of the "poison women" (*dokufu*), or sensationalized female criminals, indicated social anxiety among upper-class men concerning women and lower-class men inappropriately taking advantage of new laws and destabilizing traditional practices.[48] Similarly, when the reporters described Kanno's speaking skills, they were likely hinting at the perceived negative consequences of women's education: the creation of "poisonous" female political criminals, rather than ideally docile women. As newspapers of the time competed to capture any newsworthy part of the story, however, they provided these educated female activists with an opportunity to present themselves as a politically charged spectacle. Thus, the pages of newspapers emerged as the intersection of the multidirectional intentions and assumptions, with both the reporters and the reported unwittingly spreading multiple messages.

    Yomiuri mentioned Kanno's remark as also being the source of laughter, again along with the depiction of police violence:

Kanno angrily stated, "Because two policemen came holding the two flags, I pleaded with them to return them, but then they mercilessly pushed me down. When I got up, one of them severely twisted my arm and arrested me. If there were a legitimate reason, I would even accept death sentence. But I had never seen such a violent policeman before." When the judge asked if she recalled the policeman's face, she replied, "I remember his triangular shaped face," causing a burst of laughter.[49]

In order to report the laughter, regardless of the reporter's interest in police violence, he could hardly avoid contextualizing her comment about the policeman's "triangular shaped face." Consequently, he also informed readers about the brutal treatment she had received from the police. In this manner, the narrative of police violence illuminated the female socialists in the readers' imagination with a combination of pity, humor, and righteousness. Though the reporter appropriated Kanno's allusion to the policeman, the layers of dialogue in this and other articles indicate what Mikhail Bakhtin calls a "speech genre," in which any utterance "always responds (in the broad sense of the word) in one form or another to others' utterances that precede it," and is also related to "subsequent links in the chain of speech communion."[50] References to others can be situated as part of both diachronic and synchronic dialogues, which cannot be reduced to the writer's intention. Though a news report is the creation of one writer, he responds to and addresses dialogues using the shared assumption within a speech genre beyond his own capacity as an author.

The arrested women in the courtroom emerged as objects of curiosity, but this did not always involve a negative connotation mainly because of shared antagonism toward the police. *Kokumin* captured Kamikawa's angry statement that she would accept a death sentence but not for a crime that she had not committed.[51] A few days later, *Kokumin* ran an interview with Kamikawa with the headline, "Five Minutes in a Visitation Room: Meeting with a Socialist Woman." The article first described her smile and stylish attire.[52] This benign depiction and her photograph at the top center of the feature page sharply contrasts with the unfeminine remarks that she made in the report, which are all in a larger font: "Since I was in girls' high school, I greatly inclined to manly personality, and my daily behavior rather resembled that of men. . . . Such a manly taste eventually made me who I am today." The portrayal of Kamikawa's stylishness, her higher education, and her unfeminine persona may have been perplexing to readers, but the report ascribed a heroic and stoic quality to her.

The report also included a comment made by her best friend: "Some people say it was out of heartbreak and self-despair that Ms. Kamikawa began to argue for socialism. Particularly to her, however, I have never heard anything about her being involved with a love affair."[53] This also indicates that contemporaries viewed that the reason for a woman to become a socialist was some experience of "heartbreak" or "self-despair," and thus by no means a serious individual pursuit. In reality, however, the four female socialists, like many other male and female activists of the time, became politically engaged by choice. As mentioned above, the four women received education in high school or studied under senior scholars and were familiar with domestic and foreign socialist writings. This gap between general assumptions regarding female socialists and their actual background suggests that the women's activities were virtually unknown outside of their activist circle. During the court trials of the Red Flag Incident, however, the general assumption that female socialists were relatively passive figures proved advantageous. Any seemingly audacious remarks by these women made them seem even more astonishing, thereby piquing the curiosity of reporters and readers alike.

During the next trial on August 22, the scale of theatrical performance in newspapers escalated. A larger courtroom was chosen, and there were reportedly four hundred people in attendance, with another hundred waiting outside the room. Newspapers increasingly stressed the dramatic atmosphere of the trial, comparing the courtroom with a theater. *Kokumin* ran the headline "Full House, Sold-Out Trial"; *Yomiuri* stated "Great Popularity of the Trial since the [Hibiya] Riot."[54] It should also be noted that such theatrical depictions were primarily attached to the female socialists, though their male counterparts were also present at the trial.

Reported laughter was one gauge of audience reactions arising from gendered social expectations. For example, newspapers highlighted the contrast in testimony between a police witness, whose version of events was vague and unclear, and Kamikawa, who harshly attacked his obscure testimony. *Kokumin* stated that the spectators burst into laughter when the policeman could not specify which woman had been present and described how "unwomanly" the strength of the women had been when he had attempted to confiscate the flags.[55] *Asahi* wrote with sympathetic mirth, "Because he seems to have been shocked by such a strong woman as Kamikawa, he only remembered her name. . . . Only the chief judge's permission to leave the courtroom saved him from Kamikawa's harsh offense."[56] Previously, newspaper writers had focused unflattering attention on Kamikawa's "unfeminine" character. On this occasion, however, the police witness became an object of scrutiny, or even prey, as he was emasculated in front of the audience due to his deviation from the expected norms surrounding policemen, namely, physical strength and lucidity.

Theatrical metaphors were also popular, most notably in *Yomiuri*. The reporter explicitly stated his anticipation of something entertaining: "I waited with breathless interest to hear odd replies and unusual speech to shake off drowsiness."[57] In response to a series of remarks made by Kanno, for example, he wrote:

As expected, the former *Mainichi denpō* reporter, the eloquent woman Kanno Sugako, first stood up, and spread out an interrogation document in the manner of *Kanjinchō* [a Kabuki play]. "Chief judge!" she called, "Though I do not think there is any need to testify because all the facts set forth in the interrogation document have almost no traces, I want to clarify a fact, just in case. Because of my tuberculosis, however, I will feel sick even by talking slightly loudly, so please excuse me for not being so clear." By such an imposing condition, she first mystified the chief judge. The chief judge, like Togashi [the guard in *Kanjinchō*], replied, "Then you mean you have a fact to testify to. If it is difficult for you to breathe, come to the front and speak up." She stood up and said: "As I left Kinkikan, I was so sick that comrade Tokunaga suggested that I avoid the crowd because it would be too dangerous. I can never engage in any violent actions." . . . At the end, she obnoxiously exclaimed, "Because I am an anarchist, I am well prepared to be persecuted but would refuse to be incarcerated by such violent policemen, not even for one day." To this, reproved the judge, making a scary facial expression: "We will hear your explanation later. Just tell the facts for now"; thereby she, the female hero though she was, returned to her seat with flushed cheeks.[58]

Kanjinchō (The Subscription List) is a renowned Kabuki classic featuring a famous scene involving a loyal retainer, Benkei, who attempts to pass through the Ataka barrier while camouflaging his fugitive lord Yoshitsune in a group pretending to be monks. Relying on his quick wit, Benkei fools the guard, Togashi, by holding a blank sheet of paper and pretending to read aloud a prestigious Buddhist temple's subscription list that serves as a license to pass the gate.[59] The article is thus a parody of the Ataka barrier scene in which Benkei, here played by Kanno herself, solemnly recites from a blank sheet of paper or, in this case, the interrogation document. By using this analogy, the report reemphasized Kanno's assertion that there was no truth to the document.

Through the reference to her tuberculosis, Kanno's status as a dramatic activist was given another twist. At the time, popular conceptions of the disease were imbued with an idealized sense of romanticism, or even heroism, which perhaps derived from existing notions of the disease's indiscriminate nature, because it haunted not only the unhygienic and uneducated poor but also women of respectable upbringing.[60] The incongruity between Kanno's physical fragility as a tuberculosis patient and her masculine declarations delivered with a bravado matching that of Benkei gives rise to the impression of a strangely pitiful and righteous figure.

This theme of self-sacrificial righteousness and pity matched the trend in theater of the time, most notably the rising popularity of the performer of *naniwa-bushi* narrative chanting Tōchūken Kumoemon (1873–1916), whose repertoires included another classic Kabuki story of self-sacrifice, *Chūshingura* (*The Forty-Seven Ronin*).[61] The reporter created an image of Kanno not merely as an audacious woman condemning the police but also as a tragic hero enduring the pain of a fatal disease. *Asahi* also reported that she "entered the courtroom holding a medicine bottle in her left hand because of pleurisy, and the way she breathed hard looked painful."[62] By simultaneously appearing stylish, eloquent, and sick, Kanno, herself an experienced newspaper reporter, likely manipulated her own image for the purpose of delivering her message—or at least her appearance as a righteous and pitiful anarchist—to readers.

At the extreme ends of these dramatic depictions of the women were those who harshly criticized the socialists and those who were greatly sympathetic to them. *Tokyo Nichinichi shimbun*, a renowned pro-government press, accused the defendants of reviling the policemen during the trial.[63] The worker-friendly *Niroku*, in contrast, provided an overtly sympathetic message: "The painful behavior of Mr. Sakai who cried out, 'Aren't policemen also a kind of workers who live by wage?' was naturally eye-catching."[64] These articles only in passing mentioned the female socialists, thereby providing further layers of different meanings for the trials. Another newspaper, *Yorozu Chōhō*, briefly yet critically reported the incident and the trials. This disapproval is likely due to the personal relationship between *Yorozu*'s editor-in-chief and the Heiminsha leaders; *Yorozu* had once employed Sakai and Kōtoku, but they had resigned in protest to its support of the Russo-Japanese War.

Journalists wrote several versions of the trial proceedings to attract an audience. These articles were not merely the result of the reporters' agency but rather the product of dialogic interactions and assumptions emerging among different actors, including the reporters, socialists, policemen, judge, and audiences. Each of the reporters selectively adapted and modified the participants' presentations. The presence of a large number of spectators, along with the dramatic performances by the defendants, likely inspired reporters to use theatrical metaphors.

In *Kumamoto Review*, the magazine for the direct-action socialist faction, the trials were reported in careful detail, but for a purpose different from that of the popular newspapers. The overall tone of one such article reveals the writer's aim to treat the trial as seriously as possible: the author minimized laughter in parenthetical notes, and the female socialists were depicted as respectably as possible, using the suffix *-joshi*, referring to a female intellectual, after their names.[65] We also find in *Kumamoto Review* the female socialists' own responses to the incident from the police cell. Each of them equally expressed their gratitude to their comrades. Because of heavy censorship, however, they were limited to briefly stating their commitment to activism and solidarity with their comrades. For example, Kanno wrote, "I feel sorry for the authorities because they believe this persecution will stop our great movement."[66] Kamikawa stated, "Before, I was fully determined for revolution . . . but now depressively spend days in the cell without being able to express how I feel inside. . . . I will tell you many stories as a souvenir once I get out."[67] The writers of the *Kumamoto Review*, in response, praised these women and stated that the incident and the related police brutality strengthened their commitment to their political cause.

At the end of the trial, Kamikawa and Kanno were acquitted and Kogure and Ōsuga Satoko (1881–1913) were sentenced to suspended one-year prison terms, whereas the male socialists were given two- to three-year prison sentences. The media depictions of the Red Flag Incident incited readers' curiosity about the female socialists who dramatically criticized police violence. This curiosity worked on the activists' behalf, allowing for both recognition and advertising in the nationally circulating media. Though the ways in which reporters described the trial were ultimately beyond the control of the defendants, this indeterminacy was not disadvantageous for the activists because of the assurance that socialist magazines would always write "accurate" versions.

Conclusion

In September 1909, approximately a year after the trial associated with the Red Flag Incident, *Asahi* featured an interview of Kanno by sympathetic journalist Matsuzaki Tenmin (1878–1934). Though the other three female activists had ceased to be vocal in the movement, Kanno had been imprisoned for illegal publication of socialist magazines coedited by Kōtoku Shūsui and was under continual police surveillance. Matsuzaki favorably introduced her as the once-famous female socialist of the Red Flag Incident and depicted her as an activist who still challenged official notions of ideal womanhood. In the report, Kanno again linked her experience in jail to her own pitifulness and diligence as an activist. She first stated, "Ever since I went to jail, I lost a lot of weight," and "due to my tuberculosis and brain disease, I spent most of my time in a medical prison." She then called for more women's participation, claiming, "With more female socialists, we will be able to discuss women's issues and engage in interesting activities. Socialism is the total opposite of today's good-wife-wise-mother-ism."[68] Her comment indicates lingering expectations that socialist activities were inherently "interesting" (*omoshiroi*), a word that can also be translated as "funny." The interview again depicted Kanno as eye-catching, by including photographs of her face and calligraphy of her own poem.

Regardless of whether the state saw such persistent popular media portrayal of socialist activities as potentially subversive, within a year both Kanno and Kōtoku were arrested in the High Treason Incident, and they were executed in January 1911. As if in punishment for the ephemeral yet grand appeal that Kanno's popular media coverage had for the general public, the state launched a decisive counterattack through nationwide mass arrests of socialists and subsequent executions. At the time of the Red Flag Incident, the media portrayed the female socialists as objects of curiosity, reflecting their potential for social impact. In the High Treason Incident, however, the state unambiguously labeled socialists as impermissible villains—the assassins of the Meiji emperor—and newspapers widely delivered this message. Therefore, to this day, Heiminsha socialists are generally remembered as martyrs who were persecuted by the state. However, popular media coverage of the socialists' narratives of police violence has received little attention.

The female socialists emerged in the media overtly expressing their political views in the form of humorous and dramatic speeches against the police. Not sharing their political agendas and worldviews, journalists depicted these women using further exaggerations, but also unwittingly publicized these activists as an intriguing group worthy of public attention. Such an unpredictable dynamism might have inspired further attempts for control and propaganda from the state, thereby creating the potential for appropriation and transgression to emerge as a new form of spectacle from below. Several months after Kanno's execution, when a new feminist literary movement led by the Bluestockings (Seitōsha) emerged, its members also captured media attention with ambiguous messages mixing gossip and politics. Media portrayals of politically charged women after the Red Flag Incident would continue to serve as a vehicle for political inspiration for subsequent generations of female activists.

Notes

I presented a draft of this article in 2012 at the "Art and Politics of East Asia" workshop at the University of Chicago. I thank the Center for East Asian Studies at the University of Chicago and Yonsei University for supporting the research for this study. I am also grateful to the issue editors and anonymous reviewers for their guidance. To refer to the Japanese names, I follow the conventional order of family name and then first name. All translations, unless otherwise stated, are my own.

1. *Tōhoku hyōron* (*Tohoku Review*) 2, September 1908, 6.

2. Sakai Toshihiko, "Nihon shakaishugi undōshiwa" ("Historical Account of the Japanese Socialist Movement"), *Sakai Toshihiko zenshū* 3 (Tokyo: Chūō kōronsha, 1933): 269–71. For details of the High Treason Incident in English, see Ira L. Plotkin, *Anarchism in Japan: A Study of the Great Treason Affair, 1910–1911* (Lewiston, NY: Mellen, 1991); and Masako Gavin and Ben Middleton, eds., *Japan and the High Treason Incident* (London: Routlege, 2013).

3. *Kokumin shimbun*, June 24, 1908.

4. Ibid., August 24, 1908.

5. Lisa Duggan, *Sapphic Slashers: Sex, Violence, and American Modernity* (Durham, NC: Duke University Press, 2000), 2.

6. Recent studies of late Meiji media include Komori Yōichi, Kōno Kensuke, and Takahashi Osamu, eds., *Media, hyōshō, ideologii: Meiji sanjū nendai no bunka kenkyū* (*Media, Representations, and Ideologies: Cultural Studies of the Meiji Thirties*) (Tokyo: Ozawa shoten, 1997); and Kaneko Akio, Yoshida Morio, and Takahashi Osamu, eds., *Diskūru no teikoku: Meiji sanjū nendai no bunka kenkyū* (*The Empire of Discourse: Cultural Studies of the Meiji Thirties*) (Tokyo: Shinyōsha, 2000).

7. The 1907 circulation of each of the Tokyo newspapers discussed here is as follows: *Kokumin*, 34,000; *Tokyo Asahi*, 82,073; *Niroku*, 60,000; *Yomiuri*, 32,000; *Tokyo Nichinichi*, 24,000; and *Yorozu*, 87,000. James Huffman, *Creating a Public: People and Press in Meiji Japan* (Honolulu: University of Hawai'i Press, 1997), 386–87.

8. Amanda Frisken, *Victoria Woodhull's Sexual Revolution: Political Theater and the Popular Press in Nineteenth-Century America* (Philadelphia: University of Pennsylvania Press, 2011), 15.

9. The arrested male activists included such prominent socialists as Sakai Toshihiko, Yamakawa Hitoshi, and Ōsugi Sakae. For recent studies on these male leaders, see Umemori Naoyuki, ed., *Teikoku wo ute: Heiminsha 100-nen kokusai shinpojūmu* (*Shoot the Empire: International Symposium for the Centennial Anniversary of the Heiminsha*) (Tokyo: Ronsōsha, 2005); and Murata Hirokazu, *Kindai shisōsha to Taisho-ki nashonarizumu no jidai* (*The Modern Thought Society and the Era of Taisho Nationalism*) (Tokyo: Sōbunsha, 2011).

10. For the most representative studies of female socialists, see Suzuki Yūko, ed., *Heiminsha no onna tachi* (*Women of the Heiminsha*) (Tokyo: Fuji shuppan, 1986); and Vera Mackie, *Creating Socialist Women in Japan: Gender, Labour, and Activism, 1900–1937* (Cambridge: Cambridge University Press, 1997).

11. Yamaguchi was a prominent contributor to socialist magazines.

12. The Heiminsha published its organ *Weekly Heimin shimbun* from 1903 to 1905. After being dissolved in October 1905, it was reorganized in 1907 and intermittently continued until the arrest of Kōtoku in 1910. For the Heiminsha's history in English, see John D. Crump, *The Origins of Socialist Thought in Japan* (New York: Palgrave, 1983).

13. The arrested female socialists were Kamikawa Matsuko (1885–1936), a student of Russian literature; Kanno Sugako (1881–1911), a newspaper reporter; Ōsuga Satoko (1881–1913), a former medical student and an Esperantist; and Kogure Reiko (1890–1977), an apprentice of Sakai Toshihiko. Suzuki, *Heiminsha no onna tachi*, 42–48.

14. After the war, *Kokumin*'s founder lamented that his paper increasingly featured "vulgarized" news for profit. Huffman, *Creating a Public*, 317.

15. *Kokumin shimbun*, June 24, 1908.

16. Ibid.

17. For instance, *Kokumin* reported a case of "fallen male and female students" being caught by the police for flirting in the train. *Kokumin shimbun*, April 14, 1908. A mysterious female student in Tokyo's commuter train appears in the 1907 novel by Tayama Katai, "The Girl Watcher" (*Shōjo byō*), in *Columbia Anthology of Modern Japanese Literature*, ed. J. Thomas Rimer and Van C. Gessel, trans. Kenneth Henshall (New York: Columbia University Press, 2005), 254–64. For media and literary portrayal of young women in trams, see Alisa Freedman, *Tokyo in Transit: Japanese Culture on the Rails and Road* (Stanford, CA: Stanford University Press, 2011).

18. Suzuki, *Heiminsha no onna tachi*, 294.

19. The term used here is *myōrei no kajin*, "a beautiful young woman." *Tokyo Asahi shimbun*, June 23, 1908.

20. Ibid.

21. Kogure had moved into Sakai Toshihiko's house as an apprentice a few weeks before the incident. Suzuki, *Heiminsha no onna tachi*, 48.

22. Naitō Chizuko, *Teikoku to ansatsu: jendâ kara miru kindai Nihon no media hensei* (*Empire and Assassination: Modern Japanese Media Formation from the Perspective of Gender*) (Tokyo: Shinyōsha, 2005), 285–86.

23. Since the 1880s, Sophia Perovskaya frequently appeared in Japanese political novels. Tanikawa Keiichi, *Rekishi no buntai, shōsetsu no sugata* (*Style of History, Image of Novel*) (Tokyo: Heibonsha, 2008), 314. For Russian influence on Japanese intellectuals, see Sho Konishi, *Anarchist Modernity: Cooperation and Japanese-Russian Intellectual Relations in Modern Japan* (Cambridge, MA: Harvard University Press, 2013).

24. Seitō Shōji, *Bankara kidanji* (*A Bankara Eccentric Man*) (Tokyo: Daigaku kan, 1908).

25. Andrew Gordon, *Labor and Imperial Democracy in Prewar Japan* (Berkeley: University of California Press, 1991), 26–27.

26. For media reports of the riot, see Andrew Gordon, "Social Protest in Imperial Japan: The Hibiya Riot of 1905," *Asia-Pacific Journal* 12, no. 29/3 (2014): n.p, accessed June 6, 2016, http://apjjf.org/2014/12/29/Andrew-Gordon/4150/article.html.

27. *Tokyo Asahi shimbun*, February 23, 1906.

28. *Tokyo Niroku shimbun*, June 23, 1908.

29. Ibid.

30. Ibid.

31. Ibid.

32. For details of the "Low City" culture, see Edward Seidensticker, *Low City, High City: Tokyo from Edo to the Earthquake: How the Shogun's Ancient Capital Became a Great Modern City, 1867–1923* (Cambridge, MA: Harvard University Press, 1991).

33. *Shūkan Heimin shimbun*, June 20, 1904, 5.

34. *Tokyo Shakai shimbun*, July 5, 1908, 2.

35. Takeuchi Zensaku, "Kinkikan mae no katsudō" ("Activities in Front of Kinkikan"), *Kumamoto Hyōron*, July 5, 1908, 2.

36. Ibid.

37. Sakamoto Kassui, "Omoide" ("Memories"), *Kumamoto Hyōron*, July 5, 1908, 6.

38. *Kumamoto Hyōron*, July 5, 1908, 5.

39. Mackie, *Creating Socialist Women in Japan*, 43.

40. Kamikawa Matsuko, "Tomo arazu tomo" ("Even If You Have No Friends"), *Kumamoto Hyōron*, June 20, 1908, 8.

41. Nishikawa [Kamikawa] Matsuko, "25 nen mae wo kaiko shite" ("Remembering Twenty-Five Years Ago"), in Suzuki, *Heiminsha no onna tachi*, 215–16.

42. Naitō, *Teikoku to ansatsu*, 287–88.

43. Ibid., 286.

44. *Tokyo Niroku shimbun*, June 24, 1908.

45. Ibid.

46. *Yomiuri shimbun*, August 16, 1908.

47. *Kokumin shimbun*, August 17, 1908.

48. Christine L. Marran, *Poison Woman: Figuring Female Transgression in Modern Japanese Culture* (Minneapolis: University of Minnesota Press, 2007), 63–64.

49. *Yomiuri shimbun*, August 16, 1908.

50. Mikhail M. Bakhtin, "The Problem of Speech Genres," in *Speech Genres and Other Late Essays*, trans. Vern W. McGee (Austin: University of Texas Press, 2013), 94.

51. *Kokumin shimbun*, August 17, 1908, 3.

52. Ibid., August 21, 1908.

53. Ibid.

54. Ibid., August 24, 1908; *Yomiuri shimbun*, August 23, 1908.

55. *Kokumin shimbun*, August 24, 1908.

56. *Tokyo Asahi shimbun*, August 24, 1908.

57. *Yomiuri shimbun*, August 23, 1908.

58. Ibid.

59. For the latest translation of the play, see Sakurada Jisuke I, "Great Favorite Subscription List: Gohiiki Kanjinchō" in *Kabuki Plays on Stage*: Villainy and Vengeance, ed. James R. Brandon and Samuel L. Leiter, trans. Leonald C. Pronko (Honolulu: University of Hawai'i Press, 2002), 26–47.

60. The most familiar figure of an elite woman with tuberculosis was Namiko in the 1888 novel by Tokutomi Roka, *Nami-ko: A Realistic Novel* (*Hototogisu*), trans. Sakae Shioya and E. F. Edgett (Boston: Herbert and Turner, 1904).

61. Hyōdō Hiromi and Henry D. Smith II, "Singing Tales of the Gishi: Naniwabushi and the Forty-Seven Ronin in Late Meiji Japan," *Monumenta Nipponica* 61, no. 4 (2006): 460.

62. *Asahi shimbun*, August 23, 1908.

63. *Tokyo Nichinichi shimbun*, August 23, 1908.

64. *Tokyo Niroku shimbun*, August 23, 1908.

65. *Kumamoto Hyōron*, August 20, 1908.

66. Ibid., September 5, 1908.

67. Ibid.

68. Matsuzaki Tenmin, "Tokyo no onna" ("Woman of Tokyo"), in *Tokyo Asahi shimbun*, September 13, 1909.

Confronting an Enemy Abroad, Transforming a Nation at Home

Domestic Militarism in the United States, 1990–1996

Josh Cerretti

In a 1991 speech at the end of the Desert Storm operation against Iraq, US president George H. W. Bush told Congress that those who fought "set out to confront an enemy abroad, and in the process, they transformed a nation at home." But what sort of transformation "at home" arose out of this "confrontation abroad"? Here, taking the former president at his word, I ask how this war against Iraq "transformed a nation at home," recognizing *home* as a metaphor for both the land within the borders claimed by the United States and the space occupied by a heteronormative family.[1]

Beginning with the claim of "protecting children" underlying justifications for the Gulf War, I connect the transnational militarism of US intervention abroad to subsequent episodes of militarized violence within the borders of the United States, including the Los Angeles riots, Waco siege, and Oklahoma City bombing. Through a reading of government declarations and documents, print media, and cultural production, I develop the concept of domestic militarism, a term encompassing the double meaning of *domestic* by exploring episodes of state violence exercised both within national borders and to enforce a particular vision of the family. Domestic militarism is an ideology that justifies this state violence through circular

Radical History Review
Issue 126 (October 2016)   DOI 10.1215/01636545-3594345

logics of heteronormativity and settler nationalism, manufacturing perceptions of sexualized threats and helpless victims while preventing the articulation of connections between violence abroad and violence "at home." Ultimately, the article points towards a series of 1996 laws amending regulations on marriage, public assistance, immigration, and the death penalty in order to trace the concrete effects of this new, post–Cold War militarized heterosexuality, which manifests in spectacular and structural forms of violence ranging from state-sanctioned killing to racial inequity in child malnutrition.

Scholars including Chandan Reddy, Jasbir Puar, and Scott Morgensen have identified the increasingly convivial relationship between militaristic nationalism and certain gay and lesbian constituencies during the 1990s, but few scholars have shown interest in the intertwining of militarism and heterosexuality.[2] Even Lisa Duggan's *Twilight of Equality?*, one of the few works connecting heterosexuality to state violence, remains much more widely cited for the concept of homonormativity than for her analysis of heterosexuality.[3] I expand this work by tracing the reassertion of a reproductive heterosexuality complicit with state violence in the face of epochal change brought on by the end of the Cold War and the gains of feminist and LGBTQ movements. This article historicizes problems emblematic of the age of the War on Terror, such as police brutality, state-sanctioned killings, and reintegrating combat veterans into civilian society, by demonstrating how militarized responses to these issues became normative during the 1990s.

The often-convivial relationship between heterosexuality and militarism, as well as the normalization of heterosexuality in twentieth-century US culture and politics, complicates the project of examining militarized heterosexuality. Such a project must begin from an understanding that the relationships among heterosexuality, the state, and its violences has been constructed through historical struggles and cannot be taken for granted. Jonathan Ned Katz explains that heterosexuality transcends neither history nor culture and, instead, merely "signifies one particular historical arrangement of the sexes and their pleasures."[4] The state has been and remains enormously invested in this arrangement and consequentially works to both regulate these arrangements and simultaneously erase the mark of their influence upon them. As Margot Canaday writes regarding homosexuality, states did not "simply encounter homosexual citizens, fully formed and waiting to be counted classified, administered, or disciplined"; instead the state "was a catalyst in the formation of homosexual identity." She writes, "To uncover those processes is to challenge the law's own tendency to authorize homosexuality as somehow pregiven or even natural in its constitution."[5] Analogously, I dissect the ongoing construction of the heterosexual citizen in order to denaturalize the relationship between heterosexuality and militarism.

The primary dissonance in a specifically heterosexual form of militarism is that war produces death while heterosexuality, through the institutionalization of heteronormativity, claims a monopoly on the production of life.[6] Domestic militarism soothes the tension between these strange bedfellows by justifying the death making of war as a necessary feature of the way in which the nation-state fosters life. This framing functions by characterizing those outside of the "domestic" both as imminent threats to what Judith Butler calls "grievable life" and as ungrievavable should they face death at the hands of the state.[7] More concretely, one need only reflect on the implications of the popular antiwar slogan "Make Love, Not War"—or the more troubling "Girls Say Yes to Boys Who Say No"—to understand the potential for conflict between (hetero)sexual and militaristic imperatives. The potential for raising children in a world free of the threat of nuclear annihilation made possible by end of the Cold War produced a new disconnect between militarism and heterosexual domesticity in the early 1990s.

My central concern in this piece is to demonstrate how proponents of and apologists for state violence increasingly relied on appeals to sexuality in the last decade of the twentieth century. The tireless efforts of feminist and LGBTQ activists and thinkers had already significantly transformed the landscape of US sexualities by the time President Bush and Soviet leader Mikhail Gorbachev met at the 1989 Malta Summit to symbolically end the Cold War. Recognizing that both heterosexuality and militarism faced significant challenges in the late twentieth century that threatened their decentering, I characterize the post–Gulf War transformation of the United States as a cultural and material reinvestment in two institutions in crisis. I argue that as anticommunism and blatant white supremacy became less acceptable justifications for state violence, officials increasingly turned toward justifications for state violence grounded in underexamined assumptions about heterosexuality as natural, normal, and moral. This is not a break with the militarism and heterosexualization of Cold War ideology, but a reformed continuation of it in response to the collapse of its primary justification.

Scholars such as Edward Said, Steven Salaita, and Haunani-Kay Trask have demonstrated how the proponents of this reinvestment cited white supremacist tactics of racializing indigenous, black, and East Asian people to produce evidence of a threat in the form of Arab, Muslim, and "Middle Eastern" people.[8] Recentering the heteronormative nuclear family as the unit for which the state acts, as opposed to individual citizens or the broader public polity, proved equally important to creating the ambiance of peril underlying US policy before, during, and after the Gulf War. Furthermore, the state and media reasserted a commitment to the conventions of heterosexuality in defiance of increasingly louder calls for sexual equity and pluralism. For the purposes of this essay, I rely exclusively on the *New York Times* as the representative example of the media's role in this process. Understanding how this transformation amounted to a militarization of heterosexuality allows for clearer understandings of state violence wielded not only domestically in the 1990s but also transnationally in the 2000s.

Protecting Children in the Persian Gulf

On August 2, 1990, the *New York Times* reported that the Iraqi military had attacked Kuwait and "penetrated deeply into the country." Relations between Iraq and the United States had been declining for months.[9] In July, Senator Nancy Kassebaum argued for sanctions on Iraq, claiming, "I can't believe any farmer in this nation would want to send his products . . . to a country that has used chemical weapons and a country that has tortured and executed its children."[10] Kassebaum did not mention that the United States was the world's largest producer of chemical weapons—technology used against children in Vietnam and shared with Iraq during their war with Iran—and only recently had begun to move some of its chemical weapons stockpile toward destruction.[11] Additionally, Kassebaum's casting of the United States as defender of children belied the government's resistance to ratifying the UN Convention of the Rights of the Child (a resistance arguably related to the fact that the United States continued to execute individuals for crimes committed as juveniles).[12] Children provided justifications for military intervention in three ways: as hostages caught in the middle of the conflict, as the victims of Iraqi brutality, and as the domestic beneficiaries of transnational militarism.

At the outset of war, thousands of foreign oil workers lived in Kuwait. Joseph Treaster's September 8 article about the first US citizens to depart after the invasion staged the story as a gendered drama in which "the American men hoped that some military action would be taken" while "the women burst into tears when they were asked about the husbands they had left behind in hiding."[13] The hostages existed in a clear binary of masculine doers and feminine sobbers. In this same article, the phrase "women and children" appears eight times in ten sentences. According to Cynthia Enloe, news media unselfconsciously use the breathless phrase *womenandchildren* "because in network minds women are family members rather than independent actors, presumed to be almost childlike in their innocence about international *realpolitik*."[14] *New York Times* television critic Walter Goodman's mid-September 1990 article presumed as much in claiming that "the confrontation with Iraq has become a war of the innocents. The screen is dominated not by warriors but by wives, not men but boys, not armor but infants."[15] Thus, even before the United States officially intervened in Kuwait, the media had constructed a dichotomy contrasting the passive role of "womenandchildren" in the conflict with an active militarized masculinity that could not escape gendered tropes, even as many women and young people contributed to both sides. To incite support for that intervention against Iraq, the US government then sought to make this foreign conflict "domestic" through producing evidence of Iraqi violations of heterosexual domesticity in the form of infanticide.

As the occupation of Kuwait stretched into months, many remained unconvinced that distant Iraq posed any sort of threat to the United States.[16] Allegations of murders committed by Iraqi troops ejecting Kuwaiti infants from their incubators provided a vivid rationale for anyone seeking to justify US military action. Beginning in September 1990 with stories in the *Washington Post*, *New York Times*, and *USA Today*, multiple sources accused Iraqi soldiers of killing 15, 22, 300, or some other number of infants in a variety of fashions, usually completing their alleged crimes by absconding to Iraq with the incubators.[17] The testimony of "Nurse Nayirah" to the Congressional Human Rights Caucus on October 10 increased interest in these stories. The widely broadcasted testimony shows a young Arab woman tearfully claiming, "I volunteered at the al-Addan hospital. . . . While I was there I saw the Iraqi soldiers come into the hospital with guns. They took the babies out of the incubators, took the incubators and left the babies on the cold floor to die."[18]

A month later, President Bush further embellished her story as involving "babies pulled from incubators and scattered like firewood across the floor."[19] In December, Amnesty International issued a report confirming the existence of "300 premature babies who died because incubators were stolen." Anyone who had been reading the news would have understood Bush, on the eve of the US invasion, when he said "innocent children" were "among those maimed and murdered" by Saddam Hussein.[20] The US Senate voted to authorize war by only a five-vote majority, and seven senators cited Nayirah's testimony in their voting statements.[21]

Despite its impact, Nayirah's story was not all it had been made out to be.[22] Not only had the public relations firm Hill & Knowlton written Nayirah's testimony, but the "nurse" was a daughter of the Kuwaiti ambassador and a member of the royal family. Furthermore, no one who was actually at a Kuwaiti hospital corroborated her claims. The truth was unimportant; the US war on Iraq was balanced on a fulcrum of narrative.

Nayirah's story was so compelling in large part because it hinged on the violation of the most valued product of heterosexuality: children. War is the production of death but is best justified as the protection of life, and no symbol appears more useful for making that bait-and-switch than a child in danger. Recent work by Katherine Bond Stockton, Margaret Peacock, and Lee Edelman, all divergent in methods and results, concurs that definitions of childhood trace highly contentious power struggles and that children have been symbolically and rhetorically crucial to disguising oppression as innocence. Stockton demonstrates how adult discourse attempts to confine the messiness of childhood into clear categories that comply with hegemonic power, while Edelman argues that investments in protecting children mask a deeper investment in reproducing heteronormativity, and Peacock shows how Cold War governments used representations of children to starkly differentiate substantially similar militaristic projects.[23] In the case of the Gulf War, imagining that the war's purpose was to defend children served to obscure the war's negative consequences *for* children.

Within a month of the initial US assault, the Iraqi government began negotiating for an end to the conflict. "Iraq lies in ruins," the *New York Times* reported on March 4, and a month later the Iraqi foreign minister took to Baghdad radio to lament "the deliberate destruction of Iraq's infrastructure, including power and water plants, irrigation dams, bridges, telephone exchanges and factories producing infant formula and medicine."[24] The ensuing thirteen years of sanctions, known as the "siege," caused even more harm. "The siege touched every aspect of Iraqi life, causing death, disease, rapid economic decline, and nearly an end to any sort of human development," Haifa Zangana, an Iraqi activist, explains. "By the mid-nineties, half a million children died."[25] As Nadje al-Ali and Nicola Pratt write, the postwar years would prove especially devastating for women as, "aside from the most obvious and devastating effects, related to dramatically increased child mortality rates, widespread malnutrition, deteriorating health care and general infrastructure, unprecedented poverty, and an economic crisis, women were particularly hit by a changing social climate."[26] They detail how women and girls increasingly lost access to the job market and education while being forced to take on increased economic and cultural burdens.

As family life disintegrated in Iraq, President Bush sought to recenter it in the United States. In his 1992 State of the Union Address, Bush connected tales of his own progeny to stories of his wife's charitable work with HIV-positive children and a letter from a grateful Gulf War widow in order to insist that, despite the many challenges they may face, individuals "have responsibilities to the taxpayer . . . to hold their families together and refrain from having children out of wedlock."[27] In this framing, the transnational politics of militarized heterosexuality merge seamlessly with the politics of white supremacy and heteropatriarchy in the domestic context as, whether the problem is geopolitical disorder or blood-borne infection, the only solution remains a reinvestment in the nuclear family. Presented with a diverse range of threats to security and potential solutions, Bush asserted that "we must strengthen the family because it is the family that has the greatest bearing on our future."

What this rhetoric masks is that neither *family* (one kinship group) nor *families* (kinship groups collectively) is homogeneous or identical in interests. Furthermore, the task of "strengthening families" functions without the consent of those least empowered by the culturally specific forms the family takes (in this case, "womenandchildren"). The project of strengthening families implies that they are threatened and in need of the sort of protection the state offers, that is, militarized violence. Whereas Vietnam War–era organizations like Another Mother for Peace were able to use parenthood as a culturally sanctioned perspective from which to make an argument against sending their children to fight in war, the domestic militarism of the 1990s militarized parenthood. Being a "good mother" or a "family man" came to rely increasingly on support for militarized violence; consequently, the rhetoric of *family* became militarized through a perception that state violence is necessary to strengthen families.

The LA Riots and the "Culture of Poverty" Thesis

When making his call for more aggressive military action against Iraq to a joint session of Congress in September 1990, President Bush veered into the topic of how "our ability to function effectively as a great power abroad depends on how we conduct ourselves at home." He further explained that, for the United States, "world leadership and domestic strength are mutual and reinforcing; a woven piece, strongly bound as Old Glory."[28] Rather than dismissing this metaphor as another hackneyed bit of prose, we gain insight into the changing conditions of the 1990s by taking seriously Bush's contention that transnational militarism ("world leadership") structures the conditions of oppression within the borders of the nation ("domestic strength"). Furthermore, this leadership and strength are inextricable from practices of sexuality, or "how we conduct ourselves at home."

Three days after Bush declared "Kuwait is liberated," a Los Angeles man named Rodney King was brutally beaten by group of police officers.[29] That night's events may have lapsed into obscurity like so many other instances of antiblack violence were it not for a nearby resident sharing a videotape of the beating with a local news station. The state's subsequent failure to secure convictions against the offending officers sparked a series of riots centered in Los Angeles during late April and early May 1992. The LA riots were a "coming out" for the new, post–Gulf War domestic militarism that sought to justify the use of state violence within the borders of the United States through appeals to heterosexual normativity, and they set the stage for further militarization of heterosexuality as the decade continued.

Within hours of the "not guilty" verdicts, outrage fanned across the country, and reactions ranged from orderly protests to concerted attempts at property destruction. By April 30, thousands of police officers and the California National Guard had mobilized, soon to be joined by US Army and Marines deployed by President Bush. These forces arrived not to protect the mostly black and Latino neighborhoods of South Central Los Angeles but to wage war on them. Bush's executive order 12804, federalizing the California National Guard and ordering the Marines and Army into the city to suppress "the conditions of domestic violence and disorder," drew its constitutional legitimacy from the chapter 15 of Title 10 of the US Code, which applies only to "insurrection" and "rebellion" against the government. The riots provided an opportunity to display the effectiveness of the Army's newly reorganized Seventh Division light infantry units, which were designed with a post–Cold War mission "to react quickly to emergencies around the world" and to manage "'low spectrum' military crises in remote parts of the world where they would encounter little armored or air opposition."[30] On May 10 most of these troops withdrew, leaving the city with over fifty dead and more than $1 billion in property damage in the largest-scale armed civil conflict in the United States since the 1960s.[31] The persistence of applying a Gulf War metaphor to the urban uprising was made most clear by a reporter who observed "what had been scattered pillars of smoke" on the first day of rioting morphing into "a huge black cloud reminiscent of the burning oil wells of Kuwait during the Persian Gulf war."[32]

In the wake of the uprising, loud criticism of rioters drowned out critiques of the police and National Guard killing ten civilians. The debate after the riots instead focused on the underlying causes, and most prominent commentators endorsed domestic militarism by attributing the uprising to a Moynihanian "culture of poverty." Vice President Dan Quayle stated, "The lawless social anarchy which we saw is directly related to the breakdown of family structure, personal responsibility and social order in too many areas of our society."[33] Quayle located the source of rioters' oppositional actions and politics in their nonnormative sexualities and implied that a militarized response functioned to correct both. President Bush best summarized the intersection of militarized policing and heteronormative orderliness in a speech at the Challengers Boys' and Girls' Club in South Central LA, where he said, "Families can't thrive, children can't learn, jobs can't flourish in a climate of fear, however. And so first is our responsibility to preserve the domestic order."[34] Here, the dual modalities of *domestic* as internal to a household and internal to a nation-state become inseparable as, in Bush's estimation, the acceptable form of both is the same hierarchical order.

The riots revealed a new, post–Cold War terrain in which the external threat of communism receded, to be overtaken by anxieties about internal threats provoked by racial and sexual disorder. Concomitantly, the state abdicated the interventionist promises of the New Deal and Great Society, moving toward a leaner, neoliberal state that militarized by shedding those functions not related to a narrow concept of "national security." Both cultural anxieties and structural adjustments relied upon seemingly neutral descriptive terms like *structure, responsibility*, and *order* to mask the raced and gendered components of both policies and their unequal effects. Some of the same soldiers who went to Kuwait to avenge Iraqi depravations against children there would then battle "gangs of armed youths" and supposedly broken families in the streets of urban America to distribute the violence of the state in a way that maintains the inertial security of suburban, white nuclear families.

Long before the riots, hierarchies of sexual shame and the projection of aggression onto the oppressed consistently characterized antiblackness across many historical disjunctures. The poet Sapphire makes as much clear in the 1993 poem "Strange Juice (or the Murder of Latasha Harlins)," which links the 1991 shooting death of black teenager Latasha Harlins, an aggravating factor in the riots often marginalized like the deaths of so many black girls and women, to Billie Holiday's classic song about lynching, the African American Civil Rights struggle, and the colonization of the Americas. Rather than flattening these events into a homogeneous tale of black pain, Sapphire draws these connections to the past to point toward the future. Without infantilizing Harlins as a figure of childhood innocence, Sapphire makes an impassioned case for seeing Harlins as part of a solid intergenerational network "birthed by black people's struggle" in which she *"wasn't* pregnant, but . . . was gonna have a baby, definitely, one day."[35] African American cultural production in response to the riots established a clear precedent that "Black Lives Matter" two decades before Alicia Garza, Patrisse Cullors, and Opal Tometi brilliantly applied the phrase to the movement against another intensification of antiblack violence in 2013.

Although I now turn toward locating the ideological underpinnings of state violence directed against a predominantly white group of people in the United States, the constitutive nature of antiblack violence remains an instructive example in assessing the meaning of domestic militarism in the 1990s. Just as black-majority neighborhoods were used as a laboratory for more militaristic styles of police intervention that later became national phenomena, the United States would continue to visit violence upon its citizens in the name of children and the family throughout the decade.[36] At the same time, the state forged formal connections between transnational militarism and domestic policing through the Defense Logistics Agency Disposition Services, which increasingly distributed surplus military hardware to police forces around the country.

Children in Peril at the Waco Siege

In March and April 1993, the US public focused raptly on the headquarters of the Branch Davidians, just outside of Waco, watching a series of events unfold that would leave eighty-six people dead. Here, I connect the Branch Davidians to the people of Iraq and Los Angeles through their common relationship to domestic militarism without suggesting any equivalence between these communities. I demonstrate the contrast between the state's professed actions "in the interests of children" and the mass immolation of children at Waco.

On the morning of February 28, agents of the Bureau of Alcohol, Tobacco, and Firearms raided the Mount Carmel Center to arrest David Koresh on a weapons charge. Those who saw him as their spiritual leader were known as Branch Davidians, an offshoot of the Davidians, itself a breakaway segment of Seventh-Day Adventism, a Protestant Christian denomination. The exact theology of the group shifted depending on the teachings of successive leaders, but all shared with Adventists a focus on an apocalyptic "second coming" of Jesus.[37] While the siege was ongoing, the *New York Times* had few reservations about referring to the group as a "cult" and characterized members through such a lens.[38]

The Branch Davidians repelled the government raid, initiating a fifty-one-day standoff that provided ample opportunities for news media to speculate on the character of all involved, particularly Koresh. The "big figure in this drama, the mysterious mastermind, in fact the only interesting character" was "an odd mix of religious zealot and frustrated rock performer" comparable to "Jim Jones and Manson" or "Hitler and Stalin" who was "dangerously unstable" and had a "history of learning disabilities."[39] Despite these negative traits, Koresh "proved himself attractive," and "whatever his religious convictions, they did not preclude him from having sex . . . even after he married a 14-year-old girl."[40] Such fascination with Koresh's sexual practices became the primary route through which he was characterized as "deviant" and, consequently, deserving of state violence.

The first quote the *New York Times* provided from Koresh encapsulates much of the ensuing coverage: "I've had a lot of babies these past two years. It's true that I do have a lot of children and I do have a lot of wives." This same article includes reports, by way of hearsay, of "sexually abused girls," as well as rumors that "Mr. Koresh might have abused children of group members and . . . claimed to have at least 15 wives."[41] The number of wives grew to nineteen by the next day alongside reports of his "abusive tendencies, including sexual relations with young girls."[42] He was so thoroughly saturated in nonnormative, excess heterosexuality that even his rise to power was predicated on uncommon sexual relations: Koresh supposedly became a prophet by having sex with his predecessor Lois Roden, five decades his senior.[43] Reporters characterized Koresh as "a madman" and "David Death," but the accusations most instrumental to the standoff all focused on how Koresh related to his presumed dependents, the "womenandchildren" of the Mount Carmel Center.[44]

Domestic militarism assumes a system in which certain men present a sexualized threat and only militarized violence can save innocent children and women from them. Whether the threat rests in the body of an individual like Koresh or Saddam Hussein, or in the faceless "thugs" accused of violating the domestic order in Los Angeles, the state diverts attention from its violence by positioning itself as protector and savior. The raid that sparked the Waco conflict operated on the assumption that the Branch Davidians consisted of dangerous men and helpless "womenandchildren." Stephen Labaton and Sam Howe Verhovek's special report on the raid, explains that the Bureau of Alcohol, Tobacco, and Firearms "timed the raid to take advantage of a period when . . . the cult's routine would separate the men from both the weapons and the women and children."[45] Even though women participated actively on both sides of the raid, reducing them to their supposed helplessness served to cast militarized violence as benevolent protection.

On April 13, Verhovek reported that the FBI had no intention of assaulting the Mount Carmel Center "largely because of fears that such action could harm the 17 children inside."[46] Soon, though, the government began to execute "a plan of slowly stepping up the pressure" through the use of tear gas. US attorney general Janet Reno defended the decision: "We had information that babies were being beaten. . . . I specifically asked, 'You really mean babies' 'Yes, that he's slapping babies around.'"[47] Here, violence against infants, just as in the story of the Kuwaiti incubators, functioned as the ultimate transgression of heterosexual domesticity and an option of last resort to justify militarized violence.

Thus, on April 19, the same Bradley-model tanks used in the Gulf War "pumped tear gas through holes punched in the walls of the compound," smoke appeared in several parts of the complex, and within an hour "David Koresh and more than 80 followers—including at least 17 children—apparently perished . . . when flames engulfed the sprawling wooden complex on the Texas prairie."[48] Immediately following these deaths, government officials asserted that it had been done with the best intentions—that is, for the "womenandchildren." The *New York Times* reported that Reno "described the tear gas attack as an incremental increase in pressure on the cultists designed to encourage women and children to flee." Similarly, a spokesman for the US Department of Justice insisted on the maternal instincts of his boss, saying the factor "that drove her the most was her concern about the children."[49] President Bill Clinton also stuck to the story about ongoing child abuse ("the children who were still inside the compound were being abused significantly"), blamed the deaths on the Branch Davidians ("they made the decision to immolate themselves"), and assured his audience that what mattered most was the children ("I feel awful about the children").[50]

While federal officials insisted on the legitimacy of their conjectures about ongoing child abuse, the Justice Department's October report on the siege conceded, "There was no direct evidence indicating that Koresh engaged in any physical or sexual abuse of children during the standoff."[51] Verhovek's reporting on the children during the siege revealed that "none show any signs of physical abuse, and most seem consumed with a wish to see their parents."[52] Furthermore, "cult members have disputed that there was any child abuse or beatings at the compound, and Texas authorities who had looked into such accusations before the Feb. 28 raid had never found any proof."[53] Although the Justice Department report conceded that Reno "had made an inaccurate statement" regarding the child abuse, it insisted that unsubstantiated innuendo was "sufficient to be relevant to the decision making process."[54] Commentator William Safire was less charitable; he went so far as to claim that "she misled the public after the attack (and probably the President before the attack) by arguing that the children were being 'abused' inside."[55] While questions remain about how children were treated within the Mount Carmel Center, the inferno that killed its residents made such details obscure.

The fire's exact origin also remains a mystery, but both the US government and the *New York Times* settled on the assumption of a mass suicide by the Branch Davidians. What is clearer from accounts of the Waco siege is that the US government sought to solve problems with overwhelming force justified to the public through the logic of domestic militarism. The perception that tanks ramming into a building and spitting noxious gas "represent[s] the best way to resolve the standoff without catastrophic loss of life" concedes significant ground to militarization by imagining this sort of professional administered violence as a life-saving measure. While one reporter claimed that a "confusing swirl of political, practical, and psychological forces inevitably steered officials toward the plan," the most pertinent fact is that "no alternatives were formally presented to Attorney General Janet Reno" besides an assault with tanks and tear gas.[56] Domestic militarism was the driving force that steered officials toward the plan, not inevitably but ideologically. As other standoffs, like the 1994 Justus Township siege in Montana, revealed, loss of life is not an inevitability when citizens clash with their government, but assumptions about the dangers of nonnormative kinship arrangements and the utility of militarized violence make loss of life more likely.

Many surviving Branch Davidians can be found at the ruins of the Mount Carmel Center every April 19 to commemorate the deaths that occurred there. By 1995 the site had become a rallying point for "a political crusade, albeit one that the survivors haven't joined and don't even approve of."[57] The ranks of these crusaders, who "called themselves constitutionalists or patriots or militiamen," grew throughout the early 1990s, rallying around citizen-state conflicts like Waco and Ruby Ridge with their own militaristic fervor, brandishing firearms and peppering federal authorities with bellicose rhetoric.[58] The Branch Davidians, by contrast, stood a skeptical distance from the militiamen, "perplexed, and even offended," wary of the gun-toting militia, and totally unarmed.[59] At the same time, three hundred miles due north of Waco, one of those self-described militiamen turned April 19 into a day that would both eclipse the Waco siege in losses of human life and link the siege into a larger chain of militarized violence.

The "Baby Killer" in Oklahoma City

Just after 9:00 a.m. on April 19, 1995, a bomb made out of ammonium nitrate and fuel oil exploded in front of the Alfred P. Murrah Federal Building in downtown Oklahoma City. Hundreds of millions of dollars of property damage was overshadowed by 168 deaths. Representations of the space of the bombing, its youngest victims, and the bomber's motives for his violent act all demonstrate the historically specific linkages between state violence and heteronormativity, or what I refer to as domestic militarism.

In the aftermath of the bombing, many Oklahomans appeared most disoriented not by the tragedy of bombing itself but, rather, by where it occurred. "One by one they said the same thing," journalist Rick Bragg reported: "this does not happen here."[60] Locals had plenty of ideas about where these things *do* happen: "Beirut," "Bosnia . . . Jerusalem . . . Baghdad . . . Bolivia," and "countries so far away, so different they might as well be on the dark side of the moon."[61] The belief that Oklahoma existed as part of "America's heretofore invulnerable and innocent heartland . . . whose uncorrupted values and innocence were beyond the reach of such violence" required effacing the racialized violence that contours the history of Oklahoma, as well as the transnational exportation of that violence by the United States.[62]

In a defining moment of US-indigenous relations, the federal government began a systematic forcible displacement of the Cherokee, Seminole, Chickasaw,

Creek-Muscogee, Choctaw, and other indigenous nations to contemporary Oklahoma in 1830, causing unknown thousands of deaths on multiple "Trails of Tears." Furthermore, not only was the state a scene of the quotidian violence of Jim Crow, but it also was the scene of more spectacular forms of white supremacist violence, such as the 1921 assault on Tulsa's "Black Wall Street" that left hundreds dead and thousands more homeless. When those at the scene of the 1995 bombing claimed, "It's hard to imagine this happening in the heartland," they participated in a collective forgetting of tragedies like the Tulsa race riot that justified ongoing violence against people of color.[63] Domestic militarism requires effacing the suffering that was necessary to establish a seemingly benign "domestic order," or as Chandra Mohanty and Biddy Martin claim in reference to the concept of "being home," it requires "an illusion of coherence and safety based on the exclusion of specific histories of oppression and resistance."[64]

Histories of transnational militarism were also denied through representations of innocent Okies "newly burdened with an unfortunate sense of connection to the rest of the world."[65] The normalization of dozens of sudden deaths by explosion abroad—whether in Beirut, Baghdad, or Bolivia—arises out of the logic of domestic militarism that says the burden of violence should be borne "out there" and not within the domestic space of the United States. The idea that violence must be suffered in foreign countries existed in a mutually reinforcing relationship with the idea that violence must also originate from foreign countries, placing immediate scrutiny upon Arabs and Muslims as the search began for whoever planted the bomb.

A. M. Rosenthal encapsulated the dominant attitude of the moment: "Police do not know for certain whether the bombing is foreign terrorism or domestic. Either way . . . whatever we are doing to destroy Mideast terrorism, the chief terrorist threat against Americans, has not been working."[66] This is to say, regardless of who is responsible for the bombing, Arabs and/or Muslims (it's rarely clear) should be punished for it. Even after the US government stopped pursuing any Arab suspects and focused on a cadre of white men, Walter Goodman hedged his critique of how televised news cast "Arab-Americans" as "the suspects of first choice in terrorist attacks" by adding that this "suspicion is understandable."[67]

While many were immediately occupied with suspicion, the victims of the bombing transfixed many more, and both government and media represented children at the apex of victimhood in order to promote domestic militarism. Before any details about the bomb emerged, Rick Bragg would assert that "it was intended to murder on a grand scale: women, children, old people coming to complain about their Social Security checks."[68] Little mention was made of the Drug Enforcement Administration, Secret Service, Marine Corps, Army Recruiting Battalion, or Defense Security Service offices in the same building. Instead, "The enduring image of this tragedy" was that of bloodied one-year-old Baylee Almon being carried away from the rubble by a firefighter.[69] Photos of Almon "pierced the heart" of millions who saw the pictures through the Associated Press release and "prompted a flood of calls to newspapers from people concerned about the child's fate."[70] Sadly, Baylee Almon died as a result of the bombing and, like the eighteen other children killed in the blast, became a filter through which to look at domestic terrorism without seeing domestic militarism.

While 168 people died that day, the 19 children became "the focus, the epicenter, of the nation's bereavement over the blast and its rage and loathing at the bomber" because their unquestionable innocence made the bombing appear, as President Clinton put it, like "an attack on innocent children and defenseless civilians" rather than an attack on a centralized node of repressive state power.[71] Furthermore, centering the youngest victims facilitated an image of a "national family" bound together by the strength of fathers and the vulnerability of dependents. The first responders did not just pull Baylee Almon from the wreckage; as the *New York Times* reported, they "called [her] 'my baby,' adopting [her] on the spot, as did the entire nation."[72] The state also rhetorically adopted Almon, using her very real pain as a rhetorical resource to assuage concerns about the very real pain the US government would continue to inflict upon many children.

There was no shortage of familial metaphors in response to the bombing. Todd Purdum claimed "a disaster or security threat transforms the President instantly into a national paterfamilias" and quoted a Harvard historian as calling the attack "against our own family."[73] Clinton, the "national father figure," seemed to relish the role, surrounding himself and First Lady Hillary Clinton with children of federal workers for "a brief national teach-in on anxiety and reassurance" in which he promised that the governmental response would be "putting our children first."[74] With no foreign enemy to punish for provoking this anxiety, the United States turned toward the bombing's primary perpetrator to make sense of the tragedy, but domestic militarism obscured the most important explanations.

Timothy McVeigh, the man charged with and ultimately convicted and executed for bombing the Murrah Building, recalibrated the scale through which negative representations could be judged. Journalists called him a "lunatic," the "most detested of pariahs," "so sick," "Satan," an "evil person," "a demon," and a "monster,"[75] but no invective stuck like "baby killer." McVeigh's widely broadcast "perp walk" in Perry, Oklahoma, featured a crowd screaming, "Baby killer! Burn him!"[76] The *New York Times* fed the image of McVeigh as baby killer, speculating "the Murrah building may have been chosen specifically because its layout insured that a bomb could be placed so close to children" and claiming "McVeigh had displayed no reaction even when he had been shown photographs of maimed and dead children."[77]

In addition to the title "baby killer," a portrait emerged of Timothy McVeigh that emphasized his failed heterosexuality. McVeigh apparently was "a supremely dedicated soldier" who was "well on his way to . . . a brilliant military career" but also a "loner" who "could not imagine settling down, working, marrying, becoming 'domesticated.'"[78] According to some of the men who served with him, McVeigh "embraced the solitude of his pillow night after night" and "never had a date."[79] McVeigh's hyposexuality, his failure to be appropriately "domestic," functioned to pathologize him and mark his militaristic violence as improper and antithetical to the American military ideal. The creation of such a distinction was so important because of the way he blurred the division between his "legitimate" violence as a soldier for the state and his "illegitimate" bombing.

In a letter written a few months before his execution, McVeigh connected his military training to his actions in Oklahoma City: "Bombing the Murrah Federal Building was morally and strategically equivalent to the US hitting a government building in Serbia, Iraq, or other nations." He claimed the bombing was "no different than what Americans rain on the heads of others all the time, and subsequently, my mindset was and is one of clinical detachment."[80] The technical content of McVeigh's actions, from his familiarity with explosives to his composure under pressure, arose out of his training and attachment to militarism. McVeigh's struggle to reckon with his combat experience in Iraq, his revulsion at seeing the sort of tank he manned there used against the Branch Davidians in Texas, and his sense of himself as protecting domestic order, each a highly politicized perception, were completely evacuated before they could even be examined. As Pam Belluck wrote a few weeks after the bombing, "Any argument that Mr. McVeigh had been motivated by political opposition to some drastic Government action or injustice would be very difficult to advance, *since the bombing killed innocent women and children.*"[81] Domestic militarism maintains the cognitive dissonance necessary to disarticulate domestic terrorism from its roots in transnational militarism; it provides a framework for interpreting kinship, nation, and violence in ways that insulate the state from critique. In this way, the connections between McVeigh's combat history in Iraq and the bombing were actively avoided as many of the same people eager to punish McVeigh for the murders he committed in Oklahoma City enthusiastically encouraged the murders he committed in Iraq.

Conclusion

The 104th Congress and President Clinton created a series of laws in 1996 that reflected the changes wrought over the first half of the 1990s and helped to codify a new, post–Gulf War domestic militarism. These four pieces of legislation reflect both the progress and the fragility of militarized heterosexuality in the 1990s, affirming the values of domestic militarism, while also suggesting that the relationship between heterosexuality and militarism did not arise from the nature of either but, rather, was an active construction of the state.

I have argued that representations of and responses to state violence militarized heterosexuality during the early 1990s. I refer to this as domestic militarism, in that these events were both militarized violence used within the borders of the United States and violence used to enforce a particular vision of the family. The US government advanced, and media regularly endorsed, justifications for this violence grounded in binary gender roles, hegemonic whiteness, and genocidal ideas about indigenous people. In this final section, I demonstrate how the imagined "interests of children" provided a convenient excuse for regressive social change that ultimately increased the suffering of many children.

The Antiterrorism and Effective Death Penalty Act of 1996 (AEDPA) went from "a snail into a race horse" due to the "domestic terrorism" of the Oklahoma City bombing but focused its definition of terrorism almost exclusively on what it called "international terrorism."[82] In addition to tightening restrictions on contributions to "foreign organizations" designated as terrorists and opening up foreign governments to suit in US courts, AEDPA created new procedures for deporting immigrants suspected of terrorism through secret trials and limited the ability of people accused of terrorism to seek asylum in the United States.[83] Along with the Illegal Immigration Reform and Immigrant Responsibility Act of 1996 (IIRIA), which increased the authority of Immigration and Naturalization Services to imprison people indefinitely and the speed with which they could deport migrants, the AEDPA reshaped the legal regime governing immigration, separated countless family members from one another, and reflected contemporaneous conceptions of security and national identity.[84] These laws drew upon and reinforced white supremacist conceptions of Euro-Americans as the rightful arbiters of the land within the borders claimed by the United States while projecting the threat of violence regularly committed by the US state—"at home" and "abroad"—onto racialized, "foreign" threats.

IIRIA also sought to eliminate immigrants' access to the limited social safety in the United States,[85] a goal more effectively achieved by the Personal Responsibility and Work Opportunity Reconciliation Act of 1996 (PRWORA). The law begins with two findings: "Marriage is the foundation of a successful society," and "marriage is an essential institution of a successful society which promotes the interests of children."[86] Lest the exact sort of marriage to which this Congress referred be misconstrued, it is worth noting that a week earlier they passed the Defense of Marriage Act, which defined "marriage" as "only a legal union between one man and one woman as husband and wife."[87] This aggressive promotion of heterosexuality evident in PRWORA went hand in hand with the antiblack racism and classism identified by Dorothy Roberts in her work on race and reproduction in the United States. Roberts sees PRWORA as driven by "a set of myths about the connections between family structure, welfare, race, and poverty" toward the goal of "modifying poor people's behavior."[88]

How, then, did this law passed "to promote the interests of children" modify their lives? Quantitatively, fewer than half the number of children receiving Aid to Families with Dependent Children benefits in 1995 were receiving the post-

PRWORA Temporary Assistance for Needy Families benefits by 2000, despite a growing population and a child poverty rate exceeding 17 percent.[89] The Center for Popular Economics reported that the new welfare regime "offers no guarantee that families with young children under the poverty line will receive public assistance" even though children in poverty "are more likely to have behavioral problems . . . are more likely than other children to be overweight and suffer from other chronic health problems . . . [and] are far more vulnerable to neglect and abuse."[90] Clearly, serving children, particularly children of color and working-class children, was not the number one priority of PRWORA. As Roberts claims, "How we interpret child maltreatment is a political issue."[91]

The politics of interpreting what constitutes child maltreatment and the interests of children emerged concurrently with domestic militarism in the 1990s. Heterosexuality, through its claim of producing life, became the mechanism to excuse militarism's destruction of life. The government and media contributed to the structural power and power evasiveness of patriarchal, Euro-American heterosexuality in the way they framed outrage at the alleged maltreatment of children by the Iraqi military and the Branch Davidians. Officials and commentators attempted to excuse deploying military units within the borders of the United States during the Los Angeles riots by proposing it as the only tenable solution to the pathologies of the black family. In the cases of Waco, immigration reform, and welfare reform, the US government positioned itself as operating "in the interests of children," and, in each case, children suffered and died. The Oklahoma City bombing, in which Timothy McVeigh used the training he received abroad from the US military to kill a great number of people within the United States, showed the perverse yet inevitable results of this logic.

The use of symbolic children—bound up in the dynamics of sexuality, gender, race, and other forms of identity—allows for the rhetorical elision of the pain and death experienced by corporeal children. The "transformation at home" heralded by Bush amounted to a militarization of heterosexuality through the ideology of domestic militarism. Critically examining portrayals of state violence allows us to better understand how the representations examined here serve the interests of heteronormativity, settler nationalism, and militarism. Understanding the militarization of sexuality during the 1990s, furthermore, prepares us better to understand the importance of the ideology of domestic militarism in the contemporary War on Terror.

Notes

1.   For more on violence, heteronormativity, and "home," see Chandra Mohanty and Biddy Martin, "What's Home Got to Do with It?," in Mohanty, *Feminism without Borders* (Durham, NC: Duke University Press, 2004), 85–105; and Lynda Johnston and Robyn Longhurst, "At Home with Sex," in *Space, Place, and Sex* (Lantham, MD: Rowman and Littlefield, 2010), 41–60. For an examination of the dual meaning of *domestic* in US history,

see Amy Kaplan, "Manifest Domesticity," in *The Anarchy of Empire in the Making of U.S. Culture* (Cambridge, MA: Harvard University Press, 2002), 23–50.

2. Chandan Reddy, *Freedom with Violence: Race, Sexuality, and the US State* (Durham, NC: Duke University Press, 2011); Jasbir Puar, *Terrorist Assemblages: Homonationalism in Queer Times* (Durham, NC: Duke University Press, 2007); Scott Morgensen, *Spaces between Us: Queer Settler Colonialism and Indigenous Decolonization* (Minneapolis: University of Minnesota Press, 2011).

3. Lisa Duggan, *The Twilight of Equality? Neoliberalism, Cultural Politics, and the Attack on Democracy* (Boston: Beacon, 2004).

4. Jonathan Ned Katz, *The Invention of Heterosexuality* (Chicago: University of Chicago Press, 1995), 14.

5. Margot Canaday, *The Straight State: Sexuality and Citizenship in Twentieth Century America* (Princeton, NJ: Princeton University Press, 2009), 4.

6. See Lauren Berlant and Michael Warner, "Sex in Public," *Critical Inquiry* 24, no. 2 (1998): 547–66.

7. See Judith Butler, *Frames of War: When Is Life Grievable?* (London: Verso, 2009).

8. See Edward Said, *Covering Islam* (New York: Vintage Books, 1997); Steven Salaita, *The Holy Land in Transit: Colonialism and the Quest for Canaan* (Syracuse, NY: Syracuse University Press, 2006); Haunani-Kay Trask, "The Color of Violence," in *Color of Violence: The Incite! Anthology*, ed. Incite! Women of Color against Violence (Cambridge, MA: South End, 2006), 81–87.

9. Michael Gordon, "Iraq Army Invades Capital of Kuwait in Fierce Fighting," *New York Times* (hereafter *NYT*), August 2, 1990. Also see Samira Haj, *The Making of Iraq, 1900–1963* (Albany: SUNY Press, 1996); and Albert Hourani, *A History of the Arab People* (Cambridge, MA: Harvard University Press, 1991).

10. Gordon, "US Deploys Air and Sea Forces after Iraq Threatens Two Neighbors," *NYT*, July 25, 1990; Steven Holmes, "Congress Backs Curbs against Iraq" *NYT*, July 28, 1990.

11. "Summary of US-Soviet Agreement on Chemical Arms," *NYT*, June 2, 1990.

12. Bill Bradley, "Rights of the Child," *NYT*, December 16, 1990.

13. Joseph Treaster, "One Hundred Seventy-One Americans Arrive in Jordan from Kuwait," *NYT*, September 8, 1990.

14. Cynthia Enloe, *The Morning After: Sexual Politics at the End of the Cold War* (Berkeley: University of California Press, 1993), 166.

15. Walter Goodman, "The Iraq Conflict on American TV," *NYT*, September 17, 1990.

16. See William Safire, "Not Oil nor Jobs," *NYT*, November 19, 1990; and Jane Gross, "Berkeley; Coffee Is Strong, Opinion Is Split," *NYT*, January 14, 1991.

17. See Glenn Frankel, "Iraq, Kuwait Waging an Old-Fashioned War of Propaganda," *Washington Post*, September 10, 1990; Lisa Leff, "Weary, Wary Evacuees Bring Tales of Horror," *Washington Post*, September 11, 1990; Maureen Dowd, "World Summit for Children: Bush Is in New York for the U.N. Conference," *NYT*, September 30, 1990; and Johanna Neuman, "Kuwaiti's 'Shell of a Society,'" *USA Today*, October 1, 1990.

18. "Faked Kuwaiti Girl Testimony," YouTube, uploaded June 15, 2010, www.youtube.com /watch?v=LmfVs3WaE9Y (accessed March 11, 2012).

19. "Excerpts from Speech by Bush at Marine Post," *NYT*, November 23, 1990.

20. "Amnesty Report Says Iraqis Tortured and Killed Hundreds," *NYT*, December 20, 1990; George H. W. Bush, "Address to the Nation on the Invasion of Iraq," January 16, 1991, http://millercenter.org/president/bush/speeches/speech-3428.

21. Douglas Walton, *Appeal to Pity: Argumentum ad Misecordium* (Albany: SUNY Press, 1997).

22.   "Deception on Capitol Hill," *NYT*, January 15, 1992.

23.   Lee Edelman, *No Future: Queer Theory and the Death Drive* (Durham, NC: Duke University Press, 2004); Margaret Peacock, *Innocent Weapons: The Soviet and American Politics of Childhood During the Cold War* (Durham, NC: Duke University Press, 2014); Katherine Bond Stockton, *The Queer Child or Growing Sideways in the Twentieth Century* (Durham, NC: Duke University Press, 2009).

24.   "Reparations without Retribution," *NYT*, March 4, 1991; "Excerpts from Letter to U.N.," *NYT*, April 8, 1991.

25.   Haifa Zangana, *City of Widows* (London: Seven Stories, 2007), 73.

26.   Nadje al-Ali and Nicola Pratt, *What Kind of Liberation?: Women and the War on Iraq* (Berkeley: University of California Press, 2009), 46.

27.   Bush, "State of the Union Address," January 28, 1992, http://millercenter.org/president /bush/speeches/speech-5531.

28.   Bush, "Address to a Joint Session of Congress," September 11, 1990, http://millercenter.org /president/bush/speeches/speech-3425.

29.   Tracy Wood and Faye Fiore, "No Charges Filed against Suspect Beaten by Police," *Los Angeles Times*, March 7, 1991.

30.   Jason DeParle, "General and Troops Have Domestic Mission" *NYT*, May 3, 1992; Charles Mohr, "To Modernize, the Army Is Bringing Back Light Infantry," *NYT*, November 25, 1984.

31.   See Los Angeles Times, *Understanding the Riots: Los Angeles before and after the Rodney King Case* (Los Angeles: Los Angeles Times, 1992).

32.   Seth Mydans, "Twenty-Three Dead after Second Day of Los Angeles Riots," *NYT*, May 1, 1992.

33.   Andrew Rosenthal, "Quayle Says Riots Sprang from Lack of Family Values," *NYT*, May 20, 1992.

34.   "Excerpts from Speech by Bush in Los Angeles," *NYT*, May 9, 1992.

35.   Sapphire, "Strange Juice (or the Murder of Latasha Harlins)," in *American Dreams* (New York: Vintage Books, 1996), 156–57.

36.   See Radley Balko, *Rise of the Warrior Cop: The Militarization of America's Police Forces* (New York: Public Affairs Press, 2013).

37.   "Sect Arose from Split with Adventists," *NYT*, March 1, 1993.

38.   Sam Howe Verhovek, "Four US Agents Killed in Texas Shootout with Cult," *NYT*, March 2, 1993; Sam Howe Verhovek, "Four Hundred Law Agents Are in Standoff with Texas Cult," *NYT*, March 2, 1993; Sam Howe Verhovek, "'Messiah' Fond of Bible, Rock, and Women," *NYT*, March 3, 1993; Stephen Labaton, "Agent's Advice: Attack on a Sunday," *NYT*, March 3, 1993.

39.   Walter Goodman, "As Television, Waco Drama Had a Grim Inevitability," *NYT*, April 20, 1993; Peter Applebome, "Bloody Sunday's Roots in Deep Religious Soil," *NYT*, March 2, 1993; Sam Howe Verhovek, "Hardly Mentioned at Cultists' Trial: Their Leader," *NYT*, February 26, 1994; Verhovek, "'Messiah' Fond of Bible."

40.   "Apocalypse in Waco," *NYT*, April 20, 1993; Verhovek, "'Messiah' Fond of Bible."

41.   Verhovek, "Four US Agents Killed."

42.   Verhovek, "Four Hundred Law Agents."

43.   Adam Nossiter, "Warning of Violence Was Unheeded after Cult Leader's Gun Battle in '87," *NYT*, March 10, 1993.

44.   "The Waco Whitewash," *NYT*, October 12, 1993; Verhovek, "Hardly Mentioned."

45. Stephen Labaton and Sam Howe Verhovek, "Missteps in Waco: A Raid Re-examined," *NYT*, March 28, 1993.

46. Sam Howe Verhovek, "Texas Cult Fortress Is Becoming Prison behind Barbed Wire," *NYT*, April 13, 1993.

47. Peter Labaton, "Reno Sees Error in Move on Cult," *NYT*, April 20, 1993.

48. Peter Labaton, "Confusion Abounds in the Capital on Rationale for Assault on Cult," *NYT*, April 21, 1993; Sam Howe Verhovek, "Death in Waco: The Overview," *NYT*, April 20, 1993.

49. "Apocalypse in Waco"; Labaton, "Confusion Abounds."

50. "Excerpts from Clinton News Conference" *NYT*, April 21, 1993; Labaton, "Confusion Abounds."

51. US Department of Justice, "Report to the Deputy Attorney General on the Events at Waco, Texas, February 28 to April 19, 1993," October 8, 1993, VII-A-2, https://www.justice.gov /publications/waco/report-deputy-attorney-general-events-waco-texas.

52. Sam Howe Verhovek, "In Shadow of Texas Siege, Uncertainty for Innocents," *NYT*, March 8, 1993.

53. Labaton, "Confusion Abounds."

54. US Department of Justice, "Report to the Deputy Attorney General," VII-B-4, VII-A-1.

55. William Safire, "Waco, Reno, Iraqgate," *NYT*, October 14, 1993; see also "Waco Whitewash."

56. David Johnston, "US Saw Waco Assault as Best Option," *NYT*, April 25, 1993.

57. Dick Reavis, "Remembering Waco, and Stealing It," *NYT*, May 13, 1995.

58. See Fred Pfiel, *White Guys: Studies in Postmodern Domination and Difference* (New York: Verso, 1995); and Michael Kimmel, *Manhood in America: A Cultural History* (New York: Oxford University Press, 1996).

59. Reavis, "Remembering Waco."

60. Rick Bragg, "In Shock, Loathing, Denial: 'This Doesn't Happen Here,'" *NYT*, April 20, 1995.

61. Ibid.; "Savagery in Oklahoma City," *NYT*, April 20, 1995; Thomas Friedman, "Beirut, Okla.," *NYT*, April 23, 1995; John Kifner, "At Least Thirty-One Are Dead," *NYT*, April 20, 1995.

62. Serge Schmemann, "New Images of Terror," *NYT*, April 24, 1995.

63. Dirk Johnson, "The Care Center," *NYT*, April 20, 1995; Bragg, "In Shock, Loathing, Denial"; Kifner, "At Least Thirty-One Are Dead."

64. Mohanty and Martin, "What's Home Got to Do with It?," 90.

65. Melinda Henneberger, "Oklahoma City; Where Nothing Ever Happens, Terrorism Did," *NYT*, April 21, 1995.

66. A. M. Rosenthal, "On My Mind; Ending Forgiveness," *NYT*, April 21, 1995.

67. Walter Goodman, "Although Unrestrained in a Crisis, Television Is a Tie That Binds," *NYT*, April 28, 1995.

68. Bragg, "In Shock, Loathing, Denial."

69. "A Twisted Rage," *NYT*, April 24, 1995.

70. "Tiny Victim Shown in Dramatic Photo," *NYT*, April 21, 1995; "Child in Photo Was One-Year-Old Girl," *NYT*, April 22, 1995.

71. Rich Bragg, "Tender Memories of Day-Care Center Are All That Remain after the Bomb," *NYT*, April 20, 1995; Rich Bragg, "Statements by the President and Attorney General," *NYT*, April 20, 1995.

72. "Twisted Rage." Almon's gender was unconfirmed at first, producing pronoun confusion.

73. Todd Purdum, "Undertones of Relevance," *NYT*, April 20, 1995; Linda Greenhouse, "Exposed; Again, Bombs in the Land of the Free," *NYT*, April 23, 1995.

74. Todd Purdum, "Clinton and First Lady Offer Solace to the Young," *NYT*, April 23, 1995.

75. "Twisted Rage"; Peter Applebome, "The Pariah as Client," *NYT*, April 28, 1995; Bragg, "Tender Memories"; Rick Bragg, "Blast Toll Is No Longer in Deaths, but Shattered Lives," *NYT*, April 19, 1996; James Brooke, "All-American Defendant?," *NYT*, June 2, 1996; Jim Yardley, "Execution on TV Brings Little Solace," *NYT*, June 12, 2001; "History and Timothy McVeigh," *NYT*, June 11, 2001; Jo Thomas, "McVeigh Guilty on All Counts in the Oklahoma City Bombing," *NYT*, June 3, 1997.

76. John Kifner, "Authorities Hold a Man of 'Extreme Right-Wing Views," *NYT*, April 22, 1995.

77. Sam Howe Verhovek, "Many Theories about Choice of the Target," *NYT*, April 26, 1995; David Johnston, "Oklahoma Bombing Plotted for Months," *NYT*, April 25, 1995.

78. Robert McFadden, "A Life of Solitude and Obsession," *NYT*, May 4, 1995; Jo Thomas, "Nichols Convicted of Plot and Manslaughter Counts but Not of Actual Bombing," *NYT*, December 24, 1997; "History and Timothy McVeigh."

79. McFadden, "Life of Solitude and Obsession."

80. Rick Bragg, "On the Eve of His Execution, McVeigh's Legacy Remains Death and Pain," *NYT*, June 10, 2001. Full text of the letter is available at "McVeigh's Apr. 26 Letter to Fox News," Fox News, April 26, 2001, foxnews.com/story/0,2933,17500,00.html.

81. Pam Belluck, "McVeigh Said to Play Role in Seeking Holes in Government's Case." My emphasis.

82. Antiterrorism and Effective Death Penalty Act of 1996, S.735, 104th Congress, 1996, Title I, Title II, sec. 233(c), Title III, sec. 324(1); Neil Lewis, "Anti-terrorism Bill: Blast Turns a Snail into a Race Horse," *NYT*, April 21, 1995.

83. Antiterrorism and Effective Death Penalty Act of 1996, Title III, sec. 301, Title II, sec. 221, Title IV, sec. 401, Title IV, sec. 421.

84. Illegal Immigration Reform and Immigrant Responsibility Act of 1996, H.R. 3610, 104th Congress, 1996; Michael Welch, *Detained: Immigration Laws and the Expanding I.N.S. Jail Complex* (Philadelphia: Temple University Press, 2002).

85. Illegal Immigration Reform and Immigrant Responsibility Act of 1996, Title V.

86. Personal Responsibility and Work Opportunity Reconciliation Act, H.R. 3734, 104th Congress, 1996, sec. 101.

87. Defense of Marriage Act, H.R. 3396, 104th Congress, 1996, sec. 3.

88. Dorothy Roberts, *Killing the Black Body: Race, Reproduction, and the Meaning of Liberty* (New York: Vintage, 1999), 217, 202.

89. "Indicators of Welfare Dependence, Annual Report to Congress" (Washington, DC: Department of Health and Human Services, 2008), table TANF 1. Also see "Poverty Status of People, by Age, Race, and Hispanic Origin, 1959–2011," Department of the Census, www.census.gov/hhes/www/poverty/data/historical/hstpov3.xls (accessed October 20, 2012).

90. Jonathan Teller-Elsberg, Nancy Folbre, James Heintz, and the Center for Popular Economics, *Field Guide to the US Economy: A Compact and Irreverent Guide to Economic Life in America* (New York: New Press, 2006), 98–99.

91. Dorothy Roberts, "Feminism, Race, and Adoption Policy," in Incite!, *Color of Violence*, 44.

Fighting Back, Claiming Power

Feminist Rhetoric and Resistance to Rape in the 1970s

Catherine O. Jacquet

In early December 1970, 150 women stormed a Berkeley city council meeting and demanded a public hearing where, they said, "all the raped women of Berkeley can finally speak."[1] Organized as Women of the Free Future, the group had a list of demands, including free, frequent public bus transportation for all women from dusk to dawn; the introduction of self-defense training for all female schoolchildren in Berkeley schools; funding for Women of the Free Future to draw up, print, and circulate a pamphlet on how to prevent rape; and that women be allowed to carry loaded, concealed weapons.[2] One member of the group stood at the council chamber doors, wearing all black and carrying an unloaded Winchester rifle.

The Women of the Free Future organized one of the earliest actions of a burgeoning nationwide feminist antirape movement. This movement came in response to severely inadequate resources and overwhelming hostility toward survivors of sexual assault from the health care system, the criminal legal system, and society at large. In the early 1970s, some emergency rooms refused to admit rape victims, while most others lacked standardized health care protocols to treat survivors of sexual violence. There was little to no state or federal funding for rape prevention or response efforts, rape conviction rates were astronomically low, and women who reported rape were typically doubted, scrutinized, or blamed for their assaults. Feminist activists nationwide demanded change. They stormed city halls and dis-

Radical History Review
Issue 126 (October 2016)   DOI 10.1215/01636545-3594421
© 2016 by MARHO: The Radical Historians' Organization, Inc.

trict attorney's offices; they demonstrated in the streets and held speak-outs, conferences, and workshops; in cities and towns across the country they organized "women against rape," or WAR, groups; and they created the first rape crisis centers and hotlines to assist survivors of violence. Some took up arms, claiming their bodies as their own and angrily declaring they would defend themselves and other women by any means possible. After a decade of feminist organizing and agitation around rape, the world looked significantly different. By 1980 rape had become a topic of serious public debate, widespread social concern, and the target of sustained public policy.

Forty years in the making, the feminist antirape movement continues to this day. As a result, most scholarship on feminist antirape activism focuses on movement outcomes, analyzing its successes and failures. Largely written by sociologists, legal scholars, and political scientists, this scholarship typically paints a dismal picture. At best the movement is depicted as misguided and co-opted; at worst, it is described as a failure.[3] Like the battered women's movement, another innovation of 1970s feminist organizing, the antirape movement is often framed within a "narrative of decline"—this narrative tells a story of the movement's co-optation by the state, its depoliticization, and its eventual failure to meet its original, utopic goal to eradicate violence against women.[4] This interpretation is based largely on studies of the sweeping rape law reforms that were initiated by feminists in the 1970s and that took hold in all fifty states by the early 1980s. Many scholars rightly point out that law reform did not bring about the results that feminists had hoped for.[5] Indeed violence against women remains pervasive in the United States today.[6] Moreover, some scholars now argue that the reliance on the criminal legal system has both increased women's vulnerability to violence and had devastating effects on communities of color.[7] Yet while law reform may not have brought the revolution that feminists had hoped for, there was more to the 1970s feminist antirape movement than a push for legal reform alone. Indeed, there were significant currents within feminist organizing that both rejected and fiercely contested state-based solutions to sexual violence.

From antirape squads to self-defense training and vigilante responses, some feminists in the 1970s became vocal advocates of individual deterrence strategies rather than focusing on state-based solutions. These critical yet often overlooked feminist organizing strategies to protect women and avenge victims of sexual violence have an important place in the history of the feminist antiviolence project. Reductionist narratives that equate feminist antirape activism with law reform alone neglect these powerful calls for action and obscure what was, and continues to be, a multifaceted and complex feminist antirape movement.

This article, then, serves to expand the commonly told narrative of 1970s feminist antirape activism. While feminists responded to rape in myriad ways—such as opening rape crisis centers and creating hotlines to support survivors, holding public demonstrations, and writing extensive literature—this article focuses specifically on physical resistance and extrajudicial retaliation. The feminist actions presented here include both reported instances of resistance and urgent calls for women to fight their assailants. In pursuing and suggesting such methods, feminists created politically meaningful narratives that sought to change how women thought about themselves and the power they had in their own lives. These calls to action also challenged the state's authority by questioning who had the right to protect and defend women. In claiming this right for themselves, feminist activists reimagined women's social roles, disrupted traditional, patriarchal notions of femininity, and demanded their right to self-determination.

"Regaining Our Rights and Depriving the Rapist of His"

One of the earliest strategies of feminist resistance to sexual violence came in the form of antirape squads.[8] In response to a serial violent rapist in East Lansing, Michigan, a group of women from Michigan State University Women's Liberation announced their plan to form antirape squads during the fall of 1970. Writing in their newsletter, *Pissed Off Pink*, the women explained that these squads would be "groups of feminists dedicated to avenging the rape or other kinds of harassment perpetrated on our sisters by male supremacists."[9] By November, readers of *Pissed Off Pink* learned that a group calling itself the Kitty Genevesie (sic) Memorial Anti-Rape Squad had organized in the area. "Any woman who is harassed or attacked by a man" could report the incident to the squad, and "appropriate actions" would be taken.[10] The women of East Lansing were not alone; they announced their plan "in conjunction with our sisters in Berkeley," where one of the first documented antirape squads had formed.[11]

In August 1970 the Contra Costa Anti-Rape Squad no. 14 took to the streets.[12] Their first action was picketing the wedding of an alleged rapist. As reported in the Berkeley Women's Liberation newsletter, *It Ain't Me Babe*, the squad learned that the groom had raped a hired dancer who had performed at the bachelor party a week before the wedding. In response, members of the squad showed up at the wedding and reception and left leaflets on the cars of the friends and family of the bride and groom that read: "Women's Liberation thinks that relatives and friends should be the first to know there's a rapist in their midst, not the last. A week ago Saturday a young woman was raped by a man who sits among you today. He's the bridegroom. . . . We tried to warn Nancy [the bride] about the kind of pig she's marrying, but she didn't want to hear. Maybe it's still not too late."[13] Like the members of the Contra Costa squad, many women who joined antirape groups were motivated by a desire to retaliate against violence. The New York Women's Anti-Rape Group, for example, began in early 1972 in part to "go out and 'take care of' the men that rape."[14] Rather than rely on the state for justice, or male "protectors" for revenge, these women sought to take matters into their own hands, organize in their own defense, and fight back on their own behalf.

Stories of antirape squads offered a radical reimagining of the consequences of violence against women. In speeches at the University of Maine and the University of Maryland, New York–based radical feminist Robin Morgan claimed that a Women's Defense League operated a twenty-four-hour hotline in Chicago to protect women. "The most common call," Morgan explained, "comes around 2 or 3 a.m. It's a woman whose husband is drunk again, and who has beaten her up one side and down the other."[15] Following a phone call, black-belt-trained league members would arrive at the abused woman's house and "take care of" the man. Claiming that the incidences of rape in Chicago had dropped since the organization of the league, Morgan announced that antirape squads were putting "rapists in hospitals all over the country. . . . Rapists think twice about committing rape again after six weeks in traction."[16] In 1972, the *Chicago Tribune* and the *Washington Post* reported that the Los Angeles antirape squad had a "special way of dealing with rapists." Squad members would track down an alleged rapist, "jump him, shave his head, pour dye on him, take photographs and use them on a poster saying 'This man rapes women.'"[17] A similar story was told about a New York squad the next year.[18] A 1973 *Time* article reported that in Lansing, Michigan, a group of women spray-painted the word *rapist* across a front porch, scrawled the word on a suspect's car, and "made late-night warning telephone calls." In Los Angeles, an antirape squad adopted a "counter-harassing strategy: when a woman called to complain that a neighbor followed her whenever she went out, squad members followed the follower for three days."[19] And the *Chicago Tribune* reported in 1975 that after three women "entered the home of an accused rapist in Daytona Beach, Fla.," one of the women "proceeded to slash the man's shoulders, stomach, and arms."[20]

How numerous or how effective these antirape squads were is not clear. In their 1974 rape survivor's manual, *Against Rape*, Chicago Women Against Rape members Andra Medea and Kathleen Thompson reported that the squads in Detroit had disbanded when the "women decided that this approach was not a very practical one in terms of the time and emotional energy expended."[21] They further reported that on the West Coast all-women street patrols that tried to apprehend rapists who police had failed to arrest also typically abandoned this for other activities. Unlike other forms of feminist action, such as rape crisis lines or legal advocacy services, antirape squads were not a mainstay of the movement. By 1975 there was little mention of squads in either the feminist or mainstream press.

Yet, even if antirape squads largely went out of existence after a few short years, and even if feminists were *not* putting rapists in hospitals all over the country— Morgan's claims do seem somewhat doubtful—calls for violent resistance and retaliatory measures speak to the frustration many women felt and the lack of confidence they had in the state's ability to respond to sexual violence. Additionally, these early voices sought to shape a discourse on rape that at the time largely portrayed women as vulnerable victims. In contrast to this portrayal, narratives of antirape squads offered women a feeling of agency and access to power. By employing or suggesting various retaliatory measures, antirape squads countered the discourse of victims and victimization. With these stories, feminists invoked a scenario where there were serious consequences for male violence, and women were a force to be reckoned with.

"Everyone Has a Tiger Inside of Her"

Unlike antirape squads, self-defense did become a mainstay of the movement.[22] Self-defense strategies ran the gamut from more radical calls for women to take up arms to less controversial measures like learning the martial arts.[23] Yet no matter the form, from its earliest iterations in the late 1960s feminist advocacy for self-defense was always connected to efforts to protect women from male violence. As explained by two women who wrote of their experiences learning karate in 1969: "Women are attacked, beaten and raped every day. By Men. Women are afraid to walk certain streets after dark, and even afraid to walk into buildings where they live. It's about time that we as women got strong in order to defend ourselves."[24] Similar rhetoric accompanied feminist calls for self-defense across the nation. Many feminists understood this prevention effort as a critical piece of women's liberation. If women were to have complete autonomy over their lives, they had to be able to defend themselves. As feminist martial arts activist Dana Densmore explained in a recent interview, "Female liberation is not going to be there as long as this [male violence] is hanging over you."[25] Self-determination was the theory; self-defense was the practice.

Self-defense arrived on the feminist agenda well before a national antirape movement organized. In the summer of 1968, feminist activist Jayne West was nearly abducted by a group of men in Cambridge, Massachusetts. Following her narrow escape, she immediately began martial arts training. Her activist friends, including Dana Densmore and Abby Rockefeller, joined her in intensive training. By the end of the year, these women were giving demonstrations on self-defense at feminist workshops and conferences. Joined by several others, West, Densmore, and Rockefeller organized themselves as Cell 16, a radical feminist group that promoted martial arts training taught to women, by women, as a politically expedient step toward women's liberation.[26] Speaking to this, Densmore explained, "It was serious, and it was feminist. It was intended to be transformative, a political response to the physical assaults on women and [to men's] physical control."[27] Almost two full years before a national antirape movement organized, the women of Cell 16 were at the vanguard of an emerging movement in women's self-defense. They articulated a politics of rape that called for active resistance, focused on prevention, and sought to disrupt the male attacker–female victim paradigm. As Densmore wrote in the November 1969 issue of Cell 16's journal *No More Fun and Games*, "If even a few women, once in a while, stood up and fought back, the rapists would think twice. They are looking for certain sick thrills, and these thrills just aren't available from a woman who breaks out of his hold in one spring and drives an elbow into his solar plexus knocking him cold."[28] While Densmore erroneously suggested that women never fought back against their assailants, her statement was likely not meant to be a condemnation of individual women's behavior but, rather, a comment on women's vulnerability. Densmore suggested an alternative world where, rather than being viewed as easy targets, women could effectively defend themselves.

As the antirape movement gained traction, self-defense became an accepted form of activism and was widely promoted within the movement. By the early 1970s, self-defense permeated feminist antirape discourse and literature and would continue to do so throughout the decade. Indeed, one of the best-known posters from the early

Figure 1. Poster by Betsy Warrior, 1971.

years of organizing was radical feminist activist Betsy Warrior's graphic of a woman giving a swift kick to a man in his groin. The man is falling backward, shocked. The words "Smash Sexism, Disarm Rapists" surround the graphic. The poster was circulated nationwide and printed in the July 1971 issue of *No More Fun and Games* (figure 1).[29]

While often illustrated with female figures in karate uniforms, self-defense encompassed a range of activities from basic kicks and punches to the repurposing of keys and cigarettes as weapons. In their handbook on rape, for example, the Detroit Women Against Rape featured a twenty-page section on self-defense with illustrations explaining how to effectively ward off an attacker.[30] This included jabs, punches, stabs, kicks, and instructions on how to use everyday items

for defense. "If you smoke, forget what your mother told you about women who smoke on the street," the authors instructed. "You don't have to smoke it anyway; just carry it. It burns." An umbrella should be used "as a bayonet, not a club, and aim for his throat or stomach."[31] Similarly, in their handbook, the Chicago Women Against Rape advised women on basic principles like stance, how to use your hands, breaking a hold, and taking the offensive.[32] The authors included an illustration of a male figure with explanations detailing how to attack various parts of the body:

"Slam heel of hand up under chin or nose . . . wrench little finger; try to break it . . . kick to kneecap."[33] At the root of any method of self-defense was a belief in self-reliance and a challenge to the narrative of women as helpless victims. As New York Radical Feminist member Maryanne Manhart explained to an all-female audience at an April 1971 self-defense workshop, "It's high time we stopped being victims. . . . Since you are living in a jungle and no one may help you, be self-reliant. . . . Everyone has a tiger inside of her."[34]

As a strategy, self-defense reimagined the relationships among embodiment, vulnerability, and gender. Rather than framing women's bodies as inherently rapable, self-defense activists sought to reimagine women's bodies as forces that repelled rapists and stopped rape.[35] Like the stories of antirape squads, retaliation, and revenge, self-defense allowed women to imagine themselves as powerful agents in their own lives.

In a more extreme iteration of self-defense, some feminists advocated that women take up arms. Although not necessarily the most popular method, it is noteworthy that in the era of increasing militancy within social movements, some feminist activists also took up this call.[36] In the early 1970s, for example, the Iowa City women's liberation newsletter *Ain't I a Woman* featured drawings of women holding, aiming, or shooting guns. A September 1970 issue included a series of six drawings that instructed the reader on how to hold and shoot a pistol. A January 1971 issue featured a cartoon of a women confidently pointing and shooting a gun. The word bubble next to her read, "Sisterhood is" with a large blank space following.[37] For the feminists of Iowa City, sisterhood meant protecting themselves and one another from violence by any means necessary.

Perhaps the best example of armed resistance came from a group in Dallas, Texas, who called themselves Women Armed for Self-Protection (WASP). Formed in 1974, WASP advocated both self-defense and violent retaliation against attackers. The group's first leaflet declared, "WE ARE WOMEN. . . . WE ARE ARMED. WE SUPPORT IMMEDIATE AND DRASTIC RETALIATION AGAINST ALL RAPISTS." The group produced provocative posters of women holding rifles—a warning to rapists to beware. One WASP poster featuring a woman holding a rifle read: "Men and women were created equal . . . and Smith & Wesson makes damn sure it stays that way."

While the group faced criticism for their extreme stance, group member Nikki Craft claimed that they received letters of support from women across the country. According to Craft, four women from Chicago even traveled to Dallas to meet with WASP members to share ideas and discuss strategy. "Many women were ready for defiance," Craft explains, "They wanted to channel their anger and were ready to hear what we had to say, even if it was rhetorical and rigid."[38] With the energy and outrage of the antirape movement behind them, some feminists advocated militant means to protect themselves from rape.

"Why Have a Trial—the Criminal Is Dead"

Feminist support for women's self-defense collided head-on with the authority of the state in cases where women were brought up on criminal charges for defending themselves against sexual assault.[39] Many of these cases became feminist causes célèbres, underscoring feminist contentions about the failures of the legal system and its hostility toward women. Perhaps the best-known of these cases was that of Joan Little.[40] On August 27, 1974, twenty-year-old black inmate Joan Little escaped from the Beaufort County Jail in the small town of Washington, North Carolina, after killing Clarence Alligood, a white officer at the facility. Another officer found Alligood dead in Little's cell, naked from the waist down with ejaculate on his thigh. Little was gone. When she turned herself in to the State Bureau of Investigation one week later, Little claimed that she had acted in self-defense, stabbing Alligood eleven times with an ice pick that he had brought into her cell so he could sexually assault her. The state of North Carolina charged Little with first degree murder, a crime that held a mandatory death sentence. With a major outpouring of support from the civil rights, prisoners' rights, and women's liberation movements, the Little case gained national attention over the next eleven months. By the time of the trial in July 1975, nearly every major newspaper in the country was covering it, dozens of demonstrations for Little's innocence had taken place across the country, and the case had garnered international notoriety.[41]

When politicizing the Little case, feminists confronted what they understood as two major failures of the criminal legal system. First, in cases of rape, the legal system criminalized the victim and not the rapist. Second, the law did not support a woman's right to self-defense. As a rape victim on trial for defending her bodily autonomy, Little's case epitomized those failures. The case was equally crucial from the standpoint of racial justice. As a black woman, Little stood at the crossroads of a long history of racial and sexual injustice. Historically, black women had seen virtually no justice in cases of white sexual attack.[42] Her acquittal, therefore, would set a new precedent in particular for black rape victims of white male violence.

"Power to the ice pick!" became a rallying cry for many of Little's supporters. During the trial some of Little's feminist supporters sat in the back of the Wake County Courthouse courtroom wearing T-shirts emblazoned with the slogan. In so doing, they were supporting a woman's right to protect herself from male violence by any means necessary, a right denied by the state.[43] In a *Feminist Alliance Against Rape* newsletter article titled "Killing with Just Cause," author Sue Lenaerts, a self-defense instructor at D.C. Rape Crisis Center, sharply criticized the state's handling of self-defense cases, connecting self-defense with larger feminist goals. "We consider women found guilty of murder in a self-defense case to be political prisoners," Lenaerts wrote. "Supporting women who fight back is politically crucial for feminists. Any time the criminal justice system prosecutes a woman for fighting for her life and dignity, all women stand to lose."[44] Like Lenaerts, many feminists believed that women had a fundamental right to protect themselves. Denying that right kept all women's safety in jeopardy and further increased the levels of violence against them. As one defense committee plainly stated: "In defending themselves, women run the risk of prosecution by the state for a violent crime. As a result women often find themselves facing two violent situations: the first being the physical assault, and the second, a legal assault leading to possible imprisonment."[45] As Little's supporters proclaimed "power to the ice pick!" they rejected the state's interpretation of the crime and supported a woman's right to protect herself.

Outside the Wake County Courthouse, supporters carried picket signs with the slogan "Why have a trial—the criminal is dead."[46] According to this feminist perspective, the only crime committed was the rape, and "the case had no business coming to trial in the first place."[47] The criminal legal system wrongly portrayed Little's killing of Alligood as murder rather than the act of self-defense that it actually was. Justice could only be served, therefore, if the trial was called off. A petition circulated by the Chicago Women's Committee to Free JoAnne Little, which urged the governor of North Carolina to drop all charges, emphasized this viewpoint. The petition stated, "It is abundantly clear that the death [of Alligood] resulted from his own crime of attempted rape. The criminal is already dead."[48] Little, on the other hand, had committed no crime.

On August 15, 1975, the jury for the Joan Little murder trial acquitted the defendant of all charges. According to the jury, the state had not proven its case. This was a major victory for activists of multiple stripes. Little walked out of the Wake County Courthouse that day to the celebration of some one hundred protestors as they cheered "Freedom, freedom, freedom!"[49] National Organization for Women president Karen DeCrow hailed the verdict as the first "legal precedent for a woman's right to self-defense."[50] A significant departure from the past, Little's acquittal held enormous meaning for the movements that rallied around her. For all, the case served as a major milestone in a history of overwhelming injustice.

Self-defense cases like that of Little's sat at a critical crossroads of women's liberation and the criminal legal system. In defending themselves, women like Little claimed the right to protect their own lives and bodies. Their feminist supporters demanded that the state recognize all women's right to self-defense and self-determination. In so doing, these feminists challenged the authority of the state and rejected the notion that the state be the sole arbiter in cases of rape. When confronted with male violence, feminists believed that women had the right to defend and avenge themselves. In denying women this right, the state continued a long-standing pattern of hostility toward all women, and rape victims in particular.

Conclusion

In 1981, Minneapolis's newly founded Cleis Press published *Fight Back! Feminist Resistance to Male Violence*. With over forty contributors, the 392-page volume included accounts of women who retaliated or defended themselves against abusive husbands or rapists, accounts of antirape and battered women's activism, essays on fighting back and the self-defense movement, descriptions of community outreach efforts, and a forty-two-page directory of resource organizations. Like Berkeley's Women of the Free Future who organized over a decade before, the contributors to *Fight Back!* articulated a politics of rape that focused on prevention, advocated women's right to self-determination and self-defense, celebrated resistance, and offered complex reflections on state-based solutions to the problem of sexual violence. Their voices are a reminder that despite the fact that antirape work had turned largely to state-based efforts by the late 1970s, particularly in the form of law reform, some feminists continued to challenge the role of the state and sharply rejected the growing influence of state actors.

Throughout the 1970s, some feminists contested state intervention into antirape work, and many sought alternative means to address sexual violence. In pursuing methods like antirape squads and self-defense, they asserted their right to defend and protect themselves and their sisters, challenging the authority of the state by taking matters into their own hands. These narratives of resistance served as powerful rejections of dominant cultural constructions of women as weak, inferior, or inherently rapable. Even if those who employed combat tactics or engaged in extrajudicial revenge were few, the alternatives they presented challenged women to reconsider the way they thought about themselves and to claim their own power. The narratives of resistance and retaliation that they constructed (and sometimes enacted) did important cultural work—they offered an alternative to women that was based on their own empowerment, and reframed how women saw themselves in relation to men, as well as in relation to a state that largely failed to protect them.

Notes

The author thanks Zevi Gutfreund for his thoughtful feedback on early drafts of this article. Many thanks also to the readers and editors of the *Radical History Review* for their comments.

1.   "No More Rape: Berkeley Women Confront City Council," *Liberation News Service*, December 5, 1970, Rape—Newspaper Ephemera folder, Women's Ephemera Collection, McCormick Library of Special Collections, Northwestern University Library, Evanston, IL (hereafter WEF).

2.   "No More Rape." See also "The Most Vicious Word," *Wichita Eagle*, March 25, 1971, Rape—Newspaper Ephemera folder, WEF.

3.   Kristin Bumiller, *In an Abusive State: How Neoliberalism Appropriated the Feminist Movement against Sexual Violence* (Durham, NC: Duke University Press, 2008); Rose Corrigan, *Up against a Wall: Rape Reform and the Failure of Success* (New York: New York University Press, 2013); Nancy Matthews, *Confronting Rape: The Feminist Anti-Rape Movement and the State* (New York: Routledge, 1994); Janet C. Gornick and David S. Meyer, "Changing Political Opportunity: The Anti-Rape Movement and Public Policy," *Journal of Policy History* 10, no. 4 (1998): 367–98. Gornick and Meyer argue that the feminist antirape movement "was in sharp decline" by 1980—they go so far as to

suggest that as a result of state co-optation of feminist goals, the movement itself actually disappeared.

4. For a critique of the narrative of decline in the battered women's movement, see Gretchen Arnold and Jami Ake, "Reframing the Narrative of the Battered Women's Movement," *Violence Against Women* 19, no. 5 (2013): 557–78.

5. See Jeanne C. Marsh, Alison Geist, and Nathan Caplan, *Rape and the Limits of Law Reform* (Boston: Auburn House, 1982); Cassia Spohn and Julie Horney, *Rape Law Reform: A Grassroots Revolution and Its Impact* (New York: Plenum, 1992).

6. For recent statistics on violence against women in the United States, see Office of Justice Programs, "Full Report on the Prevalence, Incidence, and Consequences of Violence against Women," US Department of Justice, November 2000, www.ncjrs.gov/pdffiles1/nij/183781.pdf. See also the Bureau of Justice Statistics, "Selected Findings: Female Victims of Violence," US Department of Justice, October 23, 2009, www.bjs.gov/content/pub/pdf/fvv.pdf.

7. See Aya Gruber, "Rape, Feminism, and the War on Crime," *Washington Law Review* 84 (2009): 581–58; Incite! Women of Color against Violence, ed., *Color of Violence: The Incite! Anthology* (Cambridge, MA: South End, 2006); Beth Richie, *Arrested Justice: Black Women, Violence, and America's Prison Nation* (New York: New York University Press, 2012).

8. The title of this section is from Detroit Women Against Rape, *Stop Rape* (Detroit: Women Against Rape, 1973).

9. "Jack the Raper," *Pissed Off Pink*, September 1970, Special Collections, Michigan State University Library, Lansing, MI. This announcement was also printed in the October 30, 1970, issue of Iowa City Women's Liberation newsletter, *Ain't I a Woman*.

10. "Anti-Rape Squad," *Pissed Off Pink*, November 1970, Special Collections, Michigan State University Library. It is not clear if the antirape squad was a group of women from Michigan State University or a separate group entirely. It is notable that this group named themselves in memory of Kitty Genovese. In 1964, a male attacker repeatedly stabbed, raped, and eventually killed Genovese in a thirty-two-minute attack outside of her apartment building in New York City. It was reported at the time, although this has since been debunked, that thirty-eight of Genovese's neighbors had either heard or witnessed the attack, yet not a single person intervened or called the police. Antirape activists in the 1970s would take Genovese up as a martyr for the movement.

11. "Jack the Raper."

12. Contra Costa County runs adjacent to Alameda County. Dozens of town and cities sit within the borders of Alameda Country, including Berkeley, Oakland, and San Francisco.

13. "Jack the Raper," *It Ain't Me Babe*, September 4–17, 1970, 5.

14. Notes of National Organization for Women Rape Meeting, May 24, 1973, box 1, New York Women against Rape collection, Schlesinger Library, Radcliffe Institute, Harvard University, Cambridge, MA.

15. Quoted in "Feminist Praises Maine Lib Moves," *Bangor Daily News*, Dec. 10, 1971.

16. Fran Pollner, "Robin: Harbinger of a New Season," *Off Our Backs*, March 31, 1972, 23.

17. Marsha Dubrow, "Women Organize to Combat Rape and Counsel Victims," *Washington Post*, December 21, 1972. See also "Women Join to Combat Rape—the 'Condoned' Crime," *Chicago Tribune*, December 25, 1972.

18. J. Dwyer, "End of the Line for Jack the Ripper?," *Black Belt Magazine*, December 1973.

19. "Women against Rape," *Time*, April 23, 1973.

20. Patricia Anstett, "Defining Defense against Rape," *Chicago Tribune*, September 9, 1975.

Although it is unknown if these women considered themselves a "squad," they used tactics similar to those of antirape squads. Local police described the women as "vigilantes."

21. Andra Medea and Kathleen Thompson, *Against Rape* (New York: Farrar, Straus, and Giroux, 1974), 126.

22. The title of this section is taken from Grace Lichtenstein, "Feminists Hold Rape-Defense Workshop," *New York Times*, April 18, 1971.

23. The scholarship on the feminist self-defense movement is typically focused on martial arts training or street fighting and does not include armed resistance. See Patricia Searles and Ronald Berger, "The Feminist Self-Defense Movement: A Case Study," *Gender and Society* 1, no. 1 (March 1987): 61–84. See also Nadia Telsey, "Karate and the Feminist Resistance Movement," in *Fight Back! Feminist Resistance to Male Violence*, ed. Frédérique Delacoste and Felice Newman (San Francisco: Cleis Press, 1981), 184–96. For an analysis of women's self-defense in the 1990s, see Martha McCaughey, *Real Knockouts: The Physical Feminism of Women's Self-Defense* (New York: New York University Press, 1997).

24. Susan Pascalé, Rachel Moon, and Leslie B. Tanner, "Self-Defense for Women," in *Sisterhood Is Powerful: An Anthology of Writings from the Women's Liberation Movement*, ed. Robin Morgan (New York: Vintage Books, 1970), 527.

25. Dana Densmore, interview by the author, June 17, 2015.

26. Original members of Cell 16 also included Roxanne Dunbar, Betsy Warrior, and Lisa Leghorn. Many others joined the group over the years. Cell 16 was active from 1968 to 1973. They published the feminist journal *No More Fun and Games*.

27. Densmore interview.

28. Dana Densmore, "Writing a Leaflet," *No More Fun and Games*, no. 3 (November 1969): 108.

29. Susan Brownmiller, *In Our Time: Memoir of a Revolution* (New York: Dial Press, 1999), 205; Betsy Warrior, "Disarm Rapists, Smash Sexism," *No More Fun and Games: A Journal of Female Liberation*, no. 5 (July 1971): 19.

30. The Detroit Women Against Rape published *Stop Rape*, the first feminist handbook on sexual violence, in 1971. *Stop Rape* was distributed to women across the country and, according to Chicago Women Against Rape, inspired antirape activities in many communities.

31. Detroit Women Against Rape, *Stop Rape*, WEF, 16.

32. See Medea and Thompson, *Against Rape*, 73–94.

33. Ibid., 93.

34. Quoted in Lichtenstein, "Feminists Hold Rape-Defense Workshop." Manhart's self-defense workshop was part of the New York Radical Feminists' Conference on Rape, held in April 1971 in New York City. Two hundred women attended the all-day event, which included workshops on rape and the law, health and medical issues, rape and psychiatrists, incest and child molestation, a speak-out, and a self-defense workshop.

35. See Sharon Marcus, "Fighting Bodies, Fighting Words: A Theory and Politics of Rape Prevention" in *Feminists Theorize the Political*, ed. Judith Butler and Joan W. Scott (New York: Routledge, 1992), 385–403. In this essay on rape prevention, poststructuralist theorist Marcus defines self-defense as one strategy "which will enable women to sabotage men's power to rape, which will empower women to take the ability to rape completely out of men's hands" (388). Self-defense, she argues, puts the emphasis on "women's will, agency, and capacity for violence," rather than assuming women as subjects of fear and objects of male violence (395). Curiously, with the exception of one academic study published in 1985,

Marcus makes no mention of 1970s feminist calls for self-defense or of the feminist self-defense movement.

36. While there is a significant historiography on the role of violence in movements for social justice (the black freedom struggle being an excellent example), scholars of 1970s feminism have yet to address this discourse in modern feminism. There were indeed currents within 1970s feminism that supported the use of violence, as documented in this article, and there is a literature debating the use and meanings of violence and nonviolence within modern feminism. See, for example, Judith Winthrow, "Should Women Go Armed?," *Feminist Alliance Against Rape,* July/August 1978; Melanie Kaye, "Women and Violence," in Delacoste and Newman, *Fight Back!,* 160–63; D. A. Clarke, "A Woman with a Sword: Some Thoughts on Women, Feminism, and Violence," in *Transforming a Rape Culture,* ed. Emilie Buchwald, Pamela Fletcher, and Martha Roth (Minneapolis, MN: Milkweed Editions, 1993), 393–404; and Pearl Cleage, "What Can I Say," in *Words of Fire: An Anthology of African American Feminist Thought,* ed. Beverly Guy-Sheftall (New York: New Press, 1995), 429–32.

37. "Sisterhood is" cartoon, *Ain't I a Woman,* January 29, 1971.

38. Nikki Craft, "Drifting from the Mainstream: A Chronicle of Early Anti-rape Organizing," in Delacoste and Newman, *Fight Back!,* 112.

39. The title of this section is from Wayne King, "Trial Gives New Twist to Old Racial Issue," *New York Times,* August 12, 1975.

40. Little's first name was spelled differently depending on the source, sometimes Joan, JoAnne, or Joann. I use *Joan* here as that is the spelling used in the legal record. Her name is pronounced "Jo-Anne."

41. For additional scholarship on Joan Little, see Danielle McGuire, "Power to the Ice Pick!," in *At the Dark End of the Street: A New History of the Civil Rights Movement from Rosa Parks to the Rise of Black Power* (New York: Knopf, 2011), 246–78. See also Genna Rae McNeil, "'Joanne Is You and Joanne Is Me': A Consideration of African American Women and the 'Free Joan Little' Movement, 1974–75," in *Sisters in the Struggle: African American Women in the Civil Rights–Black Power Movement,* ed. Bettye Collier-Thomas and V. P. Franklin (New York: New York University Press, 2001), 259–79.

42. For an excellent analysis of white-on-black sexual violence in twentieth-century United States and antirape organizing, see McGuire, *At the Dark End of the Street.*

43. King, "Trial Gives New Twist."

44. Sue Lenaerts, "Killing with Just Cause," *Feminist Alliance Against Rape,* July/August 1976, 8–9.

45. "Free Yvonne Wanrow," box 1, Nkenge Touré papers, Sophia Smith Collection, Smith College, Northampton, MA.

46. King, "Trial Gives New Twist."

47. Karen Lindsey, "Victory for Joanne," *Off Our Backs* 5, no. 8 (1975): 2.

48. "Free JoAnne Little," Rape—Joanne Little folder, WEF.

49. Rick Nichols, "Verdict Comes Quickly," *Raleigh News and Observer,* August 16, 1975.

50. Quoted in Dennis A. Williams, "Trials: It Was the People," *Newsweek,* August 25, 1975, 29.

Protecting the Prestige of the Traditional Family

The Politics of Domestic Violence Discourse

Raphael Ginsberg

Pennies for Change is a thrift shop located in Durham, North Carolina. One of many thrift stores funding victim support services in the state of North Carolina, it donates its proceeds to funding the Durham Crisis Response Center (DCRC). The DCRC provides various forms of socioeconomic support for domestic violence victims, including counseling, emergency housing, and legal advocacy.[1] In addition to thrift store fundraising, PayPal donations are solicited on DCRC's website.

Just thirty-five miles east of Pennies for Change is the headquarters of North Carolina's prison system. Its budget situation is completely different from DCRC's. Its 2012–13 budget of $1.52 billion is funded wholly by tax dollars and requires no thrift shop support or voluntary donations.[2]

This situation is typical in the United States: public resources for prisons are ever available while funding for victims' socioeconomic support remains contingent on uncertain donation and retail revenues. For example, in 2011, the National Network to End Domestic Violence completed a census of 1,726 domestic violence programs across the nation. The census recorded the requests for services each program reported within a twenty-four-hour period, finding that there were 10,581 requests for services that the domestic violence programs could not meet, including over 6,714 requests for housing. The report notes that programs could not meet these requests because "programs did not have the resources to offer these ser-

Radical History Review
Issue 126 (October 2016)   DOI 10.1215/01636545-3594433
© 2016 by MARHO: The Radical Historians' Organization, Inc.

vices."[3] Accordingly, in the 2012 piece "VAWA Is Not Enough: Academics Speak Out about VAWA Reauthorization," leading domestic violence scholars charged that "Congress should focus efforts on economic justice,"[4] shifting its emphasis from the criminal justice system.

This gap between prison funding and victim support services can be traced in part to a series of late twentieth-century federal initiatives. In 1978, a US Civil Rights Commission hearing reflected deep concerns about the relationship between domestic violence and both male authority and female economic subordination. Conservative responses to the nascent battered women's movement in the 1980s, including debates about the 1980 Domestic Violence Prevention Act and the 1984 report of the Task Force on Family Violence,[5] portrayed domestic violence as a matter of aberrant abusers rather than an exercise of patriarchal authority or structural socioeconomic inequality. Congressional debates addressing the 1994 Violence Against Women Act (VAWA), like the task force report, also characterized domestic violence as a problem of aberrant offenders. In the process, criminality displaced gender as the primary framework for understanding domestic violence.

Battered Women: Issues of Public Policy

In the 1970s, domestic violence was treated largely as a private family matter, and arrest rates for domestic violence incidents to which officers responded averaged between 3 percent and 13 percent.[6] Assaultive men were often granted formal and informal immunities from prosecution, to protect the privacy of the family and promote "domestic harmony."[7] In response, feminists formed consciousness-raising groups to condemn domestic violence and publicize its pervasiveness. According to activist and scholar Susan Schechter, by 1977 the term *battered women* reached public prominence.[8] The movement's orientation was feminist and grassroots and articulately critical of traditional gender norms through which males perceive their dominant position as a license to abuse and women, because of their subordination, have difficulty escaping such abuse. Activists contested the lax enforcement of domestic violence laws, advocated for the creation of civil protection orders, established shelters for battered women, and created emotional support systems for victims.

It was in this context that the 1978 US Civil Rights Commission consultation "Battered Women: Issues of Public Policy" was held. The first federal examination of domestic violence, it drew on an array of experts, including law enforcement personnel, scholars, attorneys, and members of the battered women's movement (a precursor to contemporary anti-domestic violence activism). While some participants argued for changing law enforcement responses to domestic violence, many stressed the need for gender equality and socioeconomic support for victims.

The consultation took place over two days and included over thirty presenters. It received scant media attention, with no coverage in either the *New York Times* or the *Washington Post.* Its aims were diverse, including "to identify sound, existing research data, as well as research gaps, and consequently to consider research strategies; to identify necessary state legal and law enforcement reform; to identify needed short- and long-term support services for battered women; to identify, in all of the above, the appropriate Federal role; to facilitate communication among researchers, activists, policymakers, and others; and to inform the public."[9] Law enforcement was only one of many issues the consultation addressed; over two-thirds of the presenters focused on issues of socioeconomic support. The consultation's participants offered feminist, class-conscious analyses of domestic violence, locating the origins of the violence in economic inequality and traditional family roles. In her keynote address, movement activist Del Martin argued, "Marriage is the institutional source and setting in which the violence is carried out. . . . Domestic violence cannot be fully understood without examining the institution of marriage itself as the context in which the violence takes place."[10] She described American gender relations as a "patriarchal structure" in which the "dominant group [men] define acceptable roles of subordinates [women]." Marriage, Martin argued, is the arena in which "women and men are socialized to act out dominant-submissive roles that in and of themselves invite abuse. Husbands/assailants and wife/victims are merely the actors in the script that society has written for them."[11] Lisa Leghorn averred, "That the nuclear family is not working in this culture can no longer be questioned."[12]

Accordingly, participants challenged male dominance within the family. Judge Lisa Richette proposed eliminating the husband as "head of the family" from its "continuing presence in the law, in religion, in administrative procedure, and a taken for granted aspect of family life." She argued, "Full sexual equality is essential for the prevention of wife-beating."[13] Leghorn stressed the need for replacing male domination with female solidarity, hailing support services provided to abused women, which could foster "new ways of living" and the kinds "of transformation in their lives [that] is not only possible, but also necessary."[14]

Participants noted how socioeconomic challenges prevent women from leaving abusive relationships. The consultation's introduction noted that "battered women are limited often in their ability to flee their homes by financial dependence . . . [and] the lack of housing . . . services."[15] The lack of economic resources, housing, and job training constrained victims, Martin noted: "Without a place to go or means of support . . . the wife/victim is often forced to return to her violent husband," and that, in evaluating whether to leave, women are "forced to face the cold, hard fact of the poverty of her existence."[16] The consultation's participants proposed policies responsive to the needs of all women, not just victims. Monica Erler argued, "Abused women don't need treatment programs. They, like other women, need fair income for their labor, decent housing at an affordable price, competent legal advice, dependable child care and other assistance with child rearing. Government policy and funding should take these needs seriously."[17] These resources would ensure independence, which could enable women to leave abusive situations.

It was not only the consultation's battered women's activists who asserted the need for victims' support but the mainstream political figures participating in the consultation as well. Representatives from the Department of Housing and Urban Development, Department of Health, Education, and Welfare, Department of Labor, and the Legal Services Corporation gave extensive presentations about how victims could utilize federal resources to escape abuse, including information about how to find housing, welfare, and legal representation through their respective offices.

Altogether, consultation participants held that the traditional family rests on the exercise of male violence and socioeconomic inequalities that trap women in abusive situations. They proposed mechanisms enabling women to escape abuse, but these mechanisms threatened to undermine the autonomy of the family. Subsequent conservative responses absolved gender norms and socioeconomic inequality of any culpability in domestic violence.

Conservative Opposition to Federal Domestic Violence Assistance

Conservative opposition to the battered women's movement coalesced soon after the consultation took place. According to Elizabeth Pleck, in the late 1970s and early 1980s "the New Right identified domestic violence legislation with feminism, which in turn they associated with an attack on 'motherhood, the family, and Christian Values.'"[18] For example, in 1980, the Moral Majority worked with Republican senators to successfully defeat the Domestic Violence Prevention and Services Act. The proposed act provided $65 million to domestic violence shelters and programs, money that, in contrast to subsequent VAWA legislation, was entirely dedicated to victims' services.

In Senate debates about this bill, Gordon Humphrey argued that the domestic violence shelters poised to receive federal money were "opposed to traditional families"[19] and would function as "indoctrination centers" for "antifamily" ideas.[20] For Humphrey, the matter went "right to heart of the American family, which is the basis of our society."[21] Senator Jesse Helms likewise argued that shelters "encourage the disintegration of thousands of American families." Helms claimed, "This type of social engineering does not command the support of the majority of the American people and I suspect this is the primary reason why these centers have not been able to generate sufficient financial support within their local communities and now seek federal tax dollars." He concluded, "I cannot support legislation which gives every indication of supporting activities which can only further undermine the ability of many families to resolve their problems while preserving their unity."[22]

Senator Strom Thurmond asked, "Who can seriously argue that the Federal Government is better suited than family and friends, churches and community groups to cure this social ill?" He feared that the legislation "would result in dividing the family rather than uniting the family and curing domestic violence."[23] If passed, a Moral Majority lobbyist argued, "radical feminists" will "be coming to the federal trough for a $65 million feed."[24] Another Moral Majority lobbyist said their opposition to the bill was an effort to "counter the federal government's intrusion into the domestic realm."[25] The *Moral Majority Report* complained that the bill would "place undue emphasis on separation as a solution to domestic violence. This would violate a fundamental moral precept and represent a victory for humanism."[26] Howard Phillips, head of the Conservative Caucus, asserted that civil society adequately addressed domestic violence, asking, "How do you suppose the matter has been taken care of the last two hundred years? It's been largely taken care of by private organizations, religious groups, by families."[27]

The conservative defense and absolution of the traditional family took fuller form in the 1983 Final Report of President Ronald Reagan's Task Force on Family Violence.[28] The report marked only a minor moment in domestic violence discourse, as, like the events described above, it received scant media attention and passing mention in subsequent scholarly work. Nonetheless, the document marks an important moment in the growing divide between criminal-justice-based versus victim-support-oriented responses to domestic violence. In contrast to the battered women's movement activists in the 1978 consultation, the Task Force on Family Violence was composed of law enforcement personnel and members of the punishment-oriented wing of the victims' rights movement. The group included the Detroit and Phoenix police chiefs, the Suffolk County, Massachusetts, district attorney, Missouri attorney general John Ashcroft, Ursula Meese (wife of US attorney general Ed Meese), and victims' rights activists Frances Seward, Mareese Duff, and Catherine Milton.

In noting the prevalence of domestic violence, the report is consistent with the consultation. The report also addressed the unique challenges of addressing domestic violence (as opposed to anonymous violence), noting the necessity of specific criminal justice responses. Acknowledging the particular nature of intimate partner violence at all was counter to conservative antipathy for addressing domestic violence at the federal level, and in fact, some conservatives opposed it.[29] However, despite this acknowledgment, the report conformed to conservative orthodoxy concerning the family, hailing the centrality of the traditional family and remaining silent on women's socioeconomic subordination. The report's analysis of domestic violence did not foreground gender and therefore could not address the relationship between gender inequality and victims' inability to leave abusive relationships.

Instead, the report extolled the virtues of the traditional family and the necessity of its promotion and preservation. The report's epigraph quotes President Reagan: "Families stand at the center of society . . . building our future must begin by preserving families."[30] The introduction declares that "the family is the cornerstone of the American community. Preserving valuable traditions and nurturing the country's children, families are the nation's greatest strength and hope for the future" (97). And the report's conclusion reiterates the point: "America derives its strength, purpose and productivity from its commitment to family values" (119). Thus, according to the report, "As important as our families are to us individually and to the health of the nation, it is crucial that public policy support and strengthen family values and family well-being" (119).

The report protects the family's prestige by privileging criminal justice responses and arguing that lax punishment causes domestic violence, not the traditional family's dynamics. The report contains twenty recommendations for the criminal justice system, recommendations geared toward increasing prosecution and conviction rates and toward intensifying criminal sanctions. For example, the report recommends abolishing the requirement that victims testify at preliminary hearings, barring the police from interviewing children multiple times, and promoting prison terms as the appropriate sanction for perpetrators of family violence. The report claims, "Penalties imposed by the court [in domestic violence cases] do not reflect the severity of the injury or the number of prior conviction for the same offense. This under-enforcement of the law tells victims and assailants alike that family violence is not really a serious crime, if a crime at all. It is this widespread perception that has contributed to the perpetuation of violence within the family" (36). Criminal justice concerns permeate the report, including sections of the report that expressly have nothing to do with criminal justice. Recommendations in sections titled "Data Collection" and "Research" aim to increase prosecutions and convictions. For example, in the "Data Collection" section, the report recommends compelling drug and alcohol treatment providers to report when a patient admits to child abuse, a violation of federal privacy laws prohibiting the release of such confidential information.

The task force report's key rhetorical maneuver is to equate domestic violence with stranger crime. It argues, "The legal response to family violence must be guided primarily by the nature of the abusive act, not the relationship between the victim and the abuser" (4). This assertion that "crime is a crime" explicitly denies the unique nature of violence that occurs within, and sometimes as a result of, the traditional family context. Importantly, this argument characterized family violence as aberrant rather than, as the battered women's movement claimed, inherent in the conditions of the traditional family.

The final report further protects the prestige of the family by remaining vague in describing victims' services. This vagueness obscures the larger problems these services were designed to ameliorate, such as gender norms and socioeconomic inequality. For example, the report's "Victim Assistance" chapter names various forms of victims' assistance, such as "family violence prevention and intervention," "victim assistance programs," and "victim assistance services," but does not specify the purpose of such programs or what needs these services fulfill (45–62). Also, the report identifies the need for the coordination between the criminal justice system and service providers, explaining that "law enforcement officers must know where victims can be referred for emergency aid, judges must be familiar with the services that can be employed as alternatives to traditional dispositions, service agencies must know who to call at the police station" (6; see also 21). However, the report fails to define key terms, such as service agencies, emergency aid, and alternatives to traditional dispositions, and therefore does not directly or specifically acknowledge the needs that are addressed by these services and resources.

The report's proposed victims' services include drop-in centers, in-home care, and temporary shelters and childcare. However the report never advocates funding these services or any specific supporting role for the federal government in providing them. More important, such services do not enable permanent separations or enable victims to survive on their own on a permanent basis but give time for unification, perhaps because the task force privileges reunification. The support services were organized around maintaining traditional family formations rather than focusing primarily on victim needs.

The report's specificity about the role of the criminal justice system and vagueness concerning socioeconomic responses frame intimate partner violence as a problem of "bad people" who can be changed by punishment and thereafter reunited with their families. Obscuring solutions obscures the problems those solutions presuppose. The final report's emphasis on prosecuting and punishing offenders frames domestic violence as isolated acts outside of any socioeconomic and gender relationality, thereby preserving the family's autonomy and prestige.

The Violence Against Women Act

The Family Violence Task Force final report's valorization of the family and the criminal justice system reflected the Reagan administration's broader glorification of both. Because Democrats historically avoided family values discourses when supporting a modest welfare state, there was ideological room for domestic violence policy drafted by Democrats to look different. However, the Democratic Party's primary federal response to domestic violence, VAWA, embraced the task force's reliance on criminal justice responses to domestic violence rather than socioeconomic support for victims, while remaining silent on the traditional family.

Feminist scholars contend that "battered women's activists played a major role in crafting VAWA,"[31] despite its limitations as described above and below. The White House declared 1994's original VAWA "landmark" legislation.[32] In contrast to the historical moments discussed above, VAWA received massive media attention and represents a consensus between Republicans and Democrats about the federal government's role in addressing domestic violence.

Introduced by Senator Joe Biden in 1990, VAWA created two federal crimes:

crossing state lines to commit acts of domestic violence and crossing state lines to violate protection orders. It also mandated that any civil protection order receive full faith and credit in every state. VAWA provided funds for socioeconomically supporting victims and changing criminal justice responses to domestic violence. Importantly, however, funding for the criminal justice system dwarfed funding allocated to support victims.

For example, the 2005 version of the act contained $75 million per year for encouraging mandatory domestic violence arrest practices, $55 million per year for rural domestic violence and child abuse enforcement grants, and $225 million per year for Services and Training for Officers and Prosecutors grants. By contrast, VAWA contained no money for temporary shelters, only $40 million per year for transitional housing, and $10 million for grants to develop long-term housing for victims.[33] In the fiscal year 2012, the amount available for transitional housing fell to $25 million, while funding for criminal justice efforts remained constant. While in 2000 over two thousand shelters and transitional housing programs existed, federal funding filled only a tiny portion of shelter and transitional housing program needs.[34] Further, VAWA lacks funds for long-term housing, employment, medical and mental health care, transportation, substance abuse treatment, financial assistance, and child care, all central needs for victims to escape abusive situations.

Democratic rhetoric during congressional VAWA hearings shared the Task Force on Family Violence's focus on criminal justice responses and the "crime is a crime" ethos. For example, Biden argued in the 1990 Senate Judiciary Committee hearing concerning VAWA that the act "uses federal grant money to encourage States to treat domestic violence as a crime and not as a quarrel."[35] In a 1994 statement provided to the House Subcommittee on Crime and Criminal Justice of the Committee on the Judiciary hearing, Biden argued, "For too long, violence in the home has not been treated as seriously as violence in the street . . . while a stranger might serve a lengthy jail term for an assault, a spouse of boyfriend will all too often be neither arrested nor prosecuted for the very same conduct."[36] Similarly, in his speech opening same hearing, Representative Charles Schumer hailed VAWA's criminal justice orientation, declaring, "If there is one message I would like everyone to hear today it is that batterers must be treated like the criminals they are."[37]

Neither Schumer nor Biden discussed patriarchal norms or gender inequality. Like the Task Force on Family Violence, they focused on the criminal justice system's investigation, prosecution, and conviction of abusers, presuming that privileging punishment alone will substantially reduce future victimization and improve abused women's lives. Meanwhile, few of the consultation's ideas about domestic violence are found in VAWA: helping women means little other than enhancing prosecutions and intensifying punishment.

Perhaps unsurprisingly, Republican statements during VAWA hearings mirrored Biden's and the task force "Final Report's" rhetoric, employing the "crime is

a crime" ethos and supporting prosecution and criminal sanctions as remedies for
domestic violence. For example, in a 1991 hearing, Chuck Grassley said, "We must
impose swift, sure, and strict punishment for criminals at least as tough as the crime
itself," and "getting tough on the crime means getting tough on the criminal."[38]
Strom Thurmond demanded that "vicious acts against women be dealt with by
enacting tough crime penalties which harshly punish perpetrators and deter these
violent crimes."[39] In the 1994 hearing, Steven Schiff justified treating domestic violence identically to stranger crime by reference to his prosecutorial experience: "I
issue[d] instructions to our office and law enforcement agencies in our district that
domestic relations violence was violence . . . a charge of assault and battery should
be treated like a charge of assault and battery and the relationship between the
accused and the victim were [*sic*] not relevant."[40]

Needless to say, not one of them argued for robust socioeconomic support
for victims or reformulated gender norms. This approach to domestic violence has
continued to leave women vulnerable to abuse. As Donna Coker argues, inadequate
resources are a primary reason women do not leave abusive situations. To remedy
this, Coker proposes submitting every anti-domestic violence law and policy to a
"material resources test," to find if a policy "improves women's access to material
resources," thereby reducing victimization.[41] The test shows that criminal justice
responses to victimization are ineffective and harmful for victims. For example,
requiring that police officers arrest someone at a domestic violence scene risks victims' arrest as well, with severe familial and financial consequences that outweigh
the material benefits of the policy (1042–1049).

Instead of costly criminal justice responses, Coker recommends transportation, housing, childcare, and food assistance (1053). She reasons that "inadequate
material resources render women's choices more coerced than would otherwise be
the case" (1020). Ultimately, "the obvious impact of applying the material resources
test is to shift significant monies to direct aid for victims and to target more significant aid to poor women," and away from the criminal justice system (1052). Studies
affirming Coker's arguments demonstrate that access to material resources reduces
revictimization. For example, employed victims with stable housing are considerably
less likely to suffer future victimization by their batterers, because they are materi-
ally capable of staying away from them.[42] Very little of this perspective made it into
the VAWA policy.

Domestic Violence and Family Values

Instead of the socioeconomic approach, the more conservative "family values" tilt
guided VAWA implementation. The state has taken the position that the traditional
family cultivates the values necessary for economic success, and members of nontraditional families are doomed to socioeconomic failure and dependence on government support. Martha Fineman argues that "images of the traditional family per-

vade contemporary discourse" attacking social spending programs and that "it is the intimate unit in policy and legal discussions that is exclusively designated as what is normatively desirable."[43] This discourse includes the 1965 Moynihan Report (which blames black poverty on nontraditional and thus "dysfunctional" families) through President Reagan's treasured *Losing Ground*, written in 1985 by Charles Murray (which holds that welfare causes fathers to leave families, leaving children without proper behavioral models), to welfare reform debates in the 1990s.

Protection of traditional marriage was the cornerstone of these debates. As Senator Phil Gramm argued, "We need to promote marriage. I believe there are only two things that can prevent or eliminate poverty: work and family. No great civilization has ever risen that was not built on strong families."[44] One of the four stated goals of the 1996 welfare reform was to "encourage the formation and maintenance of two-parent families."[45] This discourse endures today. For example, a 2014 House Budget Committee publication claimed that "poverty is most concentrated among broken families."[46] The Heritage Foundation declared in 2015, "A major reason for the nation's lack of success for the last half century has been the collapse of marriage."[47] As 2016 presidential candidate Marco Rubio put it in 2015, "You cannot have a strong country without strong people. You cannot have strong people without strong families."[48]

By absolving the culture of traditional patriarchal family of any responsibility, US policy from Reagan to VAWA treats domestic violence as an aberration, a crime perpetrated solely by individual men. Within this framework, punishment becomes the appropriate response. But when policy makers privilege criminal justice responses, they deemphasize victims' services and starve service providers of the funding needed to provide services preventing victimization and revictimization.[49]

Notes

1. For information on Durham Crisis Response Center, see its website, durhamcrisisresponse .org/ (accessed July 8, 2015).

2. For more information about North Carolina's prison system's budget, see the Office of State Budget and Management's website, osbm.nc.gov/thebudget (accessed July 8, 2015).

3. National Network to End Domestic Violence, "Domestic Violence Counts 2011: A 24-Hour Census of Domestic Violence Shelters and Services," 2012, 1, nnedv.org/downloads/Census /DVCounts2011/DVCounts11_NatlReport_BW.pdf.

4. Caroline Bettinger-Lopez, Donna Coker, Julie Goldscheid, Leigh Goodmark, Valli Kalei Kanuha, James Ptacek, and Deborah Weissman, "Academic Speak Out about VAWA Reauthorization," February 27, 2012, www.feministlawprofessors.com/2012/02/academics -speak-about-vawa-reauthorization/ (accessed December 11, 2015).

5. William L. Hart, John Ashcroft, Ann Burgess, Neman Flanagan, Ursula Meese, Catherine Milton, Clyde Narramore, Ruben Ortega, Frances Seward, *Attorney General's Task Force on Family Violence, Final Report* (Washington DC: Department of Justice, 1984).

6. Barbara Fedder, "Lobbying for Mandatory-Arrest Policies: Race, Class, and the Politics of the Battered Women's Movement," *NYU Review of Law of Social Change*, 23 (1997): 283.

7. Elizabeth Schneider, *Battered Women and Feminist Lawmaking*. (New Haven: Yale University Press, 2002).

8. Susan Schechter, *Women and Male Violence: The Visions and Struggles of the Battered Women's Movement* (Boston: South End, 1982), 3.

9. *Battered Women: Issues of Public Policy: A Consultation Sponsored by the United States Commission on Civil Rights* (Washington, DC: US Civil Rights Commission, 1978), III–IV.

10. Del Martin, "Overview: Scope of the Problem," in *Battered Women*, 11.

11. Ibid., 11.

12. Lisa Leghorn, "Response to Lisa Richette," in *Battered Women*, 140.

13. Lisa Richette, "Support Services: Long-Term Needs for Battered Women—Underpinnings or Foundations for New Structures?," in *Battered Women*, 425.

14. Leghorn, "Response," 459.

15. *Battered Women*, II.

16. Martin, "Overview," 10.

17. Monica Erler, "Response," in *Battered Women*, 113.

18. Elizabeth Pleck, *Domestic Tyranny: The Making of American Social Policy against Family Violence from Colonial Times to the Present* (Urbana: Illinois University Press, 2004), 197.

19. Quoted in Ruth Colker, "Marriage Mimicry: The Law of Domestic Violence," *William and Mary Law Review* 47, no. 2 (2006): 1852.

20. Quoted in Ellen Goodman, "Is a Broken Home Worse than a Broken Wife?," *Boston Globe*, September 30, 1980.

21. Gordon Humphrey, *Congressional Record*, August 25, 1980, S22796.

22. Jesse Helms, *Congressional Record*, September 4, 1980, S24120.

23. Strom Thurmond, *Congressional Record*, September 4, 1980, S24123.

24. L. B. Weiss, "'Moral Majority' Leads Lobby Blitz on Bill," *Congressional Quarterly*, September 13, 1980, 4.

25. "Conservatives Kill Domestic Violence Bill." *CQ Almanac 1980* (Washington, DC: Congressional Quarterly, 1981), 443-45.

26. "Senate Jeopardizes Family Values," *Moral Majority Report*, March 14, 1980.

27. Quoted in Judy Mann, "Help for Battered Women Encounters Opposition," *Washington Post*, May 9, 1980.

28. *President's Task Force on Victims of Crime, Final Report*, December 1982, http://www.ovc .gov/publications/presdntstskforcrprt/87299.pdf.

29. See Mary Thornton, "Task Force Created on Domestic Violence," *Washington Post*, September 20, 1983.

30. *Attorney General's Task Force on Family Violence, Final Report*, i. Further cites to this work in this section appear in parentheses in text.

31. Leigh Goodmark, *A Troubled Marriage: Domestic Violence and the Legal System* (New York: New York University Press, 2012), 19.

32. "Fact Sheet: Violence Against Women Act," www.whitehouse.gov/sites/default/files/docs /vawa_factsheet.pdf (accessed June 14, 2016).

33. National Coalition against Domestic Violence, "Comparison of VAWA 1994, VAWA 2000 and VAWA 2005 Reauthorization Bill," January 16, 2006, talkingback2restrainingorders.files .wordpress.com/2012/08/vawa_94_00_05.pdf (accessed March 20, 2013).

34. Amy Farmer, Amandine Sambira, and Jill Tiefenthaler, "Services and Intimate Partner Violence in the United States: A County-Level Analysis," *Journal of Marriage and Family*, 67 (2005).

35. Joseph Biden, "Opening Statement—Women and Violence," in "Legislation to Reduce the Growing Problem of Violent Crime against Women," hearing before the Committee on the Judiciary, US Senate, 1990, 4.

36. Joseph Biden, "Statement—Domestic Violence: Not Just a Family Matter," in "Domestic Violence: Not Just a Family Matter," hearing before the House Subcommittee on Crime and Criminal Justice of the Committee on the Judiciary, 1994, 35–36.

37. Charles Schumer, "Statement—Domestic Violence: Not Just a Family Matter," in "Domestic Violence," 45.

38. Charles Grassley, "Statement—Violence against Women: Victims of the System," in "Violence against Women: Victims of the System," hearing before the Committee of the Judiciary, US Senate, 1991, 3.

39. Strom Thurmond, "Statement—Violence against Women: Victims of the System," in "Violence against Women," 19.

40. Steven Schiff, "Statement—Domestic Violence: Not Just a Family Matter," in "Domestic Violence," 5.

41. Donna Coker, "Shifting Power for Battered Women: Law, Material Resources and Poor Women of Color," *U.C. Davis Law Review* 33 (2000): 1009-55.

42. See Neil Websdale and Byron Johnson, "Reducing Woman Battering: The Role of Structural Approaches," in *Domestic Violence at the Margins: Readings on Race, Class, Gender, and Culture*, ed. Natalie Sokoloff (New Brunswick, NJ: Rutgers University Press, 2005); and Christina Gibson-Davis, Katherine Magnuson, Lisa Gennetian, and Greg Duncan, "Employment and the Risk of Domestic Abuse among Low-Income Women," *Journal of Marriage and Family* 67, no. 5 (2005): 1149–68.

43. Martha Fineman, "Masking Dependency: The Political Role of Family Rhetoric," *Virginia Law Review* 81 (1995): 2183.

44. Statement of Phil Gramm, in "Family Self-Sufficiency Act," *Congressional Record* 141 (August 7, 1995): S11747.

45. Thomas Gabe, "Welfare, Work, and Poverty Status of Female-Headed Families with Children: 1987–2011," report CRS R41917 (Washington, DC: Congressional Research Service,November 21, 2014).

46. House Budget Committee, "The War on Poverty: 50 Years Later," March 3, 2014, budget .house.gov/uploadedfiles/war_on_poverty.pdf.

47. Robert Rector, "Married to the Welfare State," February 10, 2015, www.heritage.org /research/commentary/2015/2/married-to-the-welfare-state.

48. Chris Adams, "Rubio Makes 2016 Pitch to Evangelicals," McClatchy News Services, June 18, 2015, www.mcclatchydc.com/2015/06/18/270477/rubio-makes-2016-pitch-to-evangelica l.html#storylink=cpy.

49. Rebecca Macy, Mary Giattina, Natalie Johns Montijo, and Dania Ermentrout, "Domestic Violence and Sexual Assault Service Agency Directors' Perspectives on Services That Help Survivors," *Violence against Women* 16, no. 10 (2010): 1138–61.

Which Black Lives Matter?

Gender, State-Sanctioned Violence, and "My Brother's Keeper"

Xhercis Méndez

The death of Trayvon Martin and the subsequent acquittal of his murderer sparked a series of responses across the United States, including an explosion of social media, mass protests, the birth of grassroots movements such as Black Lives Matter (BLM), and state-sponsored initiatives such as My Brother's Keeper (MBK). For many invested in the long struggle for black liberation, the acquittal symbolized the extent to which the American legal system was built on structural injustice and inequality, more often than not providing state support to vigilantes as long as those in the crosshairs were people of color. Martin was seen as yet another casualty in the war on black life and a reminder of the extent to which black lives were deemed disposable, killable, and structurally less worthy within the context of the United States. Indeed, his death, the trial, and acquittal served as yet another reminder of the structural inequalities that introduce violence into communities of color and the urgent need for a radical transformation in a system of legal and state governance that thrives on the demise of black life.

In response to Martin's death and the outrage that followed the acquittal, the nascent BLM movement, spearheaded by three black queer women, Patrisse Cullors, Alicia Garza, and Opal Tometi, proposed a grassroots movement that would broaden the scope of black liberation and address the wide array of struc-

Radical History Review

Issue 126 (October 2016)   DOI 10.1215/01636545-3594445

© 2016 by MARHO: The Radical Historians' Organization, Inc.

tural inequalities that produce violence within black communities. For instance, structural inequalities can best be understood as the sets of conditions (persistent poverty, lack of access to health care, school-to-prison pipeline) and institutions (the legal system, heteropatriarchy) that ensure some communities or group members are systematically denied access to their full rights as citizens and relegated to a lesser humanity. It refers to the conditions that produce some communities or group members as disposable and therefore more available for exploitation. The statement and approach put forth by BLM is noteworthy in that they have foregrounded the concerns of women of color, queer and gender-nonconforming folks of color, trans-folks, and differently abled bodies of color and ultimately centered the voices of those that have been historically marginalized even within the context of liberatory struggle. As a result, BLM seeks to address the diversity of structural inequalities impacting communities of color writ large. These are not limited to the issue of police brutality—they also include prisons, food security, anti-immigrant policy, transphobia, the assault on disabled community members, unequal access to health care and education, wage disparities, and reproductive justice for women of color.

In contrast, President Barack Obama responded to the collective outrage and protest by launching MBK, an initiative whose purpose was to primarily address the challenges facing young men and boys of color. In many ways, overlooking the broader community concerns being put forth by the women of BLM, the initiative was and continues to be an effort to address the *individual* barriers to social mobility for racialized males. These efforts have included providing mentorship and employment opportunities to create a path toward the middle class and creating policies that would work to minimize the disparities for youth of color.[1] Toward these ends, the initiative established a task force and issued a national call to businesses, individuals, nonprofits, and local agencies to come together, bring any and all available resources, and make concrete commitments to change the lives of young men and boys of color throughout the United States.

The response to MBK was and continues to be overwhelming. After only one year, the Obama administration reported raising over $300 million to advance the vision and objectives of MBK. In response to the call, "more than 60 superintendents of the largest urban school districts have pledged to develop aligned strategies. And nearly 200 mayors, county executives, and tribal leaders have accepted [the] challenge to develop locally driven, comprehensive cradle-to-college-and-career strategies aimed at improving the life outcomes [for young men of color]."[2]

As the attention to structural inequality continues to grow, grassroots movements such as BLM and state-sponsored initiatives such as MBK have proposed not only different framings of the problem but also necessarily different approaches to the solution. While throughout this article I reference the BLM movement, I focus primarily on MBK for two reasons. First, many who are wary of grassroots protest have hinged their hopes on MBK as a state-sponsored initiative that seems to be a "step in the right direction." Second, and more important, as a federally sanctioned response MBK has the resources and potential to create necessary change, making it all the more pressing to hold its aims accountable.

For these reasons, this article seeks to consider to what extent MBK misses a real opportunity to improve the lives of youth of color by recycling much of the problematic logic, reasoning, and assumptions of its 1965 predecessor, the Moynihan Report, the controversial government document that aimed to reduce poverty in black communities through an initiative to "reintegrate" the black family.[3] As a matter of accountability for a program with such potential impact, certain key questions must be raised, such as how rehashing central aspects of the Moynihan Report works to derail us from examining the intersectional forms of institutionalized and state-sanctioned racialized gender violence prevalent in the contemporary moment, the very issues that the BLM movement is calling attention to. In other words, to what extent does MBK keep us from examining and altering the structural forms of violence that consistently wreak havoc in the lives of both young women and men of color, regardless of gender identity? To what extent does MBK fall prey to assumptions that reinforce structural inequalities, regardless of intention, thus laying the ground for an oppositional sexual politics by creating yet another set of conditions whereby men and women of color are pitted against each other in a competition for access to resources? And in what ways does MBK serve as strategy to contain and restrict protest and ultimately transformation? Altogether, these concerns carry new significance in the context of continued protests against state-sanctioned violence targeting black lives and black life.

My Brother's Keeper: Moynihan All Over Again?

In an effort to address the "persistent opportunity gaps" that prevent boys and men of color from achieving their full potential, MBK unfortunately recycles key assumptions of the Moynihan Report. In both reports, women of color are presumed to be faring better in terms of education and jobs than their male counterparts.[4] For this reason, women of color have been excluded from the projected program to address racial inequality and structural disparities. Moynihan argued that the United States needed to focus on improving opportunities for African American men because "ours is a society which presumes male leadership in private and public affairs. . . . A subculture, such as that of the Negro American, in which this is not the pattern, is placed at a distinct disadvantage."[5] For Moynihan, the relative success of black women not only hindered the progress of black men but also served as a measure of the pathology of black families. MBK, it seems, is built upon some of the same assumptions.

The claim that women of color are faring better and that they therefore do not need resources directed at improving their lives simply isn't true. The statistics proclaiming the relative success of women of color compared with men of color come at a time when black girls are being suspended from school at six times the rate of white girls and women of color have become the fastest rising prison population.[6] According to a Prison Policy Initiative report, the women's prison population has nearly tripled since the 1990s, the majority of whom are women of color.[7] To assert the relative success of women of color in the contemporary moment is to overlook the series of physical and nonphysical forms of violence that women of color face, including but not limited to being funneled into the prison system at alarming rates, persistent poverty, racialized gender wage gaps, and being marginalized within state institutions such as public schools and health care systems. Indeed, these are the structural inequalities that BLM has identified as hindering the progress of youth and communities of color.

One of the reasons that this misperception persists, as eloquently highlighted by the African American Policy Forum brief "Say Her Name: Resisting Police Brutality against Black Women," is that there are presently no accurate databases collecting accounts of how state institutions also target women of color.[8] The brief's authors contend that the tendency to focus on young men of color leaves us with an incomplete picture of state-sanctioned violence. For example, similar to the cases of young black men who have been murdered with impunity, black women have also been assaulted for "driving while black," being poor, and having mental health issues. The brief brings together cases that illustrate the ways in which black women have also been construed as "dangerous" and "criminal," in addition to more intersectional concerns such as being penalized for defending themselves against domestic violence and having their sexualities policed.[9]

As the brief's authors note, not only are there no readily available databases detailing the particularities of how black women are profiled by police, but there are no databases documenting how black women, as well as nonblack women of color, are vulnerable to other forms of state-sanctioned violence, such as sexual assault and being profiled as sex workers by police.[10] This is not to suggest that men of color are not victims of structural racial inequality; rather, the assumption that they are the *primary* victims allows us to understand only a very small portion of the overall problem. The insistence that women of color on the whole suffer "less" from, or fare better within, structural racial inequality not only keeps us from examining the intersectional forms of institutionalized and state-sanctioned racialized gender violence prevalent in the contemporary moment but also justifies policy initiatives that can only lead to partial solutions.

Moreover, the assumption that women of color are "faring better" creates the conditions for an oppositional sexual politics that undermines collective efforts, such as those of BLM, to improve the conditions of communities of color more broadly. This is a concern in both black and nonblack communities of color. It is also an example of how MBK falls prey to assumptions that reinforce, rather than dismantle, structural inequalities. MBK lays the ground for an oppositional sexual politics by paradoxically putting women of color in the position to argue that they are indeed doing as badly (or perhaps worse) than men of color in order to access state support, resources, and be deemed worthy of investment. Women of color who attempt to correct this misconception are accused of undermining efforts to improve the lives of men of color. *They* become the enemy, not the structural dynamics that pit men and women of color against each other in the battle for resources.

For instance, Roland S. Martin has argued that those pushing to make MBK more inclusive to minority girls "look silly," especially when the Obama administration has established the White House Office on Women and Girls to address the impact of policy on women and girls.[11] And yet, as Kimberlé Williams Crenshaw and others have pointed out, the White House Office on Women and Girls has no initiatives that directly deal with the challenges facing girls and women of color (not to mention queer, gender-nonconforming, or trans folks of color who fall outside of both MBK and any initiatives coming out of the White House Office on Women and Girls), nor do they have nearly the same level of resources, cache, and mobilization as does MBK.[12] On the whole, the myopic focus on men and boys of color in the effort to address structural racial inequalities illustrates the extent to which women of color's lives continue to be marginalized and devalued. Grassroots activists that form part of BLM and the "Say Her Name" brief have consistently identified this as a problem that will only lead us to partial solutions. While I agree that not all initiatives need to be inclusive of everyone, any initiative that claims to address the structural disparities that keep youth of color systemically marginalized needs to also *center* women and girls of color.

It is here that indigenous (Aymara) lesbian feminist Julieta Paredes's argument becomes particularly instructive. In her book *Hilando Fino: Desde el Feminismo Comunitario*, Paredes begins from the assumption that "women are (minimally) half of everything."[13] She stresses this because she and others in her community noticed that when women are being discussed they are treated as though they comprise a minority sector among larger and or more important concerns. An example of this would be to say, "We are going to create policy for the indigenous, for peasants, and for women,"[14] as though women were not also indigenous or peasants. Applying this understanding to MBK, we can argue that if MBK is about telling young people of color that their lives matter, then it is important to remember that women of color do not comprise a smaller or even negligible portion of the people negatively impacted by systemic inequality.

Missing the (Structural) Forest for the (Individual) Trees

In addition to leaving women of color out of the articulated vision to address opportunity gaps and structural inequalities, Obama's promotion of MBK reframed the persistence of poverty in terms of the "absence of fathers" (the breakdown of the black family, in Moynihan's terms) and lack of male role models in communities of color.[15] Implicit in this rhetoric is the idea that the integration of individual men of color into the economy will somehow increase marriage rates for heterosexual African American couples, resolve the issue of "absent fathers," and in the process decrease the level of opportunity gaps for youth of color. Toward these ends, MBK focuses on "fixing" individuals within communities of color. As a result the list of goals primarily focuses on improving the boys themselves, by getting them to read better by the third grade, keeping them from dropping out of high school, and encouraging them to pursue postsecondary education and training.[16] However, the focus on young men of color's individual improvement circumvents the need to address the structural inequalities that introduce both physical and nonphysical forms of violence into their lives or the multiplicity of ways in which black lives are systemically marginalized and targeted for demise throughout the United States.

For instance, MBK fails to address the racialized gender wage gaps that have women of color at the bottom of the global economy and that keep youth of color in conditions of poverty in the first place. In addition, it does little to address the structural dynamics that allow black youth to be assaulted by police while in school (e.g., the teenage girl assaulted at Spring Valley High School in South Carolina by officer Ben Fields) or that have led to the deaths of black children at the hands of police, such as Tamir Rice and Aiyana Jones. It fails to address the fact that the life expectancy for black transwomen is thirty-five years of age. It fails to address the sets of conditions that criminalize black queer, gender-nonconforming, and trans youth of color for carrying condoms, profiling them as sex workers and funneling them into the prison system precisely because they are not "easily" integrated into the heternormative global economy.

Finally, MBK fails to address the fact that even when its stated objectives are met, it is not enough to protect black youth. Certainly, in the case of Trayvon Martin, in whose memory MBK was launched, having an active father and growing up in a middle-class neighborhood were not enough to either prevent his murder or hold his murderer accountable. As Jamelle Bouie notes in his article "The Flaws of My Brother's Keeper," young men like Trayvon Martin and Jordan Davis "didn't die because their parents weren't involved enough; they died because they lived in a country where their lives were feared and devalued."[17]

Rather than proffering a solution for structural inequality, MBK seems to be more about recycling Moynihan's strategies of containment and discipline. Moynihan was particularly concerned with the black liberation struggles of the time that were not opposed to mass militancy and armed self-defense as a means for liberation. He expressed concern that without a resolution to the deep and deepening levels of poverty being experienced by black communities, as well as other communities of color, impoverished communities of color would turn to "more dangerous" alternatives such as the Nation of Islam (what he referred to as the black Muslim doctrines) and Chinese communism.[18] In addition to the social movements taking place within the US, the anticolonial and black liberation struggles taking place on an international scale were also being tracked by Moynihan. With these movements in mind, he wrote that world events would undoubtedly be affected by how successfully African Americans were "peacefully assimilated" into American society, and he urged America to decide if the "Negro [would] be her liability or her opportunity."[19]

In what seems to be a haunting regurgitation of Moynihan's logic and concerns, Obama argues that America's future depends on us caring about the successful integration of men of color into the economy. According to Obama, these men and boys are "our future workforce. . . . [They] are going to be taxpayers. They're going to help build our communities. They will make our communities safer. They aren't part of the problem, they're *potentially part of the solution.*"[20] Although seemingly positive, similar to the Moynihan Report, I would argue that MBK is invested in containing and disciplining what are perceived to be "dangerous" protestors and a "criminal" masculinity on the verge of bubbling over. On the one hand, the initiative seeks to contain and appease the outrage of protestors by offering men and boys of color the carrot of future employment and by telling them that "their lives matter," even as these things fail to address the immediate conditions of poverty and violence in their lives. At the same time, although the focus on young men and boys of color may be psychologically satisfying in that it suggests somebody cares, it also serves a disciplinary function. While the funneling of youth of color into postsecondary education carries with it no guarantee of employment, it almost certainly carries with it a guarantee of debt. The current economic crisis is such that fewer and fewer jobs are available to those graduating with postsecondary educations. Without a significant restructuring of the economy, we end up with an initiative that makes youth of color increasingly exploitable by adding new layers of debt to their already precarious circumstances.

Obama claims that MBK is about introducing a new value system that will redefine who we are as a nation and that will transform liberty, justice, and equality for all into more than rhetoric. But ultimately it misses the mark. By recycling many of the problematic assumptions and values of the Moynihan report, MBK sacrifices a very real opportunity and requirement to address the structural inequalities undermining the well-being and future of youth of color, especially as it relates to black life and lives.

Departing from Moynihan's Logic:
Reframing Black Liberation as a Collective and Communal Project
Even in the face of state initiatives that undermine collective struggle, black feminists, gender-nonconforming and queer folks of color, and men of color invested in broader conceptions of black liberation have, since the Moynihan Report, done the work of promoting communal alternatives that are open to and include all black lives. For instance, the open letter widely circulated on the Internet, the "Letter of

Two Hundred Concerned Black Men Calling for the Inclusion of Women and Girls in 'My Brother's Keeper'" respectfully asked Obama for a vision of racial justice that also included black girls and women and that would not express empathy and commitments to "only half of [the black] community."[21] In an inspiring attentiveness to how such initiatives often prioritize one marginalized group at the expense of others, the letter stated,

As African Americans, and as a nation, we have to be as concerned about the experiences of single Black women who raise their kids on sub-poverty wages as we are about the disproportionate number of Black men who are incarcerated. We must care as much about Black women who are the victims of gender violence as we do about Black boys caught up in the drug trade. We must hold up the fact that Black women on average make less money and have less wealth than both White women and Black men in the United States just as we must focus on the ways in which Black men and women are disproportionately excluded from many professions.

The letter went on to suggest that "if the denunciation of male privilege, sexism and rape culture is not at the center of our quest for racial justice, then we have endorsed a position of benign neglect towards the challenges that girls and women face that undermine their well-being and the well-being of the community as a whole." Thus, challenging the long history of state sponsored initiatives purporting to "save" black men at the expense of black women, the letter called for an expansion of the initiative to include the heterogeneity and multiplicity of circumstances negatively impacting black communities as a whole.

In addition to the letter signed by "Two Hundred Concerned Black Men"—arguably one of the more successful efforts to challenge state-sponsored initiatives that pave the way for oppositional sexual politics and undermine collective struggle—is the BLM campaign. The BLM movement has been self-defined as a strategic effort to revitalize the politics of black liberation but in a way that takes up the complexity and diversity of black life. This movement draws from the lessons of the black liberation struggles of the 1960s, as well as from black feminisms and queer of color activism, to promote a much broader vision of black liberation and communal inclusion. According to its founders Cullors, Garza, and Tometi, BLM is a political project that

goes beyond the narrow nationalism that can be prevalent within Black communities, which merely call on Black people to love Black, live Black and buy Black, keeping straight cis Black men in the front of the movement while our sisters, queer and trans and disabled folk take up roles in the background or not at all. Black Lives Matter affirms the lives of Black queer and trans folks, disabled folks, black-undocumented folks, folks with records, women and all Black lives along the gender spectrum. It centers those that have been

marginalized within Black liberation movements. It is a tactic to (re)build the
Black liberation movement.[22]

Indeed, as they assert, if black lives matter, then *all* black lives matter.

As a result, the BLM movement has pushed the debate on racial inequality
to include how systemic poverty, anti-immigrant policies, prison, the assault on black
children and families, transphobia, and state-sponsored experimentation on differently abled bodies also constitute forms of state violence targeting black bodies that
need to be centered and addressed. BLM, unlike MBK, is clear that any program
or initiative that purports to improve the lives of youth of color cannot solely focus
on "fixing" individuals but must address the concerns and structural inequalities
impacting communities of color as a whole. Challenging the tendency to primarily
center males of color in the discussion on racial inequality, their approach takes into
account how racialized gender violence manifests differently depending on your
body, how you choose to inhabit that body, and how others read your body. More
importantly it reframes black liberation as a communal project that refuses to leave
anyone behind.

Notes

I extend my sincerest gratitude to my reviewers, Erica Ball, Nikolay Karkov, and Ganessa James, for their thoughtful feedback and reflections on this article.

1. Arne Duncan and Broderick Johnson, *My Brother's Keeper Task Force: One-Year Progress Report to the President* (Washington, DC: My Brother's Keeper Task Force, 2015), introductory letter, n.p.
2. Ibid.
3. See Daniel P. Moynihan, *The Negro Family: The Case for National Action* (Washington, D.C.: Office of Policy Planning and Research, 1965).
4. Ibid., 31.
5. Ibid., 29.
6. Kimberlé Williams Crenshaw, "The Girls Obama Forgot: My Brother's Keeper Ignores Young Black Women," *New York Times,* July 29, 2014.
7. Aleks Kajstura and Russ Immarigeon, "States of Women's Incarceration: The Global Context," Prison Policy Initiative, www.prisonpolicy.org/global/women/ (accessed December 1, 2015).
8. Kimberlé Williams Crenshaw and Andrea J. Ritchie, "Say Her Name: Resisting Police Brutality against Black Women" (New York: African American Policy Forum, 2015), 4.
9. Ibid., 8–24.
10. Ibid., 4.
11. Roland S. Martin, "Black Elites Look Silly over 'My Brother's Keeper' Criticism," *Roland Martin Reports* (blog), June 21, 2014, rolandmartinreports.com/blog/2014/06/roland-s -martin-black-elites-look-silly-over-my-brothers-keeper-criticism/.
12. Crenshaw, "Girls Obama Forgot."
13. Julieta Paredes, *Hilando Fino: Desde el Feminismo Comunitario* (La Paz: CEDEC, 2008).
14. Ibid., n.p.
15. Moynihan, *Negro Family,* 35–38.

16. "The President Speaks at the Launch of the My Brother's Keeper Alliance," YouTube, posted May 4, 2015, www.youtube.com/watch?v=c9_RYZ_54A4.

17. Jamelle Bouie, "The Flaws in My Brother's Keeper," *Daily Beast*, February 27, 2014, http://www.thedailybeast.com/articles/2014/02/27/the-flaw-in-my-brother-s-keeper.html

18. Moynihan, *Negro Family*, 1.

19. Ibid., prelude, n.p.

20. "President Speaks," emphasis added.

21. See "Letter of Two Hundred Concerned Black Men Calling for the Inclusion of Women and Girls in 'My Brother's Keeper,' May 28, 2014," posted at *NewBlackMan (in Exile)* (blog), newblackman.blogspot.com/2014/05/letter-of-200-concerned-black-men.html.

22. Patrisse Cullors, Alicia Garza, and Opal Tometi, "About the Black Lives Matter Network," blacklivesmatter.com/about/ (accessed December 1, 2015).

"Stubborn Masculine Women"

Violence, Slavery, the State, and Constructions of Gender in Graaff-Reinet, 1830–1834

Carla Tsampiras

In 1832, Lea, a twenty-six-year-old slave from the Camdeboo area of Britain's Cape Colony, complained to the assistant protector of slaves that she had been struck and beaten on the back and other parts of her body by her female owner, Saartjie van der Merwe. Lea claimed that the beating, administered with a piece of wood and a thong, had resulted in her having a miscarriage during the eight days that she walked through the harsh Karoo landscape to the town of Graaff-Reinet to lay a complaint of physical violence against Saartjie.

Lea was able to lay her complaint because of changing colonial legislation in the 1820s and 1830s, framed as ameliorative measures to benefit slaves, that saw, among other amendments, the creation of "protectors" or "guardians" of slaves. One of the protectors' roles was to enforce new restrictions relating to the nature and amount of punishment owners could inflict on slaves. The new legislation regulated how many lashes slaves could receive and—for the first time—distinguished between the types and amounts of punishments that female and male slaves could be subjected to.

The particular experiences and identities that bring these two women to our attention in this instance relate directly to their (gendered) bodies.[1] Lea's pregnant body experienced the pain of a beating but was healthy enough to sustain her through eight days of walking. Saartjie's body was strong enough for her to inflict

Radical History Review

Issue 126 (October 2016)   DOI 10.1215/01636545-3594457

© 2016 by MARHO: The Radical Historians' Organization, Inc.

violence on Lea. It was specifically because the law defined Lea's body as female that Saartjie could be held accountable for inflicting this violence. Inherent in their case are multiple notions of the body and how it is constituted by individuals, societies, laws, and researchers. When examining their cases, we see bodies as sites of political contestation, bodies as legal persons, bodies as violent and violated, bodies as gendered, and bodies as sites of academic research.

Scholars of slavery beyond the borders of the Cape Colony caution that research that does not seriously engage with the gendered experience of slaves and slave owners provides only partial analyses of slaveholding societies. Others have proved the same thing for slaveholding societies in the Cape, while challenging historians to think well beyond existing boundaries (geographic and otherwise) and reimagine various aspects of the historical landscape.[2] These and other works have generated discussions about intimacy in slave societies, evident in household relations, paternalism, patriarchy, violence, and masculinities.[3] Some of the existing literature focuses, appropriately, on the violence of male owners (male owners as perpetrators of violence) and the experiences of violence of female slaves, particularly relating to sexual violence. This work reveals the complex terrains that bodies—both enslaved and free—had to negotiate at various points in the Cape Colony's slave history.

As women, however, Lea and Saartjie complicate this scholarship, as they insist on a different reading of their gendered bodies. Lea emerges as a woman slave who was not just a survivor of violence but also an active, resisting political agent; Saartjie, as a woman slave owner who was neither a passive participant in a violent society nor dependent on a male figurehead to imbue her with authority, but an active perpetrator of violence.[4] The case was not atypical. In at least one district in the colony women slaves used gendered laws to complain about the violence women owners inflicted on them, thus disturbing state efforts to create "feminine" women and threatening to disturb our understanding of state, gender, slavery, and violence.

Using Graaff-Reinet as a case study, this essay explores complaints of violence brought by female slaves against female owners. Social relations evident in the cases reveal ways in which slaveholding households constituted gender and violence and, specifically, women's behaviors relating to violence. Finally, it considers how the disturbances created by Lea, Saartjie, and others might lead to new lines of inquiry into violence, slavery, the state, and gender.

Graaff-Reinet, the Cape Colony, and the Empire: Setting the Scene

One of the eleven districts that made up the Cape Colony in the early 1830s, the District of Graaff-Reinet covered a large area beyond the borders of the town and included the outlying Camdeboo region. It was an important frontier town under the colony's Eastern Division, home to at least two Voortrekker leaders and an important source of sheep and cattle for the rest of the colony.[5] As such, stock farming constituted the region's primary economic activity, alongside tobacco and wheat farming. Khoena people, not slaves, provided most of the labor in the district, but almost 6 percent of the colony's slave population resided in the area, typically in households with fewer than eight slaves each.[6] The dominance of stock farming shaped the experiences of the inhabitants of the town and surrounding areas in ways different from those of urban-based inhabitants or other rural areas with different farming activities. In districts such as Stellenbosch, where wheat farming and vineyards dominated, slaves and workers were subjected to the rigorous demands of planting and harvesting. Work in stock-farming districts, such as Graaff-Reinet and other districts of the Eastern Cape, involved a different type of regime, one that could put some slaves and workers beyond the sight of their owners/employers. Unlike urban areas, farming districts with their isolated farms could also put some slaves beyond the sight and assistance of officials and administrators.

Proximity to the town mediated the ability of people to access services, resources, information, or figures of authority within the district of Graaff-Reinet. In March 1831 a letter from Anthony Berrange, the assistant protector of slaves for Graaff-Reinet, to the Slave Registry Office in Cape Town indicated that 29 percent of the registered slaveholders lived within three hours, on horseback, from the town; 60 percent lived between three and twenty-one hours, and 11 percent from twenty-one to thirty-nine hours from town.[7]

As Lea's determination to lay a complaint shows, these vast distances may have deterred slaves but did not prevent them from making use of new ameliorative legislation to lay their complaints. So what did the new legislation offer slaves, and what did the state-issued orders and proclamations related to state-sanctioned violence have to do with the construction of gender in the Cape Colony?

The early 1830s, both in Graaff-Reinet and throughout the colony, was a period of increased agitation between slaves, slave owners, local officials, and the colonial government, especially in relation to the rights of, or over, slaves. The ameliorative measures, starting in the 1820s and eventually leading to the conditional emancipation of slaves in 1834, challenged the nature of the existing relationships between owners and slaves in ways that fueled resentment against imperial British rule.[8] The amelioration measures of 1823, 1826, 1830, and 1831 (effective in 1832) prompted negative responses from slave owners throughout the colony, ranging from petitions and deputations to government officials, meetings, and even a riot.[9]

Each proclamation or order of the King in Council issued between 1823 and 1834 altered dimensions of slaves' personal, domestic, and working lives and their standing in legal spheres. The legislation regulated the labor they undertook, altered the status of slaves' testimonies in courts of law, allowed for changing interpersonal relationships and family formations, and outlined the type and amount of violent punishment that the state was willing to sanction.[10]

In 1823, punishment of slaves was restricted and meant to be in the form of "mild domestic correction," with a maximum of twenty-five lashes permitted, with a twenty-four-hour respite between punishments. For the first time, in Ordinance 19 of 1826, the punishments permitted for adult slaves were differentiated for female and male slaves. The maximum lashes for male slaves remained twenty-five, but female slaves could no longer be flogged in public and were to be subjected to "moderate," private whipping across the shoulders.[11]

Slave complaints were to be heard by the newly appointed office of the Guardian of Slaves, located in Cape Town, or assistant guardians located in each region. The guardians would examine cases brought to them by slaves, make decisions on whether they were worth pursuing, and either attempt to resolve the conflict themselves through mediation between the slaves and their owners or place the case before the resident magistrate's court.[12] The complaints brought to each guardian were recorded for each district in a standard format and sent to London every six months.

By 1832, the guardians had been renamed "protectors of slaves," slave owners were required to keep punishment record books, and punishment had been further restricted. The maximum number of lashes a male slave could receive was reduced from twenty-five to fifteen, and it became illegal to beat female slaves.[13] Inherent in these restrictions were particular ideas about male and female bodies, their relationship to violence, and their construction as subjects of the state.

Mary Rayner has shown that the amelioration laws themselves were by-products of complex shifts in global economic systems that saw a move from mercantile capitalism to industrial capitalism, with Britain featuring as a major political power.[14] Throughout the empire, slave labor was to be transformed into wage labor, even as the metropole sought to manage and contain tensions between existing and emerging classes. Central strategies for the metropole and colonies drew on notions of moral transformation, an emphasis on the family as a means of social organization and moral regeneration, and changing state methods of disciplining and punishing populations.[15]

Pamela Scully notes that the amelioration programs and associated legislation passed after emancipation "focused on the slave family, women's sexuality, and on the promotion of patriarchal familial structures and gender relations which officials believed conducive to the reproduction of a stable and industrious working class."[16] Throughout this period, then, both colony and metropole governments ascribed and created gender roles and identities along with new relationships among subjects, the state, and the apparatus of state authority.

Amelioration laws framed the physical violence that the state would sanction around ideas about the status and capacity of an imagined and idealized male and female slave body, essentially gendering the type of violence that could be experienced and how often it could be experienced. The language in the laws frames gender and gender roles in particular ways that can be read as echoes of normative ideas of patriarchy, masculinities, and femininities, mediated by conferred status in an imagined hierarchy of state and subjects. For example, Article 13 of Ordinance 19 prohibited flogging, contained the use of solitary confinement, and limited the whipping for female slaves to a manner analogous to that used in "correcting" children in schools.[17] Article 13 moves the spectacle of violence against female slaves out of the public sphere and into the private realm, there to cohabit with (marginally) less publicly sanctioned acts of violence, such as rape.[18] Inscribed in this article is a frailer female requiring greater care than a stronger male and the same protection as a child.

Article 14 of the same ordinance addressed reductions in owners' abilities to undertake violent acts by noting that it would be illegal for anyone other than the owner, employer, or overseer of a slave to punish a slave, "except in cases where the Owners or Employers . . . are Females, or infirm, or suffering under disease, or are upwards of Sixty Years of Age."[19] This article links acts of violent punishment to male owners and, by extension, masculinities while assuming that female owners are unable to inflict violent punishment.

The orders of 1830 and 1831 further (en)gendered violence and constructed "men" and "women" slaves. They reduced the maximum number of lashes for male slaves and made it illegal to beat female slaves at all. Regardless of the existing experiences slaves and slaveholders had of gender and violence, the amelioration laws enforced state-determined understandings of gender roles and held owners accountable to them.

Major George Jackman Rogers, protector of slaves for the Cape Colony, was quick to recognize the implications of the changes in what types of violence could be used against which types of slaves, and his comments reflected ideas of women slaves at odds with the ones imagined by colonial officials in the metropole. In his December 1830 report he observed:

It is certainly highly desirable that the flogging [of] female slaves should be wholly discontinued, but some punishment should be substituted adequate to the degree of the offences which many of these stubborn masculine women commit. The reduction of food and domestic confinement for short periods are insufficient and with Mahomedans [*sic*] are at particular times no punishment at all, and it is very inconvenient and sometimes not possible to have stocks in private houses. The consequence is that very many Female slaves have become very insolent and most of them highly insubordinate. They will go out at unreasonable hours, and be Guilty of many serious offences, for which there is now no adequate punishment, and they put their Owners therefore at defiance.[20]

In his assessment Rogers straddles a line: he pays lip service to the official position making it illegal to beat female slaves yet articulates what he sees as the realities of the colony. For all the metropole's desire to grant females different protections as a means of entrenching ideas about womanhood or femininity, Rogers maintains that in the Cape Colony female slaves are stubborn, masculine, prone to committing offences, and used to being short of food. For Rogers, removing the threat of physical violence raises the specter of undisciplined, unpunishable women who were becoming increasingly difficult to control instead of turning into compliant, feminine women who could be easily controlled without violence.

A year later Rogers reiterated these ideas in a report that praised the slaveholders for not resorting to greater violence against female slaves. In relation to the lack of cases of "serious" violence committed by owners he observed: "Considering how extremely difficult it is to keep some of the masculine Females in any order since corporal Punishment has been prohibited, it is very satisfactory that so few breaches of the Law are committed by Slave Owners in this respect, when the provocation is so frequent, and often so galling, and the Punishment by putting into stocks or placing them under restraint or low diet, is not felt either as a disgrace, Punishment or Privation."[21] Regardless of the intentions of the laws, Rogers viewed female slaves as too masculine, troublesome, and difficult to control without physical violence. In addition, they failed to evince an "appropriate" sense of feminine shame. He did, however, hold out hope that the next generation of female slaves might be more "susceptible" to shame.[22] Considering the harsh realties of slave life, and slave women's gendered experiences of slavery particularly in relation to notions of family, the domestic sphere, morality, and bodily integrity, it is unsurprising that some slaves continued to resist by not being "well behaved."

Case Studies: Women and Violence in Graaff-Reinet

Far from the chambers in London in which the orders in council were debated and created, and the protectors' office in Cape Town in which the legislation and "masculine" female slaves were critiqued, Lea and others came to the assistant protector to complain. In Graaff-Reinet, between 1830 and 1834, 250 cases of complaint were brought by slaves and recorded by the assistant protector.[23]

Slaves in the district complained about a wide variety of abuses: being made to work when ill, being separated from their families, receiving insufficient food and clothing, being owed money or stock, not being allowed to visit their partners or parents, being overworked, punished, and ill-treated.[24] Most cases included some form of violence—in this context physical acts intended to inflict bodily pain or cause discomfort as a means of retribution or control. These violent acts included beatings with fists, floggings, and whippings with *riemme* (belts or thongs), *sjamboks*, sticks, or other items and, less frequently, sexual violence.[25]

Lea was one of 990 female slaves in Graaff-Reinet who lived alongside 1,257 male slaves and constituted 44 percent of the total slave population in the district. Male slaves complained differently than female slaves and appear to have experienced violence and their owners' discipline differently, too. Of the 134 cases brought by male slaves, the overwhelming majority (128 cases, 96 percent) were against male owners and almost evenly split between complaints of violence and other incidents not related to violence. Only six cases were against female slave owners, and only one of those six cases related to physical violence.

By contrast, of the 116 cases of complaint brought to the assistant protector by female slaves (46 percent of the total 250 cases), 66 cases (57 percent) were complaints against male owners, and the remaining 50 cases (43 percent) were against female owners. Far more of the female slaves' complaints related specifically to violence: 72 percent of those against female slave owners and 45 percent of those against male owners.

The nature of the violence attributed to female slave owners included placing female slaves in stocks, slapping slaves with open hands, beating slaves with fists, and whipping or flogging female slaves. A closer look at the complaints laid by female slaves against female owners reveals complex subjectivities and relationships between these two groups inherent in the maintenance and creation of hierarchical and gendered roles. Rogers made no comments on the masculinity, stubbornness, or inappropriate behaviors of female slave owners in his reports; the cases make clear that neither female slaves nor female slave owners performed the imagined femininities or "womanliness" alluded to in the amelioration acts.

Body Politics: Lea's Story

When Lea laid her complaint against Saartjie van der Merwe on March 24, 1832, the assistant protector noted in his report that she had no marks of violence on her body but nonetheless sent her case on to the resident magistrate.[26] Lea called two witnesses to verify her claims. One denied having seen Lea being beaten. The testimony of a second, Hanna (a Khoena woman), corroborated the beating with the thong and a small twig but not with a piece of wood. Hanna recounted that Lea had been sent to fetch wood and on her return was engaged in cleaning out a pot when Saartjie came in and demanded to know why Lea had stayed away for so long. Lea did not reply, and Saartjie then picked up a twig "no thicker than a quill" and hit Lea. The twig broke on the second blow, and Saartjie then picked up a thong used by Lea to collect the wood and struck Lea "about five blows over her back . . . over her clothes, and apparently not with much violence" (472–73).

In her testimony, Saartjie denied having beaten Lea at all and stated that she had merely threatened to beat her with the thong as "she had stayed away much longer than was necessary when she was sent to fetch some herbs for her Master who was sick" and because she had refused to answer Saartjie's question. Saartjie was fined £10 sterling for being in breach of the order of the King in Council, and the case was closed.

Lea's determination in bringing this complaint becomes evident in the explanatory remarks made by the assistant protector. He notes that when Lea originally lodged her complaint in March she was instructed to return home and told that her case would be prosecuted before the magistrate. On the April 19, however, before the case had reached the magistrate, Lea returned to the assistant protector, informing him that she had been pregnant when she came to lay her complaint and on her way home had "miscarried on the road, and delivered a fetus [*sic*] of about six months old" (474). Lea maintained that the miscarriage was the result of Saartjie having thrown her to the ground and given her a kick during the beating. The kick apparently left a mark, which Lea claimed she had shown her husband, Constant, that same day. She had not, however, mentioned the incident when she laid her complaint or intimated that she was pregnant; when questioned Lea merely stated that she had forgotten to do so. The assistant protector sent the district surgeon, Dr. Perry, to see if Lea's story could be verified. Perry found the fetus "in such a state of putrification that nothing but the bones could be distinguished none of which were broken" (474). Witnesses Hanna and Constant both denied seeing Lea thrown to the ground and indicated that in the week after the beating she had undertaken her work on the farm as usual and without complaint. Constant also insisted that Lea had not shown him any mark on her side or mentioned being kicked (475–76).

The assistant protector noted that from Lea's statement "it appeared that when she came to the place where the abortion [*sic*] took place she had walked 32 hours in eight successive days, carrying all the time a child of hers of about two years old and having little or no food" (474). In light of this he concluded that there was "more reason to attribute the abortion [*sic*] to fatigue and hunger than to any other circumstance" (476).

The case reveals Lea's body as a site of political contestation, resistance, and determination. Lea was resolved to assert her personhood, claim her rights, and seek redress against the violence committed against her even if doing so required walking for days carrying one child and losing a fetus. It is possible that Lea's miscarriage resulted from excessive physical strain on her body during the long walk to the town, compounded by her position as a female slave in a household that may have been affected by droughts, sicknesses, and shortages. Or, perhaps Lea deliberately induced the abortion and then sought to blame it on her owner in an effort to make use of the moral economy of the district under the new amelioration agreements to bring social censure or possible social humiliation to her owners.[27] The case obscures such details and motivations. It reveals, however, that even as Lea and Saartjie participated in a state-sanctioned legal process that sought to construct them as frail women, their behaviors showed them to be active political agents who asserted their own subjectivities.

Further evidence of women asserting their political agency can be found when reading the "substance of complaints" logged in the protector's records. Phrases such as "punished without due cause" or "punished with insufficient reason" indicate that enslaved women made conscious decisions about what constituted infringements against themselves and their persons, even if these were not strictly within the bounds of the ordinances themselves.[28] As Wayne Dooling has observed, "Slaves themselves decided what constituted acceptable treatment . . . and acted in terms of . . . a 'moral economy' [requiring] . . . their actions to be assessed in terms of their perceived rights within the [owner]-slave relationship."[29] These perceptions also extended to notions of personal honor and integrity.[30]

(Un)Suitable Behavior: Malevolence, Insolence, and Indignation

The assistant protectors' reports used words like *insolence, insubordination,* and *malevolence* to describe slaves' behavior or speech in ways that judged the attitudes, actions, or tones of voice of slaves' bodies. For example, Rachel, slave of a Graaff-Reinet butcher, sought the assistant protector several times to lay complaints against both her female and male owners, on behalf of herself and her child Francina.[31] In her first complaint, Rachel accused her female owner, Anna Sophia Pienaar, of locking a chain around her leg overnight. In addition, she accused Anna of tying her daughter to a tree and punishing her with a strap over her shoulders. The assistant protector refused to entertain the first case after it transpired that Rachel had a history of deserting and her owner had learned that she was planning to make another attempt and used the chain as a preventative measure. The second case was also unsuccessful as two witnesses, and Francina herself, contradicted the claims Rachel had made. Francina admitted that her mother had instigated the complaint (despite Rachel's denial), and Rachel found herself admonished and cautioned not to make false complaints again.[32]

A month passed, and Rachel returned to lay a complaint against her male owner for putting her in the stocks overnight.[33] Rachel had again threatened to run away, and the magistrate found this sufficient reason for her to have been confined. Her owner was still fined one shilling, however, as he had contravened the law by allowing her to remain in the stocks overnight. The magistrate dismissed Rachel's fourth complaint, again against her male owner for confining her to the stocks. The magistrate judged Rachel guilty of having made "an unfounded complaint with malevolent motive" and had her imprisoned for four days on a diet of rice water.[34]

If the protector or magistrates perceived the slave to be impertinent, insolent, or less obsequious than the officials, owners, or witnesses (including other slaves) deemed "suitable," this could adversely affect the outcome of the case.[35] Eva, for example, brought a complaint against her female owner, listed only as the "widow of the late Barend Jacobus Burger," for confining her in the stocks until after sunset. Both the witnesses Eva called to corroborate the time of her confinement, and the defendant, claimed that Eva had been extremely insolent and obstinate. The magistrate observed that the defendant was completely justified in placing Eva in the stocks but had contravened the law, so he imposed a fine of one farthing.[36] This measly fine could have been intended to show the magistrates' contempt for either the complainant or the amelioration laws—or both.

The case of Amelia, a fifty-five-year-old slave of a widow from Camdeboo River, further highlights the ways that enslaved women and women owners' behavior challenged emerging notions of "ideal" gendered behavior.[37] Amelia claimed her female owner had struck her with a fist in the face and pushed her down in the mud, her bruised and blackened eye being a result of one of the blows. Amelia described how she was washing clothes when her owner scolded her and told her to take them somewhere else, as the water she was using was not clean. Amelia replied that her body was too full of pain to go further and that her owner had better go home as she had already destroyed all the strength of her body and "she was no more able to do anything." Thereafter her owner turned toward her, took hold of her, pushed her into the mud, and struck her several blows on the face with her fist.

According to the testimony of the witness Betje, the defendant verbalized her surprise at Amelia's behavior and indicated that in the sixteen years she had owned Amelia she had been "treated well," receiving punishment only once. The defendant (listed only as the widow of Piet Venter) further claimed she had attempted to pull the clothing Amelia was washing out of her hands to prevent her washing them in dirty water. Amelia let go of the wooden trough the clothes were in, seized her by the petticoat, and pulled her into the water. They both fell into the water, Amelia with her head downward, accounting for bruises and swelling as she had fallen onto some stones. The defendant denied beating her and was acquitted by the magistrate.

Amelia's definition and understanding of what it meant to be treated "well" clearly differed from the defendant's. Perhaps Amelia reached her breaking point after a lifetime of abuse and, indignant at yet another request, simply refused to comply. Or perhaps Amelia was simply tired from the day's work and felt physically incapable of moving the washing. Either way, her "insolence" in telling her owner that her work for the day was done and that she was incapable of any further tasks directly challenged her owner's authority.

Legal Subjectivity

Two additional cases show how some women utilized specific aspects of their gendered subjectivity or expected gender roles as part of their engagement with the court. The unnamed wife of Jan Vorster, for example, pleaded ignorance of the law when Christina brought a charge against her. Christina claimed she had been beaten with a stirrup leather, knocked down, and beaten again. The defendant pleaded guilty to the beating but said she had been unaware of "a law prohibiting punishment on female slaves, nor that it had ever been made known to her."[38] The magistrate did not regard ignorance of the law a sufficient defense and fined her £10.

Elisabeth Hick tried to be more sophisticated in her engagement with the law when Josephina brought a case against her on January 6, 1832.[39] Josephina was the slave of Andries Albertus Venter but was employed by Elisabeth and her husband, Jacobus. She complained to the assistant protector that Elisabeth had struck her two blows that morning with her fists in the face as she had not asked soon enough for some herbs to put with the fowls she was roasting. The case was heard before the resident magistrate on January 10, and two witnesses confirmed that Josephina had received the blows, although with an open hand, not a fist. They described Josephina's conduct as "most provoking" and said she had been frequently spoken to by the defendant but would not return any answer and turned her back toward Elisabeth.

Elisabeth and Josephina had been at loggerheads a month earlier, on December 7, 1831, when Josephina accused Elisabeth of hitting her with a stick, beating her over her shoulders, and striking her in the face with her fists.[40] The district surgeon confirmed that Josephina had recent marks on her shoulders. Elisabeth called a witness to testify that Josephina had been very disobedient and obstinate during the last month and so deployed Josephina's inappropriate behavior as one strand of her defense.

For the second strand she used a gendered reading of the law. Elisabeth claimed that she did not have the management of her husband's slaves and therefore could only be prosecuted for common assault and not for breach of the order of King in Council of February 2, 1830, as the latter only related to *master* and slave. Her defense failed, and as with the other case, she was found guilty and fined £10.

Elisabeth undoubtedly managed her husband's slaves, regardless of who they were officially registered to, and Josephina and the courts clearly viewed her as the person responsible for breaking the law. Even as Josephina used her status as a female to evoke the protection of the law, Elisabeth used hers, and the gendered language of the law, to protect herself (albeit unsuccessfully) from being held accountable for her violent act.

Disturbances and the Development of Research on Slavery, Gender, Violence, and the State

The cases from Graaff-Reinet illuminate how women slaves and owners negotiated relationships between each other, and between domestic, public, and administrative/legal spheres, that where shaped by the use of, or resistance to, different types of violence. These insights reveal the cocreation of the concepts of violence and gender across different spheres.

Furthermore, the cases reveal gender as a significant vector of power operating differently in a variety of slaveholding households. Rather than becoming compliant, feminine, and unlikely to commit offenses, some women in Graaff-Reinet (slave and owner alike) remained tenacious, active, and disposed to committing transgressions. Conceptions of gender and violence infused both the juridical and administrative management of the colony, and the daily lives of those who lived in it.

Rogers described slave women at the Cape Colony as stubborn, masculine, and prone to committing offenses, in direct contrast to sentimental constructions of female "nature" emanating from the metropole. Ironically, women slaves in the Cape Colony made use of legislation written by the imperial state that produced and prescribed gender norms to challenge the ("unfeminine") violence of women owners, some of whom had apparently embraced their roles as oppressors and "masters." The cases from Graaff-Reinet suggest that we, first, reconsider our normative ideas of patriarchy, masculinities, and femininities and, second, undertake more detailed comparisons of the implementation and manifestations of those normative ideas among embodied beings. Because the embodied beings we will be researching will occupy multiple material and intangible spaces, our work will have to cover physical spaces, like farms, frontiers, and urban areas; abstract spaces like the law, faith, and administration; and oblique spaces like loci of power, emotions, and ideas.

Notes

1. As a political marker of the socially and historically constructed notions of binary sex and the deliberate grouping of people into gendered roles linked to "women" and "men," the author asserts her preference for alternative spellings of *woman/women* such as *womyn* or *womxn*.

2. Barbara Bush, *Slave Women in Caribbean Society, 1650–1838* (Bloomington: Indiana University Press, 1990); Elizabeth Fox-Genovese, *Within the Plantation Household: Black and White Women of the Old South* (Chapel Hill: University of North Carolina Press, 1988); Pamela Scully and Diana Paton, eds., *Gender and Slave Emancipation in the Atlantic World* (Durham, NC: Duke University Press, 2005); Marcia Wright, *Strategies of Slaves and Women: Life-Stories from East/Central Africa* (New York: James Currey, 1993); Patricia Van der Spuy, "Gender and Slavery: Towards a Feminist Revision," *South African Historical Journal* 25 (1991): 184–95; Yvette Abrahams, "Disempowered to Consent: Sara Bartman and Khoisan Slavery in the Nineteenth-Century Cape Colony and Britain," *South African Historical Journal* 35 (1996): 89–114; Helen Bradford, "Women, Gender and Colonialism: Rethinking the History of the British Cape Colony and Its Frontier Zones, c. 1806–1870," *Journal of African History* 37 (1996): 351–70; Jessica Murray, "Gender and Violence in Cape Slave Narratives and Post-narratives," *South African Historical Journal* 62, no. 3 (2010): 444–62; Nicole Ulrich, "Time, Space and the Political Economy of Merchant Colonialism in the Cape of Good Hope and VOC World," *South African Historical Journal* 62, no. 3 (2010): 571–88.

3. See, for example, Clifton Crais, *White Supremacy and Black Resistance in Pre-industrial South Africa* (Cambridge: Cambridge University Press, 1992), 30–52; Wayne Dooling, "The Hegemonic Function of Law," in *Law and Community in a Slave Society: Stellenbosch District, South Africa, c. 1760–1820* (Cape Town: University of Cape Town Press, 1992), 80–82; Robert C. H. Shell, *Children of Bondage: A Social History of the Slave Society at the Cape of Good Hope, 1652–1838* (Hanover, NH: Wesleyan University Press, 1994); John Mason, "Paternalism under Siege: Slavery in Theory and Practice during the Era of Reform, c.1825 through Emancipation," in *Breaking the Chains—Slavery and Its Legacy in the Nineteenth-Century Cape Colony*, ed. Nigel Worden and Clifton Crais (Johannesburg: Witwatersrand University Press, 1994), 45–77; John E. Mason, "'Fit for Freedom': The

Slaves, Slavery, and Emancipation in the Cape Colony, South Africa, 1806 to 1842" (PhD diss., Yale University, 1992); Robert Ross, "Paternalism, Patriarchy and Afrikaans," *South African Historical Journal* 32 (1995): 34–47; and Patricia Van der Spuy, "'Making Himself Master': Galant's Rebellion Revisited," *South African Historical Journal* 34 (1996): 1–28.

4.   See Van der Spuy, "'Making Himself Master,'" 7; and Mason, "'Fit for Freedom,'" 196–98.

5.   For more on the Eastern Division (or current Eastern Cape area), see Crais, *White Supremacy and Black Resistance.* The two Voortrekker leaders were Gerrit Maritz and Andries Pretorius. More recently (1924) Graaff-Reinet was the birthplace of Mangaliso Robert Sobukwe, founder of the Pan Africanist Congress.

6.   See Wayne Dooling, "Slavery and Amelioration in the Graaff-Reinet District, 1823–1830," *South African Historical Journal*, no. 27 (1992): 78–79; "Table submitted by Major Rogers for Return of Number of Slaves Registered at the Cape of Good Hope Colony (by age), August 31, 1833," in General Observations, National Archives (hereafter NA), Colonial Office (hereafter CO), 53/57, 150. Dooling gives the total slave population as 2,836 in 1823 and 2,266 in 1828, with slaves constituting 12 percent of the total population of 19,864 people; people identified as "white" constituted 48 percent of the population, and people classified as "free blacks," 40 percent ("Slavery and Amelioration," 79). In 1830 Rogers estimated that the 32,704 square miles that constituted the District of Graaff-Reinet had 680 slaveholders who possessed 2,630 slaves, with 570 of those slave holders having fewer than 8 slaves. Western Cape Archive, Slave Office (hereafter KAB, SO), 3/6, *Report of the Protector of Slaves of the Colony of the Cape of Good Hope, 25 June–24 December 1830,* 1:625.

7.   KAB, SO, 1/22, Slave Registry Office Graaff-Reinet, 1829–1837, "Return of the Number of Slaves Registered at Graaff-Reinet on the 31st December 1830," letter from the Slave Registry Office, Graaff-Reinet, February 9, 1831.

8.   See John E. Mason, "Fortunate Slaves and Artful Masters: Labor Relations in the Rural Cape Colony during the Era of Emancipation, ca. 1825 to 1838," in *Slavery in South Africa: Captive Labor on the Dutch Frontier,* ed. Elizabeth Eldredge and Fred Morton (Boulder, CO: Westview Press, 1994): 67–91. Slaves were forced to undergo a four-year "apprenticeship" period before being completely emancipated, so strictly speaking emancipation properly occurred in 1838.

9.   The reports by the protectors of slaves mention of increasing tension between owners and slaves and between owners and themselves as government officials. See NA, CO, 53/52, General Observations, 343–61, 409–12; NA, 53/54, General Observations, 507–9; NA, CO, 53/55, General Observations, 132–34; NA, CO, 53/57, General Observations, 129–43 (deals specifically with responses to emancipation) and 341–64 (for owner and slave reactions); and NA, CO, 53/58, General Observations, 144–51. See also Dooling, "Slavery and Amelioration," 83–84; and John E. Mason, "The Slaves and Their Protectors: Reforming Resistance in a Slave Society, the Cape Colony, 1826–1834," *Journal of Southern African Studies* 17, no. 1 (1991): 108–9.

10.   For details of contents of each proclamation or order, see Dooling, "Slavery and Amelioration," 76–77; and Mason "Slaves and Their Protectors," 106–9.

11.   KAB, SO, Cape Colony Publications 6/3/1/1—Statutes, Acts, Ordinances 1825–1853, Ordinance 19 of June 1826, 4.

12.   For more on the protectors of slaves, see John E. Mason, *Social Death and Resurrection—Slavery and Emancipation in South Africa* (Charlottesville: University of Virginia Press, 2003), esp. chap. 2.

13. This was a highly contentious issue among owners, who saw this as an infringement of their property rights, and one that the protector of slaves frequently comments upon. See NA, 53/54–53/58, table A and General Observations relating to table A.

14. Mary Rayner, "Slaves, Slave Owners and the British State: The Cape Colony 1806–1834," *Collected Seminar Papers, Institute of Commonwealth Studies* 28 (1981): 15, sas-space.sas .ac.uk/4111/.

15. Ibid., 15–17.

16. Pamela Scully, *Liberating the Family? Gender and British Slave Emancipation in the Rural Western Cape, South Africa, 1823-1853* (Cape Town: David Philip, 1997), 3.

17. Ordinance 19 of June 1826, 4.

18. For more on rape and slavery in the colony, see Scully, *Liberating the Family?*; and Pamela Scully, "Rape, Race, and Colonial Culture: The Sexual Politics of Identity in the Nineteenth-Century Cape Colony, South Africa," *American Historical Review*, 100, no. 2 (1995): 335–59.

19. Ordinance 19 of June 1826, 4.

20. KAB, SO, 3/6, *Report of the Protector of Slaves . . .* , *25 June–24 December 1830*, 1:619–20.

21. KAB, SO, 3/8, *Report of the Protector of Slaves . . .* , *25 June–24 December 1831*, 3:511–12.

22. Ibid., 512.

23. The actual number of cases recorded was 263, but 13 of these were cases carried over from one annual report to the next, and these have therefore been excluded.

24. For detailed accounts of all cases see NA, 53/50–57, reports of the protectors of slaves of the Cape of Good Hope Colony for 1830–1834.

25. A *sjambok* is a long, stiff whip used throughout South Africa's history to inflict pain on human and other species. That sexual violence is reported less frequently is not to suggest it did not occur or was not common but, rather, that it was more difficult to seek legal recourse for such cases.

26. KAB, SO, 3/9, *Report of the Protector of Slaves . . .* , *24 December 1831–25 June 1832*, case no. 33 for the Graaff-Reinet District, 4:471. Further cites to this work appear in parentheses in text.

27. See Wayne Dooling, "'The Good Opinion of Others': Law, Slavery and Community in the Cape Colony, c. 1760–1830," in Worden and Crais, *Breaking the Chains*, 25–43.

28. Similarly, John Mason observes, "The slaves of the Cape Colony frequently relied not on the law's definition of legal and illegal punishment when deciding whether or not to complain, but on their own notions of just and unjust punishment" ("Slaves and Their Protectors," 122).

29. Dooling, "Slavery and Amelioration," 81.

30. See, for example, the case of Rachel of Sneeuberg, who complained because her female owner accused her of being the cause of death of her own child. NA, 53/51, case 5, 133.

31. NA, 53/54, cases 1 and 2, 193–96.

32. Ibid. As with all the narratives recounted in this article, the accounts recorded in the archive are not taken at face value. The inherent contradictions, counterclaims, and differing versions of events are not only staples of legal proceedings but also are framed by the intentions and desires of those involved in the proceedings and the sociopolitical contexts of the times. The complexity of testimonies have been explored in Van der Spuy, "'Making Himself Master'"; and Nigel Penn, "The Wife, the Farmer and the Farmer's Slaves: Adultery and Murder on a Frontier Farm in the Early Eighteenth Century Cape," *Kronos*, 28 (November 2002): 1–20.

33. NA, 53/54, case 7, 205.

34. Ibid., case 14, 217.

35. See NA, 53/50, case 9, 11; and NA, 53/56, case 18, 211.
36. NA, 53/55, case 7, 48.
37. NA, 53/57, case 25, 261.
38. NA, 53/52, case 7, 302.
39. NA, 53/54, case 13, 215. The defendant's surname may possibly have been Fick.
40. Ibid., case 6, 204.

Torture, the State, and Sexual Violence against Men in Colonial India

Deana Heath

This article aims to broaden the analysis of gendered violence in colonial India by focusing on sexual violence against men. My goal is not to pursue, as Anjali Arondekar terms it, "the additive model of subalternity," which endeavors to fill the gaps of the colonial archive with the voices of those who have been silenced while acknowledging the impossibility of such a project of recovery.[1] I wish to go, in other words, beyond efforts to mine the content of government archives to pay attention to their form and content—to view archives "as both transparencies on which power relations were inscribed and intricate technologies of rule in themselves."[2] Rather than seeking to "recover" the "submerged" history of sexual violence against men, I interrogate the traces of such violence in the colonial archive to consider how and why the sexual violation of Indian men was able to enter the colonial archive. In light, moreover, of the refusal of colonial officials to name such violence as a sex crime, I consider what a nonevent—or, rather, a "recalcitrant event"—reveals about the archive and, by extension, colonial rule.[3] I focus, in particular, on the rape of a man named Rahmat Musalli—not to formulate his subjectivity but to question the sign of rape in the colonial archive. I hope to build, therefore, on existing scholarship on the ways in which both colonialism and colonial archives are gendered.

On January 18, 1915, a theft of grain was committed in the village of Mokhal, in the northern Punjabi district of Sialkot. No police official was available to carry out an investigation, so Sub-Inspector Paras Ram, the officer in charge of the local

Radical History Review

Issue 126 (October 2016)   DOI 10.1215/01636545-3594469

© 2016 by MARHO: The Radical Historians' Organization, Inc.

police station, requested that one Tej Muhammad, who had only that day been appointed the new *zaildar*, or local revenue collector, initiate it.[4] Muhammad, however, clearly did not regard himself in need of such authority, since he had already apprehended a suspect—twenty-six-year-old Rahmat Musalli, *chowkidar* (village watchman) of Mokhal and a former employee of Muhammad.[5] Even though there was no evidence to implicate Musalli in the theft, he was tortured by the zaildar's son and two other relatives to extort a confession from him—torture that two constables, who arrived the following day, joined and in which many others, including another chowkidar, were complicit. The torture included making Musalli "sit with his arms between his legs and hold his ears" while someone sat on his back, and forcing him to stand for long periods of time. But Musalli was also subject to sexual violence, including being "struck on the penis and testicles" and raped.[6]

In the caste system as it operated in colonial India, Musallis, though Muslim, were essentially untouchable, which made Musalli a particularly vulnerable member of his community.[7] As a lower-caste man, the sexual violence that Musalli was subjected to by upper-caste men (primarily Muslim Jats) was far from unique in colonial India. Sexual violence against lower-caste men took many forms, including being stripped naked; having their testicles, penises, and buttocks beaten, burned, or cut; being raped with iron pegs or wooden sticks; having string tied to their penises, hooked over a peg, beam, or branch, and pulled; being emasculated; having chili pepper inserted into their anuses; or being made to strip naked and sit on an ant nest. That men may indeed have become inured to such forms of violence and may even have come to expect them at the hands of men in positions of authority is suggested by the action of a young man who, when brought before a British district magistrate for questioning, simply "mumbled and tried to take off his loin cloth."[8] Such an action is chillingly evocative of Sadat Hasan Manto's Partition story "Khol Do," in which a young woman, who is lying violated and bloodied in a doctor's surgery and presumed dead, hears the doctor say "khol do" ("open it") and, mistaking the doctor's request for someone to open the window as the prelude to yet another rape, starts to fumble feebly at the string of her *salwar*.[9]

Forced to confess that the grain was at his house to escape further torture and sexual violation, upon being taken there Musalli tried to commit suicide by slashing his throat and abdomen with a razor. The constables, instead of sending Musalli to the nearest hospital, sent word of his attempted suicide to Sub-Inspector Paras Ram, who upon eventually arriving in Mokhal recorded Musalli's statement as to what had occurred—in which Musalli declared, in the words of magistrate E. R. Abbott, that "an unnatural offence had been committed on him."[10] Ram then sent Musalli to a local hospital, but he died two days later of peritonitis caused by his injuries and, doubtless, by insufficient medical care.

The Erasure of Sexual Violence against Men

In the past three decades a growing body of scholarship has examined the embodied intimacies of colonialism, including intimacy between men. But the role of violence in shaping such encounters is far from clear, since the focus has primarily been on what Sara Suleri terms the "homoerotic cast assumed by the narrative of colonialism."[11] Yet as Robert Aldrich argues, "Hierarchical relations—master to slave, entrepreneur to employee, officer to subaltern, colonist to houseboy—facilitated sexual expectations and demands" and ensured that sexual encounters between men, while at times consensual, were also "part of the violence perpetrated throughout the colonial world."[12] In his analysis of a scandal in French Central Africa in the 1880s involving the torture and sexual exploitation of African men and boys, Jeremy Rich suggests that such violence was, moreover, tacitly condoned by colonial authorities, since it became a scandal only when it signaled disrespect for colonial authority.[13] The French phrase *faire passer son brevet colonial* (literally, "to give someone an examination for a colonial diploma"), which means to initiate someone into sodomy, may therefore be a particularly telling revelation of the nature of colonial power dynamics.[14]

American slavery offers an example of how hierarchical and racialized relations provided opportunities for sexual violence against vulnerable and exploited male bodies. Since legal ownership conferred control over the enslaved male body, Thomas A. Foster concludes that "no enslaved man would have been safe from the threat of sexual abuse."[15] Such abuse—which ranged from forced penetration or reproduction to sexual coercion and psychic ill treatment—was perpetrated, moreover, not only by white men but also by white women (who could "enact radical fantasies of domination over white men with the knowledge that their victim's body was legally black and enslaved, subject to the women's control").[16] The vulnerability of male bodies to sexual violence in other states of unfreedom, such as detention (as in Musalli's case) and conflict situations, is apparent in contexts ranging from Abu Ghraib to concentration camps in Sarajevo during the Bosnian war, in which as many as 80 percent of male concentration camp inmates were purportedly raped.[17]

Yet while sexual violence against men has been recognized as pervasive, widespread, and unexceptional, it is generally "hidden under [the] rubric terms of 'abuse,' 'torture,' or 'mutilation.'"[18] Three key reasons explain why sexual violence against men in India and other colonial contexts continues to be hidden under such rubrics. First, the sexual abuser is "judged by the moral status of his victim," and in the hierarchy of victimhood men are at the bottom.[19] In nineteenth-century Britain, since sexual acts between men were deemed deviant and aberrant, whether or not the victim consented to such acts, men who were the victims of sexual violence were, in effect, denied the status of victim at all.[20] In fact, since anal intercourse was penalized along with, from 1885, any sexual activity between men, and legislation on sexual abuse was explicitly gendered (which means that the law did not acknowledge rape as something that could happen to men, or sexual violation to boys), sexual violence against men was not deemed a criminal offence and was therefore only prosecutable if it was coded as a different form of embodied violence, such as assault or torture.[21] The same held true in British colonies, including India.[22] When it came to sexual violence against men, colonial law, in denying protection to male victims of sexual violence, thus served to "promote [such] violence and give it impunity."[23]

The lack of legal recourse for male victims of sexual assault helps explain the second key reason that the sexual abuse of men in colonial contexts such as India remains hidden: men rarely speak out about their abuse. Since masculinity defines men as strong, straight, and sexually dominant, "real men" cannot be raped or subject to other forms of sexual assault.[24] For male victims of sexual violence, shame about being sexually assaulted, combined with fears about their loss of masculinity and the risk that they will be blamed (and thus socially ostracized) for their violation, generally ensures their silence.[25] So does the fact that, in contrast to women, men often show no signs of having been violated (such as a ruptured hymen or pregnancy).[26] Because of their difficulty in acknowledging and articulating their experiences, men in colonial contexts have therefore tended, like the legal systems to which they are subject, to frame their violation as abuse or torture.[27]

The third reason that the sexual abuse of men in colonial contexts remains shrouded in silence is that gendered assumptions about power have led to men being framed primarily as perpetrators and women as victims, which not only reifies existing hierarchies of victimhood but also reinforces perceptions of women as inherently violable. Such assumptions therefore normalize sexual violence against women.[28] They also obscure women's sexual agency and the ways in which this is mediated by class and race. The utilization of rape as a trope for the objectification of white women has, moreover, rendered the white woman, to borrow from Jenny Sharpe, as "a category of Other" that keeps the violated bodies of colonized women *and* men "hidden from history."[29] Since acts of sexual violence are directed against individuals on the basis of their gender (not to mention, of course, their race, class, and ethnicity) regardless of the gender of the victim or the perpetrator, sexual violence against men is therefore a gendered practice. It is utilized to effeminize, destroy, and humiliate men and their communities and to delineate between "man" and "other."[30] Rather than being exceptional or aberrant, sexual violence against men is therefore part of an array of institutionalized and socially sanctioned violence that serves to empower certain groups of men as heterosexual, masculine, and dominant.[31]

Colonialism and Sexual Violence

Nowhere is such a power dynamic clearer than in the case of colonialism, in which relationships are inherently gendered and sexualized and the body is a key trope through which difference between the West and non-West is discursively constructed. Not only were "non-Western bodies . . . portrayed as weak, barbarous, unclean, diseased or infantile in comparison with the idealized bodies of the West, which were the opposite, that is strong, ordered, hygienic, healthy and mature," but nonwestern male bodies were categorized largely as effeminate, in contrast to the purported manliness of the bodies of western men.[32] In the case of colonial India, one of the ways in which such effeminacy was produced was through proclaiming British men the saviors of Indian women from patriarchal oppression. Following the Indian Rebellion of 1857 the British also developed an elaborate ethnography of what they termed "martial" and "nonmartial" races, in which certain groups of men, such as Bengalis and Hindu groups from other "settled" regions, were singled out as being effeminate. The response of such groups was to internalize effeminacy and undertake a process of remasculation, a project that unfolded predominantly in the domestic sphere, with the body of the "chaste" and "pure" Hindu woman bearing the burden of marking the difference of the Hindu from the West. While such a project sought to ensure the dominance of a predominantly upper caste, upper class, and Hindu masculinity, it "left unresolved the tensions of traditional patterns of hierarchy across caste, community, class and gender."[33] When such tensions erupted, as they did most dramatically in the Partition of India in 1947, and again in the Bangladesh Liberation War in 1971, sexual violence became a tool for constructing and negotiating power between competing groups. But as sexual violence generally occurs in contexts in which male power is unstable, it is not only to such "exceptional" moments that we should look for evidence of it. As Sarah Solangon and Preeti Patel argue, "In some societies where masculinity is associated with being powerful and being head of the family, some men who feel they have failed to live up to this role, such as unemployed men who are unable to provide for their families, may feel that sexual violence, with its connotations of force and power, allows them to regain some control over their masculinity."[34] Since colonialism is a violation of the world of the colonized, which entails a process of unworlding that includes economic upheaval (and, for many groups, economic breakdown and impoverishment), the undermining of existing social structures, the replacement of traditional law-and-order systems with an alien legal system (in which "difference" is, moreover, enshrined), and—since the British "took over precolonial coercive techniques at the local level and introduced new ones on a global scale"—wide-scale structural violence, we perhaps need, therefore, to start viewing colonialism more as a state of conflict in which violence has been normalized.[35]

What distinguished sexual violence perpetrated against or among the colonized was its sheer brutality. As Sharon Block argues in her study of rape in early America, "Both African American and Native American women were far more likely than white women to be the victims of sadistic and horrific sexual violence that . . . starkly expressed relations of subordination through intentional sexual cruelty."[36] Violence against nonwhite women often took the form of sexual torture because it was carried out by multiple attackers and could involve multiple victims.[37] Such group violence serves to engender compliance, solidarity, and social conformity among the men who participate in it. It is common in war and conflict situations and was the standard means through which sexual violence was perpetrated in colonial India in the many torture cases I have examined. Although the sexual violence that Rahmat Musalli was subjected to was perpetrated by Indian men on an Indian body, this does not make it any less a form of colonial violence. For not only do the psychological effects of colonialism produce self-hatred in the colonized, as Frantz Fanon has argued, that manifests in the form of "collective auto-destruction," but such destruction was enacted by men who arguably felt the most threatened by or had the most to gain from the social and economic upheaval unleashed by colonialism.[38] Acts of sexual violence perpetrated by groups of men also act as a form of resistance to authority.[39] That such resistance is generally directed toward the most vulnerable members of a society rather than the actual source of oppression explains why sexual violence is tacitly condoned by authorities such as the colonial regime in India.

As Andrea Smith observes in her study of the genocidal effect of sexual violence on Native Americans, sexual violence is a tool through which peoples whose bodies are conceived of as inherently degenerate or impure "become marked as inherently 'rapable.'"[40] Although sexual violence obviously predates modern European colonialism, a new form of racism—what Michel Foucault terms "state racism"—began to emerge in the second half of the eighteenth century that was inherently biopolitical in nature.[41] What is particular about this form of racism is its deployment of the concept of the "norm" to single out particular groups within a population and mark them as deviant. Sexuality was central to this process of delineating "abnormal" bodies from normative ones. While the imperative of biopolitics is to optimize life, Foucault argues that such a form of racism, which is modeled on war, made it possible to justify killing "abnormal" segments of the population that are deemed a biological threat in order to purify and strengthen the "race." Racism is therefore "bound up with the workings of a State that is obliged to use race, the elimination of races and the purification of the race, to exercise its sovereign power." Moreover, rather than emerging in Europe and being exported to Europe's colonies, such a form of racism emerged through the process of colonization—or, as Foucault puts it, through "colonizing genocide."[42] It is this biopolitical imperative that explains why not only colonized women but also colonized men have been subjected to what Smith refers to as "reign[s] of sexualized terror," ranging from direct sexual assault to state policies to usurp the land and undermine the welfare of the colonized.[43]

The Sign of Rape

Such an imperative may help explain why Rahmat Musalli's rape was silenced by E. R. Abbott, the magistrate who initially tried his torturers. Abbott disregarded Musalli's claim that "an unnatural offence had been committed on him," since he was convinced that it was "most unlikely that such an offence was committed in the circumstances." For Abbot it was more likely that a stick had been inserted into Musalli's anus—clearly not, for him, an act of sexual violence—and the Sub-Inspector, in the course of translating Musalli's Punjabi into Urdu (the language in which official records in Punjab were kept), used a "wrong translation" for what Musalli had actually said.[44] Furthermore, in light of colonial officials' inherent distrust of Indians' oral evidence, they sought truth in the Indian body, to be unveiled by British medical "experts"—and for Abbott Musalli's body belied the possibility of any such offence having been committed, since the assistant surgeon who examined it did not observe any damage to Musalli's anus (although Abbott admitted that the surgeon may not have actually looked at Musalli's anus, since up to that stage no charge of "torture" had yet been made).[45] Abbott thus sought to deny the truth of sexual violence against Indian bodies.

Because Abbott "sympathise[d]," moreover, "with the accused" (since he felt "it is not improbable that the hurt caused was no more than is frequently employed in burglary investigations when taken up with zest"), the sentences that he imposed were, not surprisingly, nominal, and these were virtually overturned on appeal.[46] But when the government of Punjab appealed against the appeal to the Punjab Chief Court (which was possible to do under Indian law), the judgment of M. Shah Din and W. Chervis broke the conspiracy of silence surrounding Musalli's rape and named it for what it was. In response to opposition from the counsel for the defendants to the introduction of a statement on the cause of Musalli's death, which referred to his violation, the judges noted in their summation that "a statement as to the cause of death, referring to the rape is relevant as against a person tried for the rape when rape and death form parts of the same transaction."[47] Musalli's violators could not be punished for rape since, as Musalli was a man, rape and death did not legally form "parts of the same transaction." Nonetheless, the Chief Court judgment enabled the truth that male bodies could be raped—and that, moreover, state agents were in part responsible for such sexual violation—to enter the colonial archive.

In the numerous Indian police torture cases that I have examined from the nineteenth and early twentieth centuries, Musalli's case is the only one in which an act of sexual violence carried out against a man is explicitly referred to as "rape." Yet what is striking about such cases is not only the sheer ubiquity—and hence banality—of references to sexual violence against male bodies (although these were always coded as "torture") but the detail with which such violence was often delineated. What explains the denial of sexual violence against Indian men in the face of the omnipresence of their violated bodies in the colonial archive? And why was Musalli's rape actually named?

We might begin to answer such questions by considering colonial discourses about rape. Narratives of rape were initially deployed by critics of the East India

Company, such as Edmund Burke, to critique company rule, but with the onset of the Indian Rebellion of 1857 a new rape narrative emerged in which the violence of colonialism was displaced from British to colonized men—from whose lustful desires English women, rather than Indian, now had to be protected.[48] Stories that detailed what rebellious native men purportedly did to English women actually reflect the horrors that British soldiers inflicted on Indian bodies as punishment and retribution for the uprising, and the ways in which spectacular forms of punishment were utilized in the exercise of sovereign power. But since "the binarism of Western civilization and Eastern barbarism is difficult to maintain when the colonizer is an agent of torture and massacre," a discourse of rape that displaced victimhood onto English women rather than Indians made it possible to project counterinsurgency as the restoration of moral order and the articulation of a feudal hierarchy as a relationship of race.[49] As Jenny Sharpe argues, colonial narratives of rape are therefore "so invested with the value of English womanhood that they strategically exclude Indians, *men and women alike.*"[50] The sexual violation of Indian men, according to such a reading, is thus unnamed in the colonial archive because colonial officials were unable to "see" such violation.

Not only do such narratives about sexual violence reveal the tremendous insecurity of colonial regimes, particularly in moments of crisis, but they also disclose considerable anxiety about British masculinity. By the second half of the nineteenth century masculinity had become "fused in an especially potent configuration with representations of British imperial identity," which led to the emergence of an aggressive, militaristic, hypermasculinity.[51] But empire also fostered fears of the male body as under threat, weakened by sexual indulgence, enervating climates, and racial intermixing, and of the consequent degeneration of the British "race." In contrast to the fetishistic depictions of English women in "Mutiny" narratives, in which they are stripped naked, sexually violated, and then subjected to a variety of horrific tortures (such as the hacking off of breasts and other body parts), there are notably no detailed descriptions of the slaughter of English male bodies since "such a fragmentation of the male body would allocate British men to the objectified space of the rape victim—a status that would negate colonial power at the precise moment that it needed reinforcing."[52] The focus on sexual crimes against women in narratives of the revolt served, therefore, to shift attention away from the deaths of English men at the hands of the rebels. Acknowledging the rapability of male bodies by according Indian men the status of rape victims would thus threaten the fragile integrity of the bodies of British men.

Since, furthermore, the meaning of masculinity is drawn from the particular power relations that masculinity is employed to replicate in any given historical context, then British masculinity must be seen as something that was not simply transplanted to colonial contexts such as India but shaped by the colonial encounter.[53] Not only was British masculinity forged through "the rupture in the different forms of male interaction, between the strong emotional bonds of the male homosocial world and the strong emotional-sexual bonds of the male homosexual world"—not to mention the "hysteria and cultural terror" generated in the British by their encounter with India—but also the dynamics of a "deferred homosexual decorum" is evident in the script of a racialized gender dynamic in which British men were figured as hypermasculinized and Indian men as effeminate.[54] It is for these reasons that colonial discourse in India relegated both Indian *and* British women to the margins of what was ultimately an exchange between men. Scholars have demonstrated the many ways in which such a homoerotic desire for nonwhite men was configured, from the construction of what Rudi C. Bleys has termed a "geography of perversion" (including, most famously, Richard Francis Burton's "sotadic zone," which encompassed most parts of the "Orient" and in which, he maintained, sodomy was endemic) to the sexual imaginary of the Cannibal Club, an inner circle of the Anthropological Society of London (formed in 1863) whose members published homoerotically charged works that functioned as both science and pornography.[55]

Flagellation featured in much of the writing of Cannibal Club members, as it did in the pornographic literature produced in Britain into the early twentieth century. Although the figure doing the flagellation in such literature is generally depicted as female, she is, according to Stephen Marcus, a surrogate for "the terrible mother, the phallic mother of childhood" whose muscular biceps, hairy arms, and hairy upper lip actually serve to conceal the real perpetrator, the father.[56] Since the figure being beaten is always a boy, Marcus reads such a fantasy as a homosexual one; thus, for Marcus, "the entire immense literature of flagellation produced during the Victorian period, along with the fantasies it embodied and the practises it depicted, represents a kind of last-ditch compromise with and defense against homosexuality."[57] Lisa Z. Sigel observes that, in the case of Cannibal Club flagellation literature, which created "a sexual practice that moved the focus from orgasm to the desire for discipline and control," such writings "worked as a pedagogical technique to teach masculine self-control"; indeed, such prose demonstrates more of a longing for discipline than for intercourse.[58] Such literature therefore reflects the shift in British conceptions of manliness (motivated in large measure by empire) during the nineteenth century from "sexual prowess and maturity" to "sexual restraint and 'cleanness.'"[59]

The displacement of sexuality from desire to discipline mirrors the way in which torture is coded. For although, as Marnia Lazreg remarks in her study of torture as a colonial counterinsurgency tool in Algeria, "the *essence* of torture is sexual," torture is coded as a form of disciplining—or of, in a colonial context, "resocializing" (in order to convince the colonized, ironically, of the justness of colonialism). The sexual violation of colonized men and women was a means, therefore, of making them into obedient colonial subjects.[60] It operates as a form of "calculated" cruelty, which Talal Asad argues was regarded as being necessary to make the colonized "fully human."[61] Torture is thus, as Darius Rejali has demonstrated, a form of physical suffering that is an integral part of a disciplinary society—and hence of the modern state.[62] If public rituals of torture are no longer, per Foucault, necessary for the maintenance of sovereign power, torture persists in secret as an aspect of policing.[63] The sexual and disciplinary nature of torture in colonial India is evident in the ways in which the alien legal regime forced Indians to speak the truth of their sexual violation, or to extract it from them by mining their bodies for hidden truths. Musalli's death prevented him from speaking the truth of his rape in a colonial courtroom, but he was forced to make no less than three confessions before he died.[64] Since magistrates were required to examine the bodies of men who wished to make a confession in order to check for marks of "ill-treatment," had Musalli survived his ordeal he would consequently have been required to submit to a further violation.[65] That violated male bodies litter the colonial archive is therefore emblematic not only of the ways in which torture was utilized to discipline Indian bodies but also of the cultures of desire and disavowal that circulated around such bodies—truths that the Punjab Chief Court judgment on Musalli's torturers served, inadvertently, to reveal.

Notes

1. Anjali Arondekar, "Without a Trace: Sexuality and the Colonial Archive," *Journal of the History of Sexuality* 14, no. 1/2 (2005): 14.
2. Ann Laura Stoler, "The Colonial Archive and the Arts of Governance," *Archival Science* 2 (2002): 87.
3. Arondekar, "Without a Trace," 22.
4. In addition to being revenue collectors, *zaildars* were also responsible for village policing.
5. *The Crown v. Faiz*, IOR/L/PJ/6/3554, British Library, London.
6. Ibid.
7. H. A. Rose, *A Glossary of the Tribes and Castes of the Punjab and North-west Frontier Province*, 3 vols. (Lahore: Civil and Military Gazette Press, 1911), 2:182.
8. *King Emperor v. Muhammad Ismail Khan*, Home, Police, B Proceedings, January 1911, no. 145–46, National Archives of India, New Delhi.
9. A salwar is a pair of loose, pleated and tapered trousers that are tied at the waist with string. Sadat Hasan Manto, "Khol Do," in *Manto: Selected Stories*, trans. Aatish Tasheer (Gurgaon, Haryana: Random House India, 2008), n.p.
10. *Crown v. Faiz*.
11. Sara Suleri, *The Rhetoric of English India* (Chicago: University of Chicago Press, 1992), 16.
12. Robert Aldrich, *Colonialism and Homosexuality* (New York: Routledge, 2003), 4, 1.
13. Jeremy Rich, "Torture, Homosexuality, and Masculinities in French Central Africa: The Faucher-d'Alexis Affair of 1884," *Historical Reflections* 36, no. 2 (2010): 19.
14. Aldrich, *Colonialism and Homosexuality*, 1.
15. Thomas A. Foster, "The Sexual Abuse of Black Men under American Slavery," *Journal of the History of Sexuality* 20, no. 3 (2011): 448.
16. Ibid., 450.
17. Sarah Solangon and Preeti Patel, "Sexual Violence against Men in Countries Affected by Armed Conflict," *Conflict, Security, and Development* 12, no. 4 (2012): 419.
18. Ibid.

19. Joanna Bourke, *Rape: A History from 1860 to the Present Day* (London: Virago Press, 2007), 48.

20. Human Rights Watch, "This Alien Legacy: The Origin of 'Sodomy' Laws in British Colonialism," 2008, 11, accessed January 18, 2016, https://www.hrw.org/report/2008/12/17 /alien-legacy/origins-sodomy-laws-british-colonialism.

21. Ibid., 20. The sexual violation of boys remained largely invisible in Victorian Britain, in spite of knowledge of its existence, because the protection of children from sexual abuse emerged from social purity and rescue organizations' endeavors to protect "fallen" women. Louise Jackson, *Child Sexual Abuse in Victorian England* (New York: Routledge, 2000), 5.

22. While section 377 of the 1860 Indian Penal Code, for example, penalized sodomy (with imprisonment up to life), it made no distinction between homosexual acts committed with or without consent, and section 375, which penalized rape, restricted the crime to the penetration of a woman by a man.

23. Human Rights Watch, "This Alien Legacy," 4. The same held true, of course, for female victims, although both British and colonial law acknowledged that, at least in certain circumstances, women and girls *could* be raped.

24. Valeria Vojdik, "Sexual Violence against Men and Women in War: A Masculinities Approach," *Nevada Law Journal* 14, no. 3 (2014): 940.

25. Solangon and Patel, "Sexual Violence," 422.

26. Bourke, *Rape*, 42.

27. Marnia Lazreg, *Torture and the Twilight of Empire: From Algiers to Baghdad* (Princeton, NJ: Princeton University Press, 2008), 124.

28. Ratna Kapur, "The Tragedy of Victimization Rhetoric: Resurrecting the 'Native' Subject in International/Post-colonial Feminist Legal Politics," *Harvard Human Rights Law Journal* 15, no. 1 (2002): 1–39.

29. Jenny Sharpe, *Allegories of Empire: The Figure of Woman in the Colonial Text* (Minneapolis: University of Minnesota Press, 1993), 130.

30. Solangon and Patel, "Sexual Violence," 427.

31. Vojdik, "Sexual Violence," 927.

32. James H. Mills and Satadru Sen, introduction to *Confronting the Body: The Politics of Physicality in Colonial and Post-colonial India*, ed. James H. Mills and Satadru Sen (London: Anthem Press, 2002), 1.

33. Indira Chowdhury, *The Frail Hero and Virile History: Gender and the Politics of Culture in Colonial Bengal* (Oxford: Oxford University Press, 2001), 3.

34. Solangon and Patel, "Sexual Violence," 426.

35. Sharpe, *Allegories of Empire*, 80.

36. Sharon Block, *Rape and Sexual Power in Early America* (Chapel Hill: University of North Carolina Press, 2006), 80.

37. Ibid., 83.

38. Frantz Fanon, *Concerning Violence*, trans. Constance Farrington (London: Penguin, 2008), 23.

39. Bourke, *Rape*, 343.

40. Andrea Smith, *Conquest: Sexual Violence and American Indian Genocide* (Cambridge, MA: South End Press, 2005), 3.

41. Michel Foucault, *"Society Must Be Defended": Lectures at the Collège de France, 1975–76*, ed. Maurio Bertani and Alessandro Fontana, trans. David Macey (New York: Picador, 1997), 257.

42. Ibid., 256, 258, 257. See also Ann Laura Stoler, *Race and the Education of Desire: Foucault's "History of Sexuality" and the Colonial Order of Things* (Durham, NC: Duke University Press, 1995).

43. Smith, *Conquest*, 8.

44. *Crown v. Faiz.*

45. Ibid. Torture was penalized in the 1860 Indian Penal Code.

46. The convictions that Abbott imposed on Musalli's torturers were reduced to a fine or imprisonment in default.

47. "Judgement in the Chief Court of the Punjab, Appellate Side, Criminal," case no. 922 of 1915, IOR/L/PJ/6/3554, British Library.

48. Nicholas Dirks, *The Scandal of Empire: India and the Creation of Imperial Britain* (Cambridge, MA: Harvard University Press, 2006); Nancy L. Paxton, "Mobilizing Chivalry: Rape in British Novels about the Indian Uprising of 1857," *Victorian Studies* 36, no. 1 (1992): 5.

49. Sharpe, *Allegories of Empire*, 6.

50. Ibid., 129; emphasis mine.

51. Graham Dawson, *Soldier Heroes: British Adventure, Empire, and the Imagining of Masculinities* (New York: Routledge, 1994), 1.

52. Sharpe, *Allegories of Empire*, 67.

53. Mrinalini Sinha, "Giving Masculinity a History: Some Contributions from the Historiography of Colonial India," *Gender and History* 11, no. 3 (1999): 454.

54. Mrinalini Sinha, "Gender and Imperialism: Colonial Policy and the Ideology of Moral Imperialism in Late Nineteenth-Century Bengal," in *Changing Men: New Directions in Research on Men and Masculinity*, ed. Michael S. Kimmel (Newbury Park, CA: Sage, 1987), 228; Suleri, *Rhetoric of English India*, 17.

55. Rudi C. Bleys, *The Geography of Perversion: Male-to-Male Sexual Behaviour outside the West and the Ethnographic Imagination 1750–1918* (London: Cassell, 1996); Lisa Z. Sigel, *Governing Pleasures: Pornography and Social Change in England, 1815–1914* (New Brunswick, NJ: Rutgers University Press), 54.

56. Stephen Marcus, *The Other Victorians: A Study of Sexuality and Pornography in Mid-Nineteenth-Century England*, 3rd ed. (London: Corgi Books, 1970), 261.

57. Ibid., 263.

58. Sigel, *Governing Pleasures*, 77.

59. Ronald Hyam, *Empire and Sexuality: The British Experience* (Manchester: Manchester University Press, 1990), 71.

60. Lazreg, *Torture and the Twilight*, 143, 120, 134; emphasis mine.

61. Talal Asad, "On Torture, or Cruel, Inhuman, and Degrading Treatment," in *Social Suffering*, ed. Arthur Kleinman, Veena Das, and Margaret Lock (Berkeley: University of California Press, 1997), 294.

62. Darius Rejali, *Torture and Democracy* (Princeton, NJ: Princeton University Press, 2007).

63. Michel Foucault, *Discipline and Punish: The Birth of the Prison*, trans. Alan Sheridan (London: Lane, 1977).

64. The criminal justice system as it emerged in India was virtually dependent on confessions to ensure convictions. Douglas Peers, "Torture, the Police, and the Colonial State in the Madras Presidency, 1816–55," *Criminal Justice History: An International Annual* 12 (1991): 48.

65. This requirement was introduced in the Indian Evidence Act of 1872.

Gendered Violence and Cultural Forgetting

The Case of the Irish Magdalenes

Jennifer Yeager and Jonathan Culleton

Irish narratives of femininity facilitate a persistent gendered violence toward women formerly incarcerated in Magdalene Laundries and continue to affect Magdalene survivors today. The case of the Magdalene Laundries illustrates how the Irish state has shaped cultural narratives of gender. Further, it demonstrates the vital role played by cultural memory in constructing these gendered identities. As Anthony Smith argues, memory "by definition is integral to identity, and the cultivation of shared memories is essential to the survival . . . of such collective identities."[1] We argue that memory and dominant national narratives are powerful cultural constructions with broad repercussions in Ireland's past and present.[2]

To understand collective memory, it is necessary to take note of "collective amnesia."[3] "Forgetting becomes part of the process of national identity formation" as "a new set of memories are accompanied by a set of tacitly shared silences."[4] The women who inhabited Magdalene Laundries are subject to this shared silence, as they are omitted from Ireland's dominant historical narrative. Not everyone is equally powerful in their ability to claim and define the past.[5] What becomes defined as the official memory reflects the power of certain groups.[6] The result is that different groups claim the same past in sometimes contradictory ways; hence, "memory can be a potential oppressor as well as a potential liberator."[7]

Restriction of archival material related to the Magdalene Laundries contributes to the invisibility of these survivors. The lack of access to the archives points to the role of the Irish state and religious orders as gatekeepers of information and key

Radical History Review

Issue 126 (October 2016)   DOI 10.1215/01636545-3594481

© 2016 by MARHO: The Radical Historians' Organization, Inc.

participants in gendered violence toward survivors. Integral to historical scholarship is the notion that knowledge of the past can inform future behaviors.[8] Political forces constrain knowledge of the past, restructuring events so that "society better remembers."[9] Championing one version of events (in this case, one that silences Magdalene women) has implications for survivors. Trauma experiences are social; recovery is a *collective* process, necessitating social support.[10] We argue that survivor oral histories (for example, those gathered as part of the Waterford Memories Project) provide a way both to understand the meaning of what happened to the Magdalene women and to provide a record of these narratives.[11] As a method, oral history is particularly appropriate for examining "subjective experiences of shifting historical periods" as it emphasizes processes of meaning making.[12]

Women in Postindependence Ireland and the Magdalene Laundries

From the 1920s, "the Irish State conceived its national identity in terms of a predominantly Gaelic and Catholic cultural ethos."[13] In particular, the Catholic Church sought control of socialization processes by "establishing a firm grip on education as well as by the doctrine of familism."[14] This meant enforcing a moral control over women, which encompassed domestic life, education, health, the arts, welfare entitlements, and religious participation.[15]

Historical discourse surrounding the sexuality of the Irish has rarely challenged the self-proclaimed belief in Irish moral superiority.[16] Evidently, those guilty of such crimes as extramarital sex contradicted the prescribed national narrative that emphasized conformity, valued community over the individual, and esteemed conservative Catholic moral values.[17] The control of sexuality (or that of Irish women, at least)—as a practice and a discourse—became one of the strategies by which the Catholic Church maintained power.[18] The interaction between notions of female sexual purity and the nation is critical. As Claudia Lenz notes, women are constructed as biological and moral bearers of the nation, responsible for its future existence, yet regarded as neither capable of coping with the challenges of public affairs nor reliable in political matters.[19] Postindependence Ireland contained what it perceived as sexual immorality by locking it away. Ireland's "architecture of containment" (after James Smith's formulation) encompassed an assortment of interconnected institutions, including mother and baby homes, industrial and reformatory schools, mental asylums, adoption agencies, and Magdalene Laundries.[20] In effect, Magdalene women were hidden from society and written out of Irish history.

With a decline in prostitution after independence (1922), Irish Magdalene asylums began to alter their orientation, and the population of inmates became increasingly diverse; "hopeless cases," "mental defectives," infanticide cases, those on remand from courts, transfers from industrial and reformatory schools, and some "voluntary" committals increasingly formed cohorts of inmates.[21] They accommodated fewer voluntary entrants, and increasing numbers were detained for longer periods (many for life). These institutions increasingly served a punitive function, containing unmarried mothers, victims of sexual assault, and girls who were "sexually aware" or "demonstrating . . . tendencies towards sexual immorality."[22] The laundries became places where those who did not fit the model of Irish morality were effectively "excluded, silenced or punished."[23]

Ten Magdalene Laundries operated in Ireland between 1922 and 1996, with the stated mission to "protect, reform, and rehabilitate."[24] According to James Smith, many of these institutions shared overriding characteristics, including "regimes of prayer, silence, work in a laundry and a preference for permanent inmates."[25] The longevity of Irish Magdalene Laundries is also noteworthy; women were still entering Irish laundries in the 1980s.[26] The Sean McDermott Street laundry was the final laundry to close in 1996.

Magdalene Laundries provided a powerful mechanism for patriarchal control by the Irish state and religious orders, which deemed sexuality the principal cause for the downfall of morality.[27] Hence, the laundries formed part of a system of moral regulation and social control.[28] Moral reformation took place through industrial discipline, which had the additional benefit of being profitable through unpaid labor.[29] Society sought to render invisible the challenges these women embodied: they were sexually active when Irish women were expected to be morally pure; they were unmarried mothers when the constitution rendered marriage and motherhood inseparable; they were the victims of abuse under a legal double standard that evaded male culpability and condemned victims.[30]

The Carrigan Report (1931), as James Smith demonstrates, was particularly important in the inauguration of a state attitude toward sexual immorality through its hegemonic discourse, which in turn encouraged public consent.[31] The report established a state-sanctioned precedent for church-state advocacy of moral purity by criminalizing sex outside marriage. The report further ensured Irish women's ignorance about biological reproduction and their rights, while simultaneously stigmatizing young women (and exculpating young men) for sexual immorality.[32] So controversial were its revelations at the time that the Department of Justice advised against its publication, believing "it might not be wise to give currency to the damaging allegations made in Carrigan regarding the standard of morality in the country."[33]

The penalty for sex outside marriage was exorbitant. If a working-class woman became pregnant outside marriage, the common practice was for her to leave home (in disgrace) and go to a Magdalene Laundry; parents who tried to stand by their daughters had the priest hammering at the door, telling them it was their Christian duty to turn their back on their child.[34] The state's responses to sexual immorality also suppressed and concealed child sexual abuse in the 1930s; this concealment continued for decades. As James Smith notes, "The precedent established between 1930 and 1935 . . . legitimized secrecy and silence as a response to child abuse and pedophilia."[35]

Survivor oral histories provide a powerful challenge to this official silencing.[36] As one survivor of the Magdalene Laundries describes her experiences:

Soon after [my mother] got married, the abuse started with my stepfather. . . . I
was taken away by the [Irish Society for Prevention of Cruelty to Children]. . . .
Instead of taking the abuser out of the home, which was a man, they took
an innocent child out of the home. And, of course, you had the church still
continuing with my mother years later when she left him, to go back to her
husband, even though he had abused me, her only, her first child, so I'm kind of
confused about the Catholic teaching.

Concealment retraumatized abused children and punished already vulnerable citizens. Additionally, girls deemed to be in danger of engaging in sexual activity were incarcerated, as were girls referred through the criminal justice system. Disposing of vulnerable women in Magdalene Laundries ensured their personal silence, while creating a larger silence that safeguarded Ireland's identity as a morally pure society.[37]

Life in the laundries was characterized by silence, prayer, and hard labor.[38] Women worked with containers of boiling water for laundering and steam from the irons while washing soiled sheets from hospitals, hotels, and other businesses.[39] The girls were kept in a constant state of emotional and psychological turmoil, often unaware of why they were there, how long they would remain, or whether they would be transferred elsewhere. For example, one survivor of the laundries describes being moved from the industrial school in Tralee to the Peacock Lane laundry in Cork: "We went in, and a nun came in and then as she was leaving she said 'be a good girl now.' . . . I wanted to run over and say to her please, please don't let me stay here, please take me away, I'll be so good, I'll be very good for you. Even though it was all abuse and starvation, and whipping and beating. But I didn't, I don't know what held me back, but I had this, such a strong urge to do it." Transferal of girls from industrial schools to the laundries was common, typically with no warning or explanation.[40] Survivors reported to the McAleese Committee that, despite conditions, they were heartbroken to leave the only place they could call home.[41] At the laundries they were under constant surveillance and deprived of privacy, education, leisure, and rest; deprived of their identity, they were assigned new names, their hair was cut, and they were provided with uniforms.[42] As one survivor recalls,

She cut my hair, bitch, she changed my name, she cut my hair, and we had to
wear a uniform. . . . I've got my name changed, I got my hair cut, and I've got
my name changed. I'm wearing this glorified sack kind of thing, from the Bible,
I call it biblical uniform. . . . It was just constant work, work, work, work, work.

Funnily enough, we didn't have a lot of prayers. When I look back, it was all
about money, it was all about raking in this bloody money.

As this reflection suggests, the laundries' economic value conflicted with its moral
project.[43] In the 1990s, shocking revelations began to crack the conspiracy of silence
about the Magdalene Laundries. In 1993 High Park Convent in Dublin was sold to
developers,[44] who discovered the unmarked graves of 133 women who had previously been in the Magdalene Laundry. The bodies of the women from High Park
were exhumed, cremated, and interred in Glasnevin Cemetery before any attempt
was made to determine their identities. More disconcerting has been the limited
public outrage regarding the treatment of these women.[45]

The following decade witnessed a series of high-profile criminal cases and
state inquiries into the abuse of children by families, in state care, and by priests.
While it is outside the scope of this article to discuss this abuse in detail, the main
inquiries are summarized in the Ferns, Ryan, Murphy, and Cloyne Reports,[46] which
document evidence of abuse. In another act of complicity between church and state,
the government signed an indemnity deal with the religious congregations in 2002,
in return for the congregations making a contribution of €128 million to the redress
scheme toward compensating those abused in institutions.[47] In a damning response
to the Ferns, Ryan, Murphy, and Cloyne Reports, Amnesty International Ireland
found "the Catholic Church was the dominant service provider for the majority of
people in the State, and remains a significant service provider. . . . The State failed
to ensure . . . proper systems of regulation and accountability. . . . In the absence of
such systems, abuse was endemic."[48]

Survivor testimony forces a reconsideration of the civic impact of the laundries, despite the indemnity deal. As one survivor reflects, "About us Irish, we love
to think we are loved around the world. We give a false impression about ourselves.
We can't accept that we are corrupt, that we are immoral, that we are . . . so wrong
about human rights." By characterizing Ireland as "wrong on human rights," survivor testimony invokes international conventions.

Such framing by survivors and advocates has power to enlist international
support. In response to reports submitted by the Justice for Magdalenes advocacy
group, in 2011 the UN Committee against Torture requested the Irish government
launch an investigation into human rights violations in the Magdalene Laundries
and consider redress for survivors. The UN recommended that

the State party should institute prompt, independent, and thorough
investigations into all allegations of torture, and other cruel, inhuman or
degrading treatment or punishment that were allegedly committed in the
Magdalene Laundries, and, in appropriate cases, prosecute and punish the
perpetrators with penalties commensurate with the gravity of the offences

committed, and ensure that all victims obtain redress and have an enforceable right to compensation.[49]

International scrutiny had some impact on internal Irish recognition of survivors. The government's response was the *Report of the Inter-departmental Committee to Establish the Facts of State Involvement with the Magdalene Laundries*. The report is limited: it attempted only to establish the facts surrounding the extent of the state's involvement. While the report includes testimony from survivors (chapter 19), "the Committee did not make specific findings in relation to [the living and working conditions in the Magdalene Laundries], in light of the small sample of women available."[50] Justice for Magdalenes and other survivor groups roundly criticized the report. Solicitors, academics, and activists responded that the evidence demonstrates that the state colluded with the laundries, provided the religious orders with support, and failed to supervise the running of the laundries.[51]

Tellingly, the Department of Justice's report placed little significance on survivor testimony. By contrast, Justice for Magdalenes' efforts to collate its own archive of survivor testimony in the form of oral histories established a clear (and oppositional) focus on understanding how survivors experienced Magdalene Laundries.[52] The group's faith in oral history as a method for exploring how people make sense of their past by contextualizing their memories in the present allows us to reflect on how participants can make both micro- and macrolevel connections between their individual memories and collective experiences (within families, cultures, nations, etc.). Similarly, oral histories collated in the Waterford Memories Project demonstrate how many of the women draw connections between their personal experiences and the mechanisms of the state and religious orders. As Paul Thompson maintains, "Once the life experience of people of all kinds can be used as its raw material, a new dimension is given to history."[53]

Impact on Survivors

Our knowledge of the Magdalene women's experiences is constrained by societal forces, restructuring events so that "society better remembers."[54] Championing one version of events (which silences Magdalene women) makes it harder for survivors to integrate their experiences into personal narratives. If trauma experiences are social, like all historical events, recovery is similarly a collective process, necessitating acknowledgment and support.[55] Further, recognizing the cultural invisibility of these survivors makes plain their reduced ability to define their own past.

While the Department of Justice report was interested in establishing "the facts" of what happened, the oral histories recorded as part of the Waterford Memories Project allow us to know how these women survived and how they lived with long-silenced trauma. Their stories reflect the very current trauma of women actively processing the meaning of their experiences. For them, this is not history per se, given its continuing impact. As one survivor insists:

> They never even saw to our education . . . they made sure we were not educated because it was all part of the plan for the Magdalene laundries. That's all. It's as simple as that. What other ulterior motive would they have not to educate us? And how long were they doing this in Irish society? How long were they doing it to children in Irish society, training them for the Magdalene laundries so Senator McAleese, as nice as he may be and all that, his work was very narrow in the sense he could have found out how far back it went the pattern. How many industrial schools there were, how many children each year came out from the industrial schools went into the Magdalene laundries. Forced in there I should say because the religious had control with their support of the government paying them for our keep in in the industrial schools, and then the payment continued because they were paying the laundries, for us anyway, 'til we were eighteen and so on.

For this survivor, the trauma of the past affects her life today; she laments not just its impact on her life but the continuing intergenerational effects. The women do not simply describe the past; they testify to its ongoing relevance.

In this sense, oral history refuses to comply with the silence surrounding these women's lives. By sharing the survivors' stories, the Waterford Memories Project makes them available inside and outside of Ireland. Videotaping (rather than audio recording) further captures the emotion inherent in the stories. Thus, we witness how the survivors construct meaning from past events in order to make sense of their current situation. For the survivor above, confronting her past involved providing testimony for the first time, recognizing her trauma, and engaging in dialogue through oral history. Where this is problematic, as in the previous quote, we see how many survivors have difficulty in making sense of the past in the absence of information about what happened; silence hinders coping.

It is the public purpose of oral history that is important in the Waterford Memories Project and other oral history projects. Collecting and displaying survivors' stories enable the women to take some control over the history of the laundries. The narration alone becomes "a subversive act, especially in light of powerful . . . forces working against it."[56] Hence, the dissemination of oral histories is an act of resistance against collective forgetting as humiliated silence; this is particularly true where broad-scale silence around an event is unacknowledged, resulting in collusive silence (as a desire to forget) and collective shame. When we consider the Magdalene institutions' presence, in conjunction with decades of silence on the subject, we are faced with "the tacit imposition of a taboo."[57] Eviatar Zerubavel notes how "washing one's community's 'dirty laundry' in public" is taboo, resulting from informal codes of silence prohibiting this act.[58] This statement works literally and metaphorically for Magdalene history: survivors literally scrubbed the community's dirty laundry while metaphorically representing what Irish society wanted hidden. Such "conspiracies of silence" often emerge after a major traumatic experience, comprising an individual's decision to remain silent, an imposed silence, and a collusion of silence between survivors and society.[59]

Reducing a person's *choice* to speak comprises meaning making, which is, like trauma, a collective process, "particularly when the shared experience is a historic event."[60] For Zerubavel, such "silent witnessing" highlights a core tension between knowledge (personal awareness) and acknowledgment (public discourse) in mutual denial.[61] Maria Ritter notes that traumatic silences in therapy can reflect both the initial disconnect with trauma and "a silencing identification with the original silencer."[62] In this way, silence around trauma is both an individual and collective experience. Survivors of trauma will often report feeling sworn to silence as "bearers of a secret" that is transferred to the next generation in a collective act of remaining silenced.[63]

Further, if the process of recovery from trauma is collective, social interaction and support are necessary for "ending" the silence.[64] Silence here must be understood at a personal, cognitive level (as a form of survival) and in terms of broader social processes. A survivor explains how she felt constrained in her ability to be heard: "The Irish government has failed in their duties. . . . Governments are not and never were thinking of any violence perpetrated against Irish women. Sadly this is in the mindset of the Irish governments. . . . Irish society is so enshrined in their negative attitudes towards women collectively . . . this mind set has . . . instilled their Catholic indoctrination, and the men in power are on a macho trip." This quote underscores how gendered violence and silencing of Irish women inherently intertwine with the patriarchal government and societal norms. This has implications for how we approach understanding collective memory. We cannot ignore the importance of social interaction and context on an individual level in understanding how public silence can promote collective forgetting. If we acknowledge the import of social contact in dealing with trauma memories, the restriction of the archives related to the laundries can be viewed as inflicting ongoing distress. Oral histories therefore constitute an organized effort to bring "meaningful history to a public audience"[65] to begin addressing the lacuna of survivor testimony in official histories of the laundries.

How Do We Remember the Magdalenes?

The modest public engagement with the history of the Magdalene laundry points to the lack of a "common historical consciousness" on the subject.[66] Analyses of the laundries are constrained by the lack of access to the records of the religious orders,[67] resulting in an absence of intervention, as well as a failure to remember officially.[68] It is also the case that the "quality and quantity of the material held in various archives varies to a great extent."[69] Thus, public engagement with Magdalene history remains, in James Smith's formulation, at the level of "story," rather than at the level of history, supported by official documentation.[70] Religious orders did submit documentation to the government as part of the compilation of the 2013 report but required that the records submitted be returned and copies destroyed. A Residential Institutions Redress Board was established after the release of the report to compensate women incarcerated in the laundries, but survivors are legally prohibited from publicly communicating their experiences of either the institutions or redress scheme; the archive collated during the report remains vulnerable and inaccessible. State and religious orders thus remain gatekeepers of information about, and participants in, the continued gendered silencing of survivors.

The statements of Magdalene survivors throughout this article reveal previously obscured relationships between gender and the state. A survivor highlights such collusion in her own reflections:

> Ireland [still hasn't asked] people like me, not just me you know, collectively, to give our versions of, of how we feel and how it should be changed. Well first all what I would like to see is if some horrible disaster struck Ireland again do not let the church get involved, nope . . . no matter how good they say they are. Do not let one specific organization be in control. Let them work side by side in honesty and in partnership and to be honest with people.

This quote emphasizes how the state, despite attempts to position itself as less culpable than the church, emerges in survivors' conviction that these "previous partners in hegemony—state and familial institutions—evaded all intimations of culpability."[71] Stephen Sloan argues that, "for the oral historian, moments of crises . . . can offer an environment when the larger weaknesses or strengths of a society are quite visible."[72] Oral histories provide a means for survivors to document emotion, thus providing insight into their experiences.[73]

Further, recording the personal accounts of these women facilitates our understanding of the meaning of these events. Only when the voices of these women enter collective memory will the nation be able to confront its gendered violence. T. W. Moody argues that history is a matter of "facing the facts of the Irish past, however painful some of them may be. . . . The study of history . . . enlarges truth about our past . . . [and] opens the mind."[74] Remembering the Magdalene women accurately necessitates a willingness to revisit our national narrative and to include that which we have forgotten through a collective "therapeutic voluntary amnesia."[75]

As their reflections make clear, Magdalene survivors actively embrace their role in realigning our collective memories by breaking the collective silence. Gathering and sharing their stories thus encourages us to focus on recording the "essential purpose of history": to "give to people who experienced history, through their own words, a central place."[76] As Mark Cave highlights, collecting oral histories validates survivors' experiences through the process of recording the story as the researcher becomes an agent of the community's collective memory.[77] This is a salient point: at the heart of oral history is empathy, on the part of both the story-teller and the researcher.

Notes

1. Anthony Smith, *Myths and Memories of the Nation* (Oxford: Oxford University Press, 1999), 10.
2. Eviatar Zerubavel, *The Elephant in the Room: Silence and Denial in Everyday Life* (Oxford: Oxford University Press), 289.
3. Charles Mills, "White Ignorance and Hermenuetical Injustice," *Social Epistemology Review and Reply Collective* 3, no. 1 (2007): 28–29.
4. Paul Connerton, "Seven Types of Forgetting," *Memory Studies* 1, no. 1 (2008): 63.
5. Brian Conway, "Active Remembering, Selective Forgetting, and Collective Identity: The Case of Bloody Sunday," *Identity: An International Journal of Theory and Research* 3, no. 4 (2003): 319.
6. Rudolf De Cillia, Martin Reisigl, and Ruth Wodak, "The Discursive Construction of National Identities," *Discourse and Society* 10, no. 2 (1999): 169.
7. Michael Kammen, "Review of Frames of Remembrance: The Dynamics of Collective Memory, by Iwona Irwin-Zarecka," *History and Theory* 34, no. 3 (1995): 253.
8. James Pennebaker and Amy Gonzales, "Making History: Social and Psychological Processes underlying Collective Memory," in *Collective Memory*, ed. James Wertsch Pascal Boyer (New York: Cambridge University Press, 2008), 110–29.
9. Alin Coman, Adam Brown, Jonathan Koppel, and William Hirst, "Collective Memory from a Psychological Perspective," *International Journal of Politics, Culture and Society* 22 (2009): 128.
10. Pennebaker and Gonzales, "Making History."
11. Oral history is a method of qualitative, in-depth interview that emphasizes the participant's narrative of personal experiences and memories of events.
12. Patricia Leavy, *Oral History: Understanding Qualitative Research* (Oxford: Oxford University Press, 2011), 23.
13. John Marsden, *Redemption in Irish History* (Dublin: Dominican, 2005), 92.
14. Patrick O'Mahony and Gerard Delanty, *Rethinking Irish History: Nationalism, Identity and Ideology* (London: Palgrave Macmillan, 2001), 66–67.
15. Ibid. See also Maryann Valiulis, "Power, Gender, and Identity in the Irish Free State," *Journal of Women's History* 6, no. 4 (1995): 117–36.
16. Maria Luddy, *Prostitution and Irish Society* (Cambridge: Cambridge University Press, 2007).
17. James Smith, *Ireland's Magdalen Laundries* (Notre Dame, IN: University of Notre Dame Press, 2007).
18. Tom Inglis, *Moral Monopoly* (Dublin: UCD Press, 1998), 157.
19. Claudia Lenz, "The Silenced Memories of the Sexualised Other in Post-war Norway," in *Minority Narratives and National Memory*, ed. Cora Doving and Nicolas Schwaller (Oslo: Unipub, 2010), 87. See also Nina Yuval Davis, *Gender and Nation* (London: Sage, 1997).
20. James Smith, *Ireland's Magdalen Laundries*.
21. Luddy, *Prostitution*.
22. Mary Raftery and Eoin O'Sullivan, *Suffer the Little Children: The Inside Story of Ireland's*

Industrial Schools (London: Continuum, 1999), 27–28; Brian Titley, "Heil Mary: Magdalen Asylums and Moral Regulation in Ireland," *History of Education Review* 35, no. 3 (2006): 9.

23. Kathryn Conrad, *Locked in the Family Cell: Gender, Sexuality, and Political Agency in Irish National Discourse* (Madison: University of Wisconsin Press, 2004), 3.

24. James Smith, *Ireland's Magdalene Laundries*, xvi; Frances Finnegan, *Do Penance or Perish* (Oxford: Oxford University Press, 2004).

25. James Smith, *Ireland's Magdalene Laundries*, xv.

26. Raftery and O'Sullivan, *Suffer the Little Children*; Finnegan, *Do Penance or Perish*.

27. Inglis, *Moral Monopoly*; James Smith, "The Politics of Sexual Knowledge: The Origins of Ireland's Containment Culture and the Carrigan Report (1931)," *Journal of the History of Sexuality* 13, no. 2 (2004): 208–33; Titley, "Heil Mary."

28. Diarmaid Ferriter, *Occasions of Sin: Sex and Society in Modern Ireland* (London: Profile Books, 2009); James Smith, *Ireland's Magdalene Laundries*; Titley, "Heil Mary."

29. Titley, "Heil Mary."

30. James Smith, *Ireland's Magdalene Laundries*, xvii.

31. James Smith, "Politics of Sexual Knowledge."

32. Ibid.

33. Finola Kennedy, "The Suppression of the Carrigan Report: A Historical Perspective on Child Abuse," *Studies: An Irish Quarterly Review* 89, no. 356 (2000): 356.

34. Finnegan, *Do Penance or Perish*.

35. James Smith, "Politics of Sexual Knowledge," 224.

36. All of the survivor quotes in this article are taken from interviews conducted by Jennifer Yeager as part of the Waterford Memories Project.

37. James Smith, "Politics of Sexual Knowledge."

38. Katherine O'Donnell, "Justice for Magdalenes" (paper presented at the Irish Human Rights Commission and Law Society of Ireland Ninth Annual Human Rights Conference, Dublin, Ireland, 2011).

39. Department of Justice, *Report of the Interdepartmental Committee to Establish the Facts of State Involvement with the Magdalene Laundries* (Dublin: Department of Justice and Equality, 2013).

40. Raftery and O'Sullivan, *Suffer the Little Children*.

41. The Irish Government established the McAleese Committee in July 2011. The committee consisted of an independent chair (Senator Dr. McAleese) and senior representatives from six centrally relevant government departments: Department of Justice and Equality; Department of Health; Department of Enterprise, Jobs, and Innovation; Department of Education and Skills; Department of Environment, Community and Local Government; and Department of Children and Youth Affairs. The purpose of the interdepartmental committee was to establish if there was state involvement with the Magdalene Laundries and to produce a report on its findings. Department of Justice, *Report of the Interdepartmental Committee*.

42. Maeve O'Rourke, "Ireland's Magdalene Laundries and the State's Duty to Protect," *Hibernian Law Journal* 200, no. 10 (2011): 200–37.

43. The Justice Department report found that the laundries "were operated on a subsistence or close to break-even basis rather than on a commercial or highly profitable basis." Department of Justice, *Report of the Interdepartmental Committee*, 993. However, this conclusion was based on figures submitted from the religious organizations and their accountants, which was not independently audited. Additionally, financial information from the laundries in New Ross, Waterford, Cork, Donnybrook, and Dun Laoghaire

"did not survive" and were not included in the report. The Justice for Magdalenes group has questioned the findings, arguing that the religious orders had an unpaid workforce and lucrative contracts. See James Smith, Maeve O'Rourke, Raymond Hill, and Claire McGettrick, "State Involvement in the Magdalene Laundries: JFM's Principal Submissions to the Inter-departmental Committee to Establish the Facts of State Involvement with the Magdalene Laundries," Justice for Magdalenes, 2013, www.magdalenelaundries.com /State_Involvement_in_the_Magdalene_Laundries_public.pdf. Without open access to the original records, clear conclusions cannot be drawn regarding the economic viability of the laundries.

44. High Park Convent ceased operations in 1991.
45. Eva Urban, "The Condition of Female Laundry Workers in Ireland 1922–1996: A Case of Labour Camps on Trial," *Études Irlandaises* 37, no. 2 (2012): 49–64.
46. Francis D. Murphy, Helen Buckley, and Larain Joyce, *The Ferns Report*, presented to the Minister for Health and Children (Dublin: Government Publications, October 2005), www .bishop-accountability.org/ferns.htm; Ryan Report, *Commission to Inquire into Child Abuse, Report*, vols. 1–4 (Dublin: Government Publications, 2009), http://www .childabusecommission.ie/rpt/pdfs/; Murphy Report, *Commission of Investigation, Report into the Catholic Archdiocese of Dublin* (Dublin: Government Publications, 2009), www .dacoi.ie/, "Dublin Archdiocese Commission of Investigation Report"; Cloyne Report, *Report into the Catholic Diocese of Cloyne* (Dublin: Government Publication, 2010), www .justice.ie/en/JELR/Cloyne_Rpt_Intro.pdf/Files/Cloyne_Rpt_Intro.pdf.
47. Ryan Report.
48. Carole Holohan, *In Plain Sight: Responding to the Ferns, Ryan, Murphy, and Cloyne Reports* (Dublin: Amnesty International Ireland, 2011), 389.
49. UN Committee against Torture, "Concluding Observations of the Committee against Torture," 46th Session, 2011, 6, https://www.magdalenelaundries.com/JFM_UNCAT _Follow%20Up_Complete.pdf.
50. Department of Justice, *Report of the Interdepartmental Committee*, 925.
51. James Smith et al., "State Involvement in the Magdalene Laundries."
52. The Justice for Magdalenes oral history project was a collaborative research project with the University College Dublin, led by Katherine O'Donnell. The project was completed in 2013. The Waterford Memories Project (led by Jennifer Yeager) focuses on collecting narratives associated with the Magdalene institutions in the southeast of Ireland.
53. Paul Thompson, *Voice of the Past: Oral History*, 3rd ed. (Oxford: Oxford University Press, 2000), 6–7.
54. Coman et al., "Collective Memory," 128.
55. Pennebaker and Gonzales, "Making History."
56. Stephen Sloan, "The Fabric of Crisis: Approaching the Heart of Oral History," in *Listening on the Edge: Oral History in the Aftermath of Crisis*, ed. Mark Cave and Stephen Sloan (London: Oxford University Press, 2014), 273.
57. Paul Connerton, "Seven Types of Forgetting," *Memory Studies* 1, no. 1 (2008): 68.
58. Zerubavel, *Elephant in the Room*, 27.
59. Jack Saul, *Collective Trauma, Collective Healing: Promoting Community Resilience in the Aftermath of Disaster* (Sussex, UK: Routledge, 2014).
60. Ibid., 134.
61. Zerubavel, *Elephant in the Room*.
62. Maria Ritter, "Silence as the Voice of Trauma," *American Journal of Psychoanalysis* 74, no. 2 (2014): 176.

63. Clara Mucci, *Beyond Individual and Collective Trauma: Intergenerational Transmission, Psychoanalytic Treatment, and the Dynamics of Forgiveness* (London: Karnac Books, 2013), 79.

64. Judith Herman, *Trauma and Recovery: The Aftermath of Violence—from Domestic Abuse to Political Terror* (New York: Basic Books, 1992); Pennebaker and Gonzales, "Making History."

65. Donald Ritchie, *Doing Oral History*, 3rd ed. (Oxford: Oxford University Press, 2015), 28.

66. Urban, "Condition of Female Laundry Workers," 2.

67. Finnegan, *Do Penance or Perish*; Luddy, *Prostitution*; James Smith, *Ireland's Magdalene Laundries.*

68. Emilie Pine, *The Politics of Irish Memory* (Basingstoke, UK: Palgrave Macmillan, 2010).

69. Luddy, *Prostitution*, 107.

70. James Smith, *Ireland's Magdalene Laundries.*

71. Ibid., 434.

72. Sloan, "Fabric of Crisis," 265.

73. Mark Cave, "Introduction: What Remains: Reflections on Crisis Oral History," in Cave and Sloan, *Listening on the Edge*, 273.

74. T. W. Moody, "Irish History and Irish Mythology," *Hermethena* 124 (Summer 1978): 18.

75. Roy Foster, *The Irish Story: Telling Tales and Making It Up in Ireland* (Oxford: Oxford University Press, 2001), 58.

76. Thompson, *Voice of the Past*, 3. See also Robert Perks and Alistair Thomson, *The Oral History Reader* (London: Routledge, 2006).

77. Cave, "Introduction," 2.

Looking beyond the Frame

Snapshot Photography, Imperial Archives, and the US Military's Violent Embrace of East Asia

Jessie Kindig

Nestled within a fairly innocuous collection of US soldiers' Brownie camera snapshots from the Korean War, most of which show everyday life in camps and bases in Korea, is a series of more than one hundred and twenty photographs of Asian women—in clubs, in bars, in bed, on the street. Taken by US Army Sergeant Richard H. Rohrbach, on "Rest & Relaxation" leave (R&R) in US-occupied Japan with his buddy Whimp, the snapshot series documents Rohrbach and Whimp's pleasure at their vacation from the war: the skies are sunny, and the anonymous women the two embrace in almost every photo usually smile for the camera when their skirts are pulled up or their breasts grabbed playfully by one of the soldiers. The series features dozens of women, some in western fashions and some in traditional Japanese dress, some embraced by one of the soldiers and some, it seems, captured for the camera as they walked down the street. The anonymous women function as interchangeable props to illustrate the soldiers' enjoyment—here are the two friends with smiling beauties at a bar, outside a restaurant, just emerged from the bedroom. Rohrbach and Whimp smile and make silly faces for the camera, and as a testament to their good time, the archival records note that Rohrbach referred to the women in these snapshots as "good pieces."

Some of these snapshots, though, reveal darker meanings of this phrase *good pieces*: the women sit uncomfortably under the camera's gaze, implicitly challenging

Radical History Review

Issue 126 (October 2016)   DOI 10.1215/01636545-3594493

© 2016 by MARHO: The Radical Historians' Organization, Inc.

Figure 1 **Photograph courtesy of the Center for the Study of the Korean War, Richard Rohrbach photograph collection, PP.901**

their designation as either cooperatively "good" or objectified "pieces" to be enjoyed. In one snapshot, Rohrbach embraces a woman by binding her arms behind her (figure 1). She stands primly with her legs together, her body held apart from his. Her black bangs frame her face as she purses her lips and looks away from the camera, pivoting toward the crowd to her left. Rohrbach, perhaps sensing her discomfort, gives a tight half smile and keeps his body angled toward the camera, attempting to direct the woman's attention there too. The woman neither resists, it seems, nor cooperates, and in this refusal she might not qualify as a "good piece."[1]

One woman in the snapshot series did qualify as "good" in the men's determinations. Dressed in a checkered skirt, white blouse, and sandals, with a fashionable modern bob, she embraces Rohrbach in front of a house with a white picket fence, using her left hand to secure his arm at her waist. Unlike the other woman, her body leans into his, and she smiles at the camera. On the back of this snapshot, Rohrbach has scrawled in uneven cursive "This was good fucking" (figure 2). She appears again in another snapshot, this time enveloped in a bear hug by Whimp, with another caption, "How about that?"[2]

How about that. These snapshots, and their captions, implore us to reconsider the historical landscape of the US military presence in East Asia during the post–World War II and Korean War period. Rohrbach and Whimp appear in nearly every photo, taking turns groping or embracing each woman, documenting the realization of their sexual fantasy of R&R. The women, many of whom are likely sex workers, are visible in the photographs because the soldiers hold them in place, sometimes willingly and sometimes less so. The snapshots prompt an interrogation of the character of this embrace, its varied shadings into coercion, and the soldiers' belief that these "good pieces" were just features of their good time. Attending to what is outside the snapshots' frames—what is not seen—helps clarify the connection between gender violence and archival silence and requires new research methodologies. If Rohr-

Figure 2 The handwritten caption on the back of this snapshot reads "This was good fucking." Photograph courtesy of the Center for the Study of the Korean War, Richard Rohrbach photograph collection, PP.957.

bach and Whimp framed the series as wartime fun, what other framings can be constructed to attend to the dissonances, the subtle coercions, the sexualized landscape, and the prurient gaze of their camera?[3] What sexualized terrain were these women negotiating?

The Violent Embrace of US Empire

Since their first introduction to the peninsula, Americans had relied on gendered metaphors to figure their relationship with Korea. In 1868, US Navy Commodore Robert W. Shufeldt described the Pacific as "the ocean bride of America" and imperialism as sexual consummation: "Let us as Americans—see to it that the 'bridegroom cometh.' . . . It is on this ocean that the East & the West have thus come together, reaching the point where search for Empire ceases & human power attains its climax."[4] In 1882, Shufeldt would be the chief American architect of the treaty "opening" Korea to American and western trade, a relationship he once described as "amicable intercourse."[5]

Since the late nineteenth century, a gendered language of sexual embrace helped naturalize the belligerent US presence in East Asia as a benevolent, guiding, and welcomed presence. Rohrbach and Whimp's snapshots can thus be read as a synecdoche of US empire. As Koreans and Japanese were embraced by an often violent US partner during the simultaneous military occupations of South Korea (1945–48) and Japan (1945–52) and the war for communist containment on the Korean peninsula (1950–53), US imperial ambitions took on intimate, sexual, or familial connotations. Historian Naoko Shibusawa has described how Japan's relationship to the United States was figured as that of a feminized, immature "geisha ally," and South Korea was understood by the US military government in Korea as the junior partner in a "big-little brother relationship."[6] Both countries, in this imperial mindset, needed to be guided on the path toward western development, wrought through their union with US empire.

Rohrbach and Whimp were typical of the many thousands of American soldiers who experienced and produced the occupations of Korea and Japan and the war in Korea through the sexualized embrace of Asian women. Soldiers moved through occupied Japan en route to and from Korea and took part as consumers in the thriving economy of sex work in Japan's geisha houses and Korea's camptowns. During their tours of duty, American soldiers learned to expect Asian women's sexual embrace as part of their mission—this was, after all, what they were told R&R was all about. Soldiers' expectations of East Asia as an erotic paradise combined with the US military's institutional policies to legitimate and normalize sexual access to Asian women. This in turn produced an unequal climate of gendered power, one in which dating and sex work became means of financial support for many women facing wartime devastation, but also one in which soldiers' expectations of sexual access to Asian women frequently led to rape.

As an imperial structure of feeling, the violent embrace combined sexual expectations and benevolent arrogance with military coercion, structuring US policy and shaping the landscape in which Asian women encountered American soldiers. Captured in Rohrbach and Whimp's photo series, this structure of feeling shaped historical narratives of US power in East Asia, obscuring both imperial power and systemic sexual violence in state archives and later historians' accounts. Archival sources, like these snapshot photographs, frame this wartime landscape as a kind of pleasure, fun, or benevolence and only hint at the scale of coercion and violence that lies outside the photograph's borders. A full accounting of the violent embrace must ask critical questions of these sources, and must look outside the frame for what isn't shown, what remains unseen or only hinted at, what is only partially divulged, and what isn't being seen at all.

"Babysan Will Be Coy and Shy about Having Her Picture Taken . . . but She Loves It"

Like many American servicemen in East Asia, Rohrbach and Whimp likely looked through a copy of Navy petty officer Bill Hume's immensely popular cartoon book, *Babysan*, to help them envision their wartime vacation. A particular favorite of troops in occupied Japan and during the Korean War, *Babysan* billed itself as a sexualized travelogue, introducing the naive and bumbling GI to "the land of the cherry blossoms" by instructing them on how to acquaint themselves with the flirtatious "Babysan"—how to be, as Hume put it, "occupied while occupying."[7] Thumbing through the pages, American soldiers could consult the pidgin Japanese glossary to figure out how to refer to parts of Babysan's body or how to greet her family respectfully. Through pseudo-pornographic cartoons, *Babysan* cheekily instructed soldiers to understand Japanese/American interaction as a sexual embrace, teaching soldiers about Japanese customs they might not understand in order to better win Babysan's affections. With her carefree charm, her exotic racial difference, and her pinup girl figure, Hume's *Babysan* introduced Americans to military duty in East Asia as first and foremost a sexual adventure.

Advances in camera technology after 1945 allowed soldiers to document this erotic adventure. Servicemen purchased Kodak's new affordable "Brownie" camera at PX stations, and one contemporary observer noted that the occupation forces in Japan shot so many photographs that a camera seemed to be a part of every American's uniform.[8] In one of Hume's cartoons, he explained "Babysan will be coy and shy about having her picture taken—at first—but she loves it."[9] Whimp and Rohrbach seemed to agree, and the roving eye of their camera, which seemed to focus on any woman or girl walking down the street, illustrates the effort to find Babysan in any woman, no matter how young, unsmiling, or unposed she might be.

Rohrbach and Whimp's search for Babysan was encouraged and sanctioned by the institutionalization of military prostitution in Japan and Korea. In US-occupied Japan, new economies emerged based around soldiers' desires and catering to their fantasies about the erotic Orient. Of the $185 million spent by American troops there, roughly half went toward the sexual procurement of Japanese sex workers.[10] Despite its illegality, prostitution in occupied Japan was tolerated by the US military, who saw it as a necessary service.[11] In South Korea, R&R facilities were built for American occupying forces starting in 1947, alongside shopping centers full of American products. Both the newly independent Republic of Korea and US military leaders encouraged the development of these camptowns outside US military installations, viewing them as a "release" for troops that improved morale and as a way to protect "virtuous" Korean women from the possibility of rape by sexually frustrated American soldiers.[12]

For soldiers like Rohrbach and Whimp, led to believe that Babysan "loved it," the culture of the violent embrace cloaked women's post–World War II dislocation and economic need in the language of romance and seduction. Sex workers in Japan emphasized not romance and pleasure but economic necessity: as Otoki, a leader of sex workers from Tokyo's Yūrakuchō district, explained in a 1947 Japanese radio broadcast, "Of course it's hard to be a hooker. But without relatives or jobs due to the war disaster, how are we supposed to live? . . . There aren't many of us who do this because we like it."[13] As the war began in Korea in 1950, dislocating and impoverishing millions of Koreans, some women found that selling sex or finding a live-in American boyfriend offered a viable form of employment, as well as access to luxury goods, gifts, and a steady stream of income from American clients, boyfriends, and husbands.[14] For others, entering the camptowns was not even a question of their own limited agency: some of the first camptown women were kidnapped or sold by poor families into prostitution or could find no other employment after being enslaved as a Japanese "comfort woman."[15]

The violent embrace transformed a landscape of dislocation and war into one of pleasure and necessity by casting servicemen's sexual "need" as natural and laudable and all Asian women as welcoming and seductive as Babysan.[16] As Brig. Gen. Bryan Milburn remarked in September 1950, it was "a problem which cannot be solved by discipline of the soldier alone," whose "comparatively new and strong sex awakening" made it "difficult for the soldier to cope" with the "abundant opportunity of attractive and submissive girls."[17]

As GIs came to see Japan as an erotic playground, sex and dating shaded easily into sexual violence. In the US military's lexicon of pleasures, R&R leave, in Korean War–era GI alliterative slang, took on variations that included "Rape & Restitution," "Rape & Ruin," "Intercourse & Intoxication," or "Booze & Broads," attempts at humor that blurred the line between consensual and coercive embrace and normalized sexual assault.[18] Japanese women, for example, reported being abducted and raped by servicemen while walking home at night, on empty buses, or in their homes.[19] Gang rape was a particularly common and brutal practice of soldiers in Japan, as it would be in Korea—in Yokohama, an eleven-year-old Japanese boy witnessed four or five US Marines rape a twenty-six-year-old woman and then take a photograph of her vagina.[20]

The US Army's small number of recorded cases is historically misleading. Between 1947 and 1949, the army received reports of 455 rapes of women in Japan by US personnel, leading to 306 arrests and 44 total convictions.[21] One Japanese estimate, however, recorded 330 sexual assaults and rapes per day during the US occupation.[22] The discrepancy may reflect the difficulty Japanese women experienced in reporting their cases: at least one Japanese woman who reported her rape said she was then treated like a prostitute and put in a guarded venereal disease hospital.[23]

In keeping with the language of the violent embrace, American officials lauded the "complete camaraderie" between Japanese and Americans.[24] Japanese women and men, however, saw the occupation differently and complained, protested, and organized against their treatment. Victims of assault lodged their cases with the Japanese police and the Supreme Commander for the Allied Powers (SCAP). Japanese citizens wrote constantly to MacArthur, SCAP, or US military officers about injustices directed toward them and asked for redress.[25] And despite SCAP's press censorship that forbade discussion of social issues criticizing the US occupation, the Japanese press reported consistently on crimes by US forces and published articles about rapes by US servicemen.[26]

With the start of the Korean War, rapes of civilian Korean women by American, South Korean, and United Nations forces also became commonplace. American troops were said to entice Korean refugee girls across the Naktong (Nakdong) River to rape them, and informal accounts describe families either hiding their daughters or trading time with their daughters to American soldiers in exchange for cigarettes or gum.[27] American Lieutenant Colonel Charles Bussey remembered overhearing his troops discussing how best to "rape a woman."[28] One US Army chaplain complained to American general Matthew Ridgway that early in the war, the murder and rape of Korean civilians was widespread because of the lax army attitude toward crimes against civilians; the chaplain reported one case of seven American soldiers caught raping Korean women in Pyongyang who were released unpunished. By winter of 1951 this violence, including rape, had increased, particularly in UN-occupied Seoul.[29] Postwar truth and reconciliation commissions in Korea have found that "sexual punishment" of suspected communist women by right-wing youth groups and US-allied South Korean military and police forces was routine during the war.[30]

Many army commanders decried American soldiers' crimes against Korean civilians, including rape, but understood these crimes as exceptions to an otherwise amicable relationship. On March 9, 1951, General Ridgway sent a letter to all subordinate commands warning that such "misconduct" and "molestation" fueled communist propaganda and debased "the honorable record of military achievement of our and other United Nations forces in Korea."[31] The idea that assault was an anomaly committed by a few lawless soldiers in an otherwise benevolent war is borne out only if the story is framed by using the army's official crime statistics. The most complete data specific to US forces in Korea is for April through August 1951, in which the provost marshal reported sixty-two rape cases over a five-month period.[32] Yet these statistics are misleadingly small: for a report to make it into military files, it would have to be a formal complaint lodged by the Korean woman or her family, an undertaking that would have been difficult at best in the midst of active combat fighting, language barriers, and mutual distrust.

Looking outside the Frame

Because of this archival record, sexual violence during the Korean War appears only sporadically, partially, or tangentially in English-language archives; the US military's own reports of investigations make it impossible to determine whether sexual violence by US soldiers in occupied Japan and Korea was rare or frequent. In fact, I doubt that an institutional history of rape cases will ever give a full accounting; as feminist legal scholars, analysts, historians, and activists have argued for decades, writing the history of gender violence demands an archive beyond state and military institutional records.[33]

Glimpses of the US military's violent embrace of East Asia appear in a traditional historical archive most often not as criminal reports or military police cases but as captions on soldiers' snapshots, in wartime slang and jokes, and as offhand references from war correspondents and in soldiers' memoirs. The violent embrace rested on just this occlusion, resolving the tension between romance and coercion, benevolence and occupation, love and war, by coding it as a kind of "good" fun or the securing of western democracy. If military occupation was "camaraderie," then assault could be pleasurable, "Rape & Restitution" could be "Rest & Relaxation," and fighting a brutal war could be, in President Truman's words, "fighting for peace."[34]

Further, this occlusion formed the way Korean War stories were and are told in the United States. War correspondents, historians, and scholars have detailed the Korean War's military violence by outlining the US and allied forces' devastating use of napalm, search-and-destroy tactics, the designation of "free-fire" zones that included rural villages, and racial violence against any Korean deemed to be a "gook."[35] Surprisingly, though, few contemporaneous American and British accounts, so intent on describing the use of napalm, guerrilla warfare, and Americans' anti-Asian racism, describe the rape of Korean women.[36] English-language histories of the war, from military histories to revisionist and contemporary ones, make only scant mention of sexual violence (or camptown prostitution, for that matter).[37] For example, sociologist and criminologist J. Robert Lilly, whose 2007 book documents incidences of GI rape in World War II's European theater, scoffed at the idea of widespread GI rape in Korea because of the lack of "verifiable sources."[38]

At times, the US government actively suppressed accounts of sexual violence during the war. In May 1951, the Women's International Democratic Federation (WIDF), a UN-affiliated network of antifascist and leftist women's organizations centered in Europe, sent a twenty-member fact-finding delegation to North Korea to investigate war crimes against Korean civilians. The delegates found evidence of the systematic use of torture and sexual torture, the destruction of food supplies and stores, targeted destruction of towns, hospitals, and schools, and the use of banned weapons—all forms of violence suppressed or sidelined in broader public discourse. The WIDF asked that their report, *We Accuse!*, be circulated to all governments, and they sent it themselves to the United Nations in June 1951, where its circulation was blocked by US representatives.[39]

Tellingly, only two rape cases reached mainstream American news, perhaps because one involved the culpability of other UN allies, not US soldiers, and the second was a racially charged case in which African American Navy steward Paul Crosslin was convicted by military court-martial for the alleged rape of a US Navy nurse, not a Korean woman. Crosslin's defense was taken up by the National Association for the Advancement of Colored People (NAACP), which recognized the case as a part of a longer American tradition of falsely accusing black men of raping white women.[40]

The silence in American accounts belies the memories of Korean women and men during the war, for whom rape forms one of the most enduring memories of the war.[41] Some women explicitly remember US soldiers calling out "saekssi, saekssi" as they looked for Korean women, using the Korean word that meant "maiden" but sounded to American ears like "sexy" and to Koreans as an intention of violation.[42] Rape and sexual exploitation of Korean women by American soldiers has become a trope in contemporary Korean fiction and film about the Korean War and postwar camptown life.[43] We might see the unnamed woman in Rohrbach and Whimp's snapshot not just embraced by the smiling GI but enfolded within a longer history of the violent embrace. This might allow space for her story to be much more than that of a "good piece" and different from my story of American militarization in East Asia. Rather, she might tell her own, complicated story.

Accommodating these new stories requires examining the silences, partial references, and traces left in the archive: it means interrogating the qualities of the embrace seen in the snapshots, asking what lies outside their frames, and theorizing what cannot be seen. Disavowal and elision were at the heart of the violent embrace, for the same framing of Whimp and Rohrbach's R&R leave as fun with "good pieces" made rape ubiquitous to US military culture, and the women who experienced it silent figures for the retrenchment of a story of American benevolence. Accommodating these new stories also calls for a recognition of the work war narratives do to reinscribe and naturalize gendered power relationships in which female bodies—particularly those already made precarious by racial and national differentiations—are made potentially violable.

In the absence of full accounts of US empire's gendered violence, Rohrbach and Whimp's photographs urge us to reconsider the framing of US power in the Pacific as benevolent or equitable. The sometimes fraught embraces in the snapshots, and Rohrbach's characterization of the women as "good pieces," bring into focus how the assertion of American democracy in Korea and Japan depended on both structural gender violence and its attendant disavowal. We need new epistemologies, new frames of vision that attend to the silences by outlining them, constructing histories that show the shape of what is lost.

Notes

I thank Moon-Ho Jung, Ellen Wu, the Histories of Violence Collective, and the History Department Colloquium at Indiana University for their comments on this piece.

1. Richard Rohrbach Photograph Collection, PP.901, Center for the Study of the Korean War, Independence, Missouri.
2. Ibid., PP.904 and PP.957.
3. Judith Butler's discussion of "frames of war" is central to my thinking: Butler, *Frames of War: When Is Life Grievable?* (New York: Verso, 2010).
4. Shufeldt's lecture quoted in Frederick C. Drake, *The Empire of the Seas: A Biography of Rear Admiral Robert Wilson Shufeldt, USN* (Honolulu: University of Hawai'i Press, 1984), 115–16.
5. Gordon Chang, "Whose 'Barbarism'? Whose 'Treachery'? Race and Civilization in the Unknown United States–Korea War of 1871," *Journal of American History* 89, no. 4 (2003): 1362.
6. Naoko Shibusawa, *America's Geisha Ally: Reimagining the Japanese Enemy* (Cambridge, MA: Harvard University Press, 2006); Korean Military Advisory Group Public Information Office, *The United States Military Advisory Group to the Republic of Korea, 1945–1955* (Tokyo: Daito Art Printing, 1956), viii, 60.

7.   Bill Hume, *Babysan: A Private Look at the Japanese Occupation* (Tokyo: Kasuga Boeki K.K., 1953), dedication and 6–7. The popularity of the text is discussed in Shibusawa, *America's Geisha Ally*, 36.

8.   Shibusawa, *America's Geisha Ally*, 17.

9.   Hume, *Babysan*, 76–77.

10.   Shibusawa, *America's Geisha Ally*, 38.

11.   A state-run system of sex work was closed after one year by US occupation authorities. John Dower, *Embracing Defeat: Japan in the Wake of World War II* (New York: Norton, 1999), 123–32; Sarah Kovner, *Occupying Power: Sex Workers and Servicemen in Postwar Japan* (Stanford, CA: Stanford University Press, 2012), chap. 1.

12.   Whitney Taejin Hwang, "Borderland Intimacies: GIs, Koreans, and American Military Landscapes in Cold War Korea" (PhD diss., University of California, Berkeley, 2010), 26–28, 89–90; Ji-Yeon Yuh, *Beyond the Shadow of Camptown: Korean Military Brides in America* (New York: New York University, 2002), 25; Seungsook Moon, "Regulating Desire, Managing the Empire: US Military Prostitution in South Korea, 1945–1970," in *Over There: Living with the US Military Empire from World War Two to the Present*, eds. Maria Höhn and Seungsook Moon (Durham, NC: Duke University Press, 2010), 41.

13.   Dower, *Embracing Defeat*, 123–24.

14.   Hwang, "Borderland Intimacies," chap. 1, esp. 38–40.

15.   Yuh, *Beyond the Shadow*, 31; Hwang, "Borderland Intimacies," 89.

16.   Hwang, "Borderland Intimacies," 25–27; Kovner, *Occupying Power*, 30–33; Susan Zeiger, *Entangling Alliances: Foreign War Brides and American Soldiers in the Twentieth Century* (New York: New York University Press, 2010), chap. 3, esp. 75.

17.   Control of Solicitors and Streetwalkers, 1950, folder 250.1 and 2, box 199, General Correspondence (GC) 1950, Adjutant General (AG), Far East Command (FEC), Record Group (RG) 554, US National Archives, College Park, MD (NACP).

18.   E. J. Kahn, *The Peculiar War: Impressions of a Reporter in Korea* (New York: Random House, 1951), 12–13; Paul Dickson, *War Slang: American Fighting Words and Phrases since the Civil War*, 2nd ed. (Dulles, VA: Brassey's, 2004), 236, 246, 253.

19.   See the complaints filed by named and unnamed Japanese women, reported in folder 250.1, "(Jan Dec) 1946 (OCC)," box 909, Official File, AG, Eighth Army, RG 338, NACP; folder 250.1, "Morals and Conduct," box 32, GC 1946–48, G-2, Eighth Army, RG 338, NACP; folder 250.1, "Alleged Misconduct of Occupation Troops against Japanese Nationals," box 199, GC 1950, AG, FEC, RG 554, NACP; folder 250.1 no. 1, box 884, Secret General Correspondence 1952, AG, FEC, RG 554, NACP.

20.   Kovner, *Occupying Power*, 50–51.

21.   The figures were tallied by the Provost Marshal Office between March 8 and 10, 1950, at the specific request of the Army Staff Branch G-1, compiled from detailed monthly crime reports prepared for each command within the entire Far East Command. Numbers of trials and convictions were prepared by the Provost Marshal Office from incomplete files of General Court-Martial orders from the Judge Advocate Section of FEC General Headquarters. Documents held in "Statistics in re: Rape," folder 250.1, "Alleged Misconduct of Occupation Troops."

22.   Charles J. Hanley, Sang-Hun Choe, and Martha Mendoza, *The Bridge at No Gun Ri: A Hidden Nightmare from the Korean War* (New York: Holt, 2001), 28.

23.   Kovner, *Occupying Power*, 54.

24.   General Omar N. Bradley, "Substance of Statements Made at Wake Island Conference on 15 October 1950, Compiled by General of the Army Omar N. Bradley, Chairman of the Joint

Chiefs of Staff, From Notes Kept by the Conferees in Washington," 13, folder 18, "Wake Island—Conference Statements," box 206, Korean War, President's Secretary's Files, Harry S. Truman Papers, Truman Library, Independence, Missouri.

25. "Unfavorable Press in Occupied Japan," November 3, 1952, folder 250.1, box 519, GC 1952, AG, Eighth Army, RG 338, NACP; "Ski Slope Beatings," March 11, 1949, folder 250.1 no. 1, box 575, Secret General Correspondence 1949, AG, FEC, RG 554, NACP; "Japanese Complaint," January 23, 1950, postcard from K. Yukashita, May 17, 1952, and case 2, Mrs. Yasuyo Onishi, folder 250.1, "Alleged Misconduct of Occupation Troops."

26. Dower, *Embracing Defeat*, 211, 410–12.

27. Hanley et al., *Bridge at No Gun Ri*, 103, 189.

28. Lt. Col. Charles M. Bussey, *Firefight at Yechon: Courage and Racism in the Korean War* (Lincoln: University of Nebraska Press, 1991), 238–43, 255.

29. Callum A. MacDonald, *Korea: The War before Vietnam* (New York: Free Press, 1986), 210, 216.

30. Bruce Cumings, *The Origins of the Korean War*, 2 vols. (Princeton, NJ: Princeton University Press, 1990), 2:702; Suzy Kim, *Everyday Life in the North Korean Revolution, 1945–1950* (Ithaca, NY: Cornell University Press, 2013), 234; Masuda Hajimu, *Cold War Crucible: The Korean Conflict and the Postwar World* (Cambridge, MA: Harvard University Press, 2015), chap. 7.

31. "Misconduct of Troops" letter, March 9, 1951, folder 250.1, box 747, Secret General Correspondence 1951, AG, RG 554, NACP.

32. See all Staff Section Report folders in box 2174, Command Reports, December 1950 to December 1952, Provost Marshal Section, Eighth Army, RG 338, NACP.

33. For example, this argument is made in Estelle Freedman, *Redefining Rape: Sexual Violence in the Era of Suffrage and Segregation* (Cambridge, MA: Harvard University Press, 2013); Judith Herman, *Trauma and Recovery: The Aftermath of Violence—from Domestic Abuse to Political Terror*, updated ed. (New York: Basic Books, 1997), 28–32; Kovner, *Occupying Power*, 55.

34. President Harry S. Truman, live television addresses from the White House, CBS network, July 19, 1950, and September 1, 1950, accessed from the Paley Center for Media database, https://www.paleycenter.org/collection/.

35. For example, see Sahr Conway-Lanz, "Beyond No Gun Ri: Refugees and the United States Military in the Korean War," *Diplomatic History* 29, no. 1 (2005): 45–81; Cumings, *Origins of the Korean War*; Réné Cutforth, *Korean Reporter* (London: Wingate, 1952); Max Hastings, *The Korean War* (New York: Simon and Schuster, 1987); Kahn, *Peculiar War*; MacDonald, *Korea*; I. F. Stone, *The Hidden History of the Korean War* (New York: Monthly Review Press, 1952); and Reginald Thompson, *Cry Korea* (London: MacDonald, 1951).

36. For a singular mention of "the bombs and the burning and the raping behind the battle line," see Cutforth, *Korean Reporter*, 189–90.

37. Bruce Cumings's valuable two-volume *Origins of the Korean War* notes that rape was "common" but adds no more (706, 904n120). However, he discusses the issue in later shorter writings: Bruce Cumings, "Silent but Deadly: Sexual Subordination in the US-Korean Relationship," in *Let the Good Times Roll: Prostitution and the US Military in Asia*, ed. Saundra Pollock Sturdevant and Brenda Stoltzfus (New York: New Press, 1993); Bruce Cumings, "Occurrence at Nogun-Ri Bridge: An Inquiry into the History and Memory of a Civil War," *Critical Asian Studies* 33, no. 4 (2001): 520. See also note 41. Several scholarly accounts tabulate rape and sexual violence in occupied Japan and discuss the Korean War as part of that context: Kovner, *Occupying Power*; Yuki Tanaka,

Japan's Comfort Women: Sexual Slavery and Prostitution during World War II and the US Occupation (New York: Routledge, 2002). Susan Brownmiller attempted to account for US Army court-martial convictions for rape, but without access to credible sources: Brownmiller, *Against Our Will: Men, Women, and Rape* (New York: Simon and Schuster, 1975), 99, 417.

38.   J. Robert Lilly, *Taken by Force: Rape and American GIs in Europe during World War II* (New York: Palgrave Macmillan, 2007), 31.

39.   Though communist propaganda often charged US and UN forces with rape, I do not believe the WIDF report can be included in this category. The report is certainly one-sided, investigating only US, ROK, and UN war crimes, but the WIDF's long history as an interwar women's organization and the commission's careful detailing of names, dates, and locations of assaults lead me to accept the report as a credible piece of reportage. Women's International Democratic Federation, *We Accuse! Report of the Commission of the Women's International Democratic Federation in Korea, May 16 to 27, 1951* (Berlin: WIDF, 1951), esp. 16, 35, 36. For the background of the WIDF, see Francisca de Haan, "The Women's International Democratic Federation (WIDF): History, Main Agenda, and Contributions, 1945–1991," in *Women and Social Movements, International, 1840–Present*, ed. Kathryn Kish Sklar and Thomas Dublin, Alexander Street Press, http://alexanderstreet .com/products/women-and-social-movements-international; Francisca de Haan, "Continuing Cold War Paradigms in Western Historiography of Transnational Women's Organisations: The Case of the Women's International Democratic Federation (WIDF)," *Women's History Review* 19, no. 4 (2010): 547–73; Suzy Kim, "Crossing Borders: A Feminist History of Women Cross DMZ," *Asia-Pacific Journal* 13, no. 1.33 (2015): 1–31. For the debate over the report's presentation to the United Nations, see "Malik Pushes Report on Korea 'Atrocities,'" *New York Times*, June 23, 1951; "US Replies to Reds," *New York Times*, July 6, 1951; US Mission to the United Nations, "Non-governmental Organizations, Consultative Status with Economic and Social Council—Women's International Democratic Federation, 4 Oct. 1946–10 April 1953 (A)," press release 1224, June 22, 1951, folder 8, box: "S-0441-0016, Registry Section/Archives and Records Service/OGS, Branch Registries—Volume I–IV, 1946–1959," UN Archives and Records Management Section, New York, New York.

40.   George Barrett, "Koreans Watch U.N. Murder Trial as Test of Curb on Unruly Troops," *New York Times*, August 21, 1951; "Navy Steward's Case to Judge Advocate," *Memphis World*, February 27, 1953; "Ask New Trial in Navy Case," *Baltimore Afro-American*, February 28, 1953. Crosslin was convicted to a ten-year term in 1951; the NAACP's lawyers petitioned to reopen the trial in 1953.

41.   Yuh, *Beyond the Shadow*, 242n36. Cumings reported that wartime rape was an enduring memory for Korean survivors of the war in an interview by Dean Lawrence Velvel on the television program *Books of Our Time* (Massachusetts School of Law/Comcast, March 20, 2011), mslawmedia.org (accessed May 2, 2013).

42.   Yuh, *Beyond the Shadow*, 242n36; Chungmoo Choi, "Nationalism and Construction of Gender in Korea," in *Dangerous Women: Gender and Korean Nationalism*, ed. Elaine H. Kim and Chungmoo Choi (New York: Routledge, 1998), 15.

43.   Choi, "Nationalism," 15–18.

Boko Haram, Refugee Mimesis, and the Archive of Contemporary Gender-Based Violence

Benjamin N. Lawrance

Nigerian Isa Muazu came to the United Kingdom in 2007. He overstayed his visitor's visa and was detained. Muazu applied for asylum protection based on his fear of death at the hands of the West African Islamist entity Boko Haram (BH), which he claimed had already killed members of his family.[1] Muazu's fears were allegedly grounded in unsubstantiated claims that BH adherents had previously subjected his wife and daughters to persecutory harms that somehow extended to his person. The Home Office rejected his application and deported him in 2013.[2] Regardless of his claims' veracity and verifiability, Muazu may have been Britain's first asylum seeker fearing BH.

Asylum seekers today witness western migration fortresses' exclusionary walls rising ever higher.[3] Protection categories in the 1951 Refugee Convention seem frustratingly immutable; access to protection in developed countries is inexorably constricted. Refugees engaging newer analytical frameworks of gender-based persecution, such as domestic violence, or even established paradigms such as genital cutting, face heavy scrutiny for credibility. Whereas in the 1990s and 2000s exotic stories of what feminist migration theorists identify as "gendered persecutory harms" gained critical attention, they have been now displaced by sensational stories about security and terrorism.[4]

Radical History Review
Issue 126 (October 2016)   DOI 10.1215/01636545-3594505
© 2016 by MARHO: The Radical Historians' Organization, Inc.

Asylum seekers, cognizant of the incredulity greeting their personal testimo-nies, employ creative strategies to anchor their narratives and render them exotically familiar.[5] Since the kidnapping of several hundred girls in Chibok in Borno State in April 2014, asylum claims increasingly cite BH. Far from exposing BH's "weakness," as pundit Andrew Noakes claimed, the kidnappings lend new agency to grander, expansive fears of abduction, rape, and forced marriage now filtering into asylum claims.[6] Although migration authorities recognize BH's extreme violence, asylum anxieties narrated in immigration courts often assert hypothetical future jeop-ardy, not enacted historical trauma.[7] By reshaping personal testimonies of gender-based violence to foreground persecution by BH, Nigerian asylum seekers actuate a mimetic strategy engaging powerful—and problematic—tropes about Africa and Africans. Absent mimesis, and as Plato conjectured, the poetics of asylum seekers risk being exposed as little more than "simple narration."[8]

Many of the asylum seeker testimonies I review in my capacity as expert wit-ness contain unique and otherwise inaccessible first-hand accounts of historical and contemporary gender-based violence. This analysis explores asylum seeking as an emergent archival form to highlight how the strategies in asylum claiming conceal a potentially rich archive of gender-based violence. Nigerian claims illustrate one such strategy, namely, how gender-based-violence asylum claimants mimetically empha-size BH as a vehicle for resistance to endemic bureaucratic suspicion, doubt, and disbelief. Echoing Luise White's inspiring analysis of rumor to reconstruct complex historical "truths," attention to strategy illustrates how mimetic asylum texts may be read as archives of gender-based violence.[9] In the mimetic invocation of BH jeopardy, a spectrum of historical and projected persecutory fears adapts current anxieties of gender-based violence. Nigerians highlight horror stories about BH to instrumentalize stereotypes of African cultures—often as primitive and endemi-cally violent—rendering gender-based violence into exotically familiar prejudices of Africa. Asylum seekers' invocations of BH operate as a mimetic enterprise, a forward-looking strategy whereby tired, often racist historical paradigms of Africa collapse into presentist anxieties of gender-based violence.

Asylum as an Archive of Gender-Based Violence

Asylum seeking is emerging as an important site of historical research.[10] African historians turn to asylum claimants, experiences narrated outside Africa, as a cre-ative way to "think more critically and imaginatively" about "Africa's post-colonial archive."[11] Asylum narratives allow historians to take the pulse of the contemporary African gendered experience; they offer new and insightful paths to see and know gender-based violence. Asylum seekers provide rich insights into the discrete worlds of grassroots resistance to patriarchy and gender-based violence and alternative sex-ualities, part of the rubric of an "emergent and tentative new conceptual bundle" of sexual rights "unfolding" in transnational globalized migrant networks.[12] Framing asylum claims as archives responds to Ann Laura Stoler's attention to archival form, notably "genres of documentation," "arts of persuasion," and "affective strains."[13]

Asylum seeking has the potential to function as an archive in several ways. First, asylum seeking offers a valuable documentation genre for evaluating lived social experiences. While asylum narratives are first-person accounts, collectively asylum claiming offers a contemporary oral historical archive of gender-based violence. Asylum claiming—including but not limited to applicant testimonies, government response letters, judgments, and other documentation—operate as "rich documentary archives tethered to discrete legal contexts," which speak to "analytical categories, constructed identities, and personal narratives of fear, trauma and violence."[14] Testimonies are multilayered: each time an asylum seeker narrates an experience, or revisits an earlier statement or interview, a contemporary archive of persecution expands. Asylum narratives—and the snowballing of documentation as claims move toward adjudication—provide a window on the changing contexts of gender-based violence.[15]

Second, asylum narratives offer a critical perspective to revisit methodological debates about gender violence histories, such as establishing the basis of complaint.[16] As asylum claims are increasingly supported by expertise, they constitute a category of persuasive art. Reports by historians, and other experts, translate narratives of "personal trauma" into persuasive acts "of political aggression," anchored to Refugee Convention articles.[17] The discipline of history, modes of historical writing, and the methodologies of historicization have powerful explanatory facility for asylum adjudicators.[18] Experts are contracted to provide analysis of the empirical details of specific claims, ranging from current state protections and capacity for enforcement to the disjuncture between objectives and on-the-ground reality. The expert may be a foil to adjudicators, evaluating the legal basis for persecution claims and the history of specific persecutory forms.[19] By comparing claims with publicly available evidence about real and purported legal remedy, experts provide a hypothetical basis for advancing a claim.

Third, as a tightly regulated formula for affecting empathy, asylum claiming demands engagement with a register of strategies. The omission of gender from the international language of refugee protection gives rise to strategies to overcome this error. Understanding asylum-seeking strategies holds the possibility of unlocking a vast archive of persecution and trauma. The routinely hostile reception granted gender-based-violence claims ironically tenders an avenue for uncovering their very meaning.[20] Asylum seekers and their advocates fashion gender-based narratives into persuasive concepts and established frameworks; as an archive they are highly problematic, and some may be of questionable reliability.[21] Asylum narratives constitute personal lived truths, buttressed by fears, hearsay, and rumors, hence the significance of identifying and problematizing one such strategy, mimesis. Disassembling strategies—as they engage, resist, and seek to subvert criticisms of claims—reveal not only the lived experience of the personal and intimate but also how refugee convention definitions restrain and conceal gender-based violence.

From Credibility to Mimesis

Asylum operates within an unbounded legal domain, and in a constant state of flux, the unanchored nature of which is revealed by policies, procedures, standards, practices, and legal challenges. Claims are co-constituted in a climate of fear in which expert, claimant, advocate, and immigration authority all operate. Assessing credibility is one key site of contestation; it reveals the unbounded, unanchored dimensions of the refugee's legal predicament. Attacks on credibility turn asylum narratives into what April Shemak calls "sites of surveillance and policing of national boundaries."[22] Mimesis has emerged as one strategy refugees themselves use to resist attacks on credibility.

Mimesis is an affective strategy of resistance and subversion of the constraints imposed on survivors of gender-based violence. Asylum seekers' strategies are inextricable from their own personal testimony and tack closely to testimony and testimonial form. The woman fleeing genital cutting has only her personal narrative of violence and persecution. When decision makers question her credibility, she adopts techniques to broaden the significance *qua* seriousness of her specific claim. One response is to stretch, embellish, or invent narratives that conform to asylum law.[23] Another is to draw on the added burden of trauma many refugees suffer, and the difficulties of communicating across both linguistic barriers and cultural dissonance add complexity to elicit empathic responses on the part of adjudicators.[24] Mimesis is another such response to incredulity.

Mimetic practices have a rich history and present throughout sub-Saharan Africa. Mimetic affect is a mechanism to assimilate, perform, mask, dissolve, and reshape.[25] Mimetic performance is neither reenactment nor deceit but self-transformative in a context of upheaval and instability.[26] In gender-based violence narratives mimesis becomes a tool to reframe the personal narrative, within a broader canvas of jeopardy. Mimesis rebuts attacks on the credibility of asylum seekers by collapsing lived experiences or future jeopardies with presentist anxieties. The recourse to mimesis in asylum seeking as a direct response to the pressures of credibility attacks and fear of incredulity was seemingly anticipated by Jean-François Lyotard when he described the violent "double bind" as a *dommage* (a tort or wrong) "accompanied by the loss of means to prove the damage."[27] Because of the "improvability" of testimony, the asylum seeker is routinely perceived as mendacious.[28] As asylum seekers are often convinced their stories will never be believed, they reframe them within a broader presentist canvas populated by terrifying fears.

to "understand how ordinary Christians" or "general supporters of the Nigerian government" may be "targets for persecution by Boko Haram." A query was posed thus: "Whether incidents committed by other persons or organizations were reported as Boko Haram actions."[39] In this example, BH is transformed into an aberration and persecutory enterprise targeting normalcy and stability. Moreover, past events are revisited, albeit hypothetically, as actions of BH.

From the perspective of the historian, the significance of transformation cannot be understated because transformation converts new things into historical practices. Protean fears, newness, and novelty are indeed a cornerstone of contemporary African asylum practice. Each instance of jeopardy embedded within any asylum application constitutes a distinct component of the archive of postcolonial African social and family life. This archive is alive and gives rise to new understandings about cultures and practices, behaviors and moralities.[40] While asylum seekers' narratives may appear, at least to western adjudicators, novel, unusual, and contested, digital information technology makes it possible for claimants to ground their need for protection in rich documentation about the absence of legal remedy or safeguards.[41]

This third mimetic formula highlights the role of experts to sustain contentions about BH. Experts mediate asylum narratives by comparing them with publicly available reports by news media, nongovernmental organizations, and government agencies. While such sources are highly problematic historical documents, adjudicators require experts to consider up-to-date "objective evidence": even historians who serve as experts must dispense with a disciplinary skepticism of such materials.[42] In so doing experts may reinvigorate established paradigms, such as slavery and witchcraft, or contribute to the emergence of perceived new analytical and social categories, such as statelessness and fraudulence.[43] In one case a BH narrative formed part of a successful asylum case. Michael C.'s lawyers transformed a confused narrative of religious and ethnic violence—hard to pin down as targeted and thus falling within Refugee Convention grounds—into a historical pattern of religious terrorism wherein BH was the teleological conclusion and future jeopardy. Michael C., a Berom man from Jos, in northern Nigeria, testified that he faced "near constant threats over more than a decade from Hausa Fulani and Boko Haram."[44] Yet allegedly Michael's cousin was killed in a 2001 massacre, an event predating BH's formation; in 2008, his home was burned in a larger attack on Berom Christians (far from any known BH activities); and in 2010, his youngest brother was allegedly killed near the family church.[45]

The fourth iteration of mimesis is presentism, whereby historical jeopardy is collapsed with current anxieties, thus making the claimant's narrative clear and real. Presentist narratives of BH deny the possibility of the recovery of the kidnapped girls by providing updates of additional kidnappings and chaos writ large. The Yoruba single mother, for example, having asserted BH's role in broad gender-based violence and the Nigerian state's failure to protect women, described the "possibility of internal relocation" in the narrowest terms. Here BH is instantiated as a nation-wide presence, in spite of considerable counterevidence.[46] In a second example, a Nigerian male—born to a Muslim father but himself a Christian convert—described how "his mother" was "killed in a Boko Haram attack." This uncorroborated allegation segued to a claim of fear of the "current situation" regarding Boko Haram.[47] In this second example BH encompasses the entire predicament of jeopardy.

Michael C.'s experience similarly illustrates the collapsing of history with presentist anxiety. Whereas he left Nigeria for Israel in 2011, returned in 2013, and then fled to the United States in February 2014, the only Jos violence with any alleged BH link was in May 2014, after his departure.[48] But the press release celebrating his triumph claimed, "Michael's case highlights the dangers Christians face in parts of Nigeria controlled by Muslim extremists including Boko Haram, which captured the world's attention last spring when it kidnapped hundreds of schoolgirls."[49] In reality, Michael C. lived far from Chibok, and the kidnappings were unrelated to his social and religious persecution. But as Chibok was in the news daily, the horrifying descriptions of rapes, forced marriage, and fears about the future children born of pregnant girls who escaped were collapsed into a presentist narrative of endemic violence into which no one may be returned.[50]

Presentism is a powerful mimetic technique because the mass abductions of 2014 invoke a general BH jeopardy, whereby the original story breathes life into other deep-seated fears. Asylum seekers may support their statements with journalistic field accounts, updates from nongovernmental organizations, and a range of so-called objective evidence that includes Amnesty International press releases, *New York Times* articles, and global terrorism surveys—the more current the better. Some submit videos from YouTube or Vimeo as substantiating "evidence." Alternatively, presentism can involve using parallel testimonies from others. Texan lawyer Linda Corchado, who represents a Nigerian preacher, claims her client fears "for her life" after "the Islamist group began killing Christians in her village." She plans to "reach out to folks from Nigeria, witnesses that were actually there when the attack happened, to help present the case in the best way possible."[51]

Presentism emphasizes continuing failures of Nigeria to protect its citizens, playing into stereotypes of failed states or worse. Presentism directs attention to alternate Nigerian state preoccupations and collapses historical failures with ongoing incompetence combating BH. Anxieties about further kidnapping are metonyms whereby Nigerian state actors explain many contemporary issues, including political paralysis. A vivid illustration of the collapsing discourse of presentism comes from self-described journalist Andrew Noakes, who wrote, "There are two insurgencies in Nigeria. There's the real insurgency that has claimed the lives of thousands of Nigerians, and then there's the insurgency that exists in the minds of much of Nigeria's political elite, to be unleashed as a tool to gain political advantage over their opponents."[52]

Conclusion

Recovering the archive of gender-based violence requires a new look at asylum seeking. Asylum narratives provide an avenue to connect to personal testimony in powerful ways. Asylum archives contain surprising histories about gender and violence, offering up stories that challenge axiomatic invocations of gender, power, and state and nonstate actors. African historians are continually frustrated by the difficulties of conducting research in the postcolonial African context. But if we look outside Africa, and to African exiles, such as asylum seekers and refugees, we will find rich personal archives of the contemporary African experience.

At the same, however, asylum claims alleging gender-based persecutory harms cannot be taken at face value. Because asylum seekers encounter institutional suspicion and bureaucratic disbelief, they employ various strategies to advance their claims. Narratives must be carefully scrutinized to preserve their archival value. Not unlike Luise White's vampire narratives that rendered the exotic familiar, Nigerian asylum seekers mimetically invoke BH to render the implausible into familiarly exotic and terrifying. Mimetic invocations of BH may or may not safeguard an asylum claim. Irrespective of success or failure, mimesis instrumentalizes unpleasant stereotypes about Africans and deep-seated racist generalizations.

Seeking asylum is no easy task, and refugees respond to credibility challenges in thoughtful and creative ways. Mimesis masks, reshapes, and reforms unsubstantiated, or unsubstantiatable, personal narratives into terrifying, shocking, present danger to affect empathy among decision-makers. Pliny the Elder's immortal proverb *ex Africa semper aliquid novi*—"always something new out of Africa"—is doubly instructive here insofar as it conveys first the idea that, at least where Africa is concerned, experiences are routinely framed as new or novel. But asylum seekers embrace this mimetically and reshape and reform their jeopardies and fears. Mimesis is not mendacity, fraud, or deceit; it is a conscious strategy to broaden a personal experience into something that may garner attention and, at its most optimistic, refugee status. Where gender-based violence is concerned, simple narration is all too often woefully inadequate.

Notes

1. "Isa Muazu Granted More Time in UK," *Guardian*, December 6, 2013.
2. "Hunger Strike Asylum Seeker Isa Muazu Deported to Nigeria," BBC News, December 18, 2013.
3. Vicki Squire, *The Exclusionary Politics of Asylum* (Basingstoke, UK: Palgrave-Macmillan, 2009).
4. For gendered persecutory harms, see Jenni Millbank and Catherine Dauvergne, "Forced

Marriage and the Exoticization of Gendered Harms in United States Asylum Law,"
Columbia Journal of Gender and Law 19, no. 3 (2011): 6. For security displacing gendered
harms, see Magnus Taylor, "Africa in the News: Weekly Analysis from the RAS: How Africa
Became All about 'Security,'" *Royal African Society* (blog), June 5, 2015.

5. Gregory Mann, "An Africanist's Apostasy: On Luise White's 'Speaking with Vampires,'"
International Journal of African Historical Studies 41, no. 1 (2008): 120.

6. Andrew Noakes, "Boko Haram's Weakness Exposed by Girls' Abduction," Think Africa
Press, May 2014, accessed June 30, 2015, https://www.facebook.com/notes/ameer-taawun
-dawood-imran/boko-harams-weakness-exposed-by-girls-abduction/322774844555534/.

7. See, e.g., UK Home Office, "Operational Guidance Note: Nigeria," 3.18, December 2013,
www.gov.uk/government/uploads/system/uploads/attachment_data/file/310454/Nigeria
_operational_guidance_2013.pdf.

8. Plato, *Republic*, Book III, 393–94.

9. Luise White, *Speaking with Vampires: Rumor and History in Colonial Africa* (Berkeley:
University of California Press, 2000).

10. Benjamin Lawrance, Iris Berger, Tricia Hepner Redeker, Joanna Tague, and Meredith
Terretta, "Law, Expertise, and Protean Ideas about African Migrants," in *African Asylum
at a Crossroads: Activism, Expert Testimony, and Refugee Rights*, ed. Iris Berger, Tricia
Redeker Hepner, Benjamin N. Lawrance, Joanna Tague, and Meredith Terretta (Athens:
Ohio University Press), 29–30.

11. Jean Allman, "Phantoms of the Archive: Kwame Nkrumah, a Nazi Pilot Named Hanna, and
the Contingencies of Postcolonial History-Writing," *American Historical Review* 118, no. 1
(2013): 106.

12. Ara Wilson, "Transnational Geography of Sexual Rights," in *Truth Claims: Representation
and Human Rights*, ed. Mark Philip Bradley and Patrice Petro (New Brunswick, NJ:
Rutgers University Press, 2002), 252.

13. Ann Laura Stoler, *Against the Archival Grain: Epistemic Anxieties and Colonial Common
Sense* (Princeton, NJ: Princeton University Press, 2009), 20.

14. Lawrance et al., "Law, Expertise," 2.

15. Benjamin N. Lawrance, "Asylum and the 'Forced Marriage' Paradox: Petitions, Translation,
and Courts as Institutional Perpetrators of Gender Violence," in *Modern Slavery and
Global Change*, ed. Joel Quirk and Anne Bunting (Vancouver: University of British
Columbia Press, 2017). See also Benjamin Lawrance, "Historicizing as a Legal Trope of
Jeopardy in Asylum Narratives and Expert Testimony of Gendered Violence," in *Politics and
Policies in Upper Guinea Coast Societies: Change and Continuity*, ed. Jacqueline Knörr,
Christian Kordt Højbjerg, and William P. Murphy (New York: Palgrave, 2016).

16. Emily Burrill, "Disputing Wife Abuse: Tribunal Narratives of the Corporal Punishment of
Wives in Colonial Sikasso, 1930s," *Cahiers d'Études Africaines* 187–88 (2007): 603–22.

17. Amy Shuman and Carol Bohmer, "Representing Trauma: Political Asylum Narrative,"
Journal of American Folklore 117, no. 466 (2004): 396.

18. Lawrance, "Historicizing."

19. See Benjamin N. Lawrance and Galya B. Ruffer, "Witness to the Persecution? Expertise,
Testimony, and Consistency in Asylum Adjudication," in *Adjudicating Refugee and Asylum
Status: The Role of Witness, Expertise, and Testimony*, ed. Benjamin N. Lawrance and
Galya Ruffer (Cambridge: Cambridge University Press, 2015), 1–24.

20. White, *Speaking with Vampires*, 43.

21. Benjamin N. Lawrance and Charlotte Walker-Said, "Resisting Patriarchy, Contesting
Homophobia: Expert Testimony and the Construction of African Forced Marriage Asylum

Claims," in *Marriage by Force? Contestation over Consent and Coercion in Africa*, ed. Anne Bunting, Benjamin N. Lawrance, and Richard L. Roberts (Athens: Ohio University Press, 2016), 199–224.

22. April Shemak, *Asylum Speakers: Caribbean Refugees and Testimonial Discourse* (New York: Fordham University), 24.

23. Meredith Terretta, "Fraudulent Asylum-Seeking as Transnational Mobilization," in Berger et al., *African Asylum*, 58–74.

24. Bruce Einhorn and S. Megan Berthold, "Reconstructing Babel: Bridging Cultural Dissonance between Asylum Seekers and Asylum Adjudicators," in Lawrance and Ruffer, *Adjudicating Refugee and Asylum Status*, 27–53.

25. Joseph Hellweg, "Manimory and the Aesthetics of Mimesis: Forest, Islam and State in Ivoirian Dozoya," *Africa* 76, no. 4 (2006): 461–84; Markus V. Hoehne, "Mimesis and Mimicry in Dynamics of State and Identity Formation in Northern Somalia," *Africa* 79, no. 2 (2009): 252–81; Ann-Marie Tully, "Becoming Animal: Liminal Rhetorical Strategies in Contemporary South African Art," *Image and Text* 17 (2011): 64–84; Sasha Newell, "Godrap Girls, Draou Boys, and the Sexual Economy of the Bluff in Abidjan, Côte d'Ivoire," *Ethnos* 74, no. 3 (2009): 379–402.

26. Sasha Newell, "Brands as Masks: Public Secrecy and the Counterfeit in Côte d'Ivoire," *Journal of the Royal Anthropological Institute* 19, no. 1 (2013): 138–54; Sasha Newell, "Le Goût des Autres: Ivoirian Fashion and Alterity," *Etnofoor* 24, no. 2 (2012): 41–56; Christina McMahon, "Mimesis and the Historical Imagination: (Re)Staging History in Cape Verde, West Africa," *Theatre Research International* 33, no. 1 (2008): 20–39.

27. Jean-François Lyotard, *The Differend: Phrases in Dispute*, trans. George van den Abbeele (Minneapolis: University of Minnesota Press, 1988), 5–6.

28. Lawrance et al., "Law, Expertise," 27.

29. Associated Press, "Nigeria's Boko Haram Kills Forty-Nine in Suicide Bombings," *New York Times*, November 18, 2015.

30. Private e-mail correspondence in possession of the author.

31. "Missing Nigerian schoolgirls 'married off,'" *Al Jazeera*, November 1, 2014, www.aljazeera .com/news/africa/2014/10/boko-haram-says-schoolgirls-married-20141031222536853563 .html.

32. David Smith, "Sixty More Women and Girls Reported Kidnapped in Nigeria," *Guardian*, October 24, 2014.

33. Private e-mail correspondence in possession of the author.

34. Kevin Rawlinson, "Nigerians Due to Be Deported, Despite Claim of Female Genital Mutilation Risk," *Guardian*, May 29, 2014.

35. Kevin Rawlinson, "Deportation Reprieve for Nigerians amid Female Genital Mutilation Fears," *Guardian*, May 30, 2014.

36. Heather Saul, "FGM Victim Afusat Saliu and Her Daughters 'Will Be Deported to Nigeria Tonight' Despite Fears for Their Safety," *Independent* (London), June 3, 2014.

37. See Jacob Zenn and Elizabeth Pearson, "Women, Gender, and the Evolving Tactics of Boko Haram," *Journal of Terrorism Research* 5, no. 1 (2013): 46–57.

38. E.g., Phyllis Chesler, "The Boko Haram Girls May Already Have Been Mutilated," May 12, 2014, Breitbart News, www.breitbart.com/national-security/2014/05/12/the-boko-haram -girls-may-already-have-been-mutilated/.

39. Private e-mail correspondence in possession of the author.

40. Lawrance et al., "Law, Expertise," 2–5.

41. Anthony Good, "Anthropological Evidence and 'Country of Origin Information' in British

Asylum Courts," in Lawrance and Ruffer, *Adjudicating Refugee and Asylum Status*, 122–44.

42. Anthony Good, "Expert Evidence in Asylum and Human Rights Appeals: An Expert's View," *International Journal of Refugee Law* 16 (2004): 358–80.

43. See several essays in Berger et al., *African Asylum*: Terretta, "Fraudulent Asylum-Seeking"; E. Ann McDougall, "'The Immigration People Know the Stories. There's One for Each Country': The Case of Mauritania," 121–40; Kate Luongo, "Allegations, Evidence, and Evaluation: Asylum-Seeking in a World with Witchcraft," 182–202; and John Campbell, "Expert Evidence in British Asylum Courts: The Judicial Assessment of Evidence on Ethnic Discrimination and Statelessness in Ethiopia," 102–20.

44. Columbia Law School, "Nigerian Man Who Faced Persecution by Boko Haram Wins Asylum in U.S.," press release, September 18, 2014, www.law.columbia.edu/media _inquiries/news_events/2014/september2014/irc-asylum-nigerian-2014.

45. Christian-Muslim violence in Jos in 2010 left 350–1,000 dead. Adam Nossiter, "Christian-Muslim Mayhem in Nigeria Kills Dozens," *New York Times*, January 19, 2010; Human Rights Watch, "'Leave Everything to God': Accountability for Inter-communal Violence in Plateau and Kaduna States, Nigeria," Human Rights Watch, December 12, 2013, https://www.hrw.org/report/2013/12/12/leave-everything-god-accountability-inter-communal -violence-plateau-and-kaduna.

46. UK Home Office, "Operational Guidance Notes."

47. Private e-mail correspondence in possession of author.

48. BH's role in the Jos bombing has never been established. See "Nigeria Violence: 'Boko Haram' Kill Twenty-Seven in Village Attacks," BBC News, May 21, 2014. BH leader Abubakar Shekau cited "incidents of cannibalism" of Jos Muslims for Christmas Day bombings. "Boko Haram: Nigerian Islamist Leader Defends Attacks," BBC News, January 11, 2012.

49. Columbia Law School, "Nigerian Man."

50. See Tulip Mazumdar, "Chibok Girls 'Forced to Join Nigeria's Boko Haram,'" BBC News, June 29, 2015.

51. Julián Aguilar, "Against the Odds, Finding Refuge in El Paso," *Texas Tribune*, September 19, 2014.

52. Andrew Noakes, "Nigeria's Boko Haram Ceasefire Deal: Too Good to Be True?," *African Arguments*, October 22, 2014, africanarguments.org/2014/10/22/nigerias-boko-haram -ceasefire-deal-too-good-to-be-true/.

Four Images of False Positives

A Visual Essay

Luis Morán (drawings) and Claudia Salamanca (text)

In first decade of the twenty-first century, Colombia moved from being a failed state to a sovereign nation, a turnaround that some US media outlets have called "the Colombian miracle."[1] Characterizing Colombia as a case of successful nation building and counterinsurgency tactics, US military analysts have praised Colombia's approach to stabilization as a strategy for the United States to emulate in other unstable areas around the world.[2] For Colombia, the success has been the result of "an uncompromising 'hard hand' against the insurgents," and the implementation of its Democratic Security and Defense (DSD) policy, an effort to consolidate state control by enhancing the technological capacity, intelligence and equipment of the Colombian armed forces.[3]

In 2008, a scandal known today as False Positives (FPs) tarnished this so-called military success. FPs are extrajudicial executions of civilians, whose corpses are made to look like guerrillas or members of illegal groups killed in combat. Perpetrated by the Colombian Army during the years of the DSD policy (2002–10), FPs inflated statistics of enemy combatants killed in action. Although this abhorrent practice has been part of the military culture in Colombia for more than twenty-five years, as reported by the CIA in 1994, the instances of FPs under the DSD policy show a systematic execution model.[4] "Recruiters" targeted Colombian males between the ages of sixteen and thirty-seven, choosing young men belonging to vulnerable populations living in marginalized areas, those with mental disabilities or substance abuse problems, and/or who were unemployed and desperate for money.

Radical History Review
Issue 126 (October 2016)   DOI 10.1215/01636545-3594517
© 2016 by MARHO: The Radical Historians' Organization, Inc.

With promises of work in countryside, recruiters lured the victims into leaving and transported them three hundred to four hundred miles away from their homes. Once in the countryside, these young men were handed over to a military unit and executed.[5] Their corpses would be dressed in fatigues, and weapons would be placed next to their bodies, which would then be photographed. A mandatory photographic record of the casualties and/or video taken at the location of the combat was part of the military armed forces protocol; those photographs were released to the press and kept in the archives for deceased and N.N. (*nomen nescio*, "name unknown") persons. Autopsy reports show that victims died between twelve and twenty-four hours from the time they were last seen by their family members.[6] Evidence suggests that these extrajudicial executions were rigorously planned and committed by a large number of military units around the country with disturbing frequency and are not, as the Colombian government asserts, the result of a few bad apples within the Colombian Army who misinterpreted the policies and goals of the DSD policy.[7]

To date, the exact number of FPs is still unconfirmed. Approximately four thousand cases have been reported to various state institutions, including the Office of the Attorney General, the Office of the Inspector General, and the Ombudsman.[8] However, organizations like the United Nations and Human Rights Watch estimate that more cases remain unreported. Relatives lack information about where and how to file FPs, and many have concerns about their own personal safety should they raise complaints against agents of the state. Relatives of many victims have received death threats to coerce them into dropping charges; some have been injured and killed for pursuing legal action, and others have relocated due to the constant fear of retribution.[9]

International organizations, such as the United Nations,[10] Amnesty International,[11] Human Rights Watch,[12] and the International Federation for Human Rights,[13] have explained FPs as the result of the formal and informal benefits, including monetary rewards, that the DSD policy set out in a series of classified directives issued by the Ministry of Defense, in exchange for successful military operations.[14] The DSD policy encouraged civilians, through its program of informants, to report the location and identity of enemy combatants in exchange for cash rewards.[15] This policy extended to the military through secret directives, based on which military units received bonuses for capturing or killing enemy combatants or for seizing any property or element that can contribute to weakening the enemy's position. In this context, FPs can be seen as instances of the body count mentality or the body count syndrome within an economy that rewards death.[16]

Although the system of benefits and rewards created by the DSD policy explains a great deal about FPs, analyzing these events based solely on the rewards and benefits given in exchange for systematic killing, and placing responsibility only on those who pulled the trigger, obscures the historical categories and social relations through which the body of a young man is turned into a commodity and his

Figure 1. Drawing by Luis Morán, 2014, copy of a photograph taken by the Colombian police. A cardboard booth with a sign that reads "rewards" and a hole in the middle is the device in which an informant poses to the press while receiving money for providing information that led to a successful military operation.

corpse photographed to create an image of the enemy. By considering the intersection between an economy of death and the construction of alterity through a fabricated image of the enemy's body, we see how the Colombian Army made these images essential for the process of claiming monetary rewards and benefits.

As part of the regular protocol, military operations are defined and planned in advance, and the information (video, photographs, and reports) related to them is an effort to further account for them.[17] The representation of an event is part of a process of accountability, explanations that come after the military operation in the field. In the case of the FPs, I argue that the photographic record was not an afterthought as it is seen in regular protocol or a side effect of the extrajudicial executions. The uniforms, boots, grenades, rifles, carbines, machine guns, and corpses were props used to fabricate an image; they were bought and prepared before the execution. Those young men were recruited and executed to construct images of dead enemy combatants, an enemy fabricated out of young unemployed males in need of money who lived on the outskirts of big cities. Those young men were fashioned into guerrillas, gang members, or paramilitary forces; identities outside the discourse of legality were inscribed on their bodies. The fabricated image of the enemy was not an afterthought but the paradigmatic image of terror. The killers

Figure 2. Drawing by Luis Morán, 2014, copy of a photograph taken by the Colombian Army. Anomaly no. 1: a corpse wears new rubber boots on the wrong feet.

of these young men knew beforehand that they were going to create an image with dead bodies; they collapsed the killing of these men—the event—and its representation. My intention is to question the status of these images, which are often trapped within the walls of accountability, transparency, and documentation as in regular protocol. As poorly staged tableaus of military victory, these images reveal apparent mistakes in the crime scenes. I want to explore what these anomalies tell us about the process of creating an imagined enemy: is this how an enemy should look and, if so, why?

Figures 2, 3, 4, and 5 reproduce actual photographs taken by the security forces of the state. These drawings are accurate reproductions of the original photographs published in the Colombian magazine *Semana* on July 17, 2010, in an article titled "The Forgotten Cases of False Positives."[18] These drawings do not add any elements or aestheticize the violence they show. These copies omit the background that appears in the photograph and highlight the foreground, which is the corpse of the victim. These drawings were commissioned specifically for my research on FPs as a tool through which I could see the violence depicted in them as the result of the imagination, as well as painfully real. Created by artist Luis Morán, these drawings compel us to separate the purported "factuality" of photography from the subject matter and Colombia's fabricated narrative of success. In other words, the photo-

Figure 3. Drawing by Luis Morán, 2014, copy of a photograph taken by the Colombian Army. Anomaly no. 2: finger on the trigger.

graphs taken by the security forces of the state exist in a framework of transparency; the state released them as proof of their success, as evidence of their actions and an account of how a military operation succeeded by killing members of illegal organizations. We see a corpse, which is connected with an explanation that signals it as a guerrilla, paramilitary, or gang member. But when these photographs are turned into drawings, the referent and the narrative of success are suspended and we get to see the elements of the image in an exercise of seeing that is different from the one we exert when confronted with a photograph issued by the state.

In viewing the photographs taken by the Colombian Army, the siblings of FP victims both recognize their loved ones and reject the person portrayed in the image. Here, there is a process of recognition through misrecognition, a disjuncture between what is apparently real and its representation. The certainty of the referent is disputed: while the corpses are indeed those of boyfriend, husband, brother, son, or father, at the same time those images do not correspond to the people. For example, in the documentary "False Positives, a Story That Could Have Been Avoided,"[19] Viviana Andrea Salcedo tells the story of her brother while holding an image of him with crutches. She says her brother went out to have a beer with a friend in a nearby store and never returned. After searching for him for two days, she went to the Technical Investigation Team office, a branch of the Office of the Attorney General of Colombia. They showed her photographs of what they claimed were images of

Figure 4. Drawing by Luis Morán, 2014, copy of a photograph taken by the Colombian Army. Anomaly no. 3: two hand grenades in his pants pockets hanging from their safety levers.

dead guerrillas killed in combat. Recognizing her brother in one of the photos, she remarked that that was impossible—her brother was not a guerrilla but a member of the Colombian Army who was on a combat-related injury leave.

The photographs of the corpses attempt to erase the signs of their previous identities. Relatives of FP victims, however, constantly point out the untruths created about their loved ones: they were not delinquents; they were not rebels; they were not members of illegal organizations; they were not drug traffickers; they were not N.N. These claims assert that the young men's lived realities did not match the ways in which they died. In "Family Portraits," Alexandra Cardona's documentary on the mothers of some of FP victims, one of the mothers states, "They [the "recruiters"] thought these kids did not have mothers, brothers, or sisters who were going to look for them."[20] This mother is voicing an identity anchored in a social context, one that could not be erased in the photographs taken by the Colombian Army. The mothers and siblings of FP victims contest images created by the security forces of the state by pointing to what is outside the frame. Very often, mothers and relatives of FP victims provide evidence that their loved ones were not members of illegal organizations with their own photographs of the victims, in high school graduation pictures, as babies, and in military uniform during the year of mandatory military

Figure 5. Drawing by Luis Morán, 2014. Copy of a photograph taken by the Colombian Army. Extra magazines are hidden inside the rubber boots.

service: anecdotes and dreams of their dead sons that speak of a living presence in another time and with others. These personal narratives and photographs contest the status of evidence and truth that the images taken by the security forces of the state seem to carry. The photographs in the family albums, as well as the pictures carried by relatives and friends of FPs during the protests against human rights violations committed by the state, open a debate by questioning the photograph taken by the state as evidence and subverting the intentions of those who took the picture.

The photographs issued by the Colombian Army exhibit a presence: a dead body on the ground. However, the absence of life enables the possibility of fabrication, a malleability that creates something other from the available corpse. The poses of those corpses in the photographs could only have taken shape as the bodies of the victims became posthumously manipulatable. Photographing the dead makes possible a situation in which corpse and image coincide, an instance of total control over the pose.

Figures 2, 3, and 4 show obvious flaws in the combat scenes. The photographs correspond to a FP attributed to the Seventh Army Division, which reported that it "neutralized six suspected members of the criminal gang Bacrim in combat" during a "military operation" in "the rural area of La India in the municipality of Chigorodó, Uraba."[21] In figure 4, we see a supposed rebel with two hand grenades in his pants pockets hanging from their safety levers; if a combatant were running with hand grenades hung from his pants like this, they could explode at any moment. In figure 2, a corpse wears new rubber boots on the wrong feet. The corpse in figure 3 has his finger on the trigger of a machine gun, but it is not squeezed as if he were shooting when shot. Should these anomalies be categorized as mistakes? Poor fabrications? The corpses generally appear with something that signals a viable threat: wires, bomb triggers, guns, explosives, and/or other weapons next to the corpses. Two grenades in each pocket, finger on the trigger, and extra magazines hidden inside the rubber boots (figure 5) are attempts to prove that killing these men was the only available recourse. These images insist on resisting ambiguity by asserting that that corpse in the ground was in fact a threat, an enemy of the state. These images, evidence of "successful" combats, attempt to substitute for verbal explanation by stating the preeminence of the referent. These photographs assert, "here is the rebel," "here he is holding a gun and wearing military fatigues," "there he is," "he was dangerous," "he is dead." These images want to teach us how an enemy looks like and to show us that he in fact is dangerous. My contention is that these images exhibit an effort to narrate the impending fear of the future; the enemy is depicted in this photograph as a potential threat that needed to be eliminated. Indeed, these images are a testimony to the past—a successful operation; nevertheless, their narration could be explained in terms of a moralizing pedagogy for future citizens and ideal spectators.

The image of the corpse, in other words, as the embodiment of a neutralized Other, is not a mere side effect of the FP. Those young men were recruited and executed solely to manufacture an image of dead enemy combatants. The uniforms, boots, grenades, the rifles, carbines, machine guns, and the corpses were props in this endeavor. The distance that these young men traveled from their hometowns to the sites of their murder enacts the distance between the real and representation. Therefore, the image is not an afterthought; it uses terror in the service of a structure of the real and its representation, embedded in modes of explanations that register violence as a means to an end outside of the violence itself. FPs use the image as a pedagogical tool, to fabricate a country with a symbolic discourse of citizenship through images of young men supposedly to be understood as the enemy, an enemy that has been killed and thus represents military victory in an unending war.

Notes

1. "After Taint of Drugs, Colombia Reinvents Itself," *Morning Edition*, National Public Radio, April 12, 2012, search.proquest.com/docview/993564663?accountid=13250; Frida Ghitis, "The Colombian Miracle: Gaining Belated Notice," *World Politics Review*, July 4, 2008, www.worldpoliticsreview.com/articles/2383/the-colombian-miracle-gaining-belated -notice; Max Boot and Richard Bennet, "The Colombian Miracle: How Alvaro Uribe with Smart U.S. Support Turned the Tide against Drug Lords and Marxist Guerrillas." *Weekly Standard*, December 14, 2009, www.weeklystandard.com/Content/Public/Articles/000 /000/017/301nyrut.asp.

2. Robert Haddick, "Colombia Can Teach Afghanistan (and the United States) How to Win," *Air and Space Power Journal* 24, no. 2 (2010): 52–56.

3. Juan Forero, "Hard-Liner Elected in Colombia with a Mandate to Crush Rebels," *New York Times*, May 27, 2002, www.nytimes.com/2002/05/27/world/hard-liner-elected-in-colombia -with-a-mandate-to-crush-rebels.html.

4. Central Intelligence Agency, Office of African and Latin American Analysis, "Colombian Counterinsurgency: Steps in the Right Direction—Intelligence Memorandum," January 26, 1994, National Security Archive, www2.gwu.edu/~nsarchiv/NSAEBB/NSAEBB266 /19940126.pdf.

5. Philip Alston, "Report of the Special Rapporteur on Extrajudicial, Summary or Arbitrary Executions," UN General Assembly, Human Rights Council, Fourteenth Session (March 31, 2010), 11, www2.ohchr.org/english/bodies/hrcouncil/docs/14session/A.HRC.14.24.Add.2 _en.pdf.

6. "Una Tesis Macabra, Conflicto Armado," *Semana*, October 4, 2008, www.semana.com /nacion/conflicto-armado/articulo/una-tesis-macabra/95879-3.

7. Alvaro Uribe Vélez, "Declaración del Presidente Álvaro Uribe, Este Jueves, desde Canadá," Presidencia de La República de Colombia, Secretaría de Prensa, June 11, 2009, web .presidencia.gov.co/sp/2009/junio/11/01112009.html.

8. Philip Alston, "Report of the Special Rapporteur"; "Las Cuentas de los Falsos Positivos," *Semana*, January 27, 2009, www.semana.com/nacion/justicia/articulo/las-cuentas-falsos -positivos/99556-3; "Más de 4 Mil Casos de Falsos Positivos Son Investigados por la Fiscalía," *El Espectador*, September 27, 2014, www.elespectador.com/noticias/judicial /mas-de-4-mil-casos-de-falsos-positivos-son-investigados-articulo-519238.

9. Both of Carmenza Gómez's sons have been killed. First Víctor Fernando Gómez disappeared in August 23, 2008, and was found dead two days later four hundred miles away from his home; he was a victim of the FPs. Five months later, her son John Nilson was killed as a result of searching for the truth about his brother's death. He received several death threats warning him to not pursue legal action. For a second case, similar to this one, see the Amnesty International, "Colombia: Murdered Man's Brother Threatened," November 5, 2009, www.amnesty.org/en/library/asset/AMR23/026/2009/en/ef9541c8-088e-4a25-857a -e2d9e87541c8/amr230262009en.html.

10. Alston, "Report of the Special Rapporteur."

11. Amnesty International: "Colombia: Murdered Man's Brother Threatened"; "Colombia: Assisting Units That Commit Extrajudicial Killings: A Call to Investigate US Military Policy toward Colombia," April 9, 2008, www.amnesty.org/en/library/asset/AMR23/016/2008 /en/116d47ce-236b-11dd-89c0-51e35dab761d/amr230162008eng.html; "Colombia: Seeking Justice: The Mothers of Soacha," January 30, 2010, www.amnesty.org/en/library /asset/AMR23/002/2010/en/ec375877-5fbf-4d3c-a074-258a79c82c9b/amr230022010en

.html; "Colombia: Impunity Perpetuates Ongoing Human Rights Violations: Amnesty International Submission to the UN Universal Periodic Review," February 14, 2013, www .amnesty.org/en/library/asset/AMR23/005/2013/en/3aaa9d53-02f5-459b-8864-dbc5e367fda7 /amr230052013es.html.

12. *Human Rights Watch World Report 2012: Events of 2011* (New York: Seven Stories, 2012), 228–35; *Human Rights Watch World Report 2011: Events of 2010* (London: Seven Stories, 2011), 227–32.

13. International Federation of Human Rights, *Colombia: The War Is Measured in Litres of Blood*, June 2012, www.fidh.org/IMG/pdf/rapp_colombie__juin_2012_anglais_def.pdf.

14. Ministerio de Defensa Nacional, República de Colombia, "Directiva 29, 2005. La Polémica Directiva de Recompensas," *La Silla Vacía—Noticias, Historias, Debate, Blogs y Multimedia sobre el Poder en Colombia,* http://lasillavacia.com/sites/default/files/media /docs/historias/Directiva_29_2005-comentado.pdf.

15. "Información de Cooperantes Permitió Realizar 21 Mil Operativos en 2005," www .mindefensa.gov.co/irj/go/km/docs/Mindefensa/noticiasold/Noticias/2006/03/C _Informacion_de_cooperantes_permitio_realizar_21_mil_operativos_en_2005.html (accessed January 17, 2013).

16. International Federation for Human Rights, *Colombia.*

17. See David Kilcullen, "New Paradigms for Twenty-First-Century Conflict," *Foreign Policy Agenda* 12, no. 5 (2007), www.america.gov/st/peacesec-english/2008/May/20080522172835 SrenoDo.8730585.html.

18. "The Forgotten Cases of False Positives," *Semana,* July 17, 2010, http://www.semana.com //nacion/articulo/los-casos-olvidados-falsos-positivos/119416-3. Quoted in Hollman Morris, "Falsos Positivos: Una Historia Que Se Pudo Evitar," *Contravía,* January 22, 2010, www .contravia.tv/Falsos-Positivos.

19. Alexandra Cardona Restrepo, *Retratos de Familia* (Karamelo Producciones, n.d.) 2013. https://vimeo.com/86939560.

20. Morris, "Falsos Positivos."

21. Ibid.

Rethinking the Egalitarian Potential of Postapartheid South Africa:

Zanele Muholi's Intervention

Efeoghene Igor

In her portrait (figure 1), Pam Dlungwana's solemn gaze defiantly confronts the camera—her eyes meet the viewer's, making her appear confident. Wearing her hair in a short bleached-blond cut with hoop earrings, she reads as youthful. In the tightly framed picture, her shoulders are bare, suggesting comfort with the photographer. Staged against a patterned backdrop, her individuality is emphasized. The photograph of Pam is a part of the series *Faces and Phases* (2006–14) by photographer Zanele Muholi. Muholi deliberately obscures the background in order to highlight the singularity of Pam's lived experience. In text accompanying the portrait in the publication *Zanele Muholi Faces + Phases 2006–14* Pam reveals to the audience that she had been raped.[1] Many black queer individuals included in Muholi's series have been raped because of their sexuality. The morning after the crime, instead of hurrying to the clinic or calling the police, Pam completed an exam at school. The seeming indifference to such a violation—by continuing her day as if nothing was wrong—underscores the frequent threat of sexual violence that confronts queer black individuals in South Africa. Juxtaposing the highly expressive portrait with the haunting narrative of sexual violence, Pam's photograph threatens the confidence of queer South Africans lobbying for recognition within an ongoing struggle to achieve an egalitarian society.

Radical History Review

Issue 126 (October 2016)   DOI 10.1215/01636545-3594675

Figure 1. Pam Dlungwana in Vredehoek, Cape Town, 2011. © Zanele Muholi. Courtesy of Stevenson, Cape Town/Johannesburg, and Yancey Richardson, New York

Faces and Phases disables the regime of social and governmental silence by rendering visual and thus legible a community exiled from popular imagination. The series showcases portraits in sober tonalities of black and white, muted backdrops, and stoic facial expressions. These images strive to normalize the presence of black queer people within the landscape. Occupying space is a critical political and ideological question within South African history. As Jennifer Beningfield posits, "There remains, however, in contemporary South Africa, a sense that the land (unmediated, untouched and natural) can still be a resource for a political reworking of the image of South Africa—a way to unify its different citizens, to connect body and nation, to enable a different conception of country and continent to emerge from the past that tainted it."[2] Muholi introduces us to the potential and ambiguity of the landscape by situating her participants in place. This effort is to preserve the lives of black queer individuals by associating them with the land. Consequently, this article examines how Muholi's work shifts the focus solely from *sight* (visibility of lesbian, gay, bisexual, transgender, and intersex persons) to *site* (the places that the photographs are taken).

By co-opting documentary style photography, a visual language perhaps most associated with antiapartheid popular politics, Muholi provides crucial introspection on the antiracist rhetoric employed by the official liberation movement during apartheid. She upsets the liberal narrative by acknowledging the antiqueer rhetoric that persists in contemporary South Africa. Rape is a technology of violence that is used to punish transgressive sexuality and gender nonconformity. As Njabulo Simakahle Ndebele artfully articulates, rape is "transformed into lasting violation. The physical invasion once ended becomes a prolonged occupation, the continuing effect of violation snuffing out a woman's life in the eternity of living it."[3] Muholi's series helps audiences acknowledge black queer individuals as the casualties of the South African liberation movement's inner contradictions.

Conventionally, the sources of antiapartheid narratives were men. Although women did rise to prominent positions within the movement, they did so within a circumscribed social field. They were typically casts as supportive and nurturing caregivers. For instance, Winnie Mandela before her political demise in the early 1990s was mythologized as the mother of South Africa.[4] The apartheid system magnified racial, gender, and sexual differences, subsequently marginalizing black queer persons from mainstream liberation efforts. The fragmentary nature of the liberation movement made race and sexuality mutually exclusive terrains.[5] Perhaps the best example of the masculinist nature of the antiapartheid struggle was the Black Consciousness Movement (BCM). The South African Students' Organization, a black student group established in 1969, emerged as a "critical center" of the antiapartheid struggle because of its ability to create a positive self-image for black (male) South Africans.[6] Steve Biko, the leader of the BCM, in an editor's note explained oppression in gendered language. To uplift the black race he suggests,

"The first step therefore is to make the black man come to himself; to pump back life into his empty shell; to infuse him with pride and dignity, to remind him of his complicity in the crime of allowing himself to be misused and therefore letting evil reign supreme in the country of his birth. . . . This is the definition of 'Black Consciousness.'"[7] BCM's alternate form of nationalism betrayed its commitment to emancipation because it demanded an unrealistic monolithic black community—that of just black men.[8] Alternatively, Muholi's work troubles the status of the heterosexual black man as an easy metaphor for the liberated national subject.

In recognizing the state's failure to protect its citizens, Muholi acknowledges the multiple ways in which the black LGBTI community is exiled from mainstream liberation discourse. She explains, "Currently, we look to our Constitution for protection as legitimate citizens in our country. However, the reality is that black lesbians are targets of brutal oppression in the South African townships and surrounding areas. We experience rape from gangs, rape by so-called friends, neighbors, and sometimes even family members."[9] Muholi's intervention is crucial in this respect as she disrupts the historical archive by harnessing the stylistic conventions of the antiapartheid movement but transforms their intentions. However, as Patricia Hayes reminds us, it is too simplistic to suggest that the polysemous South African photographic archive is homogeneous. Although there was a script that made pictures of the antiapartheid struggle desirable, it was both the demand from the West and the gendered nature of violence that dictated the limited role of women in South Africa's visual economy.[10]

Photojournalism was preoccupied with black and white realist photography; it was, as Hayes suggests, associated with "certainty and evidence."[11] The previous outlet, the newspaper, had different requirements than the gallery, which is the present-day forum for activists. Whereas photojournalism is preoccupied with perceived objectivity, the gallery is concerned with subjectivity. During postapartheid reconstruction, public history became the domain to problematize homogenizing narratives that further oppressed formally disenfranchised communities. Ciraj Rassool explains, "In South Africa after 1994, beyond the boundaries of the academy, histories began to erupt into the public sphere in museums and other arenas through the 'visuality of the spectacle.' These visual histories have tended to be understood merely as 'revelations of hidden heritage,' previously submerged by apartheid."[12] Muholi helps us reckon with this oversight by reflecting on LGBTI lived experiences without being confined to the liberal politics of outreach. There is no intention of "liberating" the person being photographed. Rather, the emphasis is on brokering an exchange between LGBTI persons and the audience.

Alongside activists during the antiapartheid struggle, Muholi strives to create an alternative visual archive by documenting from within her community. Self-identifying as a visual activist, Muholi suggests, "The series articulates the collective pain we as a community experience due to the loss of friends and acquaintances through disease and hate crimes."[13] Appropriating a documentary style of photography, she attempts to bring to the fore black LGBTI issues to a popular audience that highlight that legal equality has not translated into radically different social, economic, and political conditions for black queer individuals in the postapartheid era. Although South Africa legalized gay and lesbian marriage in 2006, the blanket declaration that South Africa is a tolerant country obscures more sophisticated mechanisms that condone homophobic rhetoric and violence. Rachel Holmes reminds us, "Within the recent history of South African politics, there is no neat teleology within which the triumph of the African National Congress (ANC) has *inevitably* led to the liberation of lesbian and gay sexual identities and to the enshrinement of lesbian and gay civil rights through the implementation of the new postapartheid political settlement."[14] Thus, Pam's willingness to be photographed prompts thoughts of irresolution; her portrait troubles the selective ways in which liberation is articulated and constructed in the postapartheid era. Operating within an evocative cultural space, the series points to the inequalities that persist in contemporary South Africa.

Yet despite photographic efforts to render legible injustices, there is no robust framework for justice and accountability for antiqueer violence in contemporary South Africa. The absence of statistical information to help gauge the severity of hate crimes, for instance, is just one example of infrastructural deficiencies in the country.[15] In May 2015 Lydia Smith of the *Telegraph* reported that "at least 32 women have been raped and murdered in the last 15 years" because they were lesbians.[16] This number is likely a gross underestimation of the severity of the violence. "Curative" rapes are a violent tactic used by perpetrators to "restore" the "natural social order," whereby men occupy the top rung of the social strata.[17] Through the series *Faces and Phases*, Muholi has begun to document hate crimes committed against LGBTI individuals. Her exhibit at the Brooklyn Museum (May 1–November 8, 2015) titled *Isibonelo/Evidence* opens by acknowledging the violent death of Disebo Gift Makau. On Friday, August 18, 2014, *Mamba Online* reported that Disebo was found dead, with a shoelace and wire wrapped around her neck and a running water hose shoved into her throat, in the Tshing location. *Mamba Online*, a local South African news outlet, reported that she appeared to have been raped.[18] Family members believe that she was murdered because she was a lesbian.[19] Transforming landscapes of knowledge relations, the lifeless body of Disebo and others murdered can be read as an assertion of dominance within a space, which signals to other potential "transgressors" the narrow gender script prescribed by patriarchy. *Faces and Phases* acts as an alternative form of reckoning, another way to imagine the possibilities of social justice by making living people rather than lifeless bodies visible.

Anelisa Mfo's portrait attests to the protracted struggles that arrest development in the postapartheid era (figure 2). The weighted absence of black LGBTI persons in the mainstream national archive is highlighted by Anelisa's presence in

Figure 2. Anelisa Mfo in Nyanga, Cape Town, 2010. © Zanele Muholi. Courtesy of Stevenson, Cape Town/Johannesburg, and Yancey Richardson, New York

Faces and Phases.[20] The close-up portrait invites reflection on the ineffective state and civil response to homophobia. Muholi's work brings to light the complexities in the construction and reconstruction of a cohesive national postapartheid South African identity. During the opening of the Innovative Women exhibition in August 2009, the former minister of arts and culture Lulama "Lulu" Xingwana left the engagement unexpectedly before her scheduled speech. She found Muholi's images of lesbian couples nakedly embracing each other distasteful.[21] The minister stated the exhibition "was immoral, offensive and going against nation-building."[22] Subsequently the minister received criticism for her actions. Meditating on Anelisa's image, here we see Muholi critique the willed amnesia that forces LGBTI individuals into hiding. Holmes astutely remarks, "Such amnesia can leave people vulnerable to new narratives of national identity that either advertently or inadvertently foster the illusion of inclusion."[23]

In anticipation of remarks similar to those made by the minister, Muholi places black queer South Africans at the vanguard of contemporary liberation struggles. Anelisa's self-confident stance and calm expression create connection but also safe distance between her and the viewer. The scar on her left side invites questions: Who hurt her? Is the scar the remains of a violent encounter? Is she is a survivor of a hate crime? The photograph is dense with visual complexity that remains unresolved. Nevertheless, Anelisa's photograph is a significant affirmation of black LGBTI existence within a hostile national terrain. The photograph's explicit mediation on space suggests that LGBTI individuals can no longer be relegated to nonexistence. Our scrutiny follows from Anelisa's political aspiration of coming out to a mainstream South African and international audience. The obscured background faintly registers a corrugated wall. The minimal greenery suggests that the photograph was taken outdoors, like most of Muholi's portraits. Anelisa appears grounded—asserting herself within a pubic space. Within the photograph Muholi blurs the line between the public and private, disrupting the enforced privacy and secrecy of black queer life. One must note that hate crimes against LGBTI persons reported in South African and international newspapers typically include the discovery of the victim's body in a public space.

In *Faces and Phases*, we witness a desire for public recognition as well as an assertion of belonging as a rights-bearing citizen. In the statement accompanying the photograph Muholi lets the audience know that the portrait of Anelisa was taken in Cape Town. Muholi's explicit naming of the space anchors Anelisa within a specifically historicized and culturally informed place, making her presence indicative of South Africa's sexual and racial diversity. The affective charge of the image is embedded in the practice of naming, while the interplay between the visual and textual successfully unsettles normative expectations of who occupies the South African landscape. *Faces and Phases* shares Muholi's aspirational vision of the future where egalitarianism in South African society is considered in relation not just to race but to genders and sexualities as well.

The administrative grip the apartheid regime had on the (in)visibility of particular communities makes Muholi's artistic renderings seductive. The ability to control how one is represented in the public domain imbues the photographs with an emancipatory zeal. Often displayed in public galleries, national and international audiences are impelled to reflect on South Africa's diversity, thus transforming the gallery into a theater of learning. Shaun de Waal and Anthony Manion have noted that visibility is essential to countering long histories of concealment and disavowal.[24] The ways in which gender, race, and sexuality intersect to produce exclusionary practices in contemporary South Africa evoke a history of apartheid violence. The Sexual Offences Act of 1957 further criminalized homosexuality, making LGBTI South Africans part of the constellation of oppressed communities targeted by the apartheid state. This repression stemmed from the need to police white masculinity as an embodiment of the ideal national subject.[25] The brutal racist system routinized forms of domination by attempting to eradicate nonmonogamous, nonreproductive, interracial, and same-sex relationships.[26] Mainstream lesbian and gay resistance to apartheid state repression was sidelined, much as feminist politics were.

However, in the 1980s growing national and international pressure compelled the movement to become multiracial. At the same time, the ANC emerged as a key player in the transition toward a democracy.[27] Although the ANC codified the protection of gay and lesbian rights, there was homophobic opposition from members within the organization.[28] The post-1994 moment inaugurated a new epoch in South African sexual politics, yet black South African LGBTI individuals would inhabit the queer archive in limited ways, if at all. *Faces and Phases* recognizes that liberatory tactics in many ways have perpetuated the subordination of black queer individuals.[29] By marking and mapping the public presence of LGBTI people and specifically black lesbians and trans men to mainstream audiences, Muholi's series reconfigures our social world to include and celebrate black queer life. She thus operationalizes the shift from nominal visibility in the constitution to material visibility in the gallery space.

The portrait of Busi Sigasa in Braamfontein, Johannesburg, commemorates her life and death (figure 3). The desolate background is slightly out of focus to further punctuate her singularity. Posed off center, she appears self-assured and insubordinate. Her gaze cast off to the distance as though preoccupied with something else. Although the black-and-white image appears timeless, her contemporary clothing prevents the viewer from displacing Busi into a distant past. Through naming, we witness the reappropriation of hostile environments that have often violated black LGBTI community members. The photograph now acts as a memorial. An

Figure 3. Busi Sigasa in Braamfontein, Johannesburg, 2006. © Zanele Muholi. Courtesy of Stevenson, Cape Town/Johannesburg, and Yancey Richardson, New York

artist in her own right, Busi was a poet and political activist. She had contracted the HIV virus after being viciously raped by so-called friends.[30] However, it is not through scrutiny of the photograph that the viewer is made aware of her diagnosis; rather, it is the blog posts and news articles surrounding her life that reveal the status of her health. The choice of subject, framing, and focus by Muholi calls attention to the empowering agency that the act of remembering and telling stories engenders. Similar to ethnographic art, the repetition of form in the series creates a sensory accessibility that conjures a sense of familiarity. Nevertheless, Muholi does not completely elide the problematic influence of ethnographic art but, rather, samples it to make room for her participants in the mainstream South African national archive. Thus these enigmatic photographs present a creative tension—they are both a parody and copy. Muholi's work provides an opportunity to examine life on the margins and reevaluate the legacy of the antiapartheid movement and liberation in the postapartheid era.

By adopting visual cues from other genres like documentary and ethnographic photography and portraiture, the images in Muholi's series take what Patricia Yaeger calls "neobaroque" form. This genre "plays with the hybrid as the source of the haunted, contemplates cultural and stylistic excess, exposes (formally and economically) the violent, decorative acquisitions of New World imperialism, and suggest the dizzying interpretation of the past and present."[31] Ultimately, *Faces and Phases* disrupts the narrative of being the possession of another that is conventional in ethnographic images of African people. Muholi's participants are neither available nor accessible in that way. Although Muholi uses an ethnographic format—unspecified backgrounds with the subjects in focus in the foreground—to build an inventory of black LGBTI persons, her work resists the conventional codes that insistently position African women against a primitive nature. Ultimately, she refuses to offer up her participants as specimens to be viewed by curious voyeurs. The portrait format signals to the audience that participants actively crafted an identity in conversation with the artist. Her optics point viewers in a more personal and subjective direction, one that incites renewed interest in aesthetic experimentation in the postapartheid moment. We do not see the undressed, eroticized, feminized, and submissive object of colonial fantasy.[32]

Instead, Muholi's series mocks the "art-in-service-to-science" narrative embedded in previous colonial images.[33] Beth Fowkes Tobin's articulation of the imperial design of eighteenth-century botany indicates "the white border and snipped twig of late-eighteenth-century botanical illustration reinforced the idea that a plant could be plucked from one cultural and ecological context and inserted into another with ease and with little regard for negative consequences."[34] The violent destruction of appropriated botany sought to erase the social, cultural, and environmental context to emphasize the *discovery* made by Western scientists. To delicately gesture toward to the violent explosion of black queer individuals in national imaginary, Muholi quotes this format to again call upon the history of representation. However, the strategic layout of Muholi's images seeks to resist the colonial normalizing gaze. The captions are essential when encountering Muholi's portraits. Without the names, places, and dates, the viewer could draw incorrect conclusions about the photographs, aligning it with imperialist photography. Borrowing Beningfield's language, Muholi's "remaking the land can therefore become a kind of remembering, but a remembering which is increasingly forced to confront the physical traces of the past."[35] In this way, Muholi's images help rewrite the history of land occupation and racial terror. Her work strives to transform the politics of inclusion in South African political discourse.

CURATED SPACES provides a focus on the relationship between visual culture and social, historical, or political subject matter.

Notes

I am grateful to Zanele Muholi and the participants of *Faces and Phases* for their continued activism and courage sharing their stories. I am also indebted to professors Daniel Magaziner, Erica James, Brian Beaton, and Bill Rankin for their encouragement and thoughtful critiques. I am thankful for the editorial support of my friends and colleagues Ayan Kassim, Beans Velocci, Jason Bell, Naomi Sussman, and Nichole Nelson. Lastly, I thank editor Conor McGrady for his encouragement and comments. Earlier versions of this article were presented at Rutgers University and Northwestern University.

1. Zanele Muholi, *Zanele Muholi Faces + Phases 2006–14* (Göttingen: Steidl Gerhard, 2014), 146-48.

2. Jennifer Beningfield, *The Frightened Land: Land, Landscape and Politics in South Africa in the Twentieth Century* (London: Routledge, 2006), 6.

3. Njabulo Simakahle Ndebele, *The Cry of Winnie Mandela: A Novel* (Oxfordshire: Ayebia Clarke, 2003), 52.

3. Rachel Holmes, "Queer Comrades: Winnie Mandela and the Moffies," *Social Text*, no. 52/53 (1997): 175.

5. Tamar Garb and Martin Barnes, *Figures and Fictions: Contemporary South African Photography* (Göttingen: Steidl Gerhard, 2011), 41.

6. Daniel R. Magaziner, *The Law and the Prophets: Black Consciousness in South Africa, 1968–1977* (Athens: Ohio University Press, 2010), 3–4.

7. Steve Biko and Aelred Stubbs, *I Write What I Like: Selected Writings* (Chicago: University of Chicago Press, 2002), 29.

8. Pumla Dineo Gqola, "Contradictory Locations: Blackwomen and the Discourse of the Black Consciousness Movement (BCM) in South Africa," *Meridians* 2, no. 1 (2001): 135.

9. Zanele Muholi, "Faces and Phases," *Transitions*, no. 107 (2012): 113.

10. Patricia Hayes, "The Form of the Norm: Shades of Gender in South African Photography of the 1980s," *Social Dynamics* 37, no. 2 (2011): 263–74.

11. Ibid., 265.

12. Ciraj Rassool, "Power, Knowledge and the Politics of Public Pasts," *African Studies* 69, no. 1 (2010): 86.

13. Muholi, "Faces and Phases," 114.

14. Holmes, "Queer Comrades," 162.

15. Tiffani Wesley, "'Corrective' Rape as Hate Crime," *Open Society Initiative for Southern Africa*, November 25, 2012, www.osisa.org/buwa/south-africa/classify-'corrective'-rape-hate-crime.

16. Lydia Smith, "Corrective Rape: The Homophobic Fallout of Post-apartheid South Africa," *Telegraph*, May 21, 2015, www.telegraph.co.uk/women/womens-life/11608361/Corrective-rape-The-homophobic-fallout-of-post-apartheid-South-Africa.html.

17. Thabo Msibi, "Not Crossing the Line: Masculinities and Homophobic Violence in South Africa," *Agenda* 23, no. 80 (2009): 51.

18. "2014 Aug. 19: Makau Family Mourns the Brutal Murder of Their Beloved," Inkanyiso, August 20, 2014, inkanyiso.org/2014/08/20/2014-aug-19-makau-family-mourns-the-brutal-murder-of-their-beloved/.

19. "Sick! SA Lesbian Hate Crime Hosepipe Killing," *Mamba*, August 18, 2014, www.mambaonline.com/2014/08/18/sick-sa-lesbian-hate-crime-hosepipe-killing/.

20. Struggle photography is a photographic form that prioritized liberation over aesthetic conventions. Darren Newbury, "'Lest We Forget': Photography and the Presentation of History at the Apartheid Museum, Gold Reef City, and the Hector Pieterson Museum, Soweto," *Visual Communication* 4, no. 3 (2005): 264.

21. Danielle de Kock, "Faces and Phases: Zanele Muholi at FRED London Ltd," *Art Throb: Contemporary Art in South Africa*, accessed June 19, 2015, artthrob.co.za/Reviews/2009/07/Danielle-de-Kock-reviews-Faces-and-Phases-by-Zanele-Muholi-at-Brodie/Stevenson.aspx.

22. "Lulu Xingwana Describes Lesbian Photos as Immoral," *Mail and Guardian: Africa's Best Read*, March 3, 2010, mg.co.za/article/2010-03-03-lulu-xingwana-describes-lesbian-photos-as-immoral.

23. Holmes, "Queer Comrades," 162.

24. Shaun de Waal and Anthony Manion, introduction to *Pride: Protest and Celebration*, ed. Shaun de Waal and Anthony Manion (Johannesburg: Jacana Media, 2006), 9.

25. Ashley Currier, *Out in Africa: LGBT Organizing in Namibia and South Africa* (Minneapolis: University of Minnesota Press, 2012), 29–30.

26. Ibid., 28.

27. Ibid., 25.

28. Ibid., 39–40.

29. Gabeba Baderoon, "Composing Selves: Zanele Muholi's Faces and Phases as an Archive of Collective Being," in *Zanele Muholi Faces + Phases 2006–14*, by Zanele Muholi (Göttingen: Steidl Gerhard, 2014), 328.

30. Andrea K. Scott, "Outlook: A South African Photographer Brings Her life's Work to Brooklyn," *New Yorker*, May 18, 2015, www.newyorker.com/magazine/2015/05/18/out-look.

31. Patricia Yaeger, "'Black Men Dressed in Gold'"—Eudora Welty, Empty Objects, and the Neobaroque," *PMLA* 124, no. 1 (2009): 14.

32. The visual legacy left by the images of Saartjie Baartman is salient to note here. The violence that has fixed Baartman in the colonial archive points us to the lineage of institutional power quoted in Muholi's series. One of Baartman's audiences among many was the scientific community, along with artists—together, they confirmed her status as

an ethnographic specimen. The spectacle went beyond entertainment. Needless to say, Baartman's inferiority was a figment of collective imagination—she became a phantasmal figure used to naturalize the subordination of black people. Witnessing here is a part of colonial violence. Her images remain a poignant relic of conquest.

33. Lisa Gail Collins, *The Art of History: African American Women Artists Engage the Past* (New Brunswick, NJ: Rutgers University Press, 2002), 13.

34. Beth Fowkes Tobin, *Picturing Imperial Power: Colonial Subjects in Eighteenth-Century British Painting* (Durham, NC: Duke University Press, 1999), 179.

35. Beningfield, *Frightened Land*, 6.

Lisa Arellano is an associate professor of American studies and women's, gender, and sexuality studies at Colby College. Her research focuses on comparative social movements, critical historiography, and violence studies. Her book, *Vigilantes and Lynch Mobs: Community, Nation and Narrative*, was published in 2012. Arellano's current book manuscript, "Disarming Imagination: Violence and the American Political Left," focuses on rape revenge cases, antiviolence activism, militant political movements, and dis/utopian political literature.

Erica L. Ball is professor of American studies at Occidental College. She is author of *To Live an Antislavery Life: Personal Politics and the Antebellum Black Middle Class* (2012) and the coeditor of the forthcoming "Reconsidering *Roots*: Race, Politics, and Memory." She is currently completing an interpretive biography of Madam C. J. Walker.

Josh Cerretti teaches in the history department at Western Washington University, where he is also affiliated faculty with women, gender, and sexuality studies. He earned his PhD in global gender studies at SUNY University at Buffalo in 2014, where he organized around issues of sexual justice, prison abolition, and affordable public education. His work has appeared in the *Feminist Wire* and *Peace and Conflict Monitor* and is forthcoming in *Gender and History*.

Jonathan Culleton is a lecturer in sociology and criminal justice studies at Waterford Institute of Technology. His main research interests are the interactions between conceptions of race and national identities. Culleton has considerable experience of working with various marginalized social groups, including religious and ethnic minority communities, former (and current) prisoners, and Travelers. Jonathan also coordinates the Wexford-Savannah Axis Research Project, an archival study in Irish migration, at WIT.

Amanda Frisken, professor of American studies at SUNY College at Old Westbury, is author of *Victoria Woodhull's Sexual Revolution: Political Theater and the Popular Press in Nineteenth Century America* (2004). Her current book project is tentatively titled "Sensationalism and Modern Culture." "'A Song without Words:' Anti-Lynching Imagery in the 1890s African American Press," based on a chapter of that book, was published in the *Journal of African American History* in 2012.

Raphael Ginsberg is associate director of the University of North Carolina at Chapel Hill's Correctional Education Program, which brings UNC-Chapel Hill courses into prisons for credit. He is also a lecturer in UNC-Chapel Hill's Department of Communication Studies and teaches through the Correctional Education Program. He received his PhD in communication studies from the University of North Carolina at Chapel Hill, focusing on cultural studies.

Deana Heath is senior lecturer in Indian and colonial history at the University of Liverpool. She is the author of *Purifying Empire: Obscenity and the Politics of Moral Regulation in Britain, India, and Australia* (2010), and coeditor of *Communalism and Globalisation in South Asia and its Diasporas* (2011) and "South Asian Governmentalities: Michel Foucault and the Question of Postcolonial Orderings" (forthcoming). She is currently working on a book on torture in colonial India.

Efeoghene (Efe) Igor is currently a doctoral student in the departments of history and women's, gender, and sexuality studies at Yale University. Her work examines the interplay between race, aesthetics, form, and identity in apartheid South Africa. Her dissertation pays attention to the particular ways in which the scientific gaze informed aesthetic conceptions of the black body.

Catherine O. Jacquet is assistant professor of history and women's and gender studies at Louisiana State University. She is currently revising her book manuscript, which examines social movement activism in response to rape in the United States, 1950–80. She has previously published "The Giles-Johnson Case and the Changing Politics of Sexual Violence in the 1960s United States" in the *Journal of Women's History* (Fall 2013).

Jessie Kindig is visiting assistant professor of history at Indiana University and an assistant editor at the *Journal of American History*. Her current book project tracks the emergence of US empire across the post-1945 Pacific by interrogating political and cultural struggles over the meaning and visibility of the Korean War's violence. She is a founding member of the Histories of Violence Collective.

Benjamin N. Lawrance is Conable Chair in International Studies and professor of history and anthropology at the Rochester Institute of Technology. His research examines trafficking, citizenship, and asylum. His recent books include *Amistad's Orphans* (2014), the collection *Adjudicating Refugee and Asylum Status* (2014, edited with Galya Ruffer), *Citizenship in Question* (2016, edited with Jacqueline Stevens), and the collection *Marriage by Force?* (2016, edited with Annie Bunting and Richard L. Roberts).

Jen Manion is associate professor of history at Amherst College. Manion is author of *Liberty's Prisoners: Carceral Culture in Early America* (2015) and coeditor of *Taking Back the Academy: History of Activism, History as Activism* (2004) and has published in *Signs: Journal of Women in Culture and Society*, *Journal of the Early Republic*, and *TSQ: Transgender Studies Quarterly*.

Xhercis Méndez is an assistant professor in philosophy and African American and African studies at Michigan State University. As a scholar-activist her research brings together women of color and decolonial feminisms, sexuality studies, and Afro-Latinx/diasporic religion and philosophies in an effort to explore alternative grounds for the (re)making of social relations, histories, intimacies, and resistant possibilities. She is the author of "Notes toward a Decolonial Feminist Methodology: The Race/Gender Matrix Revisited" (2015) and "Transcending Dimorphism: Afro-Cuban Ritual Praxis and the Rematerialization of the Body" (2014). She is currently working on her manuscript, "An Other Humanity: Decolonizing Feminism through Methodological Interventions from the Dark Side."

Luis Morán is an artist interested in fiction and visual studies. His work in illustration, graphic novels, and video focuses on experimental forms of narrative.

Claudia Salamanca is an artist, writer, and researcher whose work engages geopolitics and visual studies. She holds a PhD in rhetoric from the University of California, Berkeley and is currently assistant professor at Pontifical Xavierian University in Bogotá, Colombia, in the Department of Visual Arts. Her most recent research analyzes the modes of perception of the territory in the Colombian war conflict during 2002–10. She is also interested in experimental forms of writing specifically within the arts.

Tomoko Seto is an assistant professor of modern Japanese history at the Underwood International College, Yonsei University, South Korea. Her research interests include early socialism and anarchism, gender relations in social movements, and popular media such as gossip newspapers, theater performances, and oral narratives. She is currently working on a book that deals with the relationship between the late Meiji socialist movement and popular culture in Tokyo.

Carla Tsampiras is a historian inhabiting the position of senior lecturer in medical humanities in the Primary Health Care Directorate at the University of Cape Town. She is currently writing a book on the early years of AIDS in South Africa.

Jennifer Yeager is a lecturer in social, abnormal, and forensic psychology at the Waterford Institute of Technology. Her research focuses on how victimology and trauma are remembered and narrated by survivors and wider society. She has worked extensively with survivors of sexual assault across multiple projects and is the principal investigator of the Waterford Memories Project, an oral-history-driven study in digital humanities.

DOI 10.1215/01636545-3594699

The Near Futures Series from Zone Books

Examining the impact of neoliberal thought on contemporary society

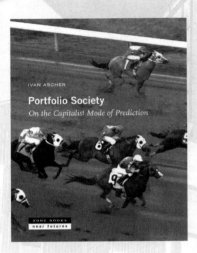

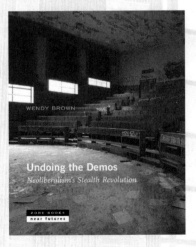

PORTFOLIO SOCIETY
On the Capitalist Mode of Prediction
by Ivan Ascher

With a focus on risk and securities rather than labor and commodities, *Portfolio Society* extends Marx's *Capital* into the age of derivative finance.

"I have never seen restrained horror, gallows humor, and elegant prose so deftly combined in political theory."
—FRANK PASQUALE, AUTHOR OF *THE BLACK BOX SOCIETY*

UNDOING THE DEMOS
Neoliberalism's Stealth Revolution
by Wendy Brown

"Brilliant and incisive... Brown has written a book that deserves to be widely read." —BOOKFORUM

FAMILY VALUES
Between Neoliberalism and the New Social Conservatism
by Melinda Cooper

Distributed by MIT Press. Online at zonebooks.org

Musicians in Transit
Argentina and the Globalization
of Popular Music
MATTHEW B. KARUSH
20 illustrations, paper, $24.95

*"Karush reveals the individual footpaths and
transnational bridges essential for decoding the
relationship between music, capital, and nation."*
—**Eric Zolov**

Punk and Revolution
Seven More Interpretations of
Peruvian Reality
SHANE GREENE
63 illustrations, 8 page color insert, paper, $23.95

*"[A] screamed prose-theory-anthropology-zine-
poem to punk, and a daring mosh pit stage dive of
an experimental ethnography."*—**Orin Starn**

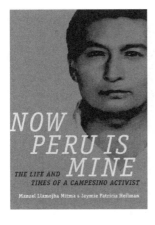

Now Peru Is Mine
The Life and Times of a
Campesino Activist
MANUEL LLAMOJHA MITMA
and **JAYMIE PATRICIA HEILMAN**
Narrating Native Histories
24 illustrations, paper, $23.95

*"Now Peru Is Mine makes a brilliantly original
contribution to the study of twentieth-century
Peru."*—**Paulo Drinot**

dukeupress.edu | 888-651-0122 | 🐦 @DUKEpress

DUKE UNIVERSITY PRESS

The Colombia Reader
History, Culture, Politics
**ANN FARNSWORTH-ALVEAR,
MARCO PALACIOS,** and
ANA MARÍA GÓMEZ LÓPEZ, editors
The Latin America Readers
103 illustrations (incl. 8 page color insert), paper, $29.95

*"In this stunning textual and visual compilation of
daily historical moments, the Colombian people
come alive, so that they may finally be understood
alongside their fellow Latin Americans."*
—Herbert Braun

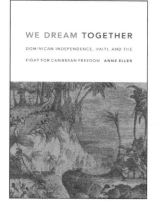

We Dream Together
Dominican Independence, Haiti, and the
Fight for Caribbean Freedom
ANNE ELLER
11 illustrations, paper, $26.95

"This is the *book that tells the story of the Dominican
Republic's independence."*— **Laurent Dubois**

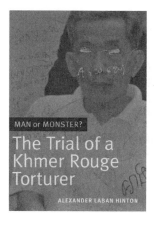

Man or Monster?
The Trial of a Khmer Rouge Torturer
ALEXANDER LABAN HINTON
22 illustrations, paper, $26.95

*"[A] finely observed and elegantly meditative study
of the Duch trial before the Khmer Rouge Tribunal...*
Man or Monster? *is a singular achievement."*
—Lawrence Douglas

dukeupress.edu | 888-651-0122 |  @DUKEpress

DUKE UNIVERSITY
PRESS

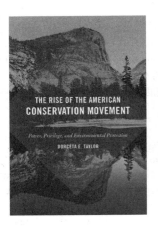

The Rise of the American Conservation Movement
Power, Privilege, and Environmental Protection
DORCETA E. TAYLOR
paper, $29.95

"This book will inspire you to reconsider nearly everything you think you know about environmental history."—**David Naguib Pellow**

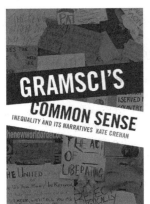

Gramsci's Common Sense
Inequality and Its Narratives
KATE CREHAN
6 photographs, paper, $23.95

"An essential text in Gramscian studies, Gramsci's Common Sense *will generate transdisciplinary interest across the humanities and social scientists."*—**Marcus E. Green**

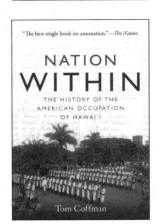

Now published by Duke University Press:
Nation Within
The History of the American Occupation of Hawai'i
TOM COFFMAN
68 illustrations, paper, $26.95

"This book gives us the untold story, the history we were not given in school, placing Hawai'i inside the larger picture of U.S. expansion into the Pacific. What we learn is sobering and fascinating."—**Howard Zinn**

dukeupress.edu | 888-651-0122 | 🐦 @DUKEPRESS

DUKE UNIVERSITY PRESS

MUSIC HANDBOOK
for the
ELEMENTARY SCHOOL

MUSIC HANDBOOK
for the
ELEMENTARY SCHOOL

Marvin Greenberg

and

Beatrix MacGregor

PARKER PUBLISHING COMPANY, INC.

West Nyack, N.Y.

PRINTED IN THE UNITED STATES OF AMERICA

ISBN 0-13-608042-1

B & P

Preface

This handbook is a practical guide for teaching music in the elementary school. It uses the discipline of music as a point of departure for developing understandings about, and appreciation of the subject.

The first section in the book—"Introduction: A Conceptual Approach"—outlines the structure and basic concepts which serve as a foundation for the music curriculum. Attention is given to planning lessons in which goals are stated in terms of desired student behaviors.

Part I—"Developing an Understanding of Music"—devotes a chapter each to tonal, rhythmic, melodic, harmonic, formal, and stylistic and associative concepts. Understandings essential to each concept are specified, with appropriate musical examples given. These understandings are ordered according to levels of complexity within the structure of the subject. This organization provides for sequential learning and individual student progress, and eliminates the need for grade level placement of subject matter. Activities designed to foster conceptual growth in music accompany each understanding. Teaching techniques drawn from the authors' experiences with children are suggested.

Part II—"Approaches to Musical Experiences"—presents a detailed description of how the processes of listening to, performing, and creating music are used to develop musical understanding. Teaching suggestions are offered for each approach.

Appendices contain a curriculum scope and sequence chart, a source list of songs and recordings referred to in the text, and sources of information for basic instructional materials. The scope and sequence chart provides an overview of the conceptual understandings mentioned in the text and offers guidelines for using the handbook for overall planning. Definitions of terms are given in context throughout the book and are located by referring to the Index.

The handbook is intended primarily for the in-service elementary classroom teacher who has the responsibility for teaching music. Conceptual understandings and activities are explained in much detail in order to help the teacher with limited musical background become more effective in teaching music. The material should also prove valuable to college students majoring in elementary or music education, and to music specialists working with general music classes at both the elementary and intermediate school levels.

In using the handbook the teacher should first read the introductory section to gain an understanding of the conceptual framework on which the curriculum is based. He should then skim through Parts I and II to become acquainted with the understandings and approaches used in the program. Those aspects which apply to the teacher's instructional situation should be selected and used in both his overall and daily planning.

The authors extend their grateful appreciation to: Odean Jones, for several illustrations used in the text; Mrs. Thelma Yoshida, principal of Hahaione Elementary School, Honolulu, for photographs of children engaged in music activities; Curt McClain, Honolulu, Harry Yoshioka of Harry's Music Store Inc., Honolulu, Kamaka Hawaii, Inc., Honolulu, M. Hohner Inc., Hicksville, New York, and Ludwig Drum Co., Chicago, for photographs of instruments; and C. F. Peters Corporation, Theodore Presser Co., and Sing Out, Inc., for use of copyrighted materials.

MARVIN GREENBERG
BEATRIX MACGREGOR

Introduction:

A Conceptual Approach

So you're getting ready to prepare a music program for your children. This handbook should help you. Before proceeding to the "how-to-do-it" sections, let us consider the principles and approach from which the materials in this book are derived.

A POINT OF VIEW

The foundation of the music program rests upon the following basic assumptions:

- Music plays a significant role in the life of man.
- Musical instruction is essential to the education of all children.
- Every child can grow musically.
- The focus of music education should be on the development of each student's potential to enjoy and understand music as an aesthetic experience.
- This aesthetic response is achieved when the student understands the ways in which the tonal and rhythmic elements of music have been organized to achieve tonal beauty.
- All learning about music as a tonal art should originate with the *aural* experience.

WHAT TO TEACH

We can obtain clues as to the content of the music program by first identifying the various components of the subject and how they are organized into a field or discipline of knowledge (*Figure A*). This organization or *structure* includes:

- the fundamental *elements* of tone, rhythm, melody, harmony, form, and style
- the key *concepts* or ideas about the elements and their interrelatedness in a musical work
- the set of unique *symbols and vocabulary* which identifies the basic concepts
- the *processes* or means of interacting with the tonal and rhythmic patterns of music, including creating, performing, and listening to music

All activities will have as their main purpose the furthering of insight into music and its structure. Through these activities two types of concepts, or basic ideas, will emerge in the mind of the learner, as shown in Figure A.

- *THE ANALYTICAL CONCEPTS*, relating to those aspects of the inner organization or structure of music which are capable of being aurally perceived and analyzed, as concepts about tone, rhythm, melody, harmony, form, tone color, dynamics, and style
- *THE ASSOCIATIVE CONCEPTS*, dealing with what can be said about the importance of music to society and the individual

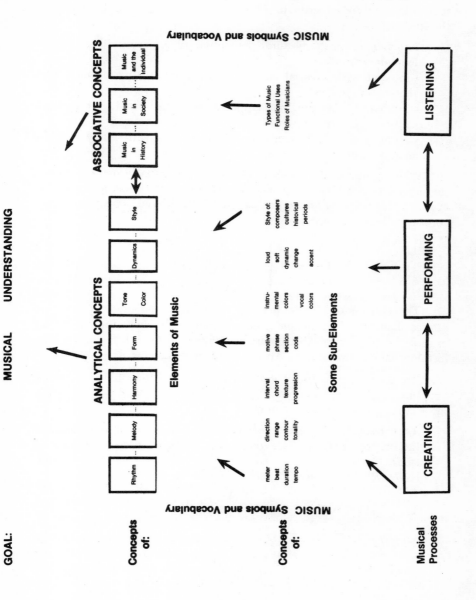

Figure A

PLANNING THE PROGRAM

An effective music program will result when emphasis is placed upon sequential conceptual growth. This process is implemented by having the student:

- participate in many aural perceptual experiences with all of the elements of music
- interact with musical content by listening to, performing, and creating music
- gradually integrate musical ideas in a sequential, yet cyclical manner to derive new concepts
- refine and enlarge concepts as experiences with many types of music literature become more complex

When planning the lesson to facilitate conceptual growth, consider the objectives, materials, sequences of activities to be used, and ways to evaluate the extent to which goals have been achieved. This plan, then, consists of four sections:

The Lesson Plan

- OBJECTIVES
- MATERIALS
- ACTIVITIES
- EVALUATION

The *objectives* of a lesson are concerned with changing the student's musical behavior. This change is based upon the learner's understanding of some aspect of musical structure as attained through listening to, performing, or creating music. An objective may have as its emphasis:

(1) a response shown to an *understanding* of a particular aspect of the structure of music, or (2) an ability to perform a *musical skill*. The following is a model for stating lesson objectives:

AN OBJECTIVE EMPHASIZING A *RESPONSE TO AN UNDERSTANDING*

> *The student will indicate an understanding that (insert the conceptual understanding to be grasped) by (insert desired student behavior(s) which demonstrates his awareness of the understanding)*

AN OBJECTIVE EMPHASIZING *A SKILL*

> *The student will indicate an ability to (insert the skill to be achieved) by (insert desired student behavior(s) which demonstrates his ability to perform the skill)*

Four sample objectives using the above model are given on p. xi. Although all the objectives deal with harmony, the first two focus on behavior dealing with understandings about harmony and the last two focus on performing abilities in specific musical skills related to harmony:

Understandings

• *The student will indicate an understanding that* the accompanying chords of a melody may change *by* saying "change" each time a different chord is heard in "Clementine."

• *The student will indicate an understanding that* the F major triad consists of three tones which are an interval of a third apart *by* selecting and playing the F, A, and C tones of the resonator bells when the symbol "F" appears above the notes of "Clementine."

Skills

• *The student will indicate an ability to* finger the F and C_7 chords on the Autoharp *by* playing these chords for the accompaniment of "Clementine."

• *The student will indicate an ability to* sing in harmony *by* singing a given harmony part to the last two measures of "Clementine."

An examination of the above illustrations reveals that an objective for a lesson should contain:

• a specific statement of the understandings to be grasped and/or skills to be attained

• a specific behavior or activity through which the student demonstrates his understanding (as saying "change" each time a different chord is heard—a *verbal* response) or an ability to perform a particular skill (as fingering the Autoharp—a *non-verbal* response)

• an aural experience as the *basis* of the response (as listening to chords or singing in harmony)

• a musical example such as a song, a specific chord progression, or an extended instrumental work which the student performs or listens to as he demonstrates his progress in attaining the objective

Every music lesson should have at least one objective focusing on the tonal and rhythmic design of the music. Concepts about music's role in the life of man and society should not be included as primary objectives of the lesson. These understandings will be used only to enhance or enrich the aural experience.

Process-related skills involving listening to, performing, and creating music provide the approaches to musical understanding. They become the focus of objectives *only* when there is a need to emphasize them in order to develop musical concepts. When used incidentally in a lesson, these skills need not appear in the objectives.

Once the lesson objectives have been determined, *materials* must be organized and *activities* planned for helping students attain the stated goals. The list of materials will include the music literature to be used, as well as the equipment and supplies needed. All activities should be designed to give students an opportunity to discover, explore, and generalize about the various facets of a musical work. Although listening to, performing, and creating music serve as the major approaches in the lesson, additional activities which do not involve aural musical experiences may be used. Discussing the meaning of repetition and contrast by using a painting, and copying the notation of a tune after singing it are examples of these activities.

The concluding activity in the lesson plan sequence may serve as the *evaluation* or means of measuring whether objectives have been attained. When each student's ability is taken into account, it may be necessary to offer several behaviors to test a particular understanding and/or skill. For example, different behaviors indicating an understanding that the beats of "Clementine" move in metric units of three (1^{23}) might include: (1) conducting the $\frac{3}{4}$ meter of the tune; (2) designing the 1^{23} pattern in the air or on the chalkboard ($|^{11}|^{11}$); (3) stamping on the first beat and clapping on the two weaker beats; and (4) saying 1^{23} in time with the music.

    *   *   *   *

This introductory section has set the stage for both the "what" and "how" of teaching music. The remaining sections of the handbook provide the specific content and activities for implementing the program.

Contents

MUSIC HANDBOOK
for the
ELEMENTARY SCHOOL

Part One

DEVELOPING AN UNDERSTANDING OF MUSIC

This section outlines the basic elements of music—*tone, rhythm, melody, harmony, form,* and *style.* In addition, the role of music in society is discussed. Each chapter presents the basic concepts, generalizations, and understandings pertinent to the particular musical element. These are followed by activities through which the concepts can be developed. The excerpt below, from Chapter One, Tone, illustrates this organization.

A CONCEPT OF TONE

I-III	(*major generalization*)	A *tone*—the basic building-block of music—is a sound having the characteristics of *duration, pitch, intensity,* and *timbre.*
I	(*understanding*)	1. There are many different kinds of sounds in the environment, some of which have musical tone.
	(*activities*)	• Strike various objects in the room. Call attention to the distinctive sounds. • Take students for a walk to the playground, park, or neighborhood. Identify and imitate the sounds of nature, machines, human beings.

The major generalizations and understandings are ordered in five *levels* of increasing conceptual difficulty, as follows:

CONCEPTUAL LEVEL	APPROXIMATE GRADE LEVEL
I	K–1
II	2–3
III	3–4
IV	4–5
V	5–6

These levels infer that the student needs to progress through several stages of conceptual development, regardless of his age or grade level, as he achieves an understanding of music and its structure. The Roman numeral(s) shown in the left-hand margin indicates the particular level(s) at which the material is to be emphasized and developed.

The activities listed below the understandings provide experiences through which students can discover and explore a particular aspect of music. The items in each list progress from relatively simple perceptual experiences to those which are more complex. Introductory and final activities for each understanding may be applicable to other instructional levels than those designated by the numerals in the left-hand margin. The teacher should be selective in choosing those activities which seem most suitable for the level(s) of his students.

Songs and recordings which provide examples of musical learnings referred to in the activities are indicated by "S"—(songs) and "RL"—(recordings for listening). These symbols are followed by numerals which coincide with the numerical order of these works as listed alphabetically in the appropriate section of Appendix B, p. 221. For example, S—3, 9; and RL—6, 8 mean that items 3 and 9 on the song list and 6 and 8 on the recordings for listening list in Appendix B contain appropriate excerpts from which the teacher can highlight particular understandings.

The material in this section should be used for formulating objectives for the specific lesson, as a guide to long-range planning, and as a source for developing a sequential music curriculum for the elementary school.

One

TONE

BASIC CONCEPT:

    The fundamental building-block of music is *tone*—a sound with the characteristics of duration (length), pitch (highness), intensity (loudness), and timbre (color or quality).

KEY TERMS:

sound, vibration, duration, silence, rhythm, pitch, melody, intensity, dynamics, tone color.

I-III   Tone is a basic ingredient of the world of sound.

I   1. There are many different kinds of sounds in the environment, some of which have musical tone.

        • Strike various objects in the room. Call attention to the distinctive sounds.

        • Take students for a walk to the playground, park, or neighborhood. Identify and imitate the sounds of nature, machines, human beings at work and play.

        • Have students bring in and strike objects which produce interesting sounds. Note different qualities of sound.

        • Play recordings designed to acquaint students with environmental sounds; (e.g., *The World of Sound*, L100, Follett).

3

• Play "The Sound Game," asking a student to make sounds with his voice or by striking various objects. Other students close eyes and guess the nature of the sounds.

• Students play echo game by taking turns imitating musical tones sung or played by the teacher and other class members.

II-III 2. A tone is caused by the vibration of air.

• Strike a tuning fork and let students hear the pitch by placing the fork next to their ears. Note how the sound stops when vibration of the fork stops. Also hit the tuning fork and place it into water. Note the slight ripples at the point where the fork comes in contact with the water.

• Show the principle of vibration and sound waves by dropping a stone into a bucket of water and watching ripples emit from the point at which the stone was dropped.

• Discuss the meaning of vibration by plucking and observing a vibrating string, by using a stretched rubber band, or by placing a paper on a drum or piano string and watching it move as the instrument is played.

• Note the effect of playing a triangle or cymbal when it is suspended and when it is grasped in the hand. Relate to freedom of movement needed for a vibrating body.

• Ask students to touch their throats and feel the vibration while they sing or speak. Develop awareness of the mechanisms involved in vocal production.

I-V A tone may be relatively long or short. The length of time assigned to a tone is known as its *duration*.

I-II 1. Tones may be long or short. Some tones may be held longer than others.

• Sing a short tone followed by a long tone, and note difference. Ask students to sing two tones—one long and one short. Also experiment with singing or playing a tone on an instrument, and making the sound longer or shorter in length.

• Compare duration of sounds in the environment and those produced by striking various objects and instruments.

• Clap or play a rhythm pattern on the drum. Students clap this pattern and raise hands for the longest tone. Also raise hands when the longest (or shortest) tone(s) in a melody is heard. Sing any song and ask students to identify the word(s) which has the longest (or shortest) tone(s).

• Students create a rhythmic pattern, making the first or final tone the longest in duration. Repeat, using short tones in the beginning or middle of the pattern.

• Write a tune such as "Hot Cross Buns" in *"blank"* (*line*) *notation* (see Ex. 1–1 and ensuing discussion). Note where the longest and shortest tones are heard and notated. Continue to use "blank" or line notation to symbolize varying lengths of tones in many melodies.

Ex. 1-1. The Rhythm of "Hot Cross Buns"

in "blank" notation

in standard notation

(1)   (2)   (3)   (4)

(5)   (6)   (7)   (8)

• Identify the long or short tones in recorded works—
MANY LONG TONES: RL—97, 121, 173, 182, 297
MANY SHORT TONES: RL—27, 59, 118, 146, 157, 161, 213
BOTH SHORT AND LONG TONES: RL—12, 44, 77, 78, 171, 205, 323

• Show the duration of tones through a sustained hand or bodily movement for long tones and a brief, abrupt movement for short tones.

• Ask one student to make up a bodily movement, thinking about either short or sustained tones. Other students may add rhythm instrument accompaniment to characterize this movement.

• Draw some short and long horizontal lines on the chalkboard. Ask students to sing tones representing the comparative length of lines.

• Relate the above understandings and activities to work on notating various rhythmic patterns (see pp. 41–48).

II-V 2. Duration of tone and silence can be pictured through the use of symbols called *notes* and *rests*.

II 2a. Various kinds of notes are used by musicians to picture different tonal durations. Some notes have *note-heads* which are filled in or "solid" ( ); others can be "seen through" ( ). Some notes have *flags* ( ) or *beams* ( ) on their stems; other notes have no flags beams, or stems (o). Some different kinds of notes and their parts are shown in Ex. 1–2.

Ex. 1-2. Some Notes and Their Parts

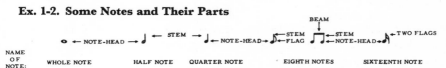

NAME OF NOTE: WHOLE NOTE   HALF NOTE   QUARTER NOTE   EIGHTH NOTES   SIXTEENTH NOTE

• Examine the musical notation of a familiar tune. Play or sing a phrase as students attempt to follow notation. Observe different kinds of notes. Introduce terms such as "note-head," "flag," and "beam" *after* students attempt description.

• Sing a familiar tune while following notation. Say: "Find a note in the music which looks like this (♩) or like this (♪)."

• Students follow notation of music which is familiar. Guide students to observe differences in the way notes are written for the shorter and longer tones.

• Use notation of familiar tune to show how the duration of any note can be shortened by adding either a flag (change ♩ to ♪ or ♪ to ♪) or stem (𝅝 to ♩), or by filling in the note-head (♩ to ♩). Observe that the kind of note-head, stem, flag, or beam on a note indicates whether it makes a longer or shorter tone than another note.

II-V

2b. There are many different kinds of notes—each of which stands for a specific duration in relation to the other notes. Some kinds of notes are:

—*the quarter note* (a solid note-head and a stem— ♩)

—*the half note* (an open note-head and a stem— ♩), having twice the duration of the quarter note (♩ = ♩ ♩)

—*the whole note* (an open note-head— 𝅝), having four times the duration of the quarter note and twice the duration of the half note (𝅝 = ♩ ♩ ♩ ♩ and 𝅝 = ♩ ♩)

—*the eighth note* (a solid note-head, a stem, and a flag— ♪), moving twice as fast as the quarter note and four times as fast as the half note (♪ ♪ = ♩ and ♪ ♪ ♪ ♪ = ♩)

—*the sixteenth note* (a solid note-head, a stem, and two flags- ♬), moving twice as fast as the eighth note and four times as fast as the quarter note (♬ ♬ = ♪ and ♬ ♬ ♬ ♬ = ♩)

—*a pitchless note*, indicating rhythmic hitting, striking, or clapping with indefinite or no pitch (♩)

—*a grace note*, usually written in small print (♪), indicating a very fast tonal movement immediately before a note of regular duration

• Develop understanding of the durational values of various notes and their relationships to each other in conjunction with study of melodic rhythm and beat (see pp. 49–51).

• Clap a sequence of basic beat-notes (see below), or set a metronome at a moderate tempo. Ask students to clap twice as fast, twice as slowly, or four times as fast or slowly. Notate this on chalkboard, as:

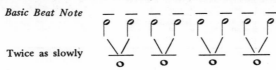

Basic Beat Note

Twice as slowly

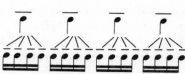

Basic Beat Note

Four times as fast

• Students may step, walk, or run to show various relationships between note values (see pp. 41–48 for detailed activities).

• Examine musical notation and ask: "How many quarter notes are on the first line of the music? How many half notes are on the page?" Also use the same or different colored chalk or crayon to circle notes which look the same or different.

• Use flash cards for identification and quick recall of note names. Place several cards together in order to have students clap the rhythmic pattern.

• Practice writing different kinds of notes by saying: "Write two quarter notes. Write two different kinds of notes, one of which goes twice as fast as the other." Clap rhythmic patterns formed by the various notes.

• Give students the opportunity to copy notation of familiar tunes. Emphasize various kinds of notes and their relationship to each other by clapping the rhythm of the tune.

• Briefly relate divisions of note values to cutting a pie in half, fourths, eighths, and sixteenths. Also relate to fractional values in mathematics.

• Make charts to show various relationships between notes, as:

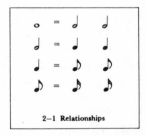

2–1 Relationships

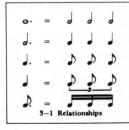

3–1 Relationships

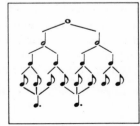

• Find examples of tunes in a very fast and very slow tempo. Note that in a very fast piece a half note can actually move more quickly than a quarter note in a slower work. In either case, the half note is held twice as long as the quarter note in the same piece.

• Differentiate between rhythms with and without pitch. Relate to notation of indefinite-pitched rhythms for rhythm instruments (see p. 177).

• Develop aural awareness of grace notes as used in music (examples: RL—52, 64, 66, 108, 171, 197, 234). Compare melody with and without a grace note(s). Students raise hands when they hear the grace note. Experiment with adding grace notes to accented tones of familiar melodies.

II-V 2c. The relative duration of silences in music may be symbolized by the use of *rests*. Rests are equal in duration to the notes bearing the same time value (quarter note—quarter rest; half note—half rest) and correspond to the time values of notes. Various types of rests are shown in Ex. 1–3.

Ex. 1-3. Types of Rests

whole rest   half rest   quarter rest   eighth rest   sixteenth rest

• Raise hands when the music rests and there is silence. Develop a crude symbolism to indicate silence in music. Later show the musical symbols of rests.

• Compare and relate time values for notes and rests. Find examples of different kinds of rests in the music. Write the rest equivalent for a given note, as: ♩ 𝄽 , ♩ ═, ♪ 𝄾 ♩. 𝄽·, ♪ 𝄾·, and ♩. ▬· . Also re-write a given rhythmic pattern using rests for notes and notes for rests. Clap the pattern and compare the effect of substituting rests for notes.

• Listen for a pause or extended rest before the end of certain works (examples: RL—75, 91, 106, 211, 224, 265) and discuss how this contributes to the resulting musical climax.

• Call attention to how the continued use of rests after tones in a pattern causes the tones to be relatively short or detached (examples: RL—29, 184, 263-theme 1, 289).

III-V 2d. The duration of a note can be prolonged by any one of three symbols—the *fermata*, the *tie*, or the *dot*. These three symbols are illustrated in Ex. 1–4.

Ex. 1-4. The Use of the Fermata, Tie, and Dot in "Steal Away"

• Sing a tune which uses a *fermata* (⌢), holding the note which has the fermata. Ask students to follow the score and state the purpose of the symbol. Discover that a *fermata* extends the note (or rest) longer than its full value (see measures 1, 2, and 4 in Ex. 1–4), and signifies a momentary interruption of the rhythmic flow.

• Experiment with placing fermatas on different tones in a familiar tune. Note effect.

• Find examples where fermatas are used to heighten the climax of a work (examples: "land of the *free*" from "The Star-Spangled Banner," "away down *South*" from "Dixie," and the "*wander*" from "I Wonder As I Wander").

• Note how the fermatas temporarily interrupt the steady beat of the music in instrumental works such as: RL—8, 94, 122, 173, 275 (theme 3).

• Apply the same technique used above for fermatas to introduce students to the aural and visual meaning of the tie and dot.

• Sing or play tunes with ties. Notice how a *tie* (⌣ or ⌢) connects two notes together on one pitch level (see measure 5 in "Steal Away" in Ex. 1–4), and increases the time value of the first note to include that of all the notes joined together by the tie (♩♩ = ♩ and ♩♩♩ = ♩. ♪)).

• Clap or sing to differentiate between ♩ ♩ and ♩ ♩ . Show how the time value for a half note can be written like this: ♩ ♩ . Continue by asking: "What other way can you write the value of a whole note (o = ♩ ♩ or ♩♩♩♩ or ♩. ♪) or a dotted half note?" (♩. = ♩♩♩ or ♩ ♪).

• Point out the difference between a tie and a *slur* (an arching line placed over a group of notes of *different* pitch to indicate the smooth connection of these notes, as in measure 5 of Ex. 1–4).

• Rewrite the rhythm of a tune using tied notes, as the following for "On Top of Old Smoky":

• Play a tune with some dotted rhythms, as students follow the notation. Observe that a *dot* extends the duration of the note (or rest) one-half its value, and that a dotted note adds the equivalent of the next shorter value to a note, as:

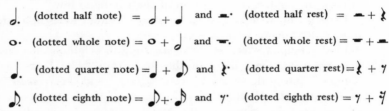

• Locate examples of dotted rhythms in familiar tunes. Practice singing and clapping rhythms containing dotted notes (see discussion on melodic rhythm, pp. 41–48).

• Teach the dotted quarter note as: ♩ ♫ ♩→♩ ♫ ♩→♩. ♪
and the dotted half note as: ♩ ♩→♩♩♩→♩♩♩→♩.

I-V A tone may be relatively high or low. The highness or lowness of a tone is known as its *pitch*.

I-II 1. The pitch of one tone may be higher or lower than the pitch of another tone.

• Strike various materials, including instruments, and compare them for highness or lowness of pitch. Determine pitch differences of objects brought from home.

• Blow into soda-pop bottles or whistles to obtain high and low pitches.

• Classify sounds in the environment and tones of rhythm instruments as being high or low-pitched; e.g., compare jingling keys with sound of large drum.

• Play three tones, two of which have the same pitch. Students raise hands on the pitch that sounds different. Also play or sing two tones whose pitches differ. Ask which tone is higher or lower in pitch.

• Students echo tonal patterns of varying pitches as sung by the teacher. Move hands high or low to show differences in pitch.

• Play two resonator or melodé bells of varying pitches. Students close eyes, listen to one of the bells, and identify which one was played. Continue activity using three or more bells.

• Distribute three resonator bells of varying pitches, as C, F♯, and A♯. Have each student play his bell to acquaint the class with the tones. Sing or play the three tones in varying order, as C, A♯, F♯, or F♯, A♯, C, or A♯, C, F♯. Students holding the bells repeat the pattern.

• Imitate sounds of cuckoo bird, siren, a whistling teakettle, the wind, a giant, a little bear, and Big Billy Goat Gruff talking. Raise or lower the hand to signify that the pitches move higher or lower.

• Use the step bells or tone bells held vertically to help visualize changes of pitch levels in familiar tunes.

• Have a student play any pitch on an instrument and then change it. Call on students to say whether the new pitch was higher or lower than the first one. Notice the many different pitches possible on the piano, the Autoharp, or the bells.

• Play many tunes on the step, resonator, and melody bells. Show that many different pitches are used in some songs. Use any bell-like instrument to compare the number of different pitches in various songs; e.g., "America"—7; "Hot Cross Buns"—3.

• Ask each student to sing at least three different pitches, including some low tones and some high tones.

• Symbolize pitch differences, using crude notation and notes (see pp. 12–17).

• Play "Follow the Leader," moving hands up and down to various pitches as the students follow you. Select several students to be leaders. Also play action games, as:

I   can   stand   tall   I   can   fall   down   Birds   fly   up   high

See me climb the stairs

• Make up a tune with a given number of pitches; e.g., use selected tones of the entire range of the piano, or only F A♭ B of the resonator bells. Point out pitch differences of the tones used.

• Use the body to respond to high and low tones of a scale or tonal pattern, a familiar tune or song, or parts of a song; e.g., tiptoe or move hands up for very high, and crouch or move hands down for very low.

• Move your hands up and down, asking students to make up a tune following your hand movements. Then call on individuals to do the hand movements as the other students sing.

• Associate high-low in pitch with right-left direction on the keyboard. Play a high-pitched tone. Ask students to find that tone on the piano. Repeat, using different pitches.

• Play a familiar tune in the low, middle, and high registers of the piano. Compare pitches and overall mood.

• Compare the moods of recorded works caused, in part, by the highness and lowness of pitch. For example, note the contrasting moods in the following works—

HIGH AND LIGHT: RL—20, 148, 170, 190, 225, 254, 255, 286, 291

LOW AND HEAVY: RL—88(beginning), 136, 172, 232, 238, 272(beginning)

HIGH–LOW CONTRASTS: RL—12, 80, 154, 174, 179, 196, 202, 268, 283, 285

• Work on *intonation* (lowering or raising the pitch) when singing to develop an accurate sense of pitch (see p. 161). Also play a pitch and then sing it out of tune. Identify intonation problem and ask for suggestions for improvement. Continue to use this activity at all instructional levels.

I-V 2. Pitch can be pictured through symbols such as lines (_ - - - _) and notes (♩ ♩ ♩ ♩ ♩).

I-II 2a. Pitch can be shown by making symbols high or low to correspond with pitch differences.

• Guide students to derive and write their own symbolization for the pitch levels of tones in their favorite tunes.

• Use lines or symbols to illustrate pitch differences in tonal patterns and tunes, as ● ● , x x x , and ♩ ♩ ♩ for "Are You Sleeping." Call attention to left-right and up-down sequence of writing symbols.

• Write a tune in crude notation on the chalkboard. Sing the tune as the students follow the notation. Stop in the middle and ask students to point to where you stopped. Also write a tune with one or more errors. Sing the tune. Have students find and correct the error(s).

• Have students place symbols on a magnetic or flannel board to indicate the various pitch levels of tones in a melody.

• Provide paper containing several up-and-down pitch patterns, as x x (with x's at varying levels), and x x x. Sing or play a pattern (as c D E in rising steps) and ask students to circle the one they hear. Repeat, using many different tonal patterns.

II-III 2b. The pitch levels of tones can be shown on a musical *staff*—five equally spaced horizontal lines enclosing four spaces.

• Students follow notes of a musical score and discover the five lines and four spaces of the staff, and the upward and downward direction of notes to signify pitch levels. Observe how the lines and spaces of the staffs are counted from the bottom to the top. Develop acquaintance with the staff by asking questions such as: "Can you point to some notes on the lines? Can you find or write a note on the first space? How many notes are on the fourth line of the staff?"

• Play musical games using the five fingers (and four spaces) of the hand held horizontally to correspond with the staff.

• Draw five parallel chalk lines on the floor. Ask students to be a note on the third line, the third space. Sing or play tones to reinforce pitch levels.

• Superimpose crude notation for pitch on the staff. Notice relationship between high and low pitches and relative positions of notes on the staff.

• Provide many opportunities for students to copy notation of familiar tunes. Stress legibility, neatness, and correct placement of notes on the staff.

• Sing a tune as students follow the notation. Ask: "Where did the tones sound the highest in pitch? How do the notes for these tones look on the staff?"

• Provide much practice in having the students point to the notation from their books, chart, or chalkboard as the tune is sung or played. Occasionally stop in the middle and ask students to point to where you have stopped. Say: "Did I stop on a high or low pitch?"

• Sing three repeated tones. Show how they appear on the staff. Continue, using ascending and descending tonal patterns. Look at the notation of a familiar tune. Find where the pitches ascend, descend, or stay the same. Reinforce by singing or playing the tune as the notes are followed.

• Examine the notation of an unfamiliar tune. Sing a pattern from the tune which illustrates a repeated, ascending, or descending sequence of tones, and ask students to locate the pattern they hear.

• Play or sing two tones "close together" in pitch. Compare with two tones "far apart." Show their notation on the staff. Use various bodily movements to show approximate distances between two tones. Also look at notation of melody. Find parts where pitches move close to or far apart from each other.

• Sing unfamiliar tune to students as they follow notation. Make occasional errors in the melody. Have students listen for and locate these errors.

II-III 2c. Each line and space on the staff represents a pitch position. The first seven letters of the alphabet—A, B, C, D, E, F, and G—are used to name the lines and spaces of the staff. The letter names used are repeated at lower or higher levels; i.e., ascending—E, F, G, *A*, B . . . , and descending—D, C, B, A, *G*, F . . . .

• Show how pitches are named by calling attention to letter names indicated on the keys of the melody or resonator bells. Ask students to find and play B, C, or F. Discuss how pitches are named.

• Identify letter names of notes in a familiar tune. Distribute resonator bells having those letter names. Each student plays his bell as the corresponding note appears in the music.

• Play game, using a two, three, four, or five-line staff. Write down any note on the staff. Say: "If this note is A, write where B would be. If this note is E, where would G be? Where would A be?"

• Show that when a note goes from a line to the next space, or from a space to the next line, the letter name used is also adjoining (exception: G to A). The same principle holds when a note skips, as from D to F or E to G (exceptions: G to B and F to A).

• Discover the need for *ledger lines*—short lines above or below the staff which are used to extend the range of written notes (see middle C in Ex. 1–5)—by experimenting with writing pitches higher than the staff's fifth line or lower than its first line. Also find examples of the use of ledger lines in notation. Practice reading and writing notes using ledger lines.

II-IV 2d. The lines and spaces of the staff have no definite meaning until a *clef* is placed on the staff. A clef sign at the beginning of the staff shows what tones are represented by the lines and spaces of the staff. The two most frequently used clefs are the *treble* and *bass* clefs. The *treble clef* (G clef) is used for relatively high voices and instruments. It locates G above middle C on the second line of the staff. The *bass clef* (F clef) is used for relatively low voices and instruments. It locates

F below middle C on the fourth line of the staff. These two clefs can be combined into the *grand staff*, consisting of eleven lines—the treble and bass clefs plus a ledger line between them (middle C), as in Ex. 1–5.

Ex. 1-5. The Grand Staff

• Find and discuss meaning of clef signs at beginning of each line of musical notation. Notice the treble clef's curve around second-line G and the two dots of the bass clef which enclose fourth-line F. Use terms "treble" and "G" clef, and "bass" and "F" clef synonymously.

• Put any note on the staff, without a clef sign. Show that it cannot be named until a clef sign is placed at the beginning of the staff. Create original clef signs to locate tones such as B and E.

• Indicate letter names for other lines and spaces after locating G or F. Start from a known note and say the letter names of the intervening lines and spaces in order.

• Use a one, two, or three-line staff for initial work in reading note names. For example, locate F on a space between two lines <u>o</u> and drill on naming E, F, and G.

• Spell words using letter names on the staff. Say: "What word am

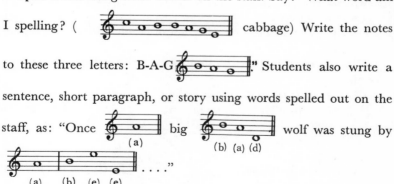

I spelling? (cabbage) Write the notes to these three letters: B-A-G   ." Students also write a sentence, short paragraph, or story using words spelled out on the staff, as: "Once   big   wolf was stung by   . . . .""

(a)   (b) (a) (d)

(a)   (b)   (e)   (e)

• Use the staff liner as a visual aid in teaching letter names of the lines and spaces. Also use a staff-lined felt board with vertically held tone bars directly related to the lines and spaces, as:

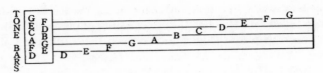

• Show visual relationship of the notes on the staff to the keyboard by superimposing a keyboard chart over a staff, as:

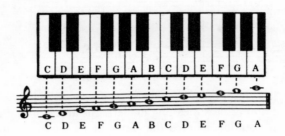

Point to specific notes on the staff. Students play corresponding keys on the piano (or melody bells). Use this activity for both treble and bass clefs, and with any familiar instrument.

• Dictate melodies to be written. Say "G, F, E, D, C . . ." for "Deck the Halls" as students write the notes for the tune.

• Play game, using the treble or bass clef. Ask: "What is the name of the note on the third line? the fourth space?" In addition, say: "I am A. What space or line am I on?" (second space, if treble clef is used). Continue, using other pitch names.

• Draw five parallel lines on the floor, and a large treble or bass clef. Ask students to be a B, D, F, and A by standing on the appropriate line or space.

• Write letter names over notation of familiar tune. Sing the tune, using letter names.

• Transpose many tunes written on the treble or bass clef to the other clef.

• Use flash cards with notes on one side and letter names on the back. Also provide self-practice, using the five fingers and four

spaces of the hand, as   for the treble clef.

• Show how letter names of spaces using the treble clef, from low to high, spell FACE, while the letter names of the lines spell E G B D F (Every Good Boy Does Fine). Also use this technique for the bass clef (A C E G or All Cows Eat Grass for the four spaces; and G B D F A or Good Boys Do Fine Always for the lines).

III-V   2e. Alterations of pitch on a given staff degree are shown by placing *accidentals* on the line or space before the note-head:

—*sharp*(♯)—raises a tone one half-step, as from C to C♯

—*flat*(♭)—lowers a tone one half-step, as from D to D♭

—*natural*(♮)—cancels other accidentals in the key signature for the duration of the measure.

In Exs. 1–6a and 1–6b notice some accidentals as they appear on the piano keyboard and in notation.

Ex. 1-6a. Some Sharps and Flats on the Piano Keyboard

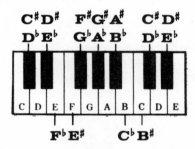

Ex. 1-6b. The Use of Accidentals in "Down by the Riverside"

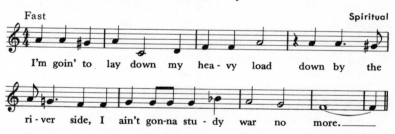

• Play F on the resonator bells. Raise F one half-step (adjoining tone) to F sharp. Show how this is notated on the staff. Repeat, using B and B sharp, C and C sharp, and D and D sharp. Use this same procedure to introduce flats.

• Find examples of music using accidentals. Play the music both with and without accidentals, and note effect. Relate need for accidentals when performing in keys other than C major, and develop this when teaching tonality and key signature (see pp. 83–84).

• Experiment with using accidentals for some tones of familiar melodies.

• Once key signatures are understood, students might attempt to rewrite a melody, inserting accidentals as they occur in the music, rather than writing the key signature at the beginning of the piece.

• Illustrate, by using the resonator bells or piano keyboard, how B sharp and C are, in essence, the same pitch. Notice how a single pitch can be notated in different ways and be called by two or more different names by using accidentals. Call the pitch an *enharmonic* tone. Some enharmonic tones, as shown in Ex. 1–6a, are B sharp and C, F sharp and G flat, and F flat and E.

• Students list as many examples of enharmonic tones as they can find by studying the keyboard. Play a tone on the resonator bells, asking students to state two ways of naming the pitch, as $F^\sharp$—$G^\flat$, or $F^\flat$—E.

• Play game, asking students to match two enharmonic tones, as:

I-V   A tone may be relatively loud or soft. The loudness or softness of a tone is known as its *intensity*.

I   1. Some sounds and tones are louder or softer than others. Changes in intensity are either toward loudness or softness.

• Compare the relative loudness of sounds such as thunder, traffic noise, an airplane, the wind, or children playing.

• Sing or play a loud tone; a soft tone. Compare differences. Show how energy level affects loudness.

• Sing or play three tones, one of which is louder (or softer) than the others. Students identify the loud or soft tone.

• Sing a sustained tone, making it gradually louder or softer through more or less breath support. Use larger bodily movements to indicate an increase in a tone's intensity. Also listen for changes in intensity of environmental sounds, as a school bell ringing or a siren screeching.

I-V   2. The relative loudness or softness of tones in a musical work is called *dynamics*.

I   2a. Some music is louder or softer than other music. Different compositions have different degrees of loudness or softness.

• Sing a tune at varying dynamic levels. Compare differences. Note effect on mood. Choose the level most appropriate for the text or intended mood. Symbolize various dynamic levels (see p. 21).

• Use large bodily movements to characterize loud dynamics, and small bodily movements to show music which is soft.

• Control dynamic level of the phonograph. Compare effects.

• Play and compare two pieces which contrast in their dynamic levels. Examples include——

SOFT: RL—59, 63, 64, 155, 176, 194, 219, 220, 229, 235, 269, 273, 308, and all lullabies (berceuses)

LOUD AND/OR ACCENTED: RL—22, 31, 49, 136, 179, 262, 263, 270, 272, and most marches

• Differentiate between meaning of highness in pitch and loudness in dynamics. Show how a loud piece may use low pitches and a soft piece may use high pitches.

I-III   2b. The degree of loudness and softness of music may change within a piece. This change may occur gradually or suddenly. Examples of dynamic changes can be seen in Ex. 1–7.

Ex. 1-7. Moussorgsky: "Samuel Goldenberg and Schmuyle" from
Pictures at an Exhibition

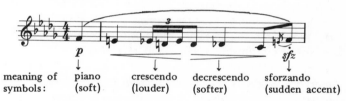

| meaning of symbols: | piano (soft) | crescendo (louder) | decrescendo (softer) | sforzando (sudden accent) |

• Listen to songs and instrumental works, and raise hands when the music becomes louder or softer, or when the dynamics change suddenly. Symbolize dynamic changes, using crude and then conventional notation (see p. 21). Instrumental pieces having obvious dynamic changes include—

SUDDEN DYNAMIC CHANGES: RL—12, 22, 75, 106, 224, 226, 268, 272, 277, 296, 322

GRADUAL DYNAMIC CHANGES: RL—11, 24, 57, 78, 98, 100, 128, 172, 251

• Compare dynamic changes in music with those used in speaking. Read poems or parts of stories aloud, and discuss why certain words or phrases are stressed.

• Use larger or smaller bodily movements to suggest music which becomes either louder or softer. Show quick changes in dynamics and dynamic accents through sudden changes in movement. Increase or decrease the number of dancers as the dynamic level becomes louder or softer.

• Distribute several types of rhythm instruments and ask students to create interesting rhythms, using contrasting dynamic levels. Also add more rhythm instruments to music which becomes louder in volume.

• Sing a song or play rhythm instruments and experiment with changing the dynamics suddenly and then gradually, as appropriate. Compare and evaluate for musical effects.

• Illustrate how dynamic accent can be achieved with the voice, or on the piano, tone block, or drum. Have students play a steady beat on various rhythm instruments, inserting occasional accents, as:

• Create a song or tune, working particularly on appropriate dynamic levels to fit the text or intended mood of the melody.

• When singing or playing musical works, experiment with varying dynamics in order to affect the music's expressiveness.

• Note that music which is soft and slow, as lullabies, suggests a quiet, peaceful mood, while music that is loud and fast, as many marches, suggests a buoyant, active mood. Compare the dynamic level of an instrumental work with the composer's title.

• Experiment with rhythm instruments to highlight the mood of a story or poem as read by the teacher. Create a piece for rhythm instruments which describes in sound a story and characters that are well-known to the students.

• Show how the song text may be an important factor in selecting appropriate dynamics. Also sing a familiar song at different dynamic levels. Compare the effect of the text on determining the most suitable level.

• Make up words to an unfamiliar tune which is played loudly. Repeat the activity for the same tune played softly.

• Listen to dynamic levels of planes, cars, or trains as they approach and leave. Show how the illusion of nearness and distance can be created through music becoming louder and then softer, as in works such as: RL—24, 128, 172.

• Call attention to how an increase in the dynamic level of the music creates tension, interest, and contributes to the climax of works such as: RL—73, 98, 100, 110, 138, 143, 157, 175, 207, 208, 296.

II-V 2c. There is a system of notation to indicate dynamic levels in music. Some common symbols are: *mp* (*mezzo-piano* or moderately soft), *mf* (*mezzo-forte* or moderately loud), *cresc.* or < (*crescendo* or louder), *decresc.* or > (*decrescendo* or softer), *dim.* (*diminuendo* or softer), *ff* (*fortissimo* or very loud).

> • Use heavy and light beat marks (**||**| or |||) to show dynamic level of music. Introduce symbols for dynamics as a shorthand for writing "loud," "soft," "accent," and other terms for dynamics.
> • Play many recorded works. Students draw symbols to express dynamic levels. Compare with symbols in the score.
> • Sing or play a tune loudly and say: "I am singing 'forte.'" Compare with singing or playing "piano" (softly). Develop meaning of these terms. Use this technique to introduce other words and symbols for dynamics.
> • Find symbols and words for dynamic levels in musical scores. Make a list of these, and practice performing music using these dynamic indications. Use symbols in original works.
> • Make a sketch of dynamic levels in a recorded work, as:
>
> $$p < f \quad p \quad mp \quad p < ff$$
>
> Stop the record in the middle of the work and ask students to point to the dynamic level where the record was stopped.
> • Ask students to make up a composition for rhythm instruments using a dynamics model, as $p < mf > p$ or $pp < ff > pp < ff$.

I-V A tone has a special quality of sound called *timbre*.

I 1. Tones may differ from each other in their tone color. For example, it is easy to tell the difference in quality between a dog's bark and the call of a bird, or the tones of a drum and an alto voice. [*Note*: See discussion and activities designed to develop recognition of sounds and tones in the environment, as listed at the beginning of this chapter, pp. 3–4. Also call attention to various tone colors in musical works, as outlined in the following pages of this chapter.]

I-III 2. Musical *tone color* or *timbre* is the characteristic quality of various sounds used in music, and is an important determinant of the expressive power of music. While vocal and instrumental media are still the most important means of producing music, many musicians today are experimenting with sounds from the environment and electronic and tape-recording processes to make music.

I-II   2a. Each type of musical media has its own characteristic sonority, quality of sound, or tone color.

• Differentiate tone colors heard live or on a recording as being vocal or instrumental (see sections 3 and 4). Also notice sounds which are from the environment, or are electronically produced (see section 5).

• Play a tone on the piano or another instrument and then sing it, trying to obtain the same degree of loudness and duration. Say: "These tones are the same in three ways. What are these ways?" (pitch, duration, intensity) "How are these tones different from each other?" (tone color or quality) Repeat, using two instruments. Develop increasingly finer discrimination as to what type of voice or instrument is being heard (see pp. 23–26). Also point out instances where various tone colors are grouped into innumerable vocal, instrumental, tape, and electronic combinations.

II-III   2b. Tone color affects musical expressiveness.

• Discuss the mood evoked by a certain piece of music, and relate the composer's use of instruments or vocal tone colors to the expressiveness of the work. Appropriate musical examples include the use of: the *harp* to suggest rippling water (examples: RL—60, 65, 235); the *harp* to evoke a quiet, peaceful mood (examples: RL—104, 273, 310); the *flute* for bird-calls (examples: RL—199, 204, 288); the *tympani* for thunder and storms (examples: RL—105, 222); and *low-pitched instruments* for slow-moving, plodding, or comical characters, or sombre and mysterious moods (examples: RL—63, 73, 98, 107, 136, 207-theme 3, 232, 238, 256-beginning).

• Vary techniques of presenting descriptive music which features certain tone colors. One method may be to ask students: "If you were a composer, what instruments might you choose to describe the feeling of a storm? Let's see what one composer did to describe a storm." Play the "Storm Music" from Rossini's *William Tell Overture* and compare. Other appropriate examples to play include: RL—57, 80, 99, 123, 148, 174, 233, 235, 243, 251, 270.

• Guide students to use appropriate rhythm instruments for various types of musical accompaniment, depending upon the instrument's timbre and the mood of the piece or section.

• Sing a song with varying tone qualities. Show that the kind of tone used in a song has much to do with establishing its mood.

• Discover how composers add instruments to achieve a more brilliant climax in musical works such as: RL—11, 82, 88, 98, 116, 136, 138, 175.

I-V   3. The human voice is an important medium of musical expression. Voices differ according to their quality and tone color.

I-IV 3a. Each person has a different quality in his singing voice.

> • Illustrate through recordings and discuss how people of all ages and occupations use their voices to make music. Sing many songs and stress the fact that we can all make music with our voices, and that each person's voice is a truly personal and valuable "instrument."
>
> • Ask one student to be "It" and sit in front of the room with his back toward the class. Another student sings the following words to any tune: "Do you know who I am?" The "It" student must repeat the tune with the words: "Yes, I know who you are." He then names the singer. Also use singing games such as "Who's That Tapping at My Window?" and "The Muffin Man" to emphasize different voice qualities.
>
> • Tape individuals singing their favorite songs. At a later date play these recordings for the class and identify names of singers.
>
> • Identify singers on recordings as a man or woman, a solo or group, or a high or low-sounding voice. Also notice voice qualities of teachers, parents, and students as they sing or speak.
>
> • Listen to vocal music recordings of entertainers and folk singers from the United States and other countries, and "pop" singers and concert artists, and compare differences in tone quality of the singers.
>
> • Listen to and identify the distinctive vocal qualities of the four basic types of adult voices—the *soprano*, the *alto*, the *tenor*, and the *bass* (see the accompanying song recordings for most basic music series, and the *RCA Basic Library for Elementary Schools: The Singing Program*, Volumes 4–6, for appropriate examples).
>
> • Call attention to the boy's changing voice (*cambiata*) at about age eleven or twelve, and its different pitch and tone quality as compared to the unchanged voice (see also p. 162).

II-V 3b. When people with different voices and qualities sing together, different vocal tone colors result.

> • Use song recordings, including those accompanying the basic music series, and note whether the song is being sung by one or many voices. Identify voices as being those of children or adults. If adult, notice whether the voices are men's, women's, or mixed. Use pictures of various groups to show arrangement of voices in choral groups.
>
> • Call attention to various tone colors of children's choral groups (boys' or girls' choirs, mixed voices).
>
> • Examine various vocal scores for choral groups. Discuss the way vocal parts are written in the score. Provide practice in following the vocal parts as the music is played.
>
> • Encourage small-ensemble singing activities in the classroom. Listen for distinctive tone colors and changes in timbre in recordings

of vocalists singing together in small groups, with each voice on a different part (as a duet, trio, or quartet).

• Invite various choral groups to perform for students. Encourage students to attend choral rehearsals and performances in the community, or watch the many choral performances on television, especially at the Christmas season.

• Play operatic excerpts (examples: RL—125, 162, 169). Call attention to voice classification and instances where duets, trios, or quartets occur.

I-V 4. The instrument is an important musical medium of musical expression. Instruments differ in their tone color.

4a. There are many different kinds of instruments. Differences in the tone quality of instruments are caused by the size of the instruments, the materials from which they are made, and the manner in which they are played.

• Whenever possible, arrange live performances by students and musicians (see p. 145). Emphasize recognition of the instruments by sight and sound.

• Play recordings highlighting specific instruments (see list below). Note particular tone color of each instrument. Show by demonstration or pictures how these instruments are played. Appropriate recordings for the most common instruments include—

VIOLIN: RL—74, 78, 96, 99, 108, 118, 213, 231, 233, 251, 278, 306, 324

VIOLA: RL—73, 130, 231(theme 2)

VIOLONCELLO (CELLO): RL—144, 207, 220, 228, 235, 269, 305

DOUBLE BASS: RL—63, 124, 232

HARP: RL—60, 61, 65, 104, 186, 214, 253, 267, 273, 298, 310

PICCOLO: RL—144(theme 2), 148, 149, 189, 196, 199, 263, 283, 288

FLUTE: RL—7, 26, 30, 60, 65, 99, 100, 148, 199, 204, 206, 213, 219, 286, 288

CLARINET: RL—15, 16, 31, 59, 84, 100, 150, 153, 199, 233, 253, 299, 301, 304, 306

OBOE: RL—16, 64, 69, 129, 130, 163, 180, 199, 246, 269, 282, 284

BASSOON: RL—16, 73, 107, 129, 199, 215, 267, 276

TRUMPET: RL—24, 28, 79, 116, 178, 221, 250, 313, 317

FRENCH HORN: RL—23, 87, 126, 127, 160, 266, 298, 319, 320

TROMBONE: RL—1(section B), 72, 108, 124, 274, 276, 318

TUBA: RL—140, 156, 172, 256, 318

TYMPANI: RL—18, 50, 121, 144(4th section), 222, 256(beginning), 277
SNARE DRUM: RL—28, 190, 250, 262, 263, 313
PIANO: RL—49, 62, 64, 85, 102, 103, 155, 230, 236, 305
ORGAN: RL—8, 83, 236(beginning)
GUITAR: RL—2, 17, 40, 302

• Students listen to and identify rhythm instruments by their distinctive tone colors.

• Notice the size, pitch, material, and manner in which various instruments are played. Discuss and illustrate similarities and differences between instruments.

• Rhythmically imitate the manner of playing a given instrument as it is heard in a recording.

• Guide students to identify the type of instrument accompanying songs sung in the classroom or on a recording.

• Compare the tones of high and low-pitched instruments; e.g., the tuba and trumpet, or violin and string bass, and relate to size of instrument.

• Compare the tone quality of an instrument being played by a beginning student and a professional musician, and a jazz musician and a symphony orchestra instrumentalist.

• Play "Instrument Bingo." Give each student a card with 25 squares. Assign the instruments to be drawn or written in each square. On separate slips of paper write the names of instruments—one name for each slip. Devise rules similar to Bingo. Identify instrumental tone colors of recorded works.

• Compare tone colors of instruments being played in their low and high registers.

• Have students who play orchestral instruments transcribe or compose tunes for their instruments and play these for the class.

• Listen to, and identify instrumental tone colors less familiar to the student, as the—

ENGLISH HORN: RL—31, 69, 130, 219, 282
BASS CLARINET: RL—108, 144(final section), 285
CONTRABASSOON: RL—70(the "frog" theme), 73, 202(the "beast" theme)
SAXOPHONE: RL—29, 84, 176, 301, 321
CELESTE: RL—123, 193, 194, 205, 274, 285

• Listen to examples of musical instruments not in common use today, as the *harpsichord* (examples: RL—95, 181, 183, 240) and *lute* (example: 71). Also play recordings featuring the *recorder*, an instrument popular during the Renaissance and enjoying a revival today (examples: RL—81, 131, 307).

• Identify unusual sounds of instruments commonly associated with particular national or ethnic groups, as the Brazilian *chocalhos*, *reco-recos* and *tamburellos* in: RL—109, 165, 315; the Hungarian *cimbalon* in: RL—142; the *Oriental drum* in: RL—130; the Japanese *koto* in: RL—239; and the American-Indian *flageolet* and *tom-tom* in several recordings of the *RCA Basic Record Library for Elementary Schools: Music of the American Indians.*

• Listen to examples of how composers have used Western-type instruments to create the illusion of non-Western music (examples: RL—144, 205-middle section, 274).

II-V 4b. Different ways of playing an instrument can produce different qualities of sound. The tone color of an instrument may be altered through means such as various bowing styles, the use of mutes, and tonguing.

• Students should be guided to discover and use the various possibilities for altering sound on classroom instruments when playing or accompanying tunes. Relate instrumental effects to various styles and moods of the music.

• Experiment with altering the sound of the piano by placing materials on the piano strings, or plucking the strings. Examples of the "prepared" piano technique include: RL—37, 55.

• Note differences between sounds of plucked and bowed string instruments, the various strummings possible on the Autoharp, guitar, or ukulele, the piano played with and without the sustaining pedal, the trumpet played with and without a mute, and percussion instruments played in unusual ways. Some tone colors which should be identified include—

PLUCKED STRINGS (pizzicato): RL—225, 255, 294, and the accompaniments to 96, 142, 189, 254
STRIKING STRINGS WITH WOOD OF BOW (col legno): RL—124, 128, 197
STRING HARMONICS: RL—87(ending), 144, 165(ending), 205
STRING TREMULO: RL—12, 106, 173, 222, 310
MUTED STRINGS: RL—148, 153, 202, 205, 206
MUTED TRUMPET: RL—108, 158, 179, 189, 196, 301
UNUSUAL PERCUSSION EFFECTS: RL—21, 61, 145, 300, 309

II-V 4c. Instruments can be classified by:
—how they are played (*blowing*—woodwinds, brasses; *striking*—percussion; *bowing*—strings; *plucking*—strings, including guitar, harp, and ukulele)
—similarities in their materials and/or the manner in which they

are played (*strings*—violin, viola, cello, string bass; *woodwinds*—piccolo, flute, clarinet, oboe, bassoon; *brasses*—trumpet, French horn, trombone, tuba; *percussion*—tympani, bass drum, snare drum, cymbals, triangle, maracas; *keyboard instruments*—piano, organ, accordion, celesta)

—their usage (*orchestral instruments; "social"* or *informal instruments*—the guitar, banjo, Autoharp, harmonica, accordion, ukulele; *band instruments; ethnic instruments*—bongo drum, bag pipes, Hawaiian pu'ili, Japanese koto, Hungarian cimbalon)

• Experiment with rhythm instruments. Classify as to similarities in sound, the material from which they are made, and the manner in which they are played, as: bell-like rhythm instruments; instruments that are beaten; or instruments with short, dry tones.

• Show pictures of many instruments. Ask students to hold pictures and regroup according to families. Make a chart of the instrumental families. Also construct a seating chart of the orchestra and color instruments of the same family the same color.

• Provide much experience in identifying tone colors of the various instrumental families, as—

STRINGS: RL—20, 29, 30, 34, 35, 53, 94, 97, 119, 184, 186, 187, 198, 241, 260, 265, 310

WOODWINDS: RL—13, 15, 16, 161, 173, 185, 191, 270, 281, 294(section B)

BRASS: RL—3, 46, 49, 50, 51, 77(the "giants" section), 83, 121. 144(4th section), 173, 210, 256(beginning), 272, 277

PERCUSSION: RL—21, 41, 105, 141, 145, 208, 209, 309, 321

• Listen to how composers alternate tone colors of two or more instrumental families in works such as: RL—10, 36, 110 and 115, 111, 152, 294, 316. Raise hands on each tone color change, and identify the instrumental family playing.

• Students write "Who Am I?" stories which describe the instruments. Also devise games to match pictures of instruments with their names and families.

• Illustrate and discuss important aspects of various instrumental families, as—

STRINGS: bow, strings, tuning, sounding board, bowing (*arco*) and plucking (*pizzicato*), string length and thickness as related to pitch, *glissando* (sliding between tones), *vibrato, harmonics* (flute-like tones obtained by touching the strings lightly), double and triple stops, and the importance of the strings to overall tone quality of the orchestra

WOODWINDS: tube length, holes, reeds, mouthpiece, tonguing

and other playing techniques, the importance of the woodwinds as "color" instruments in the orchestra

BRASSES: tube length, air column, valves, mouthpiece, tension of lips, muting, tonguing and other playing techniques, characteristic body and brilliance of sound in the orchestra

PERCUSSION: different ways of playing, manner of construction, definite and indefinite-pitched instruments, their rhythmic, climactic, and color uses in the orchestra

II-V 4d. Instrumental performers may play alone or in combination with other performers. Instruments are often combined with each other to produce varied musical effects.

• Identify whether a recorded work has one instrument (a *solo*) or many.
• Differentiate between the sound of an orchestra, band, and small ensembles. Examples include—

ORCHESTRA: The majority of works in the basic listening series for schools (see p. 228) are for orchestra
BAND: RL—47, 86, 90, 261, 264
SMALL ENSEMBLES: RL—7, 17, 39, 81, 83, 131, 241, 245, 281

• Attend rehearsals of instrumental groups in the school or community. Listen for various tone colors. Also show pictures of instrumental performing groups. Alert students to watch these groups perform in a concert or on television.
• Listen to examples of band literature (see list above). Identify predominance of woodwind and brass colors, and lack of strings (except for string bass and guitar in rock and jazz bands).
• Listen to, and compare tone colors of the various types of bands— the symphonic (concert) band, the marching band, the military band, the jazz and Dixieland band, the dance band, and the rock band.

I-V 5. Present-day composers are experimenting with new tonal effects in their compositions through various tape and electronic techniques.

• Play examples of electronic music at every instructional level, and emphasize unusual and creative ways of composing music. Note the different tone qualities and sound sources resulting from today's experimentation with tape and electronic processes. Some examples include: RL—4, 5, 6, 17, 72, 76, 308.
• Experiment with new and interesting sounds by shaking a paper bag filled with pebbles or sand, or hitting metal and wooden objects with mallets and other materials. Also use unusual vocal tones.
• Note effect on tone quality of a recording played at various speeds.

Also experiment with altering speeds of recorded music or voices on a tape recorder.

• Experiment with making unusual sounds on rhythm instruments and the piano, ukulele, or Autoharp. Tape record these sounds, and arrange them into a meaningful musical work. Devise original notational system to record the music for future reference.

• Tape record sounds in the environment, and experiment with producing distorted sounds on the tape recorder, using different speeds. Note tonal effects.

• Note the use of electronic devices with traditional instrumental or vocal tone colors (examples: RL—17, 72).

• Compare the feedback on a microphone with certain sounds used in electronic music. Experiment with the microphone and tape recorder in making original music.

• Play examples of music by modern composers who use tones of indefinite pitch, mechanical sounds, and literal sounds. Experiment with creating musical works using unusual sound sources. Devise techniques to notate these compositions.

Two

RHYTHM

BASIC CONCEPT:

Rhythm is the measured flow of tones of varying duration.

KEY TERMS:

beat, tempo, meter, melodic rhythm, rhythmic pattern, rhythmic relationships, syncopation.

I-III The *beat* is the underlying framework of regular pulses which contributes to the rhythmic flow of a musical work.

I 1. The beat is the steady recurring pulse in music. Note how the beats of "Hush Little Baby" in Ex. 2–1 coincide with the words "hush, ba-, don't, word . . . ".

> • Listen to environmental sounds having a steady beat (dripping water, ticking clock, beating heart, swishing windshield wiper). Tap the beat and imitate the object's movement.
> • Move rhythmically (clap, step, march, sway, jump, play "patty-cake" with a partner, bounce a ball, clap and snap the fingers, tap the foot and hit the knees) to a steady drum beat and to the beats of most pieces. Derive principle that most music has a steady, ongoing

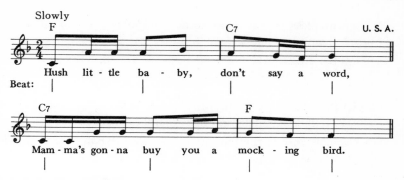

Ex. 2-1. "Hush Little Baby"

beat (notable exception: much "chance" and electronic music—see pp. 28–29).

• Use rhythm instruments to highlight the beat in music.

• Walk, run, or clap. Add drum beat and emphasize steady movement to recurring pulse.

• Picture the beat in the air or on the chalkboard as vertical (| | | |) or horizontal (– – – –) lines of the same length.

• Use a metronome to show that the beat, once established, is usually kept constant.

• Set the beat before performing a work by counting, playing chords, or moving the hands in the desired tempo (see pp. 157–158).

• Set a beat. Clap four times, rest for four beats, and clap again. Have students "think" the beat during the rests and enter on the next series of claps. Also play a recording and clap the beat. Lower volume and have students continue to clap. Turn volume up to check on the accuracy of the students' beats. Emphasize the need to keep the beat very steady. Note ongoing pulse even when the tune temporarily "rests."

I-II 2. The beat can vary considerably from piece to piece.

I 2a. The beats of one piece may move faster than those of another piece. [*Note*: for further discussion and activities on *beat* and *tempo* see this Chapter, pp. 55–58].

II 2b. Some pieces have a strong feeling of beat, while other pieces have a more subtle beat.

• Compare the subtle beats of lullabies with the definite, strong beats of most dances and marches. Use strong movements for strong beats, and limited movements for subtle beats.

• Play or sing "Silent Night," "Greensleeves," "Marching to Pretoria," and "Jingle Bells." Note differences in qualities of the beat.

Also compare instrumental works and note varying qualities of beats. Examples include—

SUBTLE FEELING OF BEAT: RL—57, 58, 63, 64, 67, 68, 78, 94, 104, 105, 206, 227, 251, 303, and many lullabies and electronic works

STRONG FEELING OF BEAT: RL—62, 74, 96, 100, 111, 189, 190, 221, 263, 319, 320, and most marches and dances

• Use appropriate rhythm instruments and dynamic levels to highlight varying beat qualities.

I-II   3. The beat within a piece may change by moving faster or slower (see discussion on *tempo* in this chapter, pp. 55–58, for related activities).

II-III   4. In a series of beats, one beat is usually stronger and more accented than other beats in the group (see next section for discussion and appropriate activities for developing this understanding of *meter*).

II-V   Music may be rhythmically organized in systematic groupings of accented and unaccented beats called *meter*.

II-III   1. Some rhythmic beats in a musical work seem stronger or more accented than others. There are both *strong* and *weak* beats in a composition, as seen in Ex. 2–2. Note that the strong beat is the stressed or accented beat (primary beat), and normally occurs on the first beat of each measure. The strong beat is also followed by one or more weak beats.

Ex. 2-2. "We Wish You a Merry Christmas," Showing Strong (—) and Weak (◡) Beats

We wish you a mer-ry Christ-mas, We wish you a mer-ry Christ-mas

• Show accented, strong beats of tunes by clapping heavily or in a "patty-cake" style with a partner; swinging arms, stamping, swaying, or bending; and doing one type of movement (jump, hit the desk) on the strong beat and another type of movement on the weaker beats.

• Chant *"strong,* weak, weak" or *"loud,* soft, *loud,* soft" to indicate the accented and unaccented beats of music moving in 3's or 2's.

• When singing, ask: "Which word or word-syllable has the strong beat?" Point to important words of the text and note how they often coincide with the strong beats.

• Use two types of rhythm instruments to accompany a piece—one for the strong beat and one for the weaker beats.

II-V   2. The accent groupings of beats usually make music swing in 2's, 3's, or multiples of these. The manner in which the accented and unaccented beats in a work are grouped may be symbolized by a *meter signature* appearing at the beginning of the music.

> • Play a steady beat on the drum, systematically accenting various beats; e.g., every other beat, or every fourth beat. Students move rhythmically to the beats, showing an accent with a stronger body movement. Determine the metric grouping of beats. Clap and move rhythmically to show grouping.
> • Relate activities described for strong, weak beats (p. 32) for determining the metric grouping of beats.
> • Sing a familiar song. Set metronome at various metric groupings or play several metric patterns on the drum. Students listen for grouping which fits the music's rhythmic flow.
> • Use the following steps to determine meter of many pieces by ear: (1) feel and clap the beat; (2) move to the strong beat; and (3) say "1" on the strong beat and "2, (3), . . . " on the weak beats, note the final number in the series, and determine the number of beats in each metric grouping.
> • Sing, play, and move to many tunes which have beats moving or swinging in units or groups of *two* (sounded "*one*-two"), with the strong beat on the first pulse and the weaker beat on the second pulse; *three* (sounded "*one*-two-three"), with the strong beat on the first pulse, and the weaker beats on the second and third pulses; and *four* (sounded "*one*-two-three-four"), with the strong beat occurring on pulse one and the weaker beats on the second, third, and fourth beats. Appropriate examples are—

MUSIC MOVING IN 2'S: S—17, 19, 20, 57, 64, 69, 70, 92, 100, 111, 121, 131, 132, 133, 135, 143, 146
RL—7, 24, 41, 46, 79, 80, 109, 118, 148, 157, 167, 181, 286, 291, 296, 304, 306, 317
MUSIC MOVING IN 3'S: S—2, 5, 29, 35, 54, 83, 91, 98, 106, 114, 118, 123, 126, 142
RL—20, 25, 47, 92, 111, 119, 147, 170, 183, 219, 232, 265, 316
MUSIC MOVING IN 4'S: S—3, 4, 6, 7, 9, 10, 21, 44, 45, 46, 63, 81, 94, 112, 120, 137, 138
RL—11, 89, 97, 98, 110, 116, 121, 132, 143, 196, 201, 251, 284, 311

> • Perform and listen to many songs and instrumental works to illustrate how musical beats may swing or move in groups of *six*, with an accent on the first beat and a lesser accent on the fourth beat (count: **1** 23 **4** 56). Note that the music is often lilting, swaying, and rocking in character. In Ex. 2–3 observe that the beats are grouped in

six, with the slight feeling of three to a group caused by the primary
and secondary accents felt on beats 1 and 4.

Ex. 2-3. "Night Herding Song"

Examples of music moving in metric patterns of six include—
SONGS: S—32, 42, 47, 58, 85, 115, 119, 129
INSTRUMENTAL WORKS: RL—60, 99, 103, 186, 235, 253

• Use ∕∕ (for 2's), ∕∕∕ (for 3's), ∕∕∕∕ (for 4's), and

∕∕∕∕∕∕ (for 6's). Also use ∕∕ , ∕∕∕ , >— , ∕² ³ , and
            1 2   1 2 3   1 2

quarter notes with lines underneath (♩ ♩ ♩ ♩) to indicate strong
and weak beats. Introduce students to the common symbolism for
strong and weak beats (— and ◡). Indicate the ∕² ³ of a metric
pattern as — ◡ ◡ .

• Recite a poem or words of a song. Locate the syllables and words
which coincide with the beat. Use activities mentioned above to
determine the meter.

• Tip hands to the meter, as ꙮ for "*1–2*," ꙮ for "*1–2–3*,"

ꙮ for "*1–2–3–4*," and ꙮ for "*1–2–3–4–5–6*."

At levels III and above, give students opportunities to conduct songs
and practice movements with recorded works moving in:

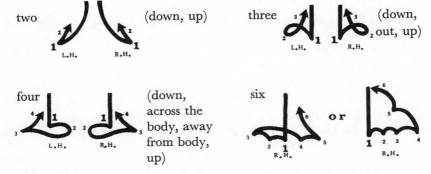

• Symbolize feeling for beats of a piece with vertical lines on the

chalkboard, as | | | | | | . Determine location of accented beats.

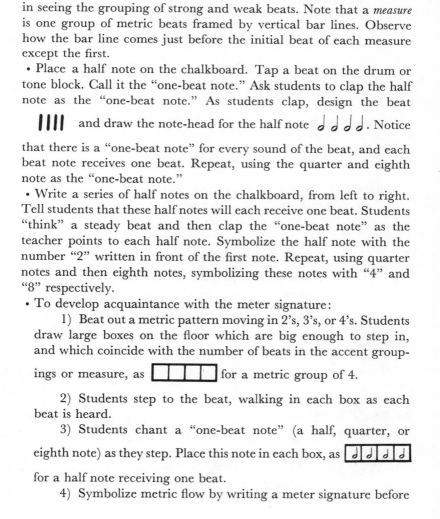

Frame each metric grouping of beats with either a box or circle, as

(1)(1)(1)(1) for music moving in two's, or |1|1| |1|1| for music

moving in 3's. Call the grouping of beats a "measure."

• Sing or play a tune. Design beats on chalkboard, using vertical lines. Determine metric grouping. Divide beat marks with vertical

bar lines, as: /   for 4,

or   / / / / / / / / / / / / / / / /   for 2. Show how *bar lines*

measure the metric flow. Introduce bar lines and measures as aids in seeing the grouping of strong and weak beats. Note that a *measure* is one group of metric beats framed by vertical bar lines. Observe how the bar line comes just before the initial beat of each measure except the first.

• Place a half note on the chalkboard. Tap a beat on the drum or tone block. Call it the "one-beat note." Ask students to clap the half note as the "one-beat note." As students clap, design the beat

| | | | and draw the note-head for the half note ♩ ♩ ♩ ♩ . Notice

that there is a "one-beat note" for every sound of the beat, and each beat note receives one beat. Repeat, using the quarter and eighth note as the "one-beat note."

• Write a series of half notes on the chalkboard, from left to right. Tell students that these half notes will each receive one beat. Students "think" a steady beat and then clap the "one-beat note" as the teacher points to each half note. Symbolize the half note with the number "2" written in front of the first note. Repeat, using quarter notes and then eighth notes, symbolizing these notes with "4" and "8" respectively.

• To develop acquaintance with the meter signature:

    1) Beat out a metric pattern moving in 2's, 3's, or 4's. Students draw large boxes on the floor which are big enough to step in, and which coincide with the number of beats in the accent group-

ings or measure, as [| | |] for a metric group of 4.

    2) Students step to the beat, walking in each box as each beat is heard.

    3) Students chant a "one-beat note" (a half, quarter, or eighth note) as they step. Place this note in each box, as [♩|♩|♩|♩]

for a half note receiving one beat.

    4) Symbolize metric flow by writing a meter signature before

the first box, placing the "2" first to show that the half note is the "one-beat note," and then a "4" above it to show that there are *four* half notes to each measure or metric group ($\frac{4}{2}$).

5) Students step to the beat, walking in each box as the beat is heard. Teacher taps simple rhythmic patterns. Students notice beats where tones move twice as fast or slow as the beat. Place the notes for these patterns in the boxes, as ♩♩♩♩♩ Continue to use this activity in developing an understanding of the 2–1, 3–1, and 4–1 relationship between notes (see p. 46).

6) Repeat, using different rhythmic patterns in the same meter. Continue with other "one-beat notes" (♩ and ♪).

7) At a later time, write meters and patterns in blocks on paper. Expand rhythmic patterns to two or more measures. Gradually eliminate boxes, and use bar lines.

• Place eight half notes on the chalkboard. Clap a metric grouping in four, accenting the first and fifth half notes. Students discover the accented and unaccented beats, and insert bar lines after the fourth and last notes of the series. Notice that the half note (♩ or "2") receives the beat, and that there are four (4) beats in each metric grouping or measure. Indicate ♩ ♩ ♩ ♩ $\frac{4}{2}$ as "four half notes."

Repeat this technique many times, using other note values (♩ and ♪) and metric groupings. Use the following symbols interchangeably until the various kinds of metric groupings have meaning:

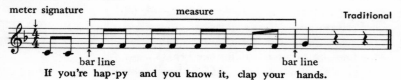

• Show that meter can be symbolized by a *meter* (*time*) *signature* found after the key signature at the beginning of the music, as in Ex. 2–4.

Ex. 2-4. "If You're Happy"

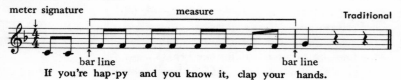

If you're hap-py and you know it, clap your hands.

• Find the two numbers in the meter signature, as $\frac{4}{4}$ (pronounced "four-four") in Ex. 2–4. Discover that the lower number indicates a certain note value, as 2 (half note—♩), 4 (quarter note—♩), or 8 (eighth note—♪), while the top number indicates the number of these notes or their rhythmic equivalent required to make a complete measure. Thus, in $\frac{4}{4}$ meter there are 4 quarter notes or their equivalent in the metric grouping, with the quarter note (4) being the basic note value. Call attention to other meter signatures:

METER SIGNATURE	BASIC NOTE VALUE	NUMBER OF THESE NOTES OR EQUIVALENT IN MEASURE

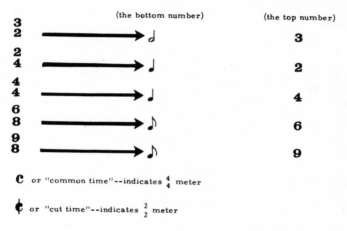

	(the bottom number)	(the top number)
3 **2**	⟶ ♩	**3**
2 **4**	⟶ ♩	**2**
4 **4**	⟶ ♩	**4**
6 **8**	⟶ ♪	**6**
9 **8**	⟶ ♪	**9**

𝐂 or "common time"--indicates $\frac{4}{4}$ meter

𝄵 or "cut time"--indicates $\frac{2}{2}$ meter

[*Note*: In many cases the top number of the meter signature is equivalent to the number of beats felt in a measure, while the bottom number indicates the note value receiving the beat. For example, in "Silent Night" (in $\frac{6}{8}$ meter) six beats to a measure are felt, with the eighth note receiving a beat. On the other hand, "Three Blind Mice," also written in $\frac{6}{8}$ meter, has a fast tempo, and the basic metric flow is felt in two (*1*, 2), as described on pp. 40–41. The number of beats felt per measure depends on the *tempo* of the music and not the meter signature.]

• Determine aurally the meter of a composition (see pp. 33–35). Find the meter signature at the beginning of the music and compare answer with the top number of the meter signature.
• Perform and observe notation of familiar tunes. Ask: "What are the two numbers at the beginning of the music? What does the top (or bottom) number mean? What note is the basic unit? How many of these notes will be found in a measure?"

• Place notation of melody on chalkboard without the meter signature or bar lines. Play the melody. Students follow notation and determine meter signature and correct placement of bar lines. For example, the meter signature for ♩♩♩♩ | ♩ ♩ | could be ⁴₄ or ²₂.

• Direct attention to metric symbols by asking questions as: "How many measures (or bar lines) are on the first line? Can you 'frame' the third measure of the second line with your fingers? What beat-note unit does the music start with? What word falls on the second beat-note unit of measure three?"

• Write a meter signature followed by rhythmic patterns on the chalkboard. Students insert bar lines in correct locations and clap the rhythm. Also place bar lines in wrong places and ask for corrections.

• Write various rhythmic patterns on chalkboard, using the appropriate meter signatures and bar lines. Students number where the basic note value or its equivalent falls, as: ⁶₄♩ ♫♩ ♩ ♩♩ |
$\quad$ 1 $\quad$ 2 $\quad$ 3 4 5 6
♬♩♩ ♩ ♩ ♫♩ ‖ . Students then clap the rhythms as
1 $\quad$ 2 3 4 5 6
the teacher sets the beat.

• Create, read, and perform rhythmic patterns written in various meters (see also pp. 41–50).

• Students fill in measures of ²₄, ³₄, ⁴₄, ²₂, ³₂, ⁴₂, ³₈, and ⁶₈ meter with rhythmic patterns, and clap these rhythms.

• Write a particular rhythm using different meter signatures, as:

⁴₄♩ ♫♩ ♩ ,   ⁴₂♩ ♩♩♩ ♩ ,   ⁴₈♪ ♫♩ ♪ ♪ .

• Find music with C or ₵ for the meter signature. Sing or play the music and move rhythmically to it. Relate this to the meter signature for music moving in 4 (C = ⁴₄) and 2 (₵ = ²₂).

• Make a chart of meter signatures and equivalent rhythmic patterns. Draw a line from the meter signature in one column to a rhythmic pattern in the second column which would use that signature.

• Listen to and sing pieces starting on beats other than the first beat, as: S—11, 17, 24, 53, 54, 106, 132, 142; and the main themes from RL—10, 46, 128, 246, 304, 319. Clap the rhythm of the tune and determine the beat number on which it starts. Practice clapping rhythms beginning on note units other than the first one (see pp. 50–51).

• Show that some accent groupings of beats in music move in five, seven, and other combinations of two and three. For example, accent groupings of beats in seven—a combination of three and four beats grouped together—can be heard in Donaldson's "Camels," in which the following rhythmic pattern in $\frac{7}{8}$ meter is played continuously by the strings as an accompaniment:

• Find examples of tunes using less common meter signatures as: $\frac{2}{2}$, $\frac{3}{2}$, $\frac{4}{2}$, $\frac{5}{4}$, $\frac{6}{4}$, and $\frac{7}{4}$; and $\frac{5}{8}$, $\frac{7}{8}$, $\frac{9}{8}$, and $\frac{12}{8}$ (see especially Books Four through Six of any of the basal music series for examples). Clap the rhythmic patterns and sing the melodies. Also listen to, move rhythmically to, and follow the notation of instrumental works using less familiar meter signatures. Examples include: RL—10, 69, 122, 124, 144(theme 3), 200, 207(theme 3), 209.

• Provide practice in following and clapping rhythms in combination meters such as $\frac{5}{4}$ and $\frac{5}{8}$, $\frac{7}{4}$ and $\frac{7}{8}$, and $\frac{11}{4}$ and $\frac{11}{8}$.

• Listen to music, including many chants and musics of primitive cultures, and electronic music, where the beats are not regularly grouped into accented and unaccented patterns, or where recurring accents are absent, as in: RL—4, 6, 42, 58, 64, 65, 67, 104, introductions to 108, 130, and 144, 173, 293, 303.

• Encourage students to create original tunes and chants which use no recurring metric pattern or meter signature.

IV-V 3. Accent groupings of beats are usually constant within a piece, but may change. Much contemporary music and music of various cultures are characterized by changing meters within a piece, and irregularity of metric groupings. The well-known "Shenandoah" in Ex. 2–5 contains several examples of metric change.

Ex. 2-5. "Shenandoah"

U. S. A.

Oh Shen-an-doah___ I long to hear you, Way hey! you roll-ing ri - ver. Oh Shen-an-doah___ I long to hear you.

• Symbolize metric changes with "line" notation, as

$\frac{4}{4}$ ⁄/// $\frac{3}{4}$ ⁄// ⁄// ⁄// $\frac{4}{4}$ ⁄/// $\frac{3}{4}$ ⁄// for "Shenandoah."

• Compare effect of saying a sentence several times, placing accents on different syllables or words. Experiment with changing accents and the meter of familiar tunes, as playing "Jingle Bells" in $\frac{3}{4}$ rather than $\frac{2}{4}$ meter. Note the effect of metric change on the character of the music.

• Practice clapping a steady beat with alternating metric groupings,

as: (musical notation)

Devise various rhythmic patterns with alternating meter signatures.

Also use accumulative accent, as (musical notation)

(musical notation) and progressive accent, as (musical notation)

(musical notation) . Devise bodily movements

to show accents.

• Use word phrases to illustrate changing meters, as:

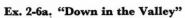
Ma - ry   likes   ice   cream, Ma - ry   likes   ice   cream

• Perform and examine notation of works whose middle sections change meter, as: S—22, 49, 125 and RL—26, 163, 192, 280, 310. Notice change of mood caused by alteration of meter and tempo. Also listen to and identify metric changes which occur frequently (RL—21, 40, 48, 124, 163, 204, 270, 276, 277) or occasionally (S—43, 116, 138 and RL—43, 87, 123, 178, 207, 209, 234, 295, 300).

V 4. Some meter signatures may indicate groupings of 2, 3, 4, 6, 9, or 12 beats, but the music may be felt in one's, two's, three's or four's if the tempo is fairly fast. In Ex. 2-6a the accent groupings are felt in three rather than nine, while in Ex. 2-6b the accent groupings are felt in two rather than four.

Ex. 2-6a, "Down in the Valley"

Ex. 2-6b. "Marching to Pretoria"

• Clap the beats of many songs. Notice the occasional discrepancy between how the beat is felt and the top number of the meter signature. Also listen to, and examine notation of songs written in one meter but moving in another meter, as $\frac{3}{4}$ meter, but moving in one: (S—13, 23, 83, 91, 102, 128); $\frac{4}{4}$ meter, but moving in two: (S—14, 34, 65, 102, 132, 133); and $\frac{6}{8}$ meter, but moving in two: (S—39, 100, 104, 110, 136, 140, 143). Play examples and move rhythmically to instrumental works written in $\frac{6}{8}$ meter, but moving in two: (RL—9, 25, 107, 176, 226, 237, 250, 252, 260, 319); $\frac{9}{8}$ meter, but moving in three: (RL—10); and $\frac{12}{8}$ meter, but moving in four: (RL—122, 200).

• Design metric grouping of fast music in meters such as $\frac{9}{8}$ ($||$ $|$

$|$ $||$ $||$) and $\frac{4}{4}$ ($|$ $|$ $|$) to show how music can be written in one meter but felt in another meter.

• Show difficulty of conducting (see p. 34) all the beats in a piece written in a meter signature of $\frac{3}{4}$, $\frac{6}{8}$, or $\frac{9}{8}$ when the main accents are felt as 1, 2, and 3, respectively. Illustrate conducting and "tipping" patterns for $\frac{3}{4}$, $\frac{6}{8}$, $\frac{9}{8}$, and $\frac{4}{4}$ which move at a fast tempo ($\frac{3}{4}$—conducted as "one"; $\frac{6}{8}$—conducted in two; $\frac{9}{8}$—conducted in three; and $\frac{4}{4}$—conducted in two).

• Indicate main beats of music written in one meter, but felt in another, by writing beat numbers under the rhythm, as in the rhythm for "When Johnny Comes Marching Home":

• Slowly play a tune in $\frac{6}{8}$ meter as "Night Herding Song" on p. 34. Increase the speed and note how the basic pulse is altered to a feeling of two beats.

I-V Tones and rests of varying duration may be organized into groups of rhythmic patterns called *melodic rhythm*. These rhythmic patterns are fused together with the beat to create the rhythmic movement in music.

I-V 1. The movement or flow of tones in a melody is the *melodic rhythm* of a piece. For example, the melodic rhythm of "America" begins:

I-II 1a. The melodic rhythm is comprised of groupings of long and short tones and silences called *rhythmic patterns*.

• Clap an interesting rhythmic pattern from any tune, as "pop! goes the weasel" ( ), "e-i-e-i-o" ( ), and "nick-nack, paddy-wack" ( ). Repeat each pattern several times and have students join in on the clapping. Step out these patterns and highlight them with rhythm instruments.

• Clap and stamp to rhythmic patterns in poems, jingles, or sentences, as "Humpty Dumpty sat on a wall," (— - — - — - - —)

or (♩. ♫ ♩. ♫ ♫♫ ♩). Design in "blank" notation (see p. 5).

• Listen to and imitate rhythmic patterns in the environment, as the gallop of horses' hoofs and the chirping of birds.

• Chant the words of both familiar and unfamiliar songs. Show how the syllables and words of a song often determine the song's rhythmic patterns and melodic rhythm. Relate hyphenation of words to rhythmic patterns.

• Clap the rhythm of a student's full name, as Timothy Jones (- - - —), and ask whose name was clapped. Compare names which have the same rhythmic pattern. Also identify and clap rhythmic patterns of other familiar words and phrases.

• Clap or play a rhythmic pattern. Devise words to suit the pattern. Also send messages, using drum rhythms to beat out the rhythm of the words.

• Clap the beat or melodic rhythm of a familiar tune, and identify which rhythmic element is being clapped. Students then join in on the clapping. Repeat procedure, using a student leader.

• Improvise rhythmic patterns over a steady drum beat.

• Sing a tune, beating out the rhythm of the first phrase on the drum. Students continue by playing or clapping the rhythm of the next phrase.

• Isolate a rhythmic pattern in a tune, as "falling down" (♩ ♩ ♩) from "London Bridge." Listen for the same pattern in other tunes, as "Are You Sleeping" (the "ding, ding, dong" pattern) and the beginning of "Jingle Bells" and "This Old Man." Repeat procedure, using other tunes:

PATTERN	WORDS OF SONGS
$\frac{4}{4}$ ♩ ♩ ♩ | ♩ ♩ ♩ |	"hot cross buns," "lightly row," "three blind mice,"
$\frac{6}{8}$ ♩ ♪♩ ♪|♩. ♩ ♪|	"eency weency spider," "I'm a little teapot,"
$\frac{4}{4}$ ♩|♩. ♫ ♩ |♩. ♫|	"O beautiful for spacious skies," "should auld acquaintance be forgot,"
$\frac{2}{4}$ ♩ ♩ |♪♩.	"Oh Susanna," "go down, Moses,"

• Clap and play a repeated rhythmic pattern to accompany songs and recordings. Use simple, then more complex patterns. Gradually add two or more contrasting rhythmic patterns.

• Clap a rhythmic pattern. Sing or play a tune and ask students to raise hands each time they hear the pattern.

• Sing a familiar song. Ask students to "think" the rhythmic pattern of a selected phrase or group of words. Clap several patterns, asking students to raise hands when the pattern which fits the phrase or words is heard.

• Design rhythmic patterns on chalkboard in "blank" (line) notation (see p. 5). Show that symbols of the same length indicate tones of the same duration, as in the beginning of "The Farmer in the Dell" (♪♩ ♪♩ ♪♩. ♩).

• Design the rhythm of a familiar tune on the chalkboard. Clap the rhythm as the students follow notation. Point to symbols. Repeat, stopping in the middle of the pattern. Students locate place where you stopped. Also design the rhythm, making an error. Students locate the error and then clap the correct rhythm as they follow the notation.

• Place several rhythms on the chalkboard, using "blank" notation. Number them. Clap one rhythm. Students indicate which rhythm was clapped. A student then claps a rhythm and chooses a classmate to point to the rhythm which was clapped.

• Clap two rhythmic patterns, with the second one being the same or different from the first. Students indicate whether the patterns are alike or contrasting.

• Ask: "What song starts like this?" and clap the rhythm of a familiar tune. Note similarities between the beginning rhythmic patterns of songs such as "Twinkle, Twinkle" and "Are You Sleeping," or "London Bridge" and "Deck the Halls."

• Ask a rhythmic question by clapping or playing a pattern as: ♩ ♩ ♫♩. Students "answer" the question by devising another rhythmic pattern, as ♫♫♩ .

• At levels III and above, sing a round or canon in two or three parts. Clap out its rhythm, as for "White Choral Bells":

Use contrasting rhythm instruments to highlight each part.

I-II   1b. A rhythmic pattern or melodic rhythm may consist of tones that are fast-moving and short (often giving a feeling of excitement and restlessness) or slow-moving and long (often giving a feeling of solemnity and peace). Rhythmic patterns frequently contain both fast and slow-moving tones, as in the opening pattern of Ex. 2–7.

Ex. 2-7. "Ten Little Indians"

• Students walk slowly. Devise rhythmic patterns which fit movement. Repeat, using movements at different speeds.

• Clap a rhythmic pattern or melodic rhythm from a familiar tune and ask questions such as: "Is this pattern fast or slow-moving, exciting or peaceful? Why? Raise your hands when the tones in the pattern move quickly (or slowly)."

• Distribute rhythm instruments. Devise exciting or quiet rhythmic patterns moving quickly or slowly.

• Play instrumental works and identify whether the melodic rhythm has fast or slow-moving tones——

FAST-MOVING MELODIC RHYTHM: RL—9, 27, 44, 54, 59, 118, 123, 157, 161, 192, 213, 243

SLOW-MOVING MELODIC RHYTHM: RL—10 (chorale theme), 89, 97, 121, 160, 173, 182, 193

II-III   1c. Rhythmic patterns and melodic rhythms may be steady and even, or unsteady and uneven (see also p. 51). Musical compositions contain a combination of steady and unsteady rhythmic movement.

• Use a steady, even bodily movement, as walking, tapping, stamping, running, or swinging to indicate an even melodic rhythm as ♩ ♩ ♩ ♩. Use an unsteady, uneven bodily movement to indicate an uneven melodic rhythm, as ♩ ♪♩ ♪ or ♩.♩♩.♩ (skipping, if in a slow tempo) and ♪♩ ♪♩ (galloping).

• Listen for even and smooth-flowing rhythmic patterns in a phrase containing the same basic note values. Identify section of the rhythm which may be uneven in movement, thereby containing notes of different duration.

• Identify the even or uneven movement of tones in the melodic rhythm and/or accompaniment of instrumental works as——

EVEN RHYTHM: RL—10(theme 1), 22, 23, 99, 156, 171, 172, 178, 187, 204, 224, 225, 228, 229, 239, and the accompaniment figure to most waltzes

UNEVEN RHYTHM: RL—25, 113, 142, 159, 186, 190, 209, 221, 260, 310, 319

Also compare sections of a single work which show a contrast in types of rhythmic movement, as: RL—26(A: even, B: uneven); 74(A: uneven, B: even); 170(A: even, B: uneven)

II-III   1d. The articulation of tones in a rhythmic pattern may vary. Frequently used methods of articulation include:

—*legato*—a smooth connection of tones without intervening pauses or accents, and indicated by a curved arch ⌒ or *slur* (see the first four notes in Ex. 2–8)

—*staccato*—a short tone, usually slightly accented, with an intervening pause between tones, and indicated by a dot above or below the note (see the dot above the E in the first and second measures of Ex. 2–8)

—*marcato*—a "marked," punched, or heavily played tone, and indicated by a small horizontal line above or below the note (see the line above the C in the last measure of Ex. 2–8)

Ex. 2-8. Massanet: "Aragonaise" from *Le Cid*

• Play a tune using *legato*, then *staccato*, and finally *marcato* articulation. Compare differences. Also listen to various pieces of music and note types of articulation used. Relate legato singing or playing to the musical phrase.

• Experiment with effect of different styles of articulation when singing or playing instruments. Emphasize the importance of articulation to help achieve the expressive content of the music.

• Identify symbols in the score which refer to articulation. Have students infer the meaning of the symbols by listening to a rendition of the work.

• Relate articulation to the various ways people speak and animals move. Also move rhythmically to music to show manner of articulation, as smooth, flowing movements for *legato*, short, light movements for *staccato*, and heavy, jagged, and accented movements for *marcato*.

• Identify various articulation styles in recorded music——

LEGATO: RL—34, 35, 52, 94, 160, 172, 176, 220, 229, 235, 251, 267, 320, and most lullabies
STACCATO: RL—98, 170, 171, 225, 254, 255, 284, 312
MARCATO: RL—12, 32, 41, 88, 98, 121, 122, 153, 172, 272, 277, 309, 317, 319

• Note how a composer can develop interest in the music through contrasting articulation. Examples include: RL—13, 65, 66, 84, 96, 110 and 115, 208, 223, 224, 231, 322.

II-V 1e. The relationship among tones and rests of different duration is an important aspect of melodic rhythm (see also p. 7). This relationship remains the same, regardless of the meter signature or tempo. Thus, ♩ = ♫, whether in $\frac{2}{4}$, $\frac{3}{2}$, or $\frac{6}{8}$ meter, or in a slow or fast tempo.

—Some tones in rhythmic patterns move twice as fast or slowly as other tones. In Ex. 2–9, the eighth notes move twice as fast as the quarter note, while the half note moves twice as slowly as the quarter note. There is a *2–1 relationship* among the time values of notes, as

$\mathbf{o} = \mathbf{\downarrow\downarrow}$ or $\mathbf{\downarrow} = \mathbf{\downarrow\downarrow}$ or $\mathbf{\downarrow} = \mathbf{\downarrow\downarrow}$ or $\mathbf{\downarrow} = \mathbf{\downarrow\downarrow}$.

Ex. 2-9. Stephen Foster: "Camptown Races"

Bet my mo-ney on the bob-tail nag, some bo-dy bet on the bay.

—Some tones in rhythmic patterns move four times as fast or slowly as other tones. In Ex. 2–9, the sixteenth notes move four times as fast as the quarter notes. There is a *4–1 relationship* among the time values of notes, as: $\mathbf{o} = \mathbf{\downarrow\downarrow\downarrow\downarrow}$, $\mathbf{\downarrow} = \mathbf{\downarrow\downarrow\downarrow\downarrow}$, $\mathbf{\downarrow} = \mathbf{\downarrow\downarrow\downarrow\downarrow}$, and $\mathbf{\downarrow} = \mathbf{\downarrow\downarrow\downarrow\downarrow}$.

—Some tones in rhythmic patterns move three times as fast or slowly as other tones, as $\mathbf{\downarrow\cdot} = \mathbf{\downarrow\downarrow\downarrow}$ or $\mathbf{\downarrow} = \mathbf{\downarrow\downarrow\downarrow}$ (*triplet*). There is a *3–1 relationship* among the time values of certain notes, as $\mathbf{\downarrow\cdot} = \mathbf{\downarrow\downarrow\downarrow}$ and $\mathbf{\downarrow} = \mathbf{\overline{\downarrow\downarrow\downarrow}}$ (see discussion of function of the dot, pp. 8, 10).

• Repeat activities utilizing "blank" (line) notation in section 2a, p. 49, substituting standard notation. Also see the many activities described in discussion of relationships between notes and their values on pp. 6–8.

• Relate sound of rhythmic patterns and corresponding physical

movements to the visual representation of tones. Basic steps include:
(1) hearing and clapping the rhythm; (2) seeing the rhythm in notation, and following it; and (3) clapping the rhythm as one follows it.

• Move to rhythmic values as "step, step, hold" (♩ ♩ ♩) or "run,
run, run, hold" (♫♫♩.).

• Use activities listed on pp. 49–50, in which stress is placed on
rhythms which move with the beat, or faster or slower than the beat.
Focus on moving two, three, or four times as fast or slow as the beat,
and notate, as appropriate.

• Students devise games for matching equivalent time values of notes,
as:

• Provide practice in following and clapping characteristic rhythmic
patterns, emphasizing note relationships, as:

Place various patterns on flash cards and charts, and provide drill
with the most common rhythmic patterns.

• Use word syllables for each type of note in a pattern, as: "ta, ti-ti,
ta-ah" for ♩ ♫♩.

• Write rhythmic patterns in "blank" notation. Guide the students
to transcribe these to standard notation by notating three aspects
of the rhythmic flow, as follows (for "Ten Little Indians," p. 44):

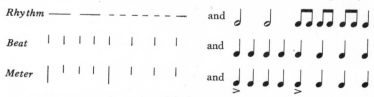

• Each student selects and notates the rhythmic pattern of a familiar
tune from his songbook. Other students clap the pattern and identify
the name of the tune.

• Devise matching game, where students draw a line matching rhythm to title of song or rhythmic pattern of words.

• Add a rhythmic accompaniment to a tune, notate it, and follow the notation as the pattern is repeated throughout the work. Guide students to read and then devise rhythm scores for accompaniments played on rhythm instruments.

• Place various patterns on the chalkboard. Clap one of them and ask students to identify the rhythm they hear. Repeat with other patterns. Individual students then select and tap a rhythm for others to identify.

• Notate and clap a rhythmic pattern and find examples of it in a tune. Also place many kinds of notes on separate pieces of large oaktag. Clap a rhythmic pattern and ask students to choose the cards which represent the rhythm.

• Students fill in several measures with interesting rhythmic patterns and then clap these patterns.

• Place rhythmic notation of familiar tune on the chalkboard, with one or more errors. Students locate these errors, correct them, and clap the rhythm.

• In analyzing and sight-reading a new song, ask questions as: "What do you notice about the rhythmic patterns in measures 1 and 5? (they are the same) Why are they the same? (they look the same) Where does the rhythm move slowly, fast? Which pattern sounds like this? (clap a pattern) Can you find a pattern with even (or uneven) movement? What pattern may be difficult for us to clap? Can you chant the words according to their rhythmic patterns?"

• Give rhythmic dictation by clapping rhythms and asking students to notate them. Also put the words of a song on the chalkboard, chant them, determine the accents and meter, and guide students to notate the rhythmic patterns. Compare with notation from song text. For example, determine the rhythmic notation of "Go Tell Aunt Rhodie":

II-V 2. There is a relationship between a musical work's rhythmic patterns and melodic rhythm, its beat, and its meter.

II 2a. The underlying steady beat of a composition coincides with the melodic rhythm to create the music's rhythmic flow.

• Use "blank" notation to differentiate melodic rhythm and beat, as:

RHYTHM — — — — — —

(for "My country, 'tis of thee")

BEAT   — — — — — —

• Sing a familiar song. Ask: "Am I clapping its beat or rhythm?" Students move rhythmically to differentiate between the two. Add rhythmic accompaniment, emphasizing the beat and then the rhythm of the tune. Divide class in half, with each group playing either the beat or melodic rhythm. Later, divide the group into three parts—for the beat, the metric accent, and the melodic rhythm. Reverse parts so that all students receive an opportunity to perform all parts of the rhythmic flow.

• Listen to and play the accompaniment to a familiar tune on the ukulele, Autoharp, or piano. Note that the accompaniment usually keeps a steady beat under the melodic rhythm.

• Write vertical lines over the rhythm to indicate where the beat occurs. Substitute these lines with the "one-beat note" (see pp. 35–36). For example:

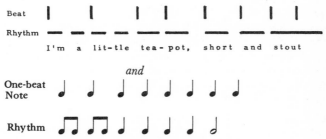

Clap the rhythm as the notation is followed.

II-III 2b. The rhythmic pattern and underlying beat of a piece are seldom identical. The tones of a rhythmic pattern may move:

—exactly with the beat, as in the beginning sections of "Are You

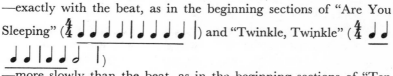

—more slowly than the beat, as in the beginning sections of "Ten

Little Indians" ($\frac{4}{4}$ 𝅗𝅥 𝅗𝅥 | ♫♫♫𝅗𝅥 |) and "Go Tell Aunt Rhodie" ($\frac{4}{4}$ 𝅗𝅥 ♩♩| 𝅗𝅥 𝅗𝅥 |).

—faster than the beat, as in "Camptown Races" ($\frac{2}{4}$ ♪| ♫♫ ♫♫ | ♫♫ ♩|) and "If You're Happy" ($\frac{4}{4}$ ♫ | ♫♫♫♫ |𝅗𝅥 𝄽 𝄽 ‖)

- Clap a steady beat with the students. Then clap a faster or slower rhythmic pattern. Identify when the rhythm moves faster or slower than the beat. Ask students to create their own rhythmic patterns against the basic beat. Step or clap to the rhythmic patterns of many tunes as the beat is played on a rhythm instrument. Note where the steps or claps coincide with, or move faster or slower than the beat.
- Walk or clap to a steady beat, and then move faster or slower than the beat. Devise a rhythmic accompaniment to a familiar tune. Ask if the accompaniment is moving with the beat, or faster or slower than the beat. Combine two, then three accompaniments—one moving faster, one moving slower, and one moving with the beat.
- Identify the word or syllable of a song where the beat occurs. Note that some beats have more than one tone (word-syllable) occurring with them.
- One group sets a steady beat, while another improvises rhythmic patterns which move faster or slower than the beat.

II-III 2c. A rhythmic pattern whose tones do not take up all of the beats will include a period of silence or rest (see discussion and activities related to the meaning of *rest* in music, p. 8).

III-IV 2d. A rhythmic pattern usually begins with its most important tone on the first beat of the metric grouping. Occasionally one, two, or three unaccented tones precede the most important tone and lead to the accented beat. Notice how the first tones of "Dixie" in Ex. 2–10 precede the first primary accent of the tune's beat.

- Compare songs beginning on the strong beat (down-beat) and weak beat (up-beat, pick-up beat, *anacrusis*). "Mary Had a Little Lamb," "Old Folks at Home," and "America" all begin on the strong beat, while "The Farmer in the Dell," "Clementine," and "America the Beautiful" begin on the up-beat. Sing familiar songs and classify them as beginning on the first beat or another beat.
- Listen to many tunes from instrumental works beginning on beats other than the primary accent (beat one), and aurally identify the beat on which the theme starts. Appropriate examples include: RL—25, 30, 47, 51, 110, 172, 179, 246, 247, 251, 284, 313.
- Look at the notation of a tune. Observe that many tunes do not begin on the first beat and that they have an incomplete measure

preceding the first bar line and a complementary measure at the end. Clap the rhythm, emphasizing the accuracy of starting on the correct beat.

III-V   2e. The beat may be divided evenly or unevenly by a tune's rhythmic patterns. The rhythmic patterns in "Dixie" in Ex. 2–10 illustrate the even and uneven subdivision of beats.

Ex. 2-10. Daniel D. Emmett: "Dixie"

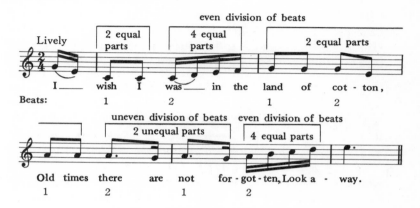

- Use activities designed to develop aural awareness of even and uneven movement of tones (see pp. 44–45).
- Clap the various rhythmic patterns in a tune, and categorize them as even or uneven in movement.
- Devise rhythmic patterns and accompaniments which evenly or unevenly divide the beat.

IV-V   2f. When a rhythmic pattern is arranged so that its most important tone does not coincide with the strong beat in the meter, the pattern is said to be *syncopated*. Syncopation results when the expected accent on a strong beat is replaced by an unexpected accent on a weak beat or between two beats. In "Swing Low, Sweet Chariot" in Ex. 2–11 the long tone (the quarter note) in measure 1 is not on the accented beat. There is a shifting of the accent to between the beats, and this accounts for the syncopated rhythmic pattern. Note that the "short-long" pattern in measure 2 is also syncopated.

Ex. 2-11. "Swing Low, Sweet Chariot"

A syncopated effect may be achieved by placing:

—a short tone on the beat, followed by a longer tone on the unaccented part of the measure (see measures 1 and 2 in Ex. 2–11)

—an accent on a tone that is normally unaccented (see the final measure of the Rimsky-Korsakov theme in Ex. 2–12)

—a rest on the beat, with tones sounding after the beat (see the beginning of Ex. 2–12, which begins on beat 5 and after the secondary accent on beat 4)

—a tie from an unaccented to an accented tone, thus sustaining the unaccented tone through the accent, and shifting the normally expected accent (see Ex. 2–12, where a tie in each measure shifts the accent from beat 4—the secondary accent in $\frac{6}{8}$ meter—to beat 3)

Ex. 2-12. Rimsky-Korsakov: "Theme" from *Scheherazade*

• Students *at all levels* should gain experience in singing and listening to syncopated rhythms. Highlight these rhythms by stepping them out, clapping them, and adding rhythm instruments to them. Examples of syncopation occur in the following——

SONGS: S—19, 23, 26, 38, 48, 55, 59, 69, 92, 107, 109, 127, 134, 137, and most Negro spirituals and songs from Latin America
INSTRUMENTAL WORKS: RL—19, 41, 62, 85, 91, 142, 147, 202, 249, 258, 259, 272, 277, 284, 301, 315, 321, and many pieces depicting or originating from Latin America, or written in the jazz idiom.

• Clap syncopated rhythms against a steady beat of an instrument or metronome.

• Teach syncopated rhythms through the use of ties, as:

• Note frequency of short—long—short patterns in syncopated rhythms, as: ♩ o ♩; ♩ ♩ ♩; ♪♩ ♪; and ♫ ♩.

• For fast pieces in ²⁄₄ or ⁴⁄₄ meter, tap the foot on the strong beat and clap on the weak or unaccented beats, thereby creating a syncopated effect with the louder clapping sound.

• Take rhythmic patterns from familiar tunes and syncopate them, using accents on weak beats, rests, and ties, as:

	Song	**Words**
A	Hot Cross Buns	Hot cross buns, hot cross buns,
B	Skip to My Lou	Skip, skip, skip to my lou,
C	Mary Had a Little Lamb	Mary had a little lamb,
D	Row, Row, Row Your Boat	Row, row, row your boat,

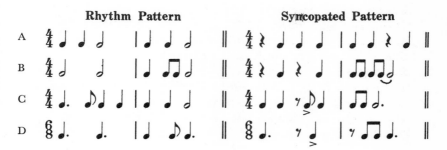

Also change selected syncopated rhythms to even movement and note effect on mood. Example: ♩ ♩ ♪ ♩. to ♩ ♩ ♩ ♩

O Su - san - na   O Su - san - na

IV-V   2g. The musics of various cultural areas (Southern United States, Latin America, the Caribbean, Southeast Asia, the Middle East, the Slavic countries), as well as jazz, popular music, and much contemporary music, are characterized by extensive use of complex rhythmic patterns, including syncopation and polyrhythms.

• Students at all levels should be given ample opportunity to listen to and respond to all types of music which have rhythmic complexity. Examples of such works, in addition to the works cited for unusual meters (p. 39), lack of regular accent (p. 39), metric change (pp. 39–40), and syncopation (pp. 51–53) are——

TWO AGAINST THREE: RL—103, 238, 257(section 2), 302
TWO SIMULTANEOUS METERS: RL—48, 109, 132, 149, 275(near the end), 302

POLYRHYTHMS: RL—21, 47(middle section), 61, 116(combination of themes 2, 3), 268, 277
JAZZ RHYTHMS: RL—21, 84, 166, 249, 276, 301, 321

• Use activities related to meter (pp. 39–40) and syncopation (pp. 51–53) to develop understandings of complex rhythms in music.

• Physically respond to the rhythmic elements of popular tunes, especially those which contain rhythmic complexity and interest. Clap the rhythmic patterns of the melody and/or accompaniment and move to the rhythm. Encourage students to bring in sheet music for rhythmic analysis of the notation.

• Play any piece of music. Encourage simple, and then more complex rhythmic accompaniments using patterns not in the melodic rhythm.

• Use rhythm instrument accompaniments to highlight rhythmic features of selected popular tunes and works in the jazz idiom.

• Have one group clap twice as fast as a given beat, while another group claps three times as fast. Switch parts. Also use metronome, having students create rhythmic patterns against the steady beat. Select those patterns which exhibit rhythmic complexity for illustrative purposes.

• Devise rhythmic rounds and canons (see p. 43). Listen for contrasting rhythms sounded together.

• Play beats or rhythmic patterns, using contrasting meters. Then combine. For example:

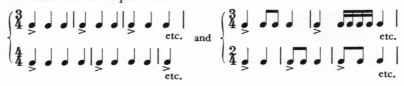

• Clap together the melodic rhythm of two or more songs in the same meter. Then use songs in different meters, as:

Also have two students play melodies of two tunes at the same time. Listen to overall effect of rhythmic elements.

I-V The rate of speed at which music moves is called its *tempo*.

I-V 1. Pieces of music can be performed at various *tempi* or *speeds*. The decisive factor in tempo is how fast the basic unit of beat is performed.

I-II 1a. A piece may move at a relatively fast, slow, or moderate speed.

  • Notice and imitate the speed of animals, mechanical toys, cars, bicycles, and the heart-beat (72 pulses per minute).
  • Experiment with slow and fast rhythmic patterns and beats on rhythm instruments. Compare familiar tunes played at various speeds. Choose the tempo most appropriate for the mood and expressive potential of the melody.
  • Note tempo of recorded works. Observe effect of experimenting with the various speeds on a phonograph or tape recorder.
  • Move rhythmically to the tempo of a work (see p. 194).
  • Provide practice in setting the tempo before performing (see pp. 157–158). "Think" the tempo by first "feeling" the beat.
  • See several activities designed to develop an understanding of the relationship between tempo and beat (pp. 30–31).
  • Tap a drum or set a metronome at a moderate speed, and sing a song. Increase the song's tempo. Note need to increase the beat on the drum or metronome. Reverse procedures, increasing the drum or metronome beat while maintaining the song's tempo.

I-II 1b. Different pieces of music have different tempi. Some compositions move faster than others.

  • Select two familiar songs with different tempi. Sing them, and compare their speeds.
  • Sing a tune at various speeds. Note effect on mood.
  • Play recordings of two works which have different speeds. Clap beat or set metronome to flow of beats. Compare metronome indications and tempi of the two works. Examples include——
SLOW TEMPO: RL—15, 34, 35, 52, 85, 93, 97, 113, 117, 155, 159, 160, 184, 206, 227, 229, 238, 239, 267, 269, 273, 282, 287
FAST TEMPO: RL—7, 9, 18, 22, 27, 30, 44, 54, 59, 67, 157, 161, 174, 180, 237, 243, 252, 259, 314, 319
  • Echo-clap rhythmic patterns, as: teacher—♩ ♩ ♫ ♩, students—♩ ♩ ♫ ♩. On the echo ask students to clap faster or slower than the first pattern. Make sure durational values and relationship of tones remain the *same*. Repeat procedures, using tonal patterns and phrases from songs.

• Note when students perform at unusually slow speeds due to unfamiliarity with an instrument, the music, and/or difficulty in reading music. Also compare tempi of songs sung in class with recorded versions of the same song.

• Listen to recorded music in various tempi. Note how tempo combines with dynamics and pitch level to create a distinct mood in pieces such as——

FAST, LIGHT, AND GAY: RL—22, 67, 148, 149, 224, 226, 254 255, 286, 291, 296
FAST, HEAVY, AND VIGOROUS: RL—12, 49, 98, 174, 221, 252, 259, 261, 262, 264, 319
SLOW AND CALM: RL—34, 35, 51, 94, 99, 113, 155, 186, 206, 229, 235, 251, 282, 285
SLOW AND HEAVY: RL—52, 111, 135, 136, 154, 156, 172, 238

• In developing the relationship of tempo to descriptive music ask students: "If you were a composer trying to describe a _____, would you make the music slow or fast? Why? Let's see what one composer did in trying to describe a _____." Use similar techniques with many unfamiliar songs and texts.

• Compare tempi and overall mood of works written to describe the same animal, person, time of day, or scene, as: RL—12, 25, 47.

• Show how the tempo of a vocal work may be affected by the meaning of the text. For example, compare the tempo of the following two texts:

"Night Herding Song" (tempo: slow)	"Camptown Races" (tempo: fast)
Go slow, little dogie, quit roving around, You have wandered and trampled all over the ground.	The Camptown ladies sing this song, Doo-dah, doo-dah.

• Create original songs and melodies. Emphasize need to decide on appropriate tempo for the lyrics and intended mood of the music.

III-V   1c. The tempo of a work may be designated through the use of terms (e.g., slow—*andante*, fast—*allegro*), and metronome markings (indicate the setting of the metronome to show the number of beat-notes per minute, as ♩ = 72, 72 quarter notes per minute, or ♪ = 60, 60 eighth notes per minute).

• Introduce terms associated with tempo with discussion as: "I'm going to sing a song at a speed called *andante*. What speed do you think *andante* indicates?" Sing the song and infer the meaning of the term ("slow"). Repeat, using other tempo indications.

• List various tempo indications on a chart or the chalkboard.

Select a song or rhythmic pattern and perform it at various speeds according to the tempo chosen. Also play a recorded work and find correct tempo indication for the piece.

• Sing songs according to various metronome indications. Decide the tempo indication most appropriate for each tune.

• Using a metronome, identify speeds of various recordings. Note tempo indications as shown by metronome markings, and notice that they fall into three main categories: slow tempi (fewer than 60 beats per minute); moderate tempi (60 to 80 beats per minute); and fast tempi (more than 80 beats per minute). Interpret metronome markings found at the beginning of the scores of most classical music pieces.

• Devise matching game, drawing line from English terms to Italian tempo markings or metronome indications.

I-V 2. The tempo within a piece may vary. While many compositions move at the same speed throughout, there are times when the tempo within a work will change. When this occurs, the beat will sound correspondingly slower or faster.

• Dramatize animals moving and how they may change speed. Add rhythm instrument accompaniment to correspond with movements.

• Observe speed changes in movements of things in the environment, as: cars, birds flying, and a child running.

• Play a steady rhythm on a rhythm instrument. Illustrate the meaning of faster and slower. Listen to instrumental works which have a steady tempo throughout, and compare with those pieces having frequent tempo changes. Discuss possible reasons for tempo changes. Appropriate examples include——

STEADY TEMPO: RL—1, 2, 20, 29, 34, 35, 39, 113, 134, 182, 183, 184, 186, 197, 198, 213, 235, 250, 252, 282, 286, 291, 308
FREQUENT TEMPO CHANGES: RL—5, 33, 36, 44, 55, 68, 144, 174, 223, 233, 234, 242, 255, 280, 281, 300, 314, 315

• Use faster or slower bodily movements or conducting patterns to coincide with tempo changes in the music.

• Set metronome to tempo of a musical work. Compare steady tick of metronome with various tempo changes in the music.

• Illustrate how a change of tempo in a musical work is one important determinant of musical form (see also pp. 120–124). For example, note the tempo changes in the second or contrasting sections of works such as: RL—32, 44, 47, 59, 60, 62, 77, 147, 158, 175, 202, 223, 231, 266, 304

• Observe that when the tempo of a piece changes, all note values maintain their same relationship. Thus, the relationship between

♩ ♫ ♩ is the same whether it is in a slow or fast tempo (see pp. 46–48 for further discussion and activities).

• Show how the tempo and beat of a piece may be affected by holding or lengthening a tone through the use of a *fermata* (see pp. 8–9 for discussion and activities).

• Listen for tempo changes in music. Discuss the resulting mood, and illustrate through bodily movements.

• Compare the conclusions of several works. Note the sense of finality caused in part by the lessening of the tempo, as in: RL—7, 9, 14, 46, 52, 57, 90, 94, 111, 176, 187, 251, 254

• Sing a song at a steady tempo. Add subtle tempo changes to increase the interest and emotional impact of the tune. Also locate the end of a phrase or the climax by ear. Experiment with tempo changes to note the effect on climax and mood.

• Observe how a change of tempo contributes to the climax of works such as: RL—73, 88, 98, 157, 163, 175, 221, 296

• Encourage students to use tempo changes in their original works in order to heighten the mood of these pieces.

• Call attention to the effect of tempo change on meter and metric accent (see pp. 8–9).

• Devise crude symbolism to indicate tempo changes. Use symbols and/or vocabulary to denote what has already been perceived through the ear.

• To develop a vocabulary to signify changes of tempo, use similar methods as those outlined on pp. 56–57 for tempo indications.

Three

MELODY

Basic Concept:

Melody is the rhythmically organized succession of single tones which vary in pitch and duration.

Key Terms:

tune, theme, song, pitch, range, melodic rhythm, tonal movement, contour, climax, tonal pattern, melodic interval, phrase, tonality, scale

I-V A melody is the tune of a vocal or instrumental composition. The infinite variety of melodies consists of tones of different pitches organized into significant tonal and rhythmic relationships. Notice that in "Clementine," Ex. 3–1, the melody has tones of both varying pitches and durations.

I-II 1. A melody is sung or played on an instrument, and is the distinguishing characteristic of most music.

> • Say the words of a song such as "Are You Sleeping." Begin singing the words in the middle of the song. Students raise hands when the melody is added to the words.
> • Add a melody to word phrases, jingles, sentences, and poems, using either the voice or a melody instrument.

Ex. 3-1. "Clementine"

- Play the accompaniment of a familiar tune. Then sing or play the melody. Students raise hands when they hear the tune.
- Play or sing the tunes of familiar songs with "la." Identify songs by title or their initial words.
- Aurally identify the melodies (themes) in a recorded instrumental work. Ask students to sing along with these tunes.
- Sing a familiar tune with "la" but change some tones. Students raise hands to note errors, and then sing corrections.
- Listen to, and identify familiar tunes in instrumental works as: RL—26, 38, 50, 92, 106, 132, 156, 158, 302. Encourage students to use excerpts from familiar tunes in their original works.
- Listen to and note difficulty of identifying the melodies of works consisting almost entirely of undeveloped melodic fragments or indefinite and obscure themes (examples: RL—21, 43, 58, 63, 66, 67, 104, 209, 276, 278, 280, 293).

I-III   2. All melodies have both high and low tones (see Chapter One—Tone—for related discussion). The distance from a melody's lowest to its highest tone is known as the *range* of the melody. The range of "Hey Betty Martin" in Ex. 3–2 is from C up to A.

Ex. 3-2. "Hey Betty Martin"

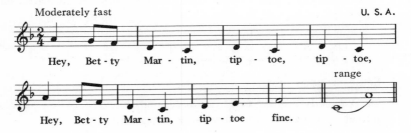

• Use activities listed for *pitch*, pp. 10–12, before developing an understanding of range.

• Raise hands or stand up on the highest tone of a melody, and sit down or touch the floor on the lowest tone. Highlight the highest and lowest tones of a melody by playing them. Play the intervening tones and note distance between the two tones. Relate meaning of melodic range to the range of a ball being tossed or the range of a rocket or gun-shot.

• Sing a scalewise progression from the lowest to highest tones possible. Compare the vocal range of the students, teacher, and other voice-types with the range of a recorder, violin, piano, or other instrument. Note how the range of a melody is often determined by whether the melody is intended for a particular voice or instrument.

• At level III and above, examine the notation of a melody and notate its range, as in Ex. 3–2.

• Compare songs with a narrow range (examples: S—5, 14, 42, 53, 56, 64, 68, 78, 79) with those having a range of an octave or more (examples: S—20, 21, 29, 33, 99, 116, 119, 123, 127, 144).

• Classify the ranges of themes of instrumental works as narrow or wide. Notice the very wide ranges of melodies in much contemporary music. Note that melodies with a limited range are generally less restless and active than melodies with a wide range. Some appropriate examples are——

NARROW RANGE: RL—15, 16, 35, 97, 130, 136, 148, 167, 187, 215, 219, 248, 257, 273, 287, 292, 314, 315

WIDE RANGE: RL—4, 9, 47, 78, 126, 157, 168, 171, 180, 197, 198, 202, 224, 234, 243, 251, 253, 265, 283, 322

I-III 3. A melody consists of tones having both pitch and rhythm.

• Play only the tones of a familiar song, or clap only its rhythm. Ask students to name the song. Note the need for both pitch and rhythm in melody. Illustrate need for other musical elements (phrase, dynamics, tempo) in a melody.

• Give students the words and tones of an unfamiliar song. Ask them to create the song's rhythm and then sing the song. Repeat, using only the words and rhythm. Compare with original song.

• Sing several tonal patterns from a song on a neutral syllable ("la" or "tay"). Ask students to provide the words which fit these patterns. Repeat, using rhythmic patterns.

I-V 4. Some melodies have words; others do not.

I-II 4a. A melody without words is called a *tune* or *theme*. When words are added to a melody, the result is a *song*.

• Listen to and/or play tunes on instruments. Compare these with songs.

• Sing a tonal pattern or the tune of a familiar song with "la." Add words to make the melody a song. Students can also make up a poem, and add an original tune to make it into a song.

I-V   4b. There are several types of melodies with words.

• Engage in musical conversations with the students, using only two or three different tones, as:

• Make up *chants* (songs in which many words are sung on a limited amount of tones) for everyday activities, adding tones for statements such as: "It's time for lunch" and "Now it's raining very hard."

• Sing common children's chants, as "Rain, Rain, Go Away" in Ex. 3–3. Also create chants for nonsense jingles.

Ex. 3-3. "Rain, Rain, Go Away"—a Chant

• Design the chant tones on the chalkboard, using line notation (as ‾ _ ‾‾ _ for "Rain, Rain, Go Away"). Note limited use of different pitches.

• Distribute two or three resonator bells, as E, G, and A, and guide students to make up a tune and add words.

• Listen to examples of religious and primitive chants, and chants from areas of the world such as Afghanistan, New Zealand (the Maoris), Hawaii, and Japan. Note limited use of tones in these chants.

• At levels III and above, draw attention to how words in songs are divided to fit the tones. Note how many songs have a separate tone for each word-syllable, as in "Rain, Rain, Go Away" in Ex. 3–3. Describe these tunes as *syllabic melodies*.

• At levels IV and V sing or play a recording of a song with some *melismatic* features (songs in which each syllable is given several tones). Raise hands when more than one tone is used for a syllable. Appropriate examples include: S—33, 41, 66, 119, 123.

• Analyze many melodies for syllabic, melismatic elements. Note the slurred line in musical notation to indicate more than one tone for one syllable. Create a melismatic melody to the words "amen" or "glory hallelujah." Also make up songs using combinations of syllabic and melismatic features.

• Listen to sections of operas and oratorios. Note the many *recitatives* (a vocal style designed for the speech-like declamations of operas and oratorios in order to advance the plot) and *arias* (an elaborate vocal work with instrumental accompaniment usually important for its musical design and vocal display rather than for its dramatic continuity). Examples include: RL—93, 114, 125, 159, 162, 169.

• Improvise a recitative style of singing to enhance the dramatic aspects of a play. Also sing several words on one or two tones, relating this to the recitative style in opera.

I-V The tones of a melody have movement and direction.

I-II 1. The tones of a melody may move in three ways—they may *go up* (rise, go higher, leap up, step up, skip up, ascend), *go down* (fall, go lower, leap down, step down, skip down, descend), and *stay the same* (stay on one level, repeat the tones, have stationary direction). The tonal movement of a melody is shown in Ex. 3–4.

Ex. 3-4. "Twinkle, Twinkle, Little Star"

• Sing a familiar song on one pitch level. Repeat, using the correct pitches. Note how the pitch direction varies. Use many activities related to increasing an understanding of pitch before working on tonal direction in a melody (see pp. 10–12).

• Distribute two or three resonator bells. Ask students to create one, two, and three-pitch melodies, with tones repeated or moving up and down. Expand tonal possibilities. Compare the effect on melodic interest and mood as tones are added.

• Use bodily movement and notation (see pp. 10–12) to picture the way tones move in a melody. Raise or lower hands, using large or small hand movements, to show tonal direction and wide or small skips and steps in the melody.

• Make a chart:

HOW TONES MOVE IN A MELODY

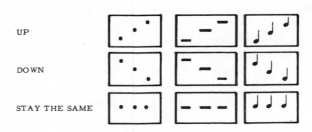

• At levels III and above observe that tones in a melody may move by step, skip, or leap, or scalewise or chordwise (see pp. 68–70).

• Play two melodies—one of which lacks melodic interest. Students evaluate the melodic movement and rhythmic elements. They then improve the uninteresting melody.

• Point out how interest is obtained in particular folk, popular, and art melodies. Note the ways the melody moves, and how this movement contributes to interest. Students then compose an interesting melody from a given tonal framework.

I-III 2. The tones of all melodies form an outline or shape known as its *melodic contour*. The contour describes the general direction and movement of the successive tones in the melody. The shape or contour of the beginning of "The Muffin Man" and "Jingle Bells" can be seen by the outlines drawn above the notes in Ex. 3–5a and 3–5b.

Ex. 3-5a. The Contour of "The Muffin Man"

Ex. 3-5b. The Contour of "Jingle Bells"

• Precede all work on contour with activities for pitch (pp. 10–12) and tonal direction (pp. 63–64).

• Listen to and sing a familiar song. Design the shape of the tune with hand movements or with symbols written on the chalkboard.

Use block-shaped outline 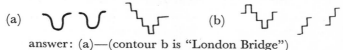 , line notation _ ⁻ ¯ _ , and

general contour lines ⌒ ⌒ .

• Draw several contours on the chalkboard. Sing or play a tune and have students match the contour to the tune. For example, ask: "Is 'This Old Man' contour (a) or contour (b)?"

answer: (a)—(contour b is "London Bridge")

• Ask students to draw the shape of a familiar tune on paper or the chalkboard. Students should also draw an outline of a tune's contour above the notation of a familiar tune.

• Write numbers or letter names to play on the resonator bells or piano, emphasizing the tune's contour, as:

	5—		5—	
	4		4	
3		3 3	3	
2		2		
1	1 1	1		

("Are You Sleeping")

		G—	
	E—		E—
			D—
C C C	C	C C C	C

("Looby Loo")

• Randomly place contours of four phrases of a tune on the chalkboard. Play or sing a tune, and rearrange contours to coincide with the tonal direction of each phrase.

• Create a melody, song, or tonal pattern using a given contour.

• List on the chalkboard two or more song titles in one column and corresponding contours in the second column. Listen to the first phrase of each tune and draw a line from the contour to the correct song title.

• When introducing new songs, relate similar contour patterns of familiar songs to the unfamiliar melodies in order to help establish the general melodic direction of the new tunes.

• Compare melodies with different contour patterns, as—

ASCENDING CONTOUR PATTERNS: S—6, 21, 25, 30, 39, 41, 54, 88, 98, 109, 122; and RL—22, 27, 78, 97, 98, 126 (beginning), 160, 172, 197, 220, 251, 298, 303

DESCENDING CONTOUR PATTERNS: S—24, 28, 51, 66, 117, 119, 126, 128; and RL—7, 42, 67, 100, 102, 121, 123, 148, 157, 167, 174, 224, 226, 285, 295, 296

SMOOTH CONTOURS: most nursery tunes and folk songs; and RL—25, 35, 94, 97, 99, 155, 186, 187, 228, 229, 235, 251
WINDING CONTOURS: RL—61 (beginning), 110, 118 (main themes), 146, 161, 213, 226, 237
JAGGED, ANGULAR CONTOURS: RL—7, 11, 74, 143, 242, 268, 278, 279, 280, 293, 321

• Identify the *climax* of a work—the point of greatest interest or tension in the music. Note that this point usually occurs during an ascending melodic line, and is accompanied by an increase in dynamics and added rhythmic and harmonic interest.

• Raise hands or respond with other bodily movements when the most exciting part of the music is heard. Discuss possible reasons for the climax, including an ascending contour, tempo and dynamic factors, instrumentation, and rhythm. Highlight the climax with rhythm instruments such as the gong, cymbals, or drum. Compare the climax of a melody or piece to the climax of a movie, story, or poem.

• After identifying the climax through aural perception, examine the notation. Observe that the melodic climax is often provided by an upward movement of melody, sometimes to a pitch higher than any of the others.

• Compare the contours of many pieces whose climaxes occur in different parts. Examples include—

ASCENDING CONTOURS AND CLIMAX IN THE MIDDLE OF THE WORK: RL—31, 61, 87, 100, 124, 126, 153, 172, 231
ASCENDING CONTOURS AND CLIMAX AT THE END OF THE WORK: RL—23, 36, 46, 94, 98, 116, 157, 175, 203, 207, 211, 260, 296

• Sing songs which have ascending contours and a climax near their endings (examples: S—5, 6, 21, 23, 30, 31, 58, 88, 110, 114, 119, 123). Note that climaxes of most tunes occur near the ending and are often followed by a downward melodic movement, suggesting relaxation and release from tension.

II-V 3. Movement and direction of tones in a melody can be pictured by the relationship of notes on a musical staff (see Chapter One—Tone—pp. 12–18 for understandings related to pitch and the staff).

II-III 3a. An ascending melodic line is symbolized by ascending notes on the staff. A descending melodic line is symbolized by descending notes on the staff. A melodic line with repeated tones is symbolized by notes on the staff which repeat at the same level.

• Use figures, designs, arrows, and line notation to indicate melodic movement, as: o ° o , x ˣ x , /\ and _ ⁻ _ . Include

varying line lengths for duration. For example, the rhythmic and

tonal movement of "London Bridge" can be symbolized as:
(—⁻—_ _—).

After much experience with crude symbolism, transfer the symbols
to the staff.

• Play tunes on step bells. Students follow the way tones rise and fall.
Also use melody or tone bells turned vertically. Move hands to tonal
direction. Symbolize melodic movement in notation.

• Sing tunes slowly and follow notation in musical score. Find sections of the melody which go up, down, or repeat.

• Show students three tonal patterns in notation—one ascending,
one descending, and one with repeated tones. Sing one of the patterns.
Students identify the pattern they hear.

• Place the notation of a familiar tune on the chalkboard. Include
one or more errors in tonal movement. Sing the tune. Students locate
the errors.

• Name a melody that begins like this: ⁻—_ (possible answers:
"Three Blind Mice," "Mary Had a Little Lamb," "The First Noel,"
"The Star-Spangled Banner," "Dixie," and others). Repeat activity,
using _ –⁻ and other patterns.

• Use a familiar tune to show relationship of tonal direction to left-
right orientation on keyboard instruments (see also pp. 12, 16, 182).

• Use activities on pp. 10–12 to develop understanding about tones
being close together or far apart.

• Experiment with creating melodies whose tones are predominantly close together or far apart.

II-III   3b. The tones in a melody may *repeat*, or may move by *step* (an interval
of a second, as from B to C or F to G), by *skip* (an interval of a third,
as from C to E or A to C), or by *leap* (an interval of a fourth or more,
as from C to F or E to B). This movement can be seen by observing
the way notes move on the staff, as in Ex. 3–6.

Ex. 3-6. Brahms: "Lullaby"—Types of Tonal Movement

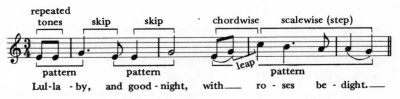

Lul-la - by,   and good - night,   with__   ro - ses   be - dight.__

• Show the meaning of step and skip by using the melody, tone, step, or resonator bells, or a chart of the piano keyboard, as:

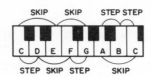

• Play various tonal patterns which move either scalewise or skipwise. Identify type of tonal movement.

• Aurally identify the scalewise, skipwise, or repeated movement of tones in works such as—

MUCH SCALEWISE MOVEMENT: S—5, 28, 31, 37, 41, 45, 52, 66, 84, 100, 102, 105, 126, 127, 136, 146; RL—10(chorale theme), 34, 51, 79, 95, 113, 181, 182, 193(theme 1), 194, 204, 229, 256(main theme), 269, 283, 287, 295, 311, 315

MUCH SKIPWISE MOVEMENT: S—29, 35, 72, 77, 92, 107, 110, 113, 114, 121, 122, 131, 132;   RL—11, 111, 124, 143, 174, 234, 250, 252, 317, 318, 319

MANY REPEATED TONES: S—1, 8, 17, 36, 39, 60, 62, 64, 65, 67, 76, 96, 133, 139, 140; RL—109, 117, 135, 183, 192, 254, 284, 292, 311, 312

• Locate tones in the notation which move stepwise (space to the next line, or line to the next space) or skipwise (line to the next line or space to the next space). Compare the notation of a melody moving mostly stepwise ("Go Tell Aunt Rhodie") with one moving primarily by repeated tones and skip ("Skip to My Lou").

• Distribute staff paper. Ask students to write tonal patterns which move stepwise or use a combination of step and skip. Students then play these patterns from the notation.

• Dictate tonal patterns for students to write. First give simple three-tone patterns which move stepwise, as F, G, F or C, D, E. Gradually expand this to four or five-tone patterns, and then to patterns with some skips. Use patterns from songs for drill material.

• Locate leaps in melodies through listening and visual reinforcement. Appropriate songs with leaps include: S—33, 55, 83, 94, 123, 142.

III-V   3c. The tones of a melody can move *conjunctly* (through the tones of a scale and called *scalewise movement*), and *disjunctly* (through the tones of a chord and called *chordwise movement*, or with larger leaps), as illustrated in Brahms' "Lullaby" in Ex. 3–6, p. 67.

• Sing a song with much scalewise movement. Students raise hands when tones move scalewise. Then play or sing the tones of a scale with numbers (1, 2, 3, . . .) or syllables (DO, RE, MI, . . .). See pp. 75–85 for background needed for developing an understanding of *scale* and *tonality*.

• Find the tones of the C chord (C, E, G) on the resonator bells. Play the tones of the C chord every time they appear in a song. Find songs in other keys which have chordwise movement (examples: S—26, 30, 74, 98, 101, 113, 121) and repeat the above activity. [*Note:* All activities regarding chordwise movement should follow the development of an understanding of chords, pp. 96–100]

• Make a chart to illustrate tonal movement:

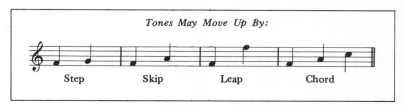

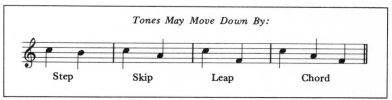

• Look at the notation of melodies and find scalewise movement by observing that the notes move from a line to the next space, or a space to the next line on the staff. Also find examples of chordwise movement by locating notes which move from one space to the next space or one line to the next line on the staff.

• Locate by ear and through notation, parts of the melody of a song or instrumental work which move conjunctly or disjunctly. Some examples, in addition to those listed for scalewise and skipwise movement on p. 68, include—

CONJUNCT MOVEMENT: RL—16, 51, 89, 109, 142, 269, 273, 295

DISJUNCT MOVEMENT (CHORDAL): RL—7, 11, 32, 36, 48 (themes 1, 5), 117, 221, 244, 246, 262 (theme 3)

DISJUNCT MOVEMENT (LEAPS): RL—5, 27, 30, 78, 174, 234, 242, 265, 268, 272, 278, 279, 319, 325

CONTRASTING TONAL MOVEMENT: RL—18(theme 1: chordal, theme 2: scalewise), 119(A: chordal, B: scalewise), 123 (theme 1: chordal, theme 2: scalewise), 165(theme 1: chordal, theme 2: scalewise), 196(theme 1: chordal, theme 2: scalewise and repeated tones)

• Repeat many activities used to develop understandings of stepwise and skipwise movement, listed on pp. 68 and 72.

• Listen for chordwise movement in a melody and harmonize the tones with that chord (see pp. 101–102), using the piano, Autoharp, ukulele, or the separate tones of the resonator bells.

• Listen to melodies in a slow tempo which remain near one level by using repeated tones and scalewise movement. Discuss how these aspects of the music produce a calm, restful mood. Examples include: S—3, 5, 43, 45, 62, 73, 87; RL—25, 34, 113, 186, 187, 219, 248, 267.

• Analyze the notation of melodies to show that almost all tunes have both conjunct and disjunct movement. Create melodies based entirely on scalewise or chordwise movement. Combine both types of movement in original tunes. Evaluate for melodic interest and mood.

• Once the meaning of triads is understood (see pp. 98–100) show that skips within a melody are usually between tones of a triad, as illustrated in Brahms' "Lullaby" in Ex. 3–6, p. 67. Sing tunes which begin with a skip or leap. Discover that almost all of these tunes begin with the triad tones of the I (tonic) chord. Some examples are: S—9, 59, 92, 98, 107, 110, 135, 145. Select and play resonator bell tones of the opening chordwise progression of a melody both separately and together for an introduction to various songs.

I-V   Tones of a melody are organized into *tonal patterns* and *phrases*.

I-III 1. The smallest group of tones used to build a melody is the *tonal pattern* (sometimes called a tonal grouping, melodic pattern, motive, tonal or melodic motive, or figure). This unit, as illustrated in Ex. 3–7, can be identified by the fact that it has at least two tones, with at least one characteristic interval; it is distinct and separable from other patterns in the melody; and it often plays an important part in the subsequent development of the melody.

• Highlight a distinctive tonal pattern in a melody with a melody instrument. Play it whenever it occurs in the music. Students can

Ex. 3-7. Schumann: "Träumerei" from *Scenes from Childhood*

sing the pattern and clap its rhythm. Distribute resonator or Swiss melodé bells for the tones of the tonal pattern. Guide students to play the pattern. Note the number of tones in the pattern and whether the movement is repeated, ascending or descending, scalewise or skipwise. Reinforce the aural experience by using line or standard notation.

• Play a tonal pattern which repeats in a melody. Students count the number of times the pattern is used in order to note its importance in the tune (see also pp. 116–117).

• Sing or play a tonal pattern. Students name songs which begin with this pattern (examples: DO MI SOL—"Michael Row Your Boat," "Did You Ever See a Lassie?" "The Marine's Hymn"). Also sing or play a characteristic tonal pattern from the middle or end of a melody and identify the tune.

• Sing or play a tonal pattern. Repeat it, altering at least one tone. Students raise hands to indicate which tones were changed.

• Sing or play an unfamiliar melody to a given point. Students then add several tones to complete the melody. Also select and sing or play a characteristic tonal pattern from a familiar tune. Students guess the words that go with this pattern. Notate the pattern. Students find the song in their songbooks and frame the pattern.

• Find repeated tonal patterns in notation, as "ding ding dong" from "Are You Sleeping" or "fa-la-la-la-la" from "Deck the Halls." Show that tonal patterns which look alike in notation sound alike, and *vice versa*.

• Provide students with a tonal pattern with which to improvise their own tunes. Encourage students to create interesting-sounding tonal patterns, and expand these to a complete melody.

• Students listen as teacher sings the beginning of a familiar song. Teacher then stops singing and students "think" the next few tones or phrases. Students begin singing on the teacher's signal or when they come to a certain tonal pattern.

II-V　2. Each tonal pattern in a melody has distinctive characteristics which add to the melody's overall structure.

II-IV　2a. A tonal pattern may have tones which move scalewise, chordwise, repeat, or move from high to low or low to high in a wide leap (see pp. 67–70 for additional discussion).

• Use many activities for developing an understanding of scalewise, skipwise, repeated, chordal, and leaping tonal movement, as outlined on pp. 68–70.

• Listen to music which has scalewise and chordwise tonal patterns.

Isolate these patterns, notate them, and play them on melody instruments when they occur in the music.

• Look at the notation of an unfamiliar tune. Teacher sings a section and asks: "What part of the melody goes this way? Point to the pattern." Also write several tonal patterns on the chalkboard. Play or sing one of them. Students guess which one was performed. Verify answers.

• Find and listen to tonal patterns which have elements of both scalewise and chordwise movement (examples: S—15, 36, 39, 72, 79, 100, 121, 123, 124, 138).

• Devise dictation exercises. Students play tonal pattern after hearing it sung. At levels I and II provide students with clues such as: "I will play a pattern using only C and G. Here is the pattern (play C C G). What did I play? Can you play it on the bells?" Expand to three or more different tones. At upper levels students should notate pattern on the staff.

• Make a separate chart for each tonal pattern or phrase in a tune. Divide class into two teams. Play a tonal pattern or phrase. One member from each team must point to pattern or phrase played.

• Make a chart and flash cards of frequently used tonal patterns in different keys based upon:

SCALEWISE MOVEMENT

do re mi fa sol,   sol fa mi re do,   mi re do ti do, sol la ti do,

sol la sol,   do ti la sol,   do ti do,   mi fa mi,

CHORDWISE MOVEMENT, especially patterns using the I (tonic) chord, as G B D in the key of G major, and the V (dominant) chord, as D F♯ A in the key of G major (see p. 96 for a discussion of chords)

do mi sol do,   do sol mi do,   do sol do,   sol ti re fa sol,

sol fa re   ti sol   re fa la   fa la do,

Also make combinations of scalewise and chordwise movement for the flash cards. Practice sight-reading these patterns.

• Create and notate tonal patterns and melodies using various types of tonal movement.

III-V 2b. A tonal pattern is made up of tones forming intervals. A *melodic interval* is the measured distance between two tones moving horizontally (see also pp. 94–96 for *harmonic intervals*). Some types of melodic intervals are shown in Ex. 3–8.

Ex. 3-8. "Rock-a-bye Baby"

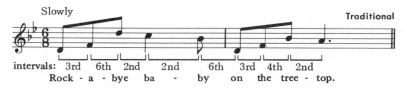

• Isolate two adjoining tones of a tonal pattern. Play them together, as an harmonic interval, and separately, as a melodic interval. Illustrate intervallic distance visually by using a melody instrument, especially the tone or step bells. See also related activities for harmonic intervals, pp. 94–96.

• Place the notes G and B on the treble staff and call the interval a "third." Discover how an interval is named, by counting: the number of letters it includes (G to B consists of G, A, and B, and is called a "third"); the beginning scale step and all the steps it includes (G is step 1, A is step 2, and B is step 3); or the lines and spaces between the two notes, including the lowest and highest notes. Provide practice in listening to and naming intervals which appear in tonal patterns.

• Make a chart giving examples of melodic intervals, such as:

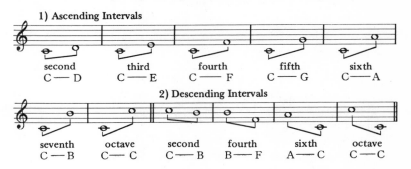

Reserve the study of interval names such as the major or minor third, the augmented fifth, and the diminished seventh for more advanced instructional levels.

• Show students various examples of one type of interval as written on the staff in several positions. Derive generalizations about the relationship between the sound of the interval and its notation on the staff which makes it easier to recognize, such as:

—a unison—the same note repeated on a line or space
—a second—a note on a space moving to an adjoining line, or on a line moving to an adjoining space, and sounding close together
—a third—a note on a line moving to an adjoining line, or on a space and moving to an adjoining space, and sounding fairly close together
—a fifth—a note on a line or space moving to a note two lines or spaces away
—a chordal pattern, as DO, MI, SOL—notes moving from line to line to line, or space to space to space
—an octave—one note will be on a line and the other on a space, and sounding far apart, but similar

• Refine interval recognition through aural drill on interval size. Begin with the second, octave, and seventh, and then the third, fifth, fourth, and sixth.
• Play the "Interval Game." Students "tune up" by singing the major scale. Then practice moving from one interval to another, as: DO-RE, DO-MI, DO-FA, . . . ; RE-MI, RE-FA, RE-SOL, . . . and other intervals, as teacher points to interval charts:

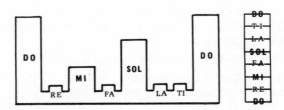

• Reinforce the sound of melodic intervals by following a score and playing them on a keyboard instrument, the tonette or recorder, and the step or tone bells. Also raise hands when a given interval is heard or played.
• Examine the keyboard or melody bells to demonstrate that a *half-step* is the distance from any tone to an adjacent tone, as from E to E flat, or F to F sharp, and that a *whole-step* is made up of two half-steps, as from E to D, or E to F sharp. Note that on the keyboard and staff half-steps occur between E and F and B and C. Use commercial or student-made keyboards to guide learning about half and whole-steps, such as:

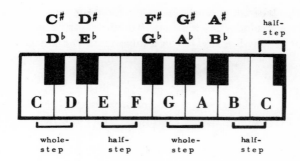

• Guide students to develop techniques for sight-reading intervallic patterns by referring to a familiar interval. For example, in singing the ascending sixth (DO to LA or 1 to 6), think of DO to SOL or 1 to 5 first, and then sing DO to LA or 1 to 6.

• Create tonal patterns made up of similar or contrasting intervals. For example, use only intervals of thirds, or a combination of seconds and fourths in a tonal pattern. Compare for tonal effects.

II-V 3. Tonal patterns in a musical work may be repeated, varied, or completely different from each other (see Form, pp. 116–118, for discussion and activities).

V-V 4. Several tonal patterns may be combined into one long musical idea, called a *phrase* (see Form, pp. 112–115, for discussion and activities).

I-V The tones of many melodies focus or center around one tone, called a tonal center. A melody can have *tonality*—an organized relationship of tones around a tonal center.

-IV 1. Most melodies have a *key center* or *home tone* (also known as tonal center, the key note or key, the first degree, the tonic, 1, or DO). This tone is the one around which all other tones seem to pull toward or gravitate. In Ex. 3–9 the D seems to be the most important tone in the melody, and is therefore the key center or home tone.

Ex. 3-9. "Joy to the World"

• Students stand and listen to a familiar tune, and sit when they feel the melody has reached its "home" or "home tone." Sing the tonal center. Locate DO on a melody instrument and raise hands or play DO every time it occurs in the melody. Repeat the melody in several keys and again locate the home tone.

• Sing or play a melody, omitting the final tone. Students supply the key tone. Also sing a scale and/or DO, MI, SOL, DO, ascending and descending. Repeat, omitting either the high or low DO. Students sing the missing tones.

• Listen to a melody having a fairly slow tempo. Indicate when the key tone is heard throughout the piece by raising hands. Ask students to sing DO at any time during the music.

• Experiment with effect of ending melodies on tones other than the key tone. Observe effect.

• Establish and develop feeling for tonality for each song by playing the I, IV, V₇ chords on an harmonic instrument (see pp. 102, 157).

• Refer to the home tone used in a piece as DO or 1. Note that the key is also the name of the line or space in which DO is located, and that the key may be on any line or space of the staff. Limit the use of the term "key" to the major and minor tonalities (see pp. 80–85 and pp. 85–87).

• Notice the tendency of some tones to move to other tones, as in "Joy to the World" in Ex. 3–9, where all the tones seem to gravitate toward the tonality core of D, F♯, and A.

• Sing tonal patterns ending on the more active second, fourth, sixth, and seventh tones of the scale. Note how the tones pull toward the more restful scale degrees of 1, 3, 5, and 8, respectively.

• Play or sing a tonal pattern, omitting the final tone, as: SOL, MI, RE, (DO); SOL, LA, TI, (DO); SOL, LA, SOL, FA, (MI); MI, RE, DO, LA, (SOL). Students sing final tone.

• Perform an unfamiliar tune, omitting certain tones. Students supply missing tones. Also sing or play a tonal pattern, omitting the final tone. Ask if the last tone should move up or down. Then sing the missing tone.

• Use many examples to show that most melodies begin with, and almost all melodies end on restful tones. Compare with works *not* beginning on DO, MI, or SOL, or ending on DO. Examples include—

NOT BEGINNING ON DO, MI, SOL: S—63, 71; RL—227, 262 (theme 1)

NOT ENDING ON DO: S—41, 59, 68, 109; RL—141, 165, 209, 246, 262 (theme 1), 280, 301

Sing melodies not ending on DO, but substitute the DO for the final tone. Evaluate the effect.

• Play many tunes and ask: "Does the melody begin on the home tone? Does it begin on DO, MI, or SOL?" Make lists of songs beginning on DO, MI, or SOL. Include songs such as—

BEGINNING ON DO: S—7, 8, 22, 25, 79, 82, 96, 111, 134, 146
BEGINNING ON MI: S—16, 52, 56, 64, 74, 76, 86, 94, 114, 121, 151
BEGINNING ON SOL: S—6, 9, 11, 13, 14, 15, 83, 119, 135, 138

• Listen to tunes which have tones other than DO as the most important tone (examples: RL—165-theme 1, 246, 262-theme 1, 300). Help students identify the tone(s) other than DO which seems very important in the theme.

• Play instrumental recordings which have either a vague tonality or a complete lack of tonality. Ask students to try to sing DO and note resulting difficulty. Use compositions such as: RL—61, 63, 65, 68, 104, 242, 277, 278, 303. Note how vague tonality or lack of tonality is frequent in music of the Impressionists (Ravel, Debussy) and modern composers.

• Identify aurally, locate in the notation, and sing the highest and lowest tones of a song or instrumental melody. Note how these tones are often either DO, MI, or SOL. Appropriate examples include: S—35, 45, 51, 54, 62, 93, 104, 107, 123, 126, 136.

• At levels IV and V students indicate when a melody shifts tonality or *modulates* (changes the home tone or tonal center). Examples include: S—38, 48, 63, 87, 122, 138, 141; RL—1, 11, 28, 33, 41, 54, 183, 216, 247, 264, 296, 313, 320. Examine notation for indications of a tonality shift (new chord markings, accidentals, new key signature).

II-V 2. Melodies are written in various tonalities and are built on contrasting scale patterns. These melodies will sound different from each other in mood and feeling. In Ex. 3–10 all three melodies have a different tonality, despite having a tonal center of D.

Ex. 3-10. Three Melodies With Contrasting Tonalities

"He's Got the Whole World in His Hands"—D Major   Spiritual

Tonal   He's got   the   whole   world___   in   his   hands.
center: D

"We Three Kings"— D Minor   Carol

Tonal   We   three   Kings   of   O - ri - ent   are.
center: D

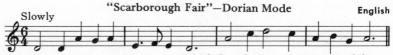

"Scarborough Fair"—Dorian Mode · English · Slowly

Tonal center: D · Are you go-ing to Scar-bor-ough fair? Pars-ley, sage, rose-mar-y and thyme

Reprinted from *Sing Out!* Used with permission.

II-III

2a. Many melodies are based on a specific organization of tones known as a *scale*. A scale is a descending or ascending pattern of tones on which a melody is built. Observe how the tones used in "The Blue-Bells of Scotland" in Ex. 3–11 outline the D major scale.

Ex. 3-11. "The Blue-Bells of Scotland"

O where, and O where is your High-land lad-die gone?

Tones used (D major scale)

• Play a familiar tune on the step or melody bells. Isolate all tones used, arranging them from low to high. Relate these tones to the idea of a scale, and show how a scale is a succession of tones arranged in ascending or descending order, usually according to a specific pattern of *half* and *whole-steps* (see pp. 74–75). Develop an understanding of the structure of various scales (see following pages).

• Distribute some resonator or melodé bells in random order. Students arrange themselves in a scalewise progression and play a scalewise pattern. Repeat, using tones of the complete scale.

• Play any scale on the step or melody bells, emphasizing tonal direction and stepwise movement. Students move hands or entire body up and down to show pitch levels. Use movement on stairs, and relate to elevator going up and down, or climbing a ladder.

• Play a scaleline progression featured in a familiar tune. Students sing the tune and raise hands when the progression occurs. Listen for, and identify scaleline passages in songs and instrumental recordings (see list of appropriate music, pp. 68, 69).

• Sing a major or minor scale with a neutral syllable. Repeat, omitting one or two tones. Notice differences, and ask students to sing missing tone(s).

• Sing or play a scale starting on various tones. Construct many scales by ear, using different starting pitch levels.

III-IV   2b. There are many kinds of scales. They differ in their sound quality according to how the intervals between the tones are arranged.

• Arrange the tones used in a song in successive order, from high to low. Determine the melody's key center. Note the half and whole-step arrangement of tones starting from the key center (see pp. 74–75 for discussion on whole and half-steps). Notice that the melody of "Canoe Song" in Ex. 3–12 contains the tones E, G, A, and B, with E as the tonal center.

Ex. 3-12. "Canoe Song"

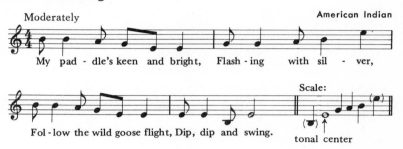

• Study the structure and scale pattern of the major, minor, chromatic, pentatonic, whole-tone, and modal scales (see discussion and activities on the following pages).
• Listen to melodies that are in the major tonality. Compare these with melodies in the minor. Play a tune in one tonality. Repeat, changing the tonality, and note effect on mood.
• Play a piece having both major and minor tonalities, such as: S—38, 122, 141, 155; RL—24, 73, 98, 110, 118, 216, 252, 255, 284, 311, 312. Raise hands when the tonality changes.
• At levels III and above call attention to the unusual sound of some melodies, due to the fact that they are written in less familiar tonalities than the major or minor scale systems (see pp. 87–91 for further discussion and activities).
• Describe a given mood or scene. Students create a melody or song to fit the mood. Use different tonalities.
• Determine the type of scale or tonality of a piece by listening to its overall quality or mood, and by recognizing differences in its half and whole-step structure.
• Listen to the tonalities of many melodies to discover that most melodies in Western music are major or minor, since they are based upon tones of either the major or minor scale.

• Students use tone bells to experiment with original scale systems, as C D♭ E♭ F G A or C D F♯ G♯ B (a "gapped" scale, which leaves out one or more letter names—see "Canoe Song" in Ex. 3–12, p. 79). Use these scales to create tunes.

III-V   2c. The most frequently used tonal system in Western music is the *major scale*—a scale of eight tones arranged so that half-steps occur between tones 3 and 4, and 7 and 8, as in Ex. 3–13.

Ex. 3-13. The Pattern of Half and Whole-Steps in a Major Scale

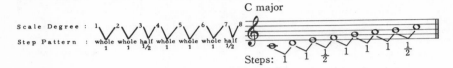

• Develop aural awareness of music in the major tonality. Call a key "major" when the tonality is based on the major scale. Identify the home tone of the major scale as 1 or DO.

• Sing or play a major scale, omitting one tone. Students sing the missing tone and name the number of the scale tone omitted. Also perform a major scale having one or more incorrect tones, and ask students to indicate which tone(s) was wrong.

• When the sound of the major scale is familiar, play the scale on the tone bells, beginning on different pitch levels. Discover need for changing certain tones to make them conform to the scale sound (see also p. 83).

• Examine the notation of various major scales, and observe that the series of eight tones begins with either A, B, C, D, E, F, or G, and always continues in alphabetical order until the first letter is repeated as the eighth tone. Note that a letter is neither skipped nor repeated. Show that the major scale is named after the tonal center or the letter name upon which the scale begins and ends.

• Build a major scale on C, using the piano or step bells. Observe the step patterns, as noted in Ex. 3–13. Discover that no sharps or flats are needed to preserve the whole and half-step pattern. Construct a major scale on D and D♭. Note the need for sharps and flats to preserve the step pattern.

• Use a chart as the following to guide students in building a major scale:

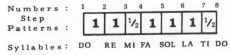

• In building a major scale on the staff use the following procedure: (1) notate eight notes, using eight consecutive letters of the alphabet, as from D to D or A♭ to A♭; (2) insert the half and whole-step pattern; and (3) add sharps or flats (do not mix them) to adjust the interval pattern between tones. This procedure is followed for building the E♭ major scale in Ex. 3–14.

Ex. 3-14. Building a Major Scale Starting on E♭

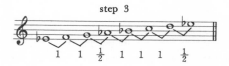

• Name the notes of the scale by using letter names, numbers, and syllables, as:

LETTER	C	D	E	F	G	A	B	C	—C MAJOR
NAMES:					or				
	E♭	F	G	A♭	B♭	C	D	E♭	—E♭ MAJOR
					or				
	G	A	B	C	D	E	F♯	G	—G MAJOR
NUMBERS:	1	2	3	4	5	6	7	8	
SYLLABLES:	DO	RE	MI	FA	SOL	LA	TI	DO	

Stress the use of numbers and syllables, since they indicate how the scale tones are related to each other and to the key tone.

• Draw a 13-step ladder on the chalkboard, relating each step to scale tones. Sing tones with numbers and syllables as the teacher points to the ladder-steps. At first, use stepwise movement; then skips and leaps.

MI	3
RE	2
DO 8	1
TI 7	
LA 6	
SOL 5	
FA 4	
MI 3	
RE 2	
8 DO 1	
7 TI	
6 LA	
5 SOL	

• Associate syllable and number names with *relative* pitch, and letter

names with *fixed* pitch. Thus, 1 2 3 or DO RE MI can be C D E or
F G A or B♭ C D or F♯ G♯ A♯. Provide practice in using all three
types of labeling. Show that the syllables and number names remain
constant in every major scale, with only the letter names and key
signature changing, as in Ex. 3–15.

Ex. 3-15. "London Bridge"

Key: C major

Letter names:	G	A	G	F	E	F	G	D	E	F	E	F	G
Numbers:	5	6	5	4	3	4	5	2	3	4	3	4	5
Syllables:	sol	la	sol	fa	mi	fa	sol	re	mi	fa	mi	fa	sol

Key: E♭ major

	B♭	C	B♭	A♭	G	A♭	B♭	F	G	A♭	G	A♭	B♭
	5	6	5	4	3	4	5	2	3	4	3	4	5
	sol	la	sol	fa	mi	fa	sol	re	mi	fa	mi	fa	sol

• Provide much experience in playing tunes on melody instruments
using a score with scale-degree numbers and/or letters, as for
"Twinkle, Twinkle":

```
                    6  6                              A  A
              5  5        5 ──  or        G  G            G ──
        1 1                          C C
```

Place numbers and letters directly on the staff as an aid in teaching
music reading.
• Develop familiarity with syllables by using "Do, Re, Mi" from
The Sound of Music. Sing tonal patterns and tone calls with syllables
and numbers.
• Fill glasses with different levels of water. Tune them to the major
scale, and label and play each tone. Also use the step bells or tone
bells turned on end for visual reinforcement of the scale and syllables.
• Use hand movements to show scale degrees for numbers-syllables:
DO-1 at belt, SOL-5 at chin, and high DO-8 at the top of the head,
with intervening scale-degrees between high and low DO. Drill on
scalewise and then stepwise patterns. Vary activity by using the five
fingers of the left hand as syllables DO through SOL or numbers
1 through 5, as the right hand points. Encourage self-drill.

• Locate a tonal pattern or phrase in notation after teacher states the syllable or number-names of the notes.

• Write the notation of a familiar song on the chalkboard. Locate DO, and place the numbers and syllable-names above each note. Sing the tune, using numbers and syllables interchangeably. Show that when DO is on a line (or space) MI-SOL-TI will also be on a line (or space), and when RE is on a line (or space) FA-LA and high DO will be on a line (or space). Note that low DO and high DO will never be both on a line or space.

• Put the first few tones of a familiar tune on the staff. Locate DO. Guide students to name the scale degrees of the notes. Ask: "What song is this?" Also write a "Mystery Tune" on the board or a chart and have students figure it out and perform it.

• Look at the notation of a tune. Ask questions such as: "Can you find a DO-MI-SOL in the notation? a MI-RE-DO? How many times does DO appear in line 1? in line 2? Can you tell when I make a mistake in singing the syllables?"

• Play a tune, such as "Twinkle," on the tone or resonator bells. First play it in the key of C (no sharps or flats) and call attention to the fact that only white keys are needed. Then play the tune beginning on D (play D, D, A, A, B, B, A—G, G, **F**, **F**, E, E, D—) and have students discover the need for F♯ rather than F. Repeat, beginning on E (where F♯ and G♯ are needed) and F (where B♭ is needed). Continue with other tunes, having students discover the need for sharps or flats in a piece where the home tone is *not* C. [*Note*: The teacher should locate DO for the students until they learn to interpret the key signature.]

• Sing, then play an ascending C major scale. Then sing an ascending major scale starting on D. Students will sing F♯ and C♯ for the third and seventh tones since they are familiar with the sound. Have students play the D major scale (many will play F and C instead of F♯ and C♯). Note need for accidentals. Transfer accidentals to *key signature* (see below). Repeat this procedure, using scales in other keys.

• Derive the principle that when a melody is written in a major tonality whose home tone or key is not C, it is necessary to use sharps or flats. Use familiar tunes to show how these sharps or flats are placed in a *key signature* following the clef, rather than as accidentals before each note requiring a sharp or flat, as illustrated in Ex. 3–16, p. 84.

• Show the relationship of key to *key signature*—a symbol comprised of one or more sharps or flats placed to the right of the clef at the beginning of each line of music to indicate the key note (home tone)

"The First Noel"
without key signature

Center of
tonality: D

The__ first____ No - el, the__ an - gels did say

with key signature

The__ first___ No - el, the__ an - gels did say

Ex. 3-16. "The First Noel"

and key in which the music is written. For example, in the major
tonality:

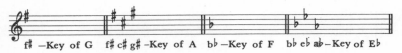

f♯ —Key of G   f♯ c♯ g♯ –Key of A   b♭ –Key of F   b♭ e♭ a♭–Key of E♭

• Guide students in identifying the key of a piece in a major tonality
by looking at the music's key signature. Observe three pieces using
three different key signatures with sharps (as one sharp—G major;
two sharps—D major; and three sharps—A major). Locate and play
DO or the key tone for each of the tunes. Notice that the last sharp
to the right in the key signature is scale step 7 or TI, and that DO is
one line or space higher, as shown in Ex. 3–17a. Apply this rule to
all key signatures with sharps.

Ex. 3-17a. The Key Signatures of Major Keys—(Sharps Only)

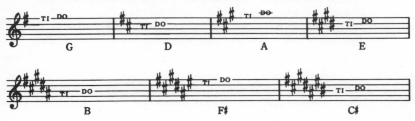

G   D   A   E

B   F♯   C♯

• Repeat above activity, using three different key signatures with
flats. Discover that the last flat to the right in the key signature is
scale-step 4 or FA, and that DO or the key tone can be found by
counting down from FA to DO. In addition, show that the next to
the last flat in a key signature with two or more flats also locates the
key tone. These rules are illustrated in Ex. 3–17b.

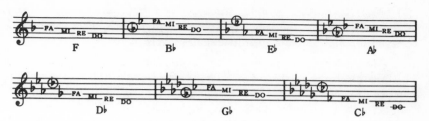

Ex. 3-17b. The Key Signatures of Major Keys—(Flats Only)

> • Discuss and experiment with various keys which are most appropriate to the students' vocal ranges.
> • Make flash cards and provide drill with key signature recognition. Find and list tunes written in certain keys. Check whether tunes are in the major tonality by looking at the final tone (the minor tonality usually ends on LA of the major key—see p. 86).

III-V 2d. Many melodies have a *minor tonality*; i.e., they use the tones of the minor scale. This scale is a frequently used tonal system in Western music. It consists of eight tones organized in a prescribed pattern of half and whole-steps, and is identified by the lowered third step (a half-step is found between the second and third tone), as illustrated in Exs. 3–18a and 3–18b.

Ex. 3-18a. The First Five Tones of Some Major and Minor Scales

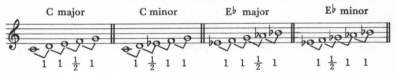

Ex. 3-18b. The Pattern of Half and Whole-Steps in an Ascending Minor Scale

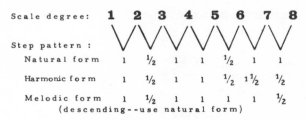

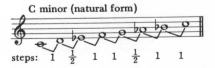

[*Note*: The rather complex study of the structure of the three forms of the minor scale—the *natural, harmonic,* and *melodic minor*—should be reserved for more advanced instructional levels.]

• Develop feeling for the minor tonality by singing, listening to, and creating tunes in the minor. The many songs in the minor tonality are frequently listed in the classified index of books in the basic music series, and include: S—36, 38, 43, 44, 65, 132. Some appropriate instrumental works in the minor tonality include: RL—7, 11, 15, 52, 73, 82, 88, 95, 96, 97, 98, 111, 121, 136, 172, 176, 206, 229, 257, 282, 287.

• Play instrumental works which have both minor and major tonality, such as: RL—1, 3, 24, 26, 32, 33, 96, 103, 146, 175, 216, 255, 256, 259, 260, 299. Identify tonality change and note how this contributes to interest and variety in the work (See Form, pp. 120–124).

• Characterize the mood of a melody written in the minor tonality as often one of sadness, mystery, or darkness. Note, however, that not all melodies in the minor elicit this mood (examples: S—36, 38, 43, 65, 132; RL—7, 32, 82, 95, 161, 226).

• Use pertinent activities related to the major tonality in order to develop understandings of the minor tonality (see pp. 81–83).

• Play a major scale on the resonator bells. Start on LA-6 to play the minor scale (related minor, natural form). Sing the minor scale and note the expressive mood and scale structure.

• Identify by ear the minor tonalities in many tunes. Examine the notation. Notice that the last tone of a melody in the minor usually ends on the sixth tone (LA) of the corresponding major scale. Although the key signature of the tune in Ex. 3–19 is for F major, the tonality is centered around D, and the final tone of the piece is D or LA (6) of the scale of F major. The melody is in the key of D minor.

Ex. 3-19. "Joshua Fit the Battle of Jericho"

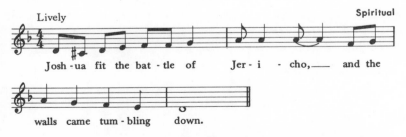

• Find examples of tunes ending on the sixth tone (LA) of the major scale, and tunes whose scale degree 5 (SOL) is raised. Discover aurally and by observing the notation that these tunes are probably in the minor tonality.

• Build a minor scale on any tone, using the prescribed order of half and whole-steps, as given in Ex. 3–18b, p. 85. Note that the minor scale is named after the tone on which it begins. Call a key "minor" when the tonality is based on some form of the minor tonality. In Ex. 3–19 the tonal center or key is D, and the tonality is minor— thus, D minor.

• Change a tune in the major tonality to the minor tonality (harmonic form) by *lowering* the third and sixth tones of the major scale, as in Ex. 3–20. Also change a tune in the minor tonality to one in the major tonality by raising the third, sixth, and possibly the seventh tones of the minor scale. Experiment with changing minor scales to major scales, and *vice versa*.

Ex. 3-20. "My Hat" in a Major and Minor Tonality

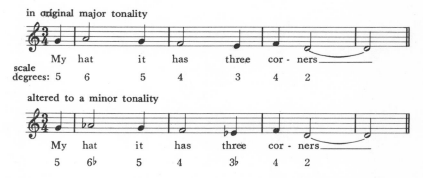

• Note that a key signature may represent a major and minor tonality. Show, for example, that the keys of G major and E minor both have one sharp (an F♯) in their key signatures.

• Sing and make up tonal patterns and tunes in the minor.

III-V   2e. Many tones of melodies outline the *pentatonic scale*—a scale consisting of five different tones corresponding to the first, second, third, fifth, and sixth scale degrees of the major scale. An example of a tune in the pentatonic tonality is found in Ex. 3–21.

Ex. 3-21. "Nobody Knows the Trouble I've Seen"—a Pentatonic Melody

No-bod-y knows but Je - sus,   No-bod-y knows the
trou-ble I've seen,   Glo - ry Hal - le - lu - jah.

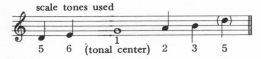

scale tones used

5   6   (tonal center)   2   3   5

• Listen to and sing tunes in the pentatonic mode, such as: S—9, 24, 27, 32, 55, 86, 92, 109, 122, 131; RL—13, 66, 99, 144, 153, 167, 205, 258, 274, 302. Identify pentatonic tonality and show scale tones on the resonator bells (1–2–3–5–6). Notice the absence of the fourth and seventh scaledegrees, making the tunes pentatonic in tonality.

• Note the frequent use of the pentatonic mode in Oriental tunes (examples: S—2, 40) and songs of the American Indians and Negroes, the cowboys, and the people of Scotland.

• Distribute the tones of the C major scale, using the resonator bells. Have each student play his tone in order of the scale. Take out scale-degree 4 (FA) and 7 (TI), and replay the scale. Note the pentatonic tonality. Also play and create pentatonic melodies on the black keys of keyboard instruments, with F♯ or G♭ being scale-degree 1 (F♯ = 1, G♯ = 2, A♯ = 3, C♯ = 5, and D♯ = 6).

• Build some pentatonic scales beginning on any tone, using only tones 1, 2, 3, 5, and 6 of the major scale. Also build a pentatonic scale on scale tone 6 (6, 7, 8, 3, and 4) for a scale used frequently in Oriental music. Practice creating Oriental-sounding tunes, using the pentatonic scale.

IV-V   2f. Many tones of melodies outline the *whole-tone scale*—a scale consisting of six different tones, each of which are a whole-step apart, as illustrated in Ex. 3–22.

Ex. 3-22. Pierné: "Entrance of the Little Fauns"

• Create sound images for clouds, dreams, or floating on air, using the whole-tone scale. Illustrate the scale on the tone or resonator bells, and note the whole-step structure and the use of six tones.

• Listen for whole-tone passages in selected works by Debussy (examples: RL—58, 64, 65, 68). Note the lack of a tonal center, and resulting vague tonality. Compare the vague, nebulous feeling with Impressionist paintings by artists such as Degas and Monet.

• Provide practice in building or writing a whole-tone scale starting on any pitch level. Encourage students to create original melodies and songs using this tonality.

IV-V 2g. A *chromatic scale* may begin on any note, and uses all twelve tones between the octave (as from C to C or F to F), each of which is one half-step apart. The chromatic scale, as shown in Ex. 3–23, uses sharps for accidentals when ascending, and flats when descending.

Ex. 3-23. The Chromatic Scale   beginning on E♭ , ascending

beginning on F , descending

• Listen to the chromatic scale beginning on several tones in order to become familiar with its sound. Build a chromatic scale from C to C or D to D. Count the number of tones and show the recurring use of half-steps. Practice singing the ascending and descending chromatic scale.

• Show how tones in the major or minor tonalities can be made chromatic by raising or lowering them one half-step. Relate this to the use of accidentals (see pp. 17–18). Add chromatic tones to basic tones of a melody for additional color and interest.

• Listen to and look at the notation of Rimsky-Korsakov's "Flight of the Bumble Bee"—a piece utilizing the chromatic scale. Identify by ear the chromatic tonal patterns found in: RL—58(theme 1), 77(theme 1), 104(themes 1, 3), 272(theme 1), 273, 280, 285.

IV-V 2h. In contemporary music some melodies use all the tones of the chromatic scale, but not in consecutive order, before any one of the twelve tones is repeated. The tones of the *12-tone melody* or *row* are not related to any tonal center and, therefore, are *atonal*. An atonal melody is illustrated in Ex. 3–24.

Ex. 3-24. Schoenberg: "Peripetia" from *Five Pieces for Orchestra*

• Play examples of music utilizing the technique of the 12-tone row, as: RL—241, 242, 300(theme 4), 303, 323. Note the absence of key feeling. Examine the notation and notice that the tunes lack key signatures.

• Use twelve resonator bells for the chromatic scale within the octave. Arrange the bells in random order. Play each one. Devise interesting rhythmic patterns and notate. Vary the melody (see pp. 124–128 for techniques) and note effect. Encourage students to compose tunes using the 12-tone technique and methods of varying a melody.

IV-V   2i. The musics of many of the world's peoples, especially those from non-Western cultures, are based upon many different types of scale systems, all of which vary in the sequence of their scale intervals. [*Note*: The detailed study of other scale systems should be reserved for more advanced instructional levels. The aim in the elementary school is to provide *aural experiences* at all levels with melodies using less familiar scale systems.]

• Listen to music of the medieval church, and note use of unfamiliar scale systems. Attend religious services of the Buddhist, Catholic, Jewish, and Moslem religions to hear modal music.

• Provide much experience in singing and playing modal tunes, and analyzing their scale systems (examples: S—12, 47, 58, 89, 95, 103, 112, 115; RL—38-"In Jerusalem" section, 129, 130, 147, 163-theme 1, 207-theme 1, 239, 310, 311-theme 2). Notate the tones used in the melody in ascending order. Play the scale and observe interval patterns, as illustrated in Ex. 3–25.

• Play examples of the "blues" effect in works such as: RL—84, 85, 166, 249, 301. Build a "blues" scale, showing that the third and seventh tones of the major scale are often flatted to cause a "blues" effect. Experiment with changing a slow melody in the major tonality into a "blues."

Ex. 3-25. "Hava Nagila"—a Modal Tune

- Play representative examples of music from many countries, peoples, and areas from both East and West. Compare scale systems used, as well as other differences in rhythm, melody, harmony, form, and tone color.
- Use selected music by Bela Bartok to illustrate how various scales have been used by a famous contemporary composer in his music (examples: RL—12, 13, 15, 16).
- Illustrate how non-Western cultures are increasing their use of the Western scale systems in their musics (examples: S—4, 75, 127). Similarly, call attention, through musical examples, to how the Beatles and other rock groups have experimented with tonalities and instrumental tone colors not commonly used in Western music.

IV-V   2j. Some compositions may use two or more tonalities simultaneously. This is known as *bitonality* or *polytonality*.

- Accompany a familiar song with chords belonging to another key. Listen for resulting dissonances and the simultaneous sounding of two tonalities. Also make up an original tune in one key. Add chords in another key and note effect.
- Play the C major chord (C, E, G) together with the F♯ major chord (F♯, A♯, C♯). Note the polyharmonic-bitonal effect of combining chords from different keys.
- Call attention to polytonal sounds and resulting dissonance in pieces such as: RL—47(section B), 132, 165, 277, 279.
- Sing or play two familiar melodies in two different keys at the same time to illustrate bitonality.

Four

HARMONY

BASIC CONCEPT:

Harmony is the simultaneous sounding of two or more tones.

KEY TERMS:

accompaniment, harmonic interval, consonance, dissonance, chord, harmonic change, harmonic cadence, texture

I-V Most musical works have tones which sound simultaneously, producing the element of *harmony*. Notice how the harmony adds depth, color, and interest to the melody of "Michael Row Your Boat" in Ex. 4–1.

Ex. 4-1. "Michael Row Your Boat"

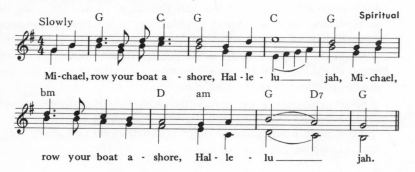

92

I-II 1. A melody may be sung or played with or without supporting tones. Harmony results when groups of two or more tones are performed at the same time.

> • Combine two or more tones on the piano, Autoharp, ukulele, or resonator bells to illustrate harmony. Discuss how two or more tones sounded together can make harmony. Listen to the harmony produced by the various parts of a band, chorus, or orchestra.
>
> • Play a tune or recording having single melodic lines followed by harmony. Students raise hands when they hear the harmony parts. Appropriate examples include: RL—88, 141, 144, 153, 178, 179, 220.
>
> • Play or sing a melody. Add accompaniment. Describe the tones played with the melody as "harmony," the melody's "accompaniment," and/or "chords" (see pp. 96–103). Note how sound in music is enhanced by harmony, which adds color, weight, richness, and depth to music. Draw two or more horizontal lines above each other to symbolize simultaneously sounding tones, such as $=_{\underline{}}=$ (for parallel thirds).
>
> • Play a melody, and then its accompanying harmony without the melody. Combine and note the more interesting and aesthetically satisfying effect.
>
> • Listen for examples of harmony in the environment; e.g., the simultaneous sounds of birds chirping and machines whirring.
>
> • Play music of primitive man, the early Church (Gregorian chant), and several ethnic groups (American Indian, some Chinese and African music, Hawaiian chant, and other Polynesian music), and call attention to the absence of harmony (see *monophony*, p. 107).
>
> • Experiment with combining two or more tones using melody and harmony instruments and/or voices.
>
> • Play a familiar tune on the tone bells. Encourage experimentation by adding a second part moving in parallel motion to the tune, using intervals as the second, third, fourth, and fifth (see also pp. 94–96).
>
> • Try to produce harmony on various instruments and by using one's voice by itself. Note that simultaneously sounding tones can be produced only on certain instruments; e.g., piano, organ, harmonica, and all string instruments.
>
> • Illustrate how harmonic accompaniments are produced on the Autoharp or ukulele by playing each tone of the chord separately, counting the tones heard, and then strumming the entire chord.
>
> • Sing songs using a variety of instrumental accompaniments. Call attention to differences in sound and texture (see pp. 106–108).
>
> • Emphasize *harmonic blend*—the smooth intermingling of various tones so that there is no perceptible separation. Work on blend when

singing in harmony and playing instruments, and help students evaluate whether blend is being accomplished.

• Observe notation where harmony is written on a second staff, as for the left hand on the piano, two or more instruments, and a chorus. Discover why there are two or more staffs of music. Observe the note-heads placed directly above each other to indicate that the tones are to be played or sung together. Also notice that the staffs are joined by a bracket.

• Encourage students at all levels to add harmony to tunes and create original works with harmony.

III-V 2. When two tones of different pitch are played simultaneously, an *harmonic interval* results.

III 2a. The combined sound of two different tones heard together results in an *harmonic interval*.

• Experiment with using various two-tone combinations played together. Compare differences in quality.

• Play F and A simultaneously on the tone bells, and name the interval a "third." Repeat, using F and G (a second), F to F (an eighth or octave) and F up to C (a fifth). In each case, name the interval. Guide students to generalize about how an interval is named. Use the same terminology to describe harmonic and melodic intervals (see pp. 73–74). Compare the differences between a melodic and harmonic interval by playing two tones successively (melodically) and simultaneously (harmonically).

III-V 2b. Some harmonic intervals sound different from other harmonic intervals.

• Note the relative *consonance* of some intervals (as the third, sixth, and octave), which gives a feeling of repose and rest; and the relative *dissonance* of other intervals (as the second and seventh), which gives the feeling of disturbance and restlessness, and a quality of tension. Play "Chopsticks" in Ex. 4–2 and note the sounding of two simultaneous tones and the quality of the intervals.

• Use activities listed for *melodic interval*, pp. 73–75, to develop understandings of how to name intervals (see Ex. 4–2.)

• Students experiment with harmonic intervals on the piano or tone

Ex. 4-2. "Chopsticks"

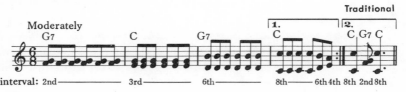

interval: 2nd———— 3rd———— 6th———— 8th———— 6th 4th 8th 2nd 8th

bells, or through vocal experimentation. Note different qualities. Write down, by letter-name and/or notation, those intervals sounding relatively more consonant than others.

• Play selected music of the twentieth century having a great deal of dissonance (examples: RL—12, 13, 21, 47, 132, 165, 167, 168, 171, 270, 272, 277, 309, 323; and many other works by contemporary composers). Note feelings of tension, conflict, and unrest. Compare with music using little dissonance (examples: RL—10, 11, 20, 57, 81, 94, 101, 175, 178, 210, 281, 290, 305, 306, 308, 310, 311, 320). Also compare frequent use of dissonance in many modern works with the few dissonances found in popular and contemporary folk music.

• Play a familiar tune, as "Au Clair de la Lune" in Ex. 4–3, and add harmonic intervals as seconds, thirds, and fifths, in parallel motion. Compare effect of harmonizing melodies with various intervals.

Ex. 4-3. "Au Clair de la Lune"

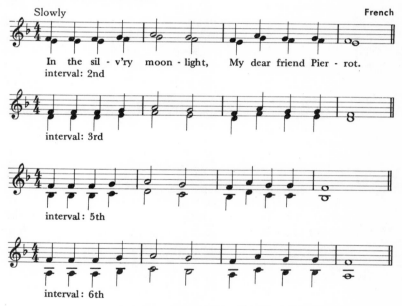

• Provide practice in recognizing a given interval. First differentiate between a unison and octave. Then play various intervals, with students raising hands whenever they hear an octave. Repeat, using harmonic seconds and sevenths, thirds and sixths, and fourths and fifths.

• Play a series of thirds. Insert another kind of interval in this series. Students raise hands when they hear this interval. Also, play a series of thirds and sixths, inserting an occasional second or seventh. Identify the dissonant interval when heard. Repeat procedures, using other intervals.

• Use various kinds of harmonic intervals in conjunction with tempo and dynamic effects to create mood and picture scenes such as anger, a summer day, a storm, or falling asleep.

• Harmonize a familiar melody with repeated intervals of a fourth or fifth. Note its Oriental quality. Play examples of music utilizing frequent intervals of the fourth or fifth, as: RL—50, 70(the "emperor" theme), 163, 207, 211, 239.

• Sing many part-songs using the relatively consonant intervals of the third and sixth. Frequently utilize these intervals when creating harmony parts to songs or original tunes (see p. 207).

• Establish a drone-like effect, using scale tones 1 and 5 simultaneously. Listen for drones in Scottish bagpipe music, music for the Japanese koto (as in "Sakura"—RL—239), and instrumental works as: RL—29, 49, 163, 274. Also experiment with harmonizing tunes, especially those of Scotland and the Orient, with the open-fifth drone.

• Play a series of intervals, alternating consonance with dissonance. Compare differences in sound and discuss how these intervals help to create tension and release. Relate this to similar aspects in life and in the arts.

• Analyze by ear and in notation the harmonic intervals occurring in two-part songs (see pp. 162–171).

II-V   The realization of harmony in most music is accomplished through the grouping of three or more tones sounded simultaneously, and called *chords*.

II-V   1. Chords provide the basis for much harmony in music. Musical accompaniment is predominantly chordal in structure.

• Play C, E, G separately and together on the piano or tone bells as students listen and observe. Use this chord as an accompaniment to "Row Your Boat" or "Three Blind Mice." Ask students to play the C, E, G on the resonator bells. Experiment by playing other chords, and see how they fit with tunes. Also encourage students to play a chord using four or more tones.

• Play a chordal accompaniment on the Autoharp, ukulele, or piano. Then change to a one-tone accompaniment. Note differences in harmonic effect. Play the tones of a chord consecutively. Call these "broken" chords or *arpeggios*. Compare a chordal accompaniment with a broken-chord and single-tone accompaniment. Note that the chordal-type accompaniments have more fullness and depth.

• Play a melody. Harmonize it in several ways, including *tone clusters* (see p. 100), *triads* (see pp. 98–100), and chords which do not fit the melody (see p. 100). Students select preferred accompaniment and discuss reasons for their choice.

• Use songs with chordwise melodic movement (see pp. 68–70 and 72) to show that the tones of a chord are often used in tonal patterns of a melody.

• Play different chords. Provide practice in singing the various tones of the chords (see *vocal chording* activities, pp. 170–171).

• Call attention to chord symbols over notation. Write the chord symbols on chalkboard. Distribute resonator bell tones, grouping them for each chord. Students play tones separately (in broken-chord style) and then together. Teacher points to each chord group as students play the appropriate chords for the melody. Other students sing the melody with the chordal accompaniment. Repeat, with students playing independently, using chord symbols. Ask volunteers to point to chord groups and switch chords when changes occur. Note chord structure. Encourage students to play by ear rather than use the chord symbols when their chord occurs. Repeat activity many times during the year. Use to develop an understanding of harmonic change, tonality, and triad construction.

• Notice how the appropriate harmony for many folk and "pop" songs is usually indicated in notation through chord symbols found above the notes where the chord is to be changed. Locate the letters above the tune which indicate the letter-name of a note on which the chord is built (see p. 102). Find examples where Roman numerals are used instead of letter-names, and discover that the numerals indicate the scale-step on which the chord is built, as illustrated in Ex. 4–4.

Ex. 4-4. "Battle Hymn of the Republic"

• Observe that when no letter-name for a chord is indicated at the beginning of a new measure (as in measure 2 in Ex. 4–4 above), the chord used for the preceding measure is repeated.

• Note differences in notating major chords (uppercase letters and

Roman numerals) and minor chords (lowercase letters and numerals), as in Ex. 4–4, p. 97, where the C or I chord is major and the dm or ii chord is minor.

• Teach the tablature system of indicating fingerings for chords on fretted instruments as the ukulele and guitar, such as:

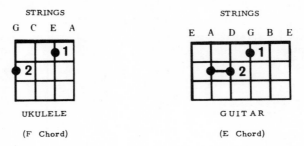

Once chord structure is understood, guide students to figure out their own fingering for chords based upon knowledge of the names of the strings, intervals, and the letter-names of the tones within a chord.

• Choose six different pitches, as E, F, D, B♭, F♯, and C. Use various combinations of three or more tones to build as many types of chords as possible. Compare chord qualities and harmonic effect of the many possible tonal groupings.

• Practice playing resonator bells for chordal accompaniments to many songs. Devise various types of accompaniments including *block chords* (a chord played for each beat or tone in the melody) and *broken chords* or *arpeggios* (each tone of the chord is sounded successively). Identify the use of block chords in instrumental works as: RL—10(the "chorale"), 47, 103, 106(the "chorale"), 126, 173, 175, 182, 203, 259, 287, 304(section B). Compare effect with frequent broken chord (arpeggio) accompaniments found in music written for the harp (RL—65, 104, 186, 215, 235, 253, 298) and piano (RL—102, 229, 235). Emphasize that the arpeggio accompaniment figures stem from the chord, and that this type of accompaniment is not as static and stationary as block-chord accompaniments.

III-V   2. There are many types of chords.

III-IV   2a. The most commonly used chord is the *triad*—a chord of three tones built up in thirds from any scale tone, as in Ex. 4–5.

• Using the resonator bells, distribute the individual tones of a triad (as C, E, G for the C chord). Sing a song which uses only one chord, as in most rounds. Students first sing the tune as they clap the beat, and then play the three tones of the triad on the beat to accompany the singing.

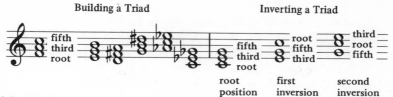

Building a Triad   **Inverting a Triad**

Ex. 4-5. Triads

• Choose a tone and build two harmonic intervals of thirds above it;
or choose every other letter-name from the first tone. Call the tone
on which a triad is built its *root*.

• Find chord symbols written above the melody, as in "Battle Hymn
of the Republic" in Ex. 4–4, p. 97. Build a triad on the letter-name
indicated, using three resonator bells. Play the chord with the
melody. Show how the triad receives its name from the letter-name
of the root note.

• Analyze a triad to show that its pitches are called the *root*, *third*
(an harmonic third above the root), and *fifth* (an harmonic fifth
above the root). Build triads by starting on any tone, skipping a
letter-name, and skipping another letter-name (as C, E, G; D, F, A;
or B, D, F).

• Play a triad. Students sing each of its three tones. Identify the
tone being sung as the root, third, or fifth. Also play a triad, and then
two tones of the triad. Students fill in missing tone by singing or
playing it.

• At levels IV and V use flashcards having numbers and syllables
of a common chordal progression on each card. Divide students into
two, and then three parts, with each group singing a different tone
of each triad in harmony.

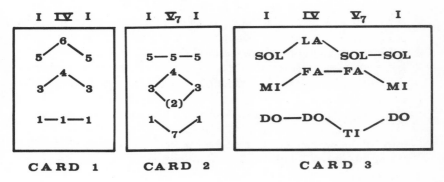

CARD 1   CARD 2   CARD 3

• Play examples from several tunes containing the V₇ chord—a
4-tone chord built on the fifth scale-step of a major or minor key
(as C₇—F major or minor; D₇—G major or minor; or G₇—C major

or minor). Discover how this chord is built by adding three thirds
above the chord root, as in Ex. 4–6a. Observe how the tone added
to the basic triad to make it a "seventh" chord is an interval of a
seventh above the chord root. Find other examples of the V₇ chord
and note how the I chord (the "home-tone chord") usually follows
it, as in Ex. 4–6b.

Ex. 4-6a. The V₇ Chord

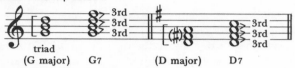

triad
(G major)   G7   (D major)   D7

Ex. 4-6b. "The Sidewalks of New York"

East   side,   West   side,   (I)   (V₇)

III-V   2b. Contemporary composers often use tone clusters and chords built
on intervals other than thirds to produce varied harmonic effects.

• Experiment with building chords upon a combination of three
or more adjacent tones called *tone clusters*. In addition, play the C
and D major chords (or any other adjacent chords) at the same
time, and note effect. Also build other *non-tertian chords* (chords built
on intervals other than thirds) by using intervals of fourths and
fifths, as:

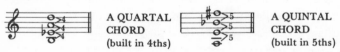

A QUARTAL CHORD (built in 4ths)   A QUINTAL CHORD (built in 5ths)

• Listen to examples of non-tertian chords in instrumental works
(examples: RL—21, 50, 132, 168, 272). Note the use of tone clusters
in works such as: RL—92 (variation 1), 242, 272, 322 (introduction
and theme 1b).
• Use techniques outlined in Melody, p. 91, to show how a piece
of music can use chords of two different keys at the same time
(*polyharmony* and *bitonality*). Compare present-day harmonic practice
in contemporary music with that prevalent in the past by comparing works of different periods.
• Experiment with harmonizing familiar tunes with tone clusters, non-
tertian chords, and chords not related to the tonality of the melody.

III-V   2c. Chords vary in their quality. Different chords and kinds of harmonies affect the mood and color of a work.

• Play a chord. Repeat it exactly or with some alteration (change a tone, add or delete a tone). Ask: "Was the second chord the same or different from the first chord?"

• Play a major chord, as C, E, G for C major, several times on the piano. Change the chord by *lowering* its third (C E♭ G). Students raise hands when change is made, and note different quality. Repeat activity, using minor chords changed to major (*raise* the third of the minor chord). Later, guide students to make these changes on resonator bells.

• Play major and minor chords and compare qualities.

• Listen to, and sing pieces using both major and minor chords, develop a "feel" for differences in harmonization, and identify the tonality of the chords.

• Describe a mood (such as gay, mysterious, noisy). Students devise chords on tone bells or piano to depict mood.

• Compare relative tension and unrest of dissonant-sounding chords with the relative rest and repose of consonant-sounding chords. Emphasize that dissonant chords are not necessarily unpleasant-sounding.

• Notice the results of accompanying a minor tune with major chords, and a tune in the major tonality with minor chords.

IV-V 3. Some chords are used more frequently and seem more important than others in harmonizing a given tune. The chordal structure helps to determine a piece's tonality (see pp. 75–91 for related learning and activities on *tonality*).

• Walk to the beat of a piece. Stop when the melody is accompanied by its home chord.

• Raise hands every time the I chord (the *tonic* chord, the keytone chord) is heard. Discover that most tunes start and end with the I chord, and that this chord helps establish the key feeling or tonality, and the overall unity of the piece. Relate the tonic chord to the keynote (DO or 1—see pp. 75–77).

• Harmonize the last tone of a song with the IV chord instead of the I chord. For example, in "On Top of Old Smoky" in Ex. 4–7, p. 102, play the F (IV) chord instead of the C (I) chord on the last tone. Note effect, and call attention to the pull of tones which seems to demand the I chord.

• Observe the predominance of the I, IV, and V₇ chords (see pp. 97–100) in harmonizing many tunes, especially folk and popular music. Establish tonality of a song by playing its I, IV, and V₇ chords (minor: i, iv, V₇), or its I, V₇, I chords (minor: i, V₇, i).

• Listen to and identify the strong feeling of conclusion at the end of sections of instrumental works caused by the use of the V₇ to I chord progression (examples: RL—1, 89, 146, 175, 183, 184, 216, 244, 246, 247, 248, 259, 263, 264, 297, 313, 320, 325).

• Listen to and examine the notation of many tunes in the major tonality to discover that most of the chords are major in quality. Compare with tunes in the minor tonality, where the chords most frequently used are minor.

• Note that almost all tunes, especially folk songs, hymns, and popular songs, end with the I chord. Call attention to the inconclusive feeling of works not ending on the I chord (examples: RL—12, 13, 165, 205, 274 and many other contemporary works).

• Derive the scale upon which a tune is built (see p. 79). Build triads on each of these tones. Label each scale tone with a Roman numeral. Note the frequency of the I, IV, and V₇ chords, as in Ex. 4–7.

Ex. 4-7. "On Top of Old Smoky"

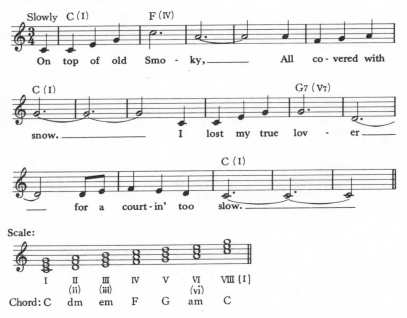

• Relabel the letter-name chord symbols found over a tune, using Roman numerals, and relate to scale-tones of a melody, as in Ex. 4–7 above. Build the I, IV and V₇ chords in various keys and play them on the Autoharp or ukulele. Accompany songs which use the I, IV and V₇ chords in keys other than the ones in which they are written.

• Use tunes with only the I and V₇ chords (examples: S—25, 35, 37,

50, 57, 72, 80, 102, 113, 121). Students put up one finger when the
I chord is heard, and five fingers when the V₇ chord is heard. Later
expand to tunes using three different chords—the I, IV, and V₇
chords (examples: S—1, 4, 23, 49, 52, 54, 60, 61, 75, 94, 134).

• Relate use of the V₇ and I chords to feelings of temporary and
final *cadence* (see p. 113). Identify when the cadence ends on the
I or V₇ chord.

II-V   A close relationship exists between the melody and its implied, supporting harmony.

II-III   1. There is a need for a change in the accompanying harmony when the
melodic structure changes. In "Tinga Layo" in Ex. 4–8 the melody seems
to imply a change of harmony in every measure.

Ex. 4-8. "Tinga Layo"

primary chords: I(C)—C E G; IV (F)—F A C; V₇ (G7)—G B D F

• Select a familiar tune, play the melody with accompaniment,
and then isolate the accompaniment. Call attention to chord changes.
Replay tune with accompaniment as students raise hands (or stand
and sit) for each chord change. Count the number of times the harmony changes.

• Play the harmony of a familiar tune on the piano or Autoharp
while saying the melodic rhythm, singing "TA," as:

Students identify tune. Use the above technique with many familiar
tunes. Call attention to chordal changes.

• Sing a familiar tune. Then strum the I chord on the Autoharp or
ukulele. Sing the tune over a repeated I chord accompaniment.
Students raise hands for those sections in which the I chord seems
inappropriate. Repeat, using many songs.

• Sing a tune while playing its accompaniment. Make one obvious
error in harmony. Students raise hands on error.

• Play a tune with accompaniment, noting harmonic changes. Repeat, clapping at the point of change. Show that chord changes frequently occur on the strong beat or primary accent.

• Distribute single resonator bells corresponding to the given chord symbols over the notation (as F, C₇—use F, C). Write on the chalkboard either the two letter-names or the sequence in which these chords occur. Point to the letters as students play the bells on the beats while the entire class sings.

• Compare the *harmonic rhythm*—the rate of change in a composition's harmonic structure—of various pieces. Note that some pieces have a relatively fast harmonic rhythm, since the chords change frequently (examples: S—11, 41, 44, 54, 109, 116, 126, 129, 137, 142). Listen and play the harmonies of many songs having a slow and relatively static harmonic rhythm because the chords change infrequently (examples: S—25, 35, 45, 49, 50, 72, 78, 92, 98, 102). For example, note that the harmonic rhythm in Ex. 4–9a is much faster and more dynamic than that of Ex. 4–9b.

Ex. 4-9a. "Praise God From Whom All Blessings Flow" ("Old Hundredth" or Doxology)

Ex. 4-9b. "A Hole in the Bucket"

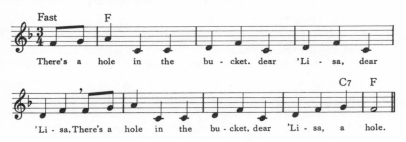

• Play a melody with chord symbols indicated, as students follow notation. Observe frequency of chord changes as symbolized above the notes, and classify tune as having a slow or fast harmonic rhythm.

• Listen to familiar and unfamiliar melodies. "Imagine" the harmony and raise hands when a change might occur. Verify answers by playing the tune with accompaniment.

IV-V   2. The tones in a melody and the harmonizing chords are related.

• Once an understanding of chords and triads is developed (see pp. 96–100), place the notation of a familiar tune on the chalkboard. Ask: "How can we figure out the chord markings for this tune?" Elicit responses, check through playing and listening, and guide students to recognize relationship between the melody and the chord structure (see the following activities).

• Write the notation of a melody and its key signature on the chalkboard. Identify the tones of the I, IV, and V_7 chords within the key, and the most important tones of each measure. Note how the tones of the melody are found in the chord tones of the harmony, as in Ex. 4–10.

Ex. 4-10. "Oh Susanna"

× = tone found in melody

• Locate the tone that receives the accent in the metric flow of a song. Show that this tone is ordinarily a tone of the required chord. In "Oh Susanna" in Ex. 4–10, the tones falling on the first beat of each measure are harmonized by appropriate chords.

• Find examples of melodies with chordwise movement (see p. 68 for list). Examine chord indications. Discover that the tones are harmonized by the chord which has these tones. Provide practice in locating and harmonizing tunes with a succession of chordal tones. For instance, note the chordwise movement of the melody, and the resulting harmony, in measures 1–3 of "Oh Susanna" in Ex. 4–10. The F-A sequence in measures 1–2 is harmonized by the F chord (containing F and A), while the G-E-C sequence in measure 3 is harmonized by the C chord (containing C, E, and G).

• Sing two *partner songs* (see pp. 163–167 for detailed discussion).

Listen to the blend of the harmonies of the two songs. Examine their notation and note reason for consonant harmonies.

• Provide a chordal background, asking students to improvise a melody over the harmony. Examples of chordal patterns can be taken from any tune, as:

"Old Folks at Home" $\frac{4}{4}$ **C ||| |F ||| |C ||| |G⁷||| etc.**

" Clementine " $\frac{3}{4}$ **F |F || |F || |F || |C⁷|| |C⁷ |F || |C⁷|| |F | ||**

• Provide experience and guidance in harmonizing a simple tune by ear, using only the I, IV, and V₇ chords. Add a harmony part to a familiar tune, basing this part on the tones of the indicated chord. Stress that the *ear* should act as the final judge as to whether the chord is correct.

III-V   An important aspect of a musical work is *texture*—the thickness or thinness of sound, and the interrelationships existing between the horizontal (melodic) and vertical (harmonic) elements of music.

III   1. Some music sounds thicker or heavier in overall sound than other music because of the presence or absence of many different tones in various registers and tone qualities.

     • Play a chord on the piano with as many tones as possible. Follow this with a triad. Compare the relative *density* of each chord. Students should experiment in making chords of high and low density.

     • Play a series of three chords, two of which have many more tones than the third. Identify the chord with the thinnest texture.

     • Listen to difference in texture between two-voiced harmony as played on the piano or resonator bells, chords as played on the Autoharp or ukulele, or as sung by a chorus, and many-voiced harmony as performed by all the instruments of a band or orchestra.

     • Compare various textures found in instrumental works, including—

RELATIVELY THICK TEXTURE: RL—12, 61, 92, 136, 143, 156, 172, 175, 211, 272, 319

RELATIVELY THIN TEXTURE: RL—42, 57, 66, 95, 149, 171, 180, 184, 203, 204, 206, 228, 232, 238, 244, 270, 282, 286, 294, 308

BOTH THICK AND THIN TEXTURES: RL—29, 36, 77, 119, 122, 130, 141, 153, 178, 202, 208, 222, 231, 275, 295, 304, 322

     • Raise hands when the texture of a work changes. Discuss why the texture seems rich and full, or thin and clear.

     • Play a triad in the low register of the piano and compare the texture with the same chord played in a higher register. Compare textures of various vocal and instrumental ensembles, and note how texture is affected when the music is written in the low or high registers.

III-V 2. Musical texture may be *monophonic, homophonic,* or *polyphonic.*

III-IV 2a. Some music has only a single unaccompanied melodic line, with no harmonic background. This music is *monophonic* in texture. See p. 62 for activities related to chant and monophonic music, and p. 93 for suggestions designed to develop recognition of harmony and its absence.

V-V 2b. A piece of music may have only a principal melody present, with all other tones supporting and enriching the melody through a subordinate, chordal-type accompaniment. This music is *homophonic* in texture. Note that in Ex. 4–11 there is only one melodic line, with the tones in the accompaniment supporting the melody.

Ex. 4-11. Tchaikowsky: "Dance of the Little Swans" from *Swan Lake*

(original key: F♯ minor)

• Play a tune with its harmony. Compare the melodic line with its supporting accompaniment by playing each one separately on the piano, ukulele, or Autoharp. Observe that the accompaniment acts as a support and a background for the more important melodic line.

• Sing and analyze the homophonic texture of the following harmonizations for songs: *chord roots, pedal tones, vocal chording, ostinato (chant), harmonic endings,* and *harmonizing in thirds and sixths* (see pp. 163–165 for discussion and illustrations). Note that the accompaniments are often repeated, lack rhythmic independence, and generally support the melody.

• Listen to music that has only a tune or theme and supportive harmony (almost all hymns, popular songs, barbershop quartet pieces, and the recorded works in the basic listening series for schools are homophonic in texture). Compare this homophonic music to music that has two or more themes present at one time (polyphonic music—see next section).

V-V 2c. A piece of music may have two or more distinct and separate musical lines sounded simultaneously, resulting in *polyphony* or a *polyphonic texture*.

• Sing the following types of songs, all of which are polyphonic in nature: *round, canon, echo song, partner song,* and *descant* or *countermelody* (see pp. 163–169 for discussion and illustrations). Note that each melodic line has rhythmic and melodic interest, and generally can be considered to be independent of the main theme. Sing and clap the rhythm of each part and note the independent themes.

• Relate polyphonic texture to the various weaves of a piece of cloth. Also note various independent lines in an art work, and show relationship of these lines to each other and to the entire work.

• Ask four students to read four different lines from a poem at the same time, with varying degrees of dynamics. Relate to separate melodic lines in a polyphonic work, each one interweaving with the others, with one more important at any given moment.

• Listen to pieces or sections of works which have polyphonic texture. Practice concentrating on only one of the themes at a time, and clapping its rhythm. Then listen to how themes are combined. Have one group clap the rhythm of one theme while another group claps the rhythm of the second theme. Examples of works with some polyphonic texture include—

ECHOING EFFECT (IMITATION OF THEME): RL—54, 83, 89, 106 (the "Oh Susanna" section), 297, 316

CANON: RL—38 (coda), 51, 75 (theme 1), 133, 147, 156, 163 (beginning), 295 (variations 9, 10).

COMBINING TWO THEMES WITHIN THE SAME WORK: RL—3(variation 4—the theme with itself), 19(fragments of themes 1, 2), 26(themes 1, 2), 31(themes 1, 2), 106("Oh Susanna" with the verse of "Old Black Joe"), 108(themes 1, 2), 109(themes 1, 2), 116(themes 1, 3), 202(themes 1, 2), 205(themes 1, 3)

COUNTERMELODY: RL—34, 75, 82, 91, 92(variation 2), 196, 204, 219, 262, 263, 282, 310(theme 2)

FUGUE: RL—11, 36(last section), middle sections of 38, 112, 231

• Identify homophonic and polyphonic textures within the same piece. The majority of works cited above are generally homophonic, but contain some polyphonic passages.

• Note how two or more contrasting rhythmic patterns sounded simultaneously make the rhythmic texture more interesting, and result in rhythmic polyphony.

Five

FORM

BASIC CONCEPT:

The result of the arrangement and organization of the elements of rhythm, melody, harmony, tone color, and dynamics in a musical work is known as the music's overall design or *form*.

KEY TERMS:

Tonal and rhythmic patterns, phrase, cadence, section, repetition, contrast, variation, forms in music.

I-V The design of a musical work consists of several divisions or parts.

I-III 1. The parts of a composition are usually clearly defined, and serve different purposes in relation to the music's overall design.

I   1a. A musical work has a beginning, a middle part, and an end.

> • Use the terms "beginning," "middle," and "ending" when singing, listening to, and playing music. Sing or play designated parts of the piece as the need arises.
> • When playing rhythm instruments or using bodily movement, stress the importance of directing one's self to the meaning of the music as soon as the music begins, and paying attention to the music until it is completed.

• Ask questions about the music, referring to the various parts, as: "Was the beginning of the music slow or fast? What happened to the speed at the end? What instrument did you hear in the middle part?"

I-II 1b. A musical work may have an *introduction* which serves as a brief opening or prelude to the main section.

• Play an introduction to a tune to set the tempo, mood, tonality, and style before the students sing. Discuss how the introduction sets the stage for the music (see also pp. 157–158).

• Raise hands when the introduction to a recorded work is completed and the main section begins. Show contrast between these two sections through creative bodily movement and changing the rhythm instrument accompaniment. Some works with introductions include: RL—28, 73, 88, 91, 108, 130, 158, 163, 176, 201, 205, 260, 282, 286, 298, 310, 314.

• Listen to a *fanfare*—a special type of introduction played by a flourish of trumpets or brass instruments, and usually found in ceremonial or military music. Appropriate examples are: RL—24, 28, 122, 190, 221, 289, 313, 317.

• At upper levels, listen to an *overture* or *prelude*, and explain how it serves to introduce the listener to an opera, operetta, or musical. Examples include: RL—126, 223, 291, 318.

I-II 1c. Some parts of a musical work have clearly identifiable melodic material called *themes* or thematic sections. These main sections are the most important part of a musical work, and are usually repeated at some time during the work.

• Listen to instrumental works having simple and definite tunes. Students raise hands each time the distinct melody is repeated. Call this the *theme* of the melodic section. Appropriate examples include: RL—1, 25, 35, 96, 108, 117, 136, 143, 148, 155, 158, 186, 187, 304, 313, 320.

• Play the theme of a work on the piano or bells. Students raise hands each time the theme is heard in the music. Sing and clap rhythm of the theme. Move rhythmically on sections which seem to contain the important or main musical ideas. Use particular rhythm instruments only on the thematic sections.

• Compare thematic sections of music to main plot and central action of a story or play.

• Use charts of themes. Follow notation of themes as they occur in the music. Count the number of times each theme appears (see pp. 148–149 for additional discussion on *theme charts*).

• Call attention to certain parts of most instrumental works where the music seems to be "connecting" or "bridging" two main thematic sections. Note how these *transitional sections* and *interludes* seem to contain less obvious thematic material.

III   1d. A musical composition may have a *coda*—a concluding passage added to the final section of the work which usually heightens the impression of finality.

• Accompany a song on the piano or Autoharp as students sing. Upon completion of the song repeat the last phrase, as in "Eeency Weency Spider" in Ex. 5–1. Call this a *coda* or ending. Continue with other songs. Also improvise a coda which may be in contrast to the last phrase of a tune.

Ex. 5-1. "Eeency Weency Spider"

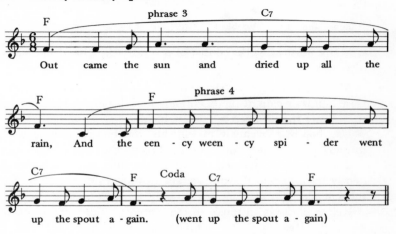

• Students experiment with adding codas to songs and instrumental works, using various types of instruments and/or their voices.

• Raise hands when the main section of the music has concluded and the coda begins. Assign students to move rhythmically on the coda. Change rhythm instrument accompaniment when the coda begins. Note frequent change of tempo, dynamics, and instrumentation, leading to a feeling of finality. Appropriate examples include: RL—19, 26, 41, 46, 78, 79, 87, 88, 121, 282, 283, 286, 298.

• Stop the music at either the introduction, main section, transitional section, or coda. Students identify point at which the music was stopped.

I-III   2. A musical work has *rhythmic* and *tonal patterns* (see pp. 41–48 and 70–75 for discussion and activities related to rhythmic and tonal patterns, respectively).

I-V   3. Most music moves in *phrases*—tonal "sentences" expressing musical ideas. The tones in a phrase flow and move toward a feeling of rest or *cadence*. Note the two distinct phrases in Ex. 5–2 and how the tones seem to move toward a point of rest (the half notes in measures 2 and 4).

Ex. 5-2. "Sing a Song of Sixpence"

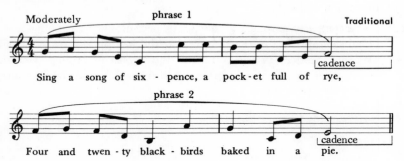

I-III   3a. Many musical works consist of several well-defined musical units called *phrases*.

• Move hands in an arc shape (⌒➤) for each phrase. Students also raise hands or clap at the beginning of each phrase. Hold up fingers to indicate the number of phrases heard.

• Use bodily movement to indicate the flow and repose of the musical phrase. Stop and change direction at end of each phrase.

• To indicate the flowing quality of the phrase use balloons tossed gently back and forth, and scarves waved as an extension of hand movements.

• Relate phrasing in music to the sentence or one line of poetry in language. Read a poem and/or song text to students, using hand movements to indicate the phrases.

• Learn how to sing phrasewise by taking a breath before each phrase and exhaling during the phrase.

• Alternate singing of phrases between the teacher and student, a student and the class, and two groups.

• Symbolize phrases by using an arc-shaped line ⌒ . Use a breath mark (❜) to indicate when to breathe for a new phrase.

• Draw phrase arcs on the board and number them, as: ₁⌒ ₂⌒ ₃⌒ ₄⌒ . Perform the tune again, as students "think" the phrases and follow the arcs. Stop in the middle and ask students to point to, or state the number of the phrase where the music stopped.

• Emphasize feeling of rest at end of phrases (see *cadences*, p. 113).

• Distribute several kinds of rhythm instruments. Have a different instrument played for the beat, accented beat, or melodic rhythm of each phrase of a tune. For example, in "Sing a Song of Sixpence" in Ex. 5–2, the four phrases can be orchestrated:

(all instruments played on the beat)   drum   rhythm stick   tone block   tambourine

   • Divide class in half. Each group moves rhythmically on alternate phrases. Choose four students to walk to the four phrases of a tune, with each student walking on a different phrase.

   • Create rhythmic phrases by clapping, or playing rhythm instruments to tell a rhythmic "idea" as: [rhythmic notation]. Later combine with rhythmic "questions" and "answers" to develop idea of antecedent and consequent phrases (see pp. 114–115).

   • Listen to many pieces to discover that not all works have clearly defined phrases (examples: RL—4, 8, 63, 67, 76, 105, 203, 268, 280, 303). Relate to discussion on melodic fragments, p. 60.

   • Note that a phrase may be longer or shorter than others in the same work. Some examples of irregular phrase lengths occur in: RL—13, 82, 110, 142, 202, 229.

III-IV   3b. The musical material of a phrase usually has a feeling of motion followed by repose. This point of rest, called the *cadence*, marks the end of the phrase and may be temporary or final in feeling. In "Sing a Song of Sixpence" (Ex. 5–2) the first cadence at the end of the first phrase seems temporary, while the second cadence at the end of the second phrase seems more conclusive.

   • Using bodily movement, emphasize the pause or rest at the end of each phrase of the music.

   • Play or sing a tune, raising hands at the point of rest at the end of the phrase. Replay tune with harmonic accompaniment and repeat activity. Note how cadence can be felt either melodically or harmonically.

   • Observe that the last tone of a phrase commonly occurs on an accented beat and is longer in duration than tones before it.

   • Clap a series of rhythms. Raise hands when the *rhythmic cadence* appears. Clap the rhythm of a phrase from a familiar tune. Identify cadence. Repeat, but alter the cadence by continuing the rhythmic flow. Note lack of cadential pause when rhythm does not stop or pause.

III-V   3c. Two adjoining phrases make up a musical unit called the *period* when the first phrase sounds like a question (the *antecedent* phrase) and the second phrase sounds like the answer (the *consequent* phrase). Observe the structural aspect of the period in Ex. 5–3, where the second phrase seems to answer and complement the first phrase. [*Note*: The study of the *double period* should be reserved for more advanced levels of instruction.]

Ex. 5-3. Humperdinck: "Susie Little Susie" from *Hansel and Gretel*

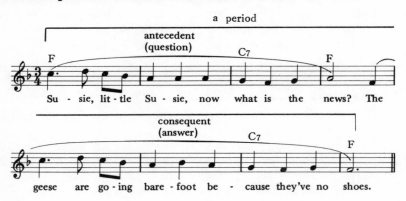

• Engage in question-and-answer clapping. Ask a question by clapping, and have students clap an answer which seems to fit the

question, as:

• Sing a question to the class. Call on students to answer with tonal patterns or phrases which seem to fit the "question" pattern, such as:

• Listen to and identify many tunes which have two phrases related to each other as antecedent and consequent. Discover that some "answers" are similar in tonal arrangement to the "questions" and some are contrasting. Examples include—

SONGS: S—25, 35, 57, 79, 81, 92, 98, 108; and the first two phrases of: 9, 19, 26, 29, 54, 82, 90, 99, 131

INSTRUMENTAL WORKS: RL—19, 41, 74, 146, 184(theme 1), 201(theme 1), 216(theme 1), 252, 262, 306, 312.

• Alternate the singing of a four-phrase tune between two soloists or groups. Note that the second and fourth phrases seem to often answer the first and third phrases. Use similar-type rhythm instruments for the "question" and "answer." Compare the antecedent and consequent phrases of a period to a question and answer or a compound sentence in language.

• One student moves rhythmically and acts out a question. Other students answer him through similar or contrasting movement. Add rhythm accompaniment.

• Students make up an "answer" phrase to a "question" phrase, using "LA" rather than words. Find a song unfamiliar to students. Sing the first and third phrases and have students make up the second and fourth phrases in a question-answer relationship.

• Compose original tunes and songs with emphasis on period construction of phrases.

II-V 4. Many musical works, especially those which are extended, are divided into *sections* (see material on sectional forms, pp. 120–129).

II-IV 4a. A *section* is a portion of the music, complete in itself, but usually part of a longer work.

• Play recordings and observe that some pieces, especially extended works, have more than one section. Raise hands when the music appears to change or have a different "part" or new idea. Describe obvious differences between the parts or sections (note differences in melody, rhythm, harmony, tempo, dynamics, mood, instrumentation). Use contrasting bodily movement and rhythm instruments to show differences. Relate the meaning of section to a paragraph in reading. Several sections (paragraphs) will comprise a movement (a chapter) or an extended work (a book).

• Develop recognition that sections are comprised of phrases and that these phrases may differ in number from one section to the next. Draw boxes and phrase-arcs on the chalkboard for each section of the music, as:

SECTION ONE   SECTION TWO   SECTION ONE

• Examine notation of songs and instrumental works with sections. Note that the close of a section is usually marked by a light double bar (‖), while the end of a piece is often marked by a light bar line followed by a heavy bar line (‖).

• Call attention to the many pieces of music which have extended forms, consisting of more than one part, scene, or movement. These types include the *opera, oratorio, sonata, symphony*, and *concerto*. Briefly explain the meaning of these works when playing excerpts from them.

III-V   4b. Some compositions have only one section or are not clearly divided into sections.

• Analyze various songs and note that many have only one section. Compare these songs (examples: S—27, 35, 40, 50, 57, 60, 62, 73, 107, 139) with those having two distinct sections (examples: S—16, 18, 23, 24, 34, 55, 64, 69, 76, 125). Note also how this *unitary, one-part form* is usually a short work of a single musical section without a break from beginning to end.

• Listen to compositions in which one or two rhythmic or melodic ideas are so skillfully handled by a composer that they form one unified piece, with no repeated or contrasted sections (examples: RL—10, 12, 15, 16, 63, 94, 98, 124, 157, 161, 176, 203, 204, 305). Compare these works with those having two or more sections (see pp. 120–124).

• Sing folk songs and hymns with several verses (examples: S—14, 27, 42, 53, 69, 105, 106, 128). Note the repetition of the music for each verse (called *stanzaic* or *strophic form*), although some variation may occur in the melody or rhythm due to the text.

I-V   Music is characterized by *repetition, contrast*, and *variation*. Musical material within a work may be *repeated*, providing *unity*; *contrasted*, providing *variety* and *interest*; and *varied*, providing both *unity* and *variety*. The arrangement and organization of the many elements of a musical composition in relation to each other and to the work as a whole determine the music's overall *form* or design.

I-III   1. The rhythmic and tonal patterns in a piece may be repeated, contrasted, or varied (see also pp. 41–55 and 70–75 for discussion on rhythmic and tonal patterns, and pp. 124–129 for ways to vary rhythmic and tonal patterns).

• Play echo games. Students repeat a rhythmic or tonal pattern as clapped or sung by the teacher. Later, ask for contrasting patterns.

• Clap or sing a predominant rhythmic or tonal pattern from a tune, as ♩♩♩♩ | o | —the "e-i-e-i-o" from "Old MacDonald." Ask students to raise hands every time the pattern is heard and/or clap the pattern when it occurs. Distribute the resonator bell tones of the tonal pattern, with students playing the pattern each time it occurs.

• Isolate various rhythmic and tonal patterns in a tune. Compare them to see if they are the same, somewhat different, or contrasting.

• Create a piece for melody and/or rhythm instruments using both repeated and contrasting patterns, as:

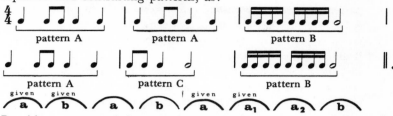

Provide a structural framework as a guide, such as: pattern 1 → pattern 2 → pattern 1 → pattern 2 (as in "Old Brass Wagon" or "Deck the Halls") or pattern 1 → pattern 2 → pattern 3 → pattern 1 (varied). Use contrasting rhythm instruments for contrasting patterns.

• Note the repeated rhythmic patterns of an accompaniment, especially in jazz, rock, and much ethnic and primitive music. Clap the repeated pattern, move to it, and add rhythm instrument accompaniment. Examples include: RL—2, 17, 69, 129, 134, 165, 176, 186, 216, 278, 282, 305.

• Observe that a melody may consist of one or two rhythmic patterns repeated over and over again. For example, "America the Beautiful"

consists entirely of the repeated pattern: ♩ |♩. ♪♩ ♩|♩. ♪♩ ♩ |♩

♩ ♩ ♩ |♩.‖. Other appropriate songs include: S—10, 18, 39, 62, 92, 93, 109, 113, 137, 139.

• Find and clap repeated patterns in notation by looking for similarities and differences in note values (for rhythmic patterns) and in the placement of the notes on the staff (for tonal patterns). Use the same colored chalk to highlight repeated patterns. Play or sing these patterns to verify similarities and differences through the ear.

• Demonstrate how tonal patterns within a melody may be repeated, but on a higher or lower pitch level, as in Ex. 5–4. This repetition is said to be in *sequence*.

Ex. 5-4. Bizet: "The Top" from *Children's Games*

Design the pattern of "land where my Father's died" from "America." Compare this with "land of the Pilgrim's pride." Note

that both patterns have the shape ‾ ‾ ‾ ‾ -_ , but the second
pattern is lower in pitch and is a *sequence* of the first pattern.

• Discover by ear the tonal patterns and phrases in songs which
move sequentially, as in the "falling down" part from "London
Bridge." Other songs with sequences include: S—31, 37, 67, 83, 109,
113, 121, 130, 140. Locate sequences in notation by observing the
same melodic contour of the patterns even though written on different lines and spaces of the staff. Compare the tonal patterns in the
sequences.

• Play or sing a short tonal pattern. Students create several sequences
by repeating the pattern at a higher or lower pitch.

• Listen for examples of sequential passages in recorded instrumental
works such as: RL—11, 19, 46, 98, 110, 111, 115, 183, 224, 246, 253,
298, 299, 315, 317, 318, 320. Listen for rhythmic and tonal variation
in many songs and recordings (see discussion, pp. 124–129).

I-V 2. Various aspects of a musical work, such as dynamics, tone color,
tempo, tonality, harmony, and texture, may be repeated or contrasted.
[*Note*: Repetition and contrast of these musical elements should be directly
related to the activities described for dynamics (pp. 18–21), tone color
(pp. 21–29), tempo (pp. 55–58), tonality (pp. 75–91), harmony (pp. 92–
106) and texture (pp. 106–108), and sectional repetition and contrast
(pp. 120–124).]

• Respond rhythmically to alterations in tempo or dynamics by
either changing the speed of the rhythmic movements for tempo, or
using large or smaller movements for dynamic changes. Represent
repetition and contrast of these elements through symbolization
(*allegro—andante—allegro*, or *f, p, mp, f*—see pp. 56–57 and 21). Relate
understandings of repetition and contrast to designs found in nature
and in works of art.

• Indicate that a particular tone color repeats in a work by raising
hands when the repetition is heard, pointing to a picture of the
instrument(s), or imitating the way the instrument is played. Use
contrasting pictures or designs on the chalkboard to show contrast.
Ask: "How many times do you hear the _____ (*insert instrumental
family*) section playing in this piece?"

• Create tunes in which various musical elements are repeated,
contrasted, or varied (see discussion, pp. 120–129).

• Listen specifically for changes in tonality, harmony, or texture in
a musical work. Use rhythmic movement or visual symbolization to
indicate repetition and contrast of these elements.

II-V 3. Phrases in a musical work may be repeated, contrasted, or varied. In
Ex. 5–5, p. 119, note the similarity in rhythm and melodic direction of
the first two phrases, and the contrast in the third phrase.

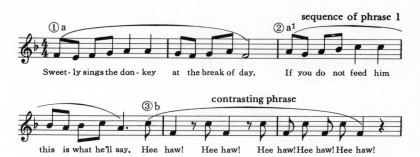

Ex. 5-5. "Sweetly Sings the Donkey"

• Sing or play a phrase from a tune in which the phrase is repeated at least once, as the first phrase of "The Marine's Hymn" or "Rock-a-bye Baby." Ask students to raise hands and listen for the number of times they hear the phrase as the tune is replayed.

• Students sing similar or repeated phrases with "LA" as they occur, while the teacher sings the contrasting phrases.

• Use various colored squares and distribute one for each of the phrases in a work. Hold up squares in turn as each phrase is heard. Use squares of the same color for identical phrases and squares of different colors for contrasting phrases. For example, the phrasing for "The Marine's Hymn" (see Ex. 5–6) may be symbolized by

RED   RED   BLUE   RED . Also sketch the phrasing on the

chalkboard, using the same design or colored chalk for similar

phrases, as ☐ ☐ ✗ ☐ or (red) (red) (blue) (red).

• Use the same rhythm instruments on phrases which are similar or the same, and contrasting rhythm instruments for contrasting phrases, as for "The Marine's Hymn":

• Listen for phrases which: (1) *repeat exactly* (phrases 1, 2, 4 of "The Marine's Hymn," phrases 1, 3 of "Sing a Song of Sixpence" and "Rock-a-bye Baby," and phrases 2, 3 of "The Riddle Song"); (2) *repeat, but with some modification* (phrases 1, 2 of "Hickory Dickory Dock," "Oh Susanna," "Old Folks at Home," and "Camptown Races"); and (3) *contrast with each other* (phrases 2, 3 of "Oh Susanna" and "Kookaburra," and phrases 1, 2 of "White Choral Bells" and "Reuben and Rachel").

• Symbolize phrases with lower-case alphabetical letters (a, b, c). Use the same letter twice if the phrase repeats exactly (a a), a numerical subscript (a a₁) if the second phrase is similar to the first phrase, and two different letters (a b) if the phrases are completely different. The labeling for the phrases of "Sweetly Sings the Donkey" is shown in Ex. 5–5, p. 119.

• Listen to and sing tunes in which all phrases seem to be different from each other, such as "Row, Row, Row Your Boat" and "America." Other songs include: S—2, 18, 33, 42, 66, 106, 116, 119, 135, 144. Use techniques mentioned above to develop understandings of contrasting phrases.

• Using the phrase as the basic structural unit, analyze the form of many folk and children's songs, as:

"London Bridge"	a	a₁		
"Oh Susanna"	a	a₁	b	a₁
"Marching to Pretoria"	a	a₁	b	b₁

• Listen to, and find examples of phrases which are repeated in *sequence* (see the first two phrases of "Sweetly Sings the Donkey" in Ex. 5–5, and discussion on pp. 117–118).

• Play a phrase. Repeat it exactly, or alter a tone, a rhythmic pattern, or the tonality. Note whether the phrase was repeated or changed, and how it was altered.

• Sing and follow notation of many tunes to discover that phrases which sound alike will look alike in notation, and that phrases which look alike will sound alike (see phrases 1–2 and phrase 3 of "Sweetly Sings the Donkey" in Ex. 5–5).

• Select a 4-phrase tune, with at least two phrases repeated (as "Deck the Halls"—phrases 1, 2; "Old Folks at Home," and "Auld Lang Syne"). Write each phrase on an oaktag strip. Randomly distribute strips. Students rearrange phrases in correct order as music is played. Note phrase repetition and identical notation.

• Play or sing, and then write the first two phrases of a short 4-phrase tune unfamiliar to the class. Ask students to complete the tune using the format: given given ⌒a⌒ ⌒b⌒ ⌒a⌒ ⌒b⌒ . Repeat activity, using the design: given given ⌒a⌒ ⌒a₁⌒ ⌒a₂⌒ ⌒b⌒ . Later, provide only one phrase and expand tune to eight measures or more. Also create tunes paying particular attention to phrase repetition, variation, and contrast.

III-V

4. Sections in music may be repeated, contrasted, or varied. Some sections of music repeat immediately. Some contrast with each other, with no repetition, while other sections repeat after contrast.

III-IV 4a. A piece may have a section which repeats immediately, or after a contrasting section.

> • Raise hands when a section repeats. Use the same colored chalk to indicate repetition, and different colors for contrasting sections. Relate to repeated patterns in art and the environment. Use the same bodily movement and/or rhythm instruments for repeated sections.
> • See pp. 122–124 for discussion and activities on some forms using repetition of material after a contrasting section (ternary and rondo forms).
> • Play and sing songs in *strophic* or *stanzaic* form—the same tune is repeated, with many verses, as in "This Old Man," "Oh Susanna," and "Deck the Halls." Other examples include: S—35, 92, 93, 108, 109, 126. Call attention to sectional repetition of musical material despite differences in text for each verse.
> • Symbolize sections in the same general manner as that described for phrases (see p. 120). Use upper-case letters to designate large sections, as A A for two repeated sections, or A B for two contrasting sections.
> • Sing or play an unfamiliar tune with repeat marks, as students follow notation. Ask: "How do you think I knew that I had to repeat the first phrase?" Refer to symbols for repetition. Illustrate some of the many ways that repetition in music may be symbolized (see "The Marine's Hymn" in Ex. 5–6), and find examples of these symbols in vocal and instrumental music.

Ex. 5-6. "The Marine's Hymn"

II-IV 4b. A piece may have two well-defined contrasting sections. This *two-part* form (A B), known as *binary form*, begins with one complete section and ends with a second, contrasting section.

> • Students raise hands when the music changes. Identify changes in tempo, dynamics, melody, tonality, rhythm, harmony, texture, tone color, and overall mood.

• Vary rhythm instrument accompaniment to show contrasting sections.

• Divide class into groups, with one group moving rhythmically on section A, and one on section B.

• Find examples and sing many songs which have a simple *stanza-refrain*, *verse-chorus* form, whereby a chorus is repeated after each verse is sung (examples: S—16, 44, 46, 55, 64, 72, 83, 91, 99, 125, 132, 146). Examine the words of songs in the binary form to show the relationship of the text to the musical form.

• Use colored chalk and diagrams ($\underset{\textbf{A}}{\square}\ \underset{\textbf{B}}{\bigcirc}$) to show sections.

• Compose a rhythmic piece in A B form by using rhythm instruments, clapping, stamping, or snapping fingers. Each section should be at least four measures long and contrast with each other.

• Identify A B form in instrumental works, and relate to songs which have an initial, and then contrasting musical idea (often chorus-verse). Examples of instrumental works in binary form include: RL— 7, 9, 13, 21, 43, 52, 87, 89, 110, 135, 163, 165, 248. Note the balance and symmetry which occur when a second section of a work answers and completes the first section.

• Discover the binary form of many folk dances learned in physical education, as: S—1, 17, 75, 95. Note the change of movement and style for the second section.

• Create tunes in binary form, experimenting with various contrasting melodic and rhythmic elements.

• Listen to and identify the two distinct sections of works in binary form in which each section repeats after contrast, resulting in an expanded form (as A B A B A B). Examples include: RL—19, 26, 79, 165.

III-V

4c. Many musical works have three well-defined sections, with a first section, a contrasting second section, and a third section which repeats the first section (form: A B A, *three-part form*, or *ternary form*). Repetition after contrast is an essential principle of form in music and the other arts.

• Listen to many instrumental works having three distinct sections, with the first and third sections alike (examples: RL—23, 44, 47, 60, 74, 77, 78, 85, 96, 103, 146, 170, 190, 193, 196, 198, 210, 257, 280, 283, 284, 286, 287, 296, 306, 310, 311, 312, and many instrumental dances and popular songs). Discover and discuss differences in the three sections. Ask: "What is interesting about the first and third sections?" Design the form, using figures ($\triangle\ \square\ \triangle$), letters (A B A), numbers (1 2 1) and colored chalk (*green, red, green*). Relate to repetition after contrast in children's art works, designs around the room, and in the human body (ear-head-ear, or arm-body-arm).

• Divide class into two groups, with one group moving on A and its repetition, and the other moving on B. Also use rhythm instruments on the beat and/or accented beat, with contrasting instruments on the middle section.

• Relate A B A in sectional works to songs which have a beginning musical idea, a contrasting idea, and repetition of the initial theme (generally using the phrase pattern a a b a), as: S—3, 15, 19, 28, 54, 77, 80, 94, 96, 128, 132.

• Distribute paper and fold into three sections. Students pictorially describe, with line, color, and design, each section of the music. Note how drawings to represent sections one and three are (or should be) the same.

• Draw three large boxes on the chalkboard. Also list terms such as: *strings, woodwinds, trumpet; loud, soft; slow, fast; major, minor;* $\frac{3}{4}$, $\frac{4}{4}$; *thin texture, thick texture;* and other words characterizing the sections of a work. Students fill in boxes with correct words, and observe A B A form. At upper levels students fill in words without help from teacher.

• Place various figures on the chalkboard, as □ × ○, □□ ×, and □ ○ □. Play a work in ternary form. Ask students which of the three patterns best fits the musical design of the work.

• Play and give the students the notation for an unfamiliar tune from the "A" section of a work in ternary form. Ask them to compose the "B" and repeated "A" parts. Play the students' works and discuss the effects of contrast and repetition. Continue by composing complete tunes in ternary form.

• Perform a simple song in ternary form, first by using the "A" melody for all three sections, and then by singing or playing it as written. Discuss the reasons for one version being more interesting.

• Locate much music in ternary form by finding *D. C. al fine* (*da capo al fine*—go back to the beginning until the word "*fine*" or end), which often appears at the end of the second section of a piece in ternary form, as in "The Marine's Hymn" in Ex. 5–6.

IV-V 4d. A piece may alternate its first section with several contrasting sections (as A B A C A . . .), resulting in a *rondo form.*

• Play a work in a rondo form, as: RL—1, 82, 91, 118, 133, 143, 149, 184, 201, 216, 297, 302. Draw boxes with colored chalk to show each section. Use the same color for the "A" section. Students discover why the same colored chalk was used. Raise hands each time the main section returns. Use the same bodily movements and/or rhythm instruments to show the return. Assign students to move on their own section, with one group moving on every other part.

• Illustrate rondo form, using geometric figures as □ × □ ○ □ + □. Play the rondo and stop in the middle, asking students to point to the correct symbol when the music is stopped. Also use various colored charts to clarify rondo form.

• Place several figures on the chalkboard, as × — × — ×, × — × ○ ×, and × □ ○ — | . Play a rondo. Ask students to match the geometric designs to the musical design. Relate the contrasting and repeated sections of the rondo to the importance of repetition (unity) and contrast (variety) in music.

• List words on the chalkboard which might describe the different sections of a rondo. Students select those words best fitting the A, B, or C parts.

• Create rhythmic rondos of various lengths, with a recurring pattern after contrasting rhythms, as:

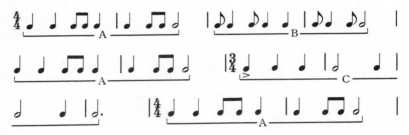

Also use contrasting rhythm instruments for the different sections.

• Students "chart" the form of a rondo on paper, using geometric figures, contrasting colors, and like and different designs. Insert words for each section to describe it. Emphasize repetition of the main section after each contrasting section.

IV-V   4e. Musical material within a work may be altered or varied, in which some musical elements remain basically the same, while others are more or less changed. A piece may consist of an opening statement of a theme, followed by several sections in which certain elements of the original statement are repeated substantially without change, while other elements are varied. This is known as *variational form*. [*Note*: Experience at levels II and III should be given in techniques of varying melodic and rhythmic elements. How this variation appears in variational forms such as the *theme and variations* should be introduced at levels IV and V. Detailed study of variational forms is reserved for more advanced instructional levels.]

• Sing a familiar tonal pattern or phrase on "LA." Resing it, varying either the tempo, dynamics, rhythm, harmony, tonality, or tonal direction, and identify what was kept the same and what was changed. For example, sing the following pattern from "The Battle Hymn of the Republic" with "LA":

Resing and identify change:

1) change in melodic rhythm

2) change in meter, melodic rhythm

3) change in melody (ornamentation)

4) change in dynamics, tempo

5) change in harmony

6) change in tonality, harmony

Also combine several changes in one rendition, and note variation.

• Play a tune with a distinctive accompaniment style (as broken chords on the piano). Replay, changing the accompaniment. Note differences. Also vary one or two chords in an harmonic pattern and notice differences from original pattern.

• Experiment with varying rhythmic patterns found in familiar tunes. For example, take the rhythmic patterns of the first phrase of "Go Tell Aunt Rhodie" (♩ ♩♩♩|♩ ♩ |♩ ♩♩♩|♩♩♩‖)

and:

— change some note values [musical notation]

— play the tones twice as fast [musical notation]

- play the tones twice as slowly [musical notation]

— lengthen (extend) the pattern [musical notation]

— shorten (fragment) the pattern [musical notation]

— change the meter [musical notation]

Repeat the above technique, using the melodic rhythm of familiar tunes.

• Note variations of rhythmic patterns in tunes caused by text changes, as in:

Verse 1   Verse 2

"Skip to My Lou"

Skip, skip,   skip, to my lou.   Lost my part-ner, what'll I   do?

[musical notation]

"Paw Paw Patch"

Where, oh where is dear lit-tle Nel-lie?   Come on boys,   let's go find her.

[musical notation]

• Create and vary a rhythmic pattern on the drum.
• Clap the recurring rhythmic pattern of "America the Beautiful"

(♩ |♩. ♪♪ ♩ |♩. ♪♪ ♩ |♩ ♩ ♩ ♩ |♩. |)—a pattern repeated in every phrase, but with varying melodic material. Take a rhythmic pattern such as $\frac{4}{4}$ ♩ ♩ ♫ ♩ |♩ ♩ ♩ | and create a tune, using the pattern throughout, but varying the melodic content. Note interest created by varied tonal patterns.

• Sing or play a familiar tune, as "Old Woman" in Ex. 5–7. Vary the melody through *ornamentation* (adding tones around the basic tones), *changing several tones*, *inverting* the melody (moving in the opposite direction), *augmenting* (enlarging) or *diminishing* (contracting) its intervals, *playing it backwards* (called "retrograde"), *playing it inverted and backwards* (retrograde inversion), *extending* the melody (adding more tones at the end), *abbreviating* the melody (shortening it by eliminating tones), *using sequences* (repeating the motive or phrase on different pitch levels), *changing the tonality, using octave displacement* (placing some pitches at least an octave lower or higher), *shifting the register* (moving it an octave or more higher or lower), and *transposing it to another key*. Some of the many ways a melody may be varied are shown in Ex. 5–7.

Ex. 5-7. "Old Woman"—Varying a Melody

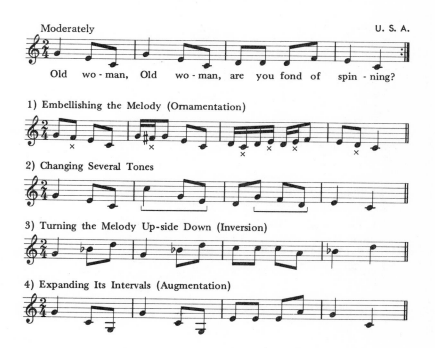

5) Contracting Its Intervals (Diminution)

6) Playing It Backwards (Retrograde)

7) Playing It Backwards and Inverted (Retrograde Inversion)

8) Extending the Melody (Extension)

9) Abbreviating the Melody (Fragmentation)

10) Using Sequences

11) Changing the Tonality (to C minor)

12) Using Octave Displacement

13) Shifting the Register

14) Transposing to Another Key (G major)

• Randomly distribute several tones of resonator bells. Students create a phrase using these tones and notate it on the chalkboard. Experiment with some of the techniques for varying melodies as mentioned above, and notate the results.

• Play a work using variational techniques, as: RL—3, 26, 38, 51, 88, 92, 117, 138, 144, 185, 245, 295. Play the theme, sing it, follow it on charts, and move rhythmically to it. Discover the many types of variational techniques within the piece. Use numerical subscripts A A_1 A_2 etc. to show similarities between sections.

• Experiment with repeating an harmonic pattern in the bass and improvising melodies over the pattern. At least one student will probably know how to play these patterns on the piano:

("Heart and Soul" Pattern)   A Vamp

C   am   dm   G   C   B♭   A♭   G

Use other simple harmonic patterns. Listen for similar-type repeated patterns in rock music and jazz (especially the "blues" and "ragtime"). Call attention to frequent repetition of harmonic patterns in popular music (examples: I I IV IV V V IV IV I I—C C F F G G F F C C; I vi ii V_7—C am dm G_7; and the "blues" harmony).

• Listen to works with ostinato-type repeated bass figures (examples: RL—23, 75, 92(variation 3), 111, 133). Sing the repeated tonal figure, play it on instruments, and clap its rhythm. Note how the melodic content is varied even though the ostinato pattern repeats continuously.

IV-V 4f. Not all music falls into forms such as unitary, binary, ternary, rondo, and variational. Some works may be clearly divisible into sections but yet have a form as A B C B or A B C.

• Play works not in unitary, binary, ternary, rondo, or variational form, such as: RL—126, 211, 226, 262, 263, 265, 320. Repeat activities described on pp. 120–124 for other forms, using rhythmic bodily movement, designs on the chalkboard, rhythm instruments, alphabetical labeling, and theme charts. Observe contrasts between sections.

• Analyze phrases of songs and locate those in which most (or all) contrast with each other (see list of works, p. 120).

• Notice contrasting sections of extended works in the style of a suite (examples: RL—56, 101, 177, 191, 271, 275, 281, 290). Repeat activities outlined above to show contrasting sections.

IV-V   4g. There are many pieces of music, dramatic and/or descriptive in nature, which have their own particular structural and formal design. These include works for both instruments and the voice.

• Play excerpts from a *suite* (a collection of short related compositions built around an idea, story, or event). Examples include: RL—48, 53, 56, 164, 177, 191, 225, 230, 271, 275, 281, 290. Note the various sections and compare a suite in music to a unit of rooms in a hotel "suite."

• Play excerpts from a *tone (symphonic) poem*—an extended descriptive or programmatic work for orchestra of a narrative nature which has the unity of a single work (examples: RL—31, 73, 104, 214, 231, 266). Identify the separate sections of the work as they relate to the description, even though no definite break in the music occurs.

• Discuss the plot and play excerpts from *operas* (examples: RL—125, 162, 169). Discover the many sections of an opera and note the important characteristics which distinguish it from a play or instrumental work.

• Listen to and sing excerpts from *operettas* (examples: RL—120 and the many works by Gilbert and Sullivan) and *musicals* (examples: RL—136, 151, 195, 217, 218). Notice how operettas and musicals are musically less complex and more popular in style than opera, with more spoken dialogue. Note similarities and differences between operas, operettas, and musicals, with particular reference to the sections and unique features of each.

• Play excerpts from *oratorios* (examples: RL—93, 112, 113, 114, 159). Note that an oratorio is an extended musical dramatic work based on a contemplative or religious subject, and performed without costumes, scenery, and acting. Observe that both an opera and an oratorio have several sections, *arias* and *recitatives* (see p. 63), and usually an *overture* (see p. 137).

V   4h. Sometimes a melody in one voice (the instrumental or vocal part) is followed by successive voices that enter separately, imitating the first voice throughout, and using distinctly polyphonic texture. The different voices overlap any phrase endings so that the music seems to be one flowing composition, with no distinct sections (see discussion on *polyphonic texture*, pp. 107–108, and *rounds* and *canons*, pp. 163, 167–168).

Six

STYLISTIC AND
ASSOCIATIVE CONCEPTS

Basic Concepts:

1) The characteristic use of musical elements by different peoples, historical periods, and composers results in a particular musical *style*.

2) Music has played a vital role in the life of all societies. As a result, a rich and extensive music literature has become an important part of our cultural heritage.

I-V Every piece of music has its own *style*—the particular and often unique results of how the elements of music such as rhythm, melody, and harmony are used and are affected by cultural and regional differences, historical periods, and the individual creative powers of the composer and performer.

II 1. The characteristic use of musical elements contributes to a music's *style* and helps to tell us whether the music we are listening to is a hymn, a march, a folk-rock piece, or a work by Mozart or his contemporaries.

   • Compare the use of musical elements which makes two works sound different from each other; e.g., note differences between a march and lullaby, and a folk song and rock music.
   • Play three works, two of which are similar in style (as two lullabies

131

and a Scottish reel, or two contemporary works and a Schubert waltz). Note similarities between two of the works and differences in style of the third piece. Relate meaning of musical style to differences in styles of living throughout the world.

• List various types of music on the chalkboard, as: hymn, dance, march, lullaby, jazz, rock, and symphonic music. Play excerpts from several of these works, with students selecting terms which fit the music.

III-V   2. Musical styles can vary according to cultures, nations, and regions. For example, Calypso music from the Caribbean area sounds very different from the music of Indonesia and Japan. Differences in the music of peoples around the world are caused by stylistic differences in the use of certain musical elements.

• Call attention to cultural, religious, and national origin of both songs and instrumental recordings used in class. Compare differences in rhythm, melody, harmony, texture, tone color, and overall mood. When singing, use appropriate tempo, dynamics, tone, and diction for the particular style performed.

• Select rhythm instruments to suit the music's style. Use appropriate accompaniments to show consideration for cultural characteristics, as maracas and claves for Latin American music, and bamboo sticks and coconut shells for Polynesian music.

• Play three recordings, two of which originate from the same culture. Note stylistic similarities and differences.

• Illustrate how the music of one group of people or cultural region may differ according to the characteristic uses of the musical elements and the intended function of the music. For example, play and sing some of the many types of musics which have originated within the United States, such as: hymn tunes, ballads, work songs, spirituals, sea chanteys, cowboy and patriotic songs, songs of the Armed Forces, rock, and art music. Note differences in use of the musical elements.

• Compare similarities and differences between lullabies, marches, and dances from various cultural groups.

• Compare stylistic differences among Asian, Pacific, and Western dances and music. For example, note the circle formation of Japanese, Israeli, and Greek dances, the partner-style of many Western dances, and the extensive use of clapping and body-slapping in the dances of Samoa. Also note differences in use of instruments and the voice.

• Play excerpts from many recordings of musics from around the world. Students classify excerpts as being Western or non-Western. Expand classification at upper levels to include Oriental, Black African, Moslem, South American, American Indian, primitive, and other groupings.

• Note the non-Western influence on popular music today (example: the use of the sitar and polyrhythms from India in some music of the Beatles and other rock groups).

• Compare selected folk music from Spain, Mexico, Latin America, and the Philippines. Notice the frequent use of the guitar and mandolin, as well as syncopated rhythms. Relate to Spanish influence on various regions of the world.

• Capitalize on the rich diversity of cultures and peoples within the community. Invite students, parents, and ethnic groups to perform music of their heritage. Compare predominant musical features of each type of music performed.

• Play and note the use of certain musical characteristics associated with the musics of particular countries, regions, or cultural groups in instrumental works such as: RL—19, 109, 165, 314(all Latin American in style); 226, 237(both depicting an Italian dance); 121, 153, 257, 258(American Indian in style); 70, 205, 239, 274(distinctly Oriental in mood)

IV-V 3. Each historical period has had its characteristic musical style. The music of one particular historical period will sound different from music of another period. [*Note*: Only a general awareness of the differences in the musical styles of various periods of history will take place in the elementary grades.]

• Relate selected works played or sung to historical times, as "Dixie" to the Civil War, "Yankee Doodle" to the Revolutionary War, or minuets to the formal dances of the 1700's.

• Listen to, sing, and compare musics of various historical periods, noting differences and similarities in the rhythms, melodic lines, harmonies, tone colors, and overall expression.

• Listen to and sing representative contemporary folk music identified with the freedom and human-rights movements (examples: S—27, 59, 134).

• Relate art works of various art periods to musical style. For example, the Impressionist works of Debussy can be better understood by using the art works of some of the Impressionist painters (Monet and Degas).

• Discuss and illustrate the new sounds of contemporary art music—aleatory or "chance" music, and electronic music (see discussion, pp. 28–29).

• Listen to examples of music played on the harpsichord or the lute (see list, p. 25). Note how the use of instrumentation in music has changed throughout the centuries, due to man's constant search for new and more varied means for creating sound.

• Note stylistic differences in popular dance music of the 1920's (the Charleston), the 1940's (the lindy and fox-trot), the 1950's (the mambo and cha-cha-cha), and the present. Also play examples of early and contemporary jazz and compare styles.

• Play some chants (*oli*) of ancient Hawaii, followed by modern hula-style music, to show the influence of Westernization on various musical elements. Similarly, use Japanese classical music and the music of today.

IV-V 4. The musical style of a given work is shaped, to a large extent, by the individuality of the composer. A composer's taste and ability, as well as the musical resources available to him at a certain time in history, determine his musical style.

• At levels I and II play a recorded selection and discuss the notion that composers are musicians who write (compose) music. Note that each composer writes music in his own way, and that composers create various kinds of music—art music, "pop" music, background music for the movies and television, and music for commercials.

• Learn about the lives and music of both classical and contemporary composers by playing their music and using story material, portraits, films and slides, and reference books, as needed.

• Compare two works by two composers who lived at different historical periods (as Bach and Copland, or Ravel and Haydn). Note that the music of one composer may sound very different from the music of another, and that this is due to how each composer uses the musical elements within his work. Play excerpts from three works, two of which were written by the same composer. Compare stylistic similarities and differences.

I-V Music has played an essential role in the life of man and society throughout history. As a result, a rich heritage of music literature has developed.

[*Note*: The following material on the *associative concepts* should be presented only as it enhances the student's understanding of the aural experience. These concepts should not be used as the focus of any lesson. See pp. x–xii for further discussion.]

1. All cultures and societies have had some form of music.

• When introducing a new piece of music provide some background on the music's place of origin and function. Identify the music with a country, ethnic group, composer, or daily events and activities in the lives of people.

• Speculate on what the world would be like without music, and the effect this would have on the students' lives. Ask students to describe how people they know engage in musical activities. Note how every person can find enjoyment and fulfillment in music.

• Sing and listen to folk songs from many countries. Discuss how the lyrics often reflect the daily life of the people.

• Discuss the three most important ways in which people participate in music—as *composer*, or creator of the music; as *performer*, or interpreter of the music; and as *listener*, or receiver (consumer) of the music. Note how each one is vital to the musical art.

• Learn about music in our society by inviting individual and group performers to talk and play for the students, examining printed materials for information on the music of today, attending and reporting about a concert, making oral and written reports on books about music, writing letters to contemporary composers and musicians, keeping a monthly calendar of musical events, referring to a schedule of musical events on radio and television, collecting and reading program notes for concerts, and developing a record collection. Discuss possible reasons for so much musical activity in the community.

• Enumerate and illustrate the many worthwhile and important occupations related to music, including: the composer, the performer, the conductor, the teacher, the musicologist, the ethnomusicologist, the music theorist, the music publisher, the music arranger, the therapist who uses music in his work, the salesman in the music store, the music textbook writer, the technician in a recording studio, and the instrument manufacturer.

• Encourage students to share their recordings with the class. Delay the playing of each recording until a meaningful musical lesson can be prepared (see also pp. 146–147).

• Note the importance of music to the dance, especially in relation to form and design, unity and variety, tension and release, and climax.

• Stress that different peoples in the world and different people in our own society prefer various types of music. Discuss need to understand and respect these differences.

• When studying the culture of a country include its music, art, and dance.

• Attend youth concerts, providing students with adequate background prior to the performance, and follow-up activities after the concert (see also p. 145).

• Compare events in the lives of composers with comparable historical and social events, as appropriate. Make a time chart to develop historical perspective of when the composers lived. Insert the names of composers as their music is played and studied, as follows:

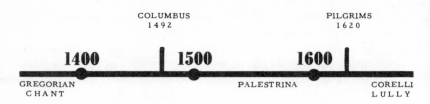

I-V   2. There is extensive music literature which has been written throughout the years, encompassing a wide range of musical expression. This music may be classified into various types.

I-V   2a. Music can be classified by its characteristic use of a musical element, as vocal, instrumental, aleatory ("chance"), and electronic music; homophonic or polyphonic music; and music with a strong rhythmic or melodic element (see discussion and activities related to *tone color*, pp. 21–29, *texture*, pp. 107–108, *rhythm*, pp. 30–58, *melody*, pp. 59–91, and *harmony*, pp. 92–107).

I-V   2b. Music can be classified as to its functional or non-functional intent.

        • Play a work, asking students if they think the music was written for a funeral, a celebration, or a dance. Ask: "What in the music gives you a hint?" Emphasize that a great deal of music is written for the pure enjoyment of tonal and rhythmic elements, and *not* for functional use.
        • Discuss and provide examples of some music which has been composed specifically to be used with or for an event, as marches, dance music, funeral music, religious music, and background music for films and the theater.
        • Discuss and illustrate some of the many types of marches, as the military, funeral, processional, wedding, triumphal, descriptive, and religious march. Examples include: RL—1, 28, 41, 46, 79, 89, 90, 122, 128, 135, 152, 182, 190, 197, 216, 263, 289, 311, 313, 317.
        • When playing or singing a vocal work refer to its particular classification or type, such as: the *lullaby* or *berceuse* (examples: S—57, 110); the *carol* (examples: S—42, 88); the *action song* (examples: S—84, 135); the *singing game* (examples: S—72, 82); the *foreign language song* (examples: S—48, 75); the *patriotic song* (examples: S—6, 10); the *nursery song* (examples: S—52, 81); the *folk song* (examples: S—16, 24); the *fun* or *nonsense song* (examples: S—11, 60); the *holiday song* (examples: S—9, 142); the *hymn* (examples: S—87, 105); the *community song* (examples: S—80, 140); the *popular song* (examples: S—31, 91); the *round* and *canon* (examples: S—33, 136); the *ballad*

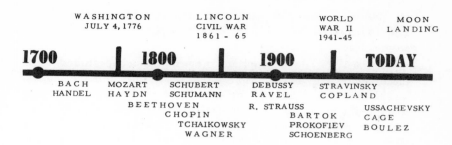

(examples: S—26, 126); the *spiritual* (examples: S—44, 131); the *chantey* (examples: S—13, 116); and the *art song* (examples: S—21, 74).

• Play various sacred and secular works. Discover differences in musical style. Introduce appropriate terms to classify these works. Note the importance of the text in religious works such as hymns, carols, anthems, chants, masses, oratorios, and sacred songs. Discuss the role of music in religious services of churches and temples. If possible, arrange for student attendance at rehearsals of church choirs. Ask students to pay particular attention to the music at their own church services.

• Refer to the various classifications and functions of instrumental works when excerpts from these are played, as the: *overture* (examples: RL—223, 291); the *orchestral prelude* (examples: RL—126, 318); the *duo, trio,* or *quartet* (examples: RL—6, 39, 131, 241); the *symphony* (examples: RL—18, 86, 117, 295); the *concerto* (examples: RL—40, 102, 316); the *sonata* (example: RL—240); the *barcarolle* (examples: RL—186, 227); and the *romanze* (example: RL—184).

• Listen, move to, and if possible, learn the basic steps of dances such as: the bolero, bossa nova, fox trot, gavotte, highland fling, mazurka, minuet, polonaise, reel, square dance, tango, tarantella, and waltz, among others.

• Listen to the musical sound-track of a film. Discuss how background music can aid in presenting a more convincing aura of time and place, how it underlines the thoughts of a character or the ensuing plot, how it serves as a quiet background for mood, and how it is used to build a sense of continuous action. Play background music. Infer what action is taking place.

• Provide experiences in creating music for various school functions (graduation march, pep song, background music for a play).

III-V   2c. Music can be classified as being programmatic or non-programmatic in content.

• Play examples of music intended to express moods or ideas (RL—

16, 106); descriptions of places (RL—180, 208) or characters (RL—179, 194); or stories (RL—73, 214). Classify this type of music as *program music*.

• At times provide appropriate programmatic background for a piece before it is played. More often, delay this until the musical meanings are first listened for and discussed. Encourage listening to program music with the musical elements and design in mind, rather than the descriptive content. Concentrate on *how* the musical elements have been used by the composer to evoke the mood or description.

• Place various adjectives on the chalkboard which might describe a musical work. Play a piece of program music and select words fitting the music.

• Discuss how much music has been written without the intent of telling a story or describing a scene. In this type of music the attention is given to the use of musical elements to create tonal beauty and aesthetic design. This non-program music, also called *absolute* or *abstract* music, does not refer or relate to anything outside the music itself. Nevertheless, feelings and pictures evoked in the mind of the listener should be recognized regardless of the type of music played.

III-V   2d. Music may be classified by *geographic* or *cultural* origin, as American Indian music, Irish music, Western music, or hillbilly music; by *historical period*, as music of the Renaissance, the Romantic period, or contemporary music; or by *composer*, as the music of Bach, Mozart, or Bartok (see this chapter, pp. 132–134, for discussion and activities).

V   2e. Music may be classified by its form, as a ternary form, rondo, or theme and variations (see pp. 120–129 for discussion and activities).

Part Two

APPROACHES TO
MUSICAL EXPERIENCES

In Part I the relationship of conceptual development to the structure of music was discussed. Many experiences in the processes of *listening*, *performing* (singing, playing instruments, moving rhythmically), and *creating* appropriate to the discovery and analysis of specific concepts of music were suggested. This section devotes a separate chapter to each of these approaches, and describes the values, objectives, skills, and techniques for teaching.

The materials in this section are to be used in conjunction with Part I. Once the conceptual understandings and related activities are identified, the teacher will refer to this section for specific techniques suitable to the desired learning situation. Regardless of the approach used in a particular lesson, the focus should be placed upon the development of concepts of:

TONE—duration, pitch, intensity and dynamics, tone color
RHYTHM—beat, meter, rhythmic patterns and melodic rhythm, tempo
MELODY—tonal direction, contour, tonal patterns and phrases, interval, melodic climax, tonality
HARMONY—simultaneously-sounding tones, chords and triads, harmonic accompaniments, harmonic change, texture

FORM—repetition, contrast, and variation of musical elements; introductions, interludes, codas, and sections; phrases; forms such as binary (A B), ternary (A B A), and rondo

STYLE—the characteristic use of tonal, rhythmic, melodic, and harmonic elements in the music of certain cultural groups, historical periods, and composers

Seven

LISTENING

Listening is fundamental to all musical experience. The student needs to listen as he sings, tunes his ukulele, claps the beat, or creates an original melody. Listening is also the means of increasing the student's understanding and enjoyment of all types of music. Every student will *not* become an accomplished performer or composer, but he *can* grow in his ability to grasp the tonal and rhythmic patterns of music as performed by others. The goal of the listening program is to increase each student's desire to listen to music and obtain aesthetic satisfaction in this experience. This can be accomplished by developing the student's awareness of patterns of tension and release in the music as accomplished by the particular uses of various musical elements. The purpose of this chapter is to show ways by which this goal can be attained through *directed listening* to music literature of many types and styles.

PLANNING THE LISTENING EXPERIENCE

Formulating Objectives

Each objective for a listening lesson should be stated in terms of the general guidelines given in the Introduction, pp. x–xii. It will focus upon an expected student response to a listening experience related to a specific aspect of musical structure. The following model illustrates how an objective for a listening lesson can be stated:

144   LISTENING

OBJECTIVE:

THE STUDENT WILL INDICATE AN UNDERSTANDING THAT:
[a section of a work may repeat after contrast

BY: ┌using the same rhythm instrument accompaniment each of
       │ the four times the main section of Kodaly's "Viennese Musical
       └Clock" is heard

The above objective, stated in terms of a desired student behavior, suggests certain activities which can be used to achieve the goal. These might include:

• listening for the overall mood of the work, and how the specific musical elements contribute to this feeling
• moving rhythmically to the rhythmic flow of the music, and choosing appropriate rhythm instruments to highlight the music's mood and beat
• playing the chordwise theme for the students, noting its tonal direction, clapping its rhythm, singing it on a neutral syllable, and designing it on the chalkboard
• raising hands each time the main theme is heard, and moving creatively to only those sections which feature the main theme (sections 1, 3, 5, and 7)
• playing the same rhythm instruments only on the sections in which the main theme occurs

Several basic points for planning any listening experience can be drawn from the above outline:

• Listening experiences are developed in relation to achieving an understanding and enjoyment of the total musical structure and design, even though the music may be programmatic, descriptive, or functional in type.
• While guided listening is the main approach used in a listening lesson, some singing, movement, music reading, playing instruments, and creating may take place within the musical setting. Several approaches may be used to accomplish the lesson objective.
• The evaluative activity at the conclusion of the lesson is the same as the one stated in the objective, and is used to determine whether the objective has been accomplished.
• Understandings gained in the listening experience may be shown through a *non-verbal* as well as a verbal response.

Selecting Music and Materials

The music chosen for a listening lesson should be appropriate for the stated objective. A balance of representative music is recommended. Some types of music which should be played for students at *all* levels of instruction include: art music, folk music, popular and semi-Classical music, jazz, and ethnic music of both Western and non-Western cultures; vocal, instrumental, aleatory ("chance"), and electronic music; program and non-program ("absolute") music; music of all historical periods, including the Middle Ages, the Renaissance, and the contemporary era; monophonic, homophonic, and polyphonic music (see pp. 107–108); sacred and secular music; selected works by many composers; and functional music, such as music for the dance, theater, and ceremonial occasions. For students with a limited background in directed listening, music should be chosen which will arouse interest through its definite rhythm, tuneful melody, obvious contrasts, or unusual tone colors.

There are many sources from which to obtain materials for the listening program. These include:

- recordings with accompanying guides found in several listening series for schools (see list, p. 226)
- recordings and teaching suggestions for listening lessons which accompany some of the newer basal music series for the elementary schools (see p. 219)
- supplementary record series (see Appendix C for sources)
- recordings from libraries and personal collections
- tape recordings
- audio-visual aids, such as charts, slides, filmstrips, films, and pictures of instruments and composers
- books in which information is given about the composers, the music of other countries, the science of sound, and various performing media

One extremely valuable source of music which is frequently overlooked in the listening program is *live music*. Here the students can see, as well as hear a soloist, small ensemble, choral group, band, or orchestra perform. In addition, there is often an opportunity to discuss the music and instrumentation with the performer, conductor, or composer. Several sources of live music are available, including other teachers and students within the school who are capable performers, visiting performing groups from neighboring schools, and parents, college groups, and amateur and professional musicians in the community.

The teacher should also encourage students to bring in records from home, whether they be classical, folk, or rock. In this way the teacher can develop an air of acceptance and respect for all music. In addition, the judicious use of the music most familiar to the students can serve as a bridge to open newer musical horizons for each student. After careful preparation, the teacher should present the student's recording to the class, and use the work to reinforce or introduce understandings about the structure of music.

Preparing for the Lesson

In order to present successfully the listening experience, the teacher must become familiar with the music so that he has a real "working acquaintance" with the musical elements affecting its design. He will find it helpful to listen to the music several times, read the accompanying teacher's guide (when available), and note the musical elements which are particularly related and pertinent to the form of the music. He should then develop some familiarity with certain aspects associated with the music, such as facts about the composer, or historical and ethnic influences, so that the listening experience can be enriched.

Following this preparation, the teacher must plan the activities to introduce the piece and get the students "into" the music as soon as possible. The number of ways of involving students with the music is limited only by the creativity and enthusiasm of the teacher. If he is truly excited about the music, he will be able to motivate students to enjoy the selection with him.

The teacher should follow a *cyclical sequence* that challenges students to move from the obvious and known to the subtle and unknown in seeking answers to questions regarding the music and its form. In general, a recommended sequence for a listening lesson is:

(1) introduce the work, providing motivation and presenting background material

(2) pose a problem, asking students to listen for the overall musical effect and discover the more obvious musical elements within the work

(3) discuss what has been heard, with particular reference to possible answers to the initial question raised

(4) reset the stage for further discovery by asking students to listen for specific elements of the music and how they relate to the overall musical design

(5) repeat the above steps, each time having students develop increasingly broader understandings about the use of the musical elements in this particular piece

(6) apply these understandings to new musical experiences

Through this *cyclical approach* the teacher is encouraging discovery of musical elements which might otherwise have been ignored. This approach helps students to direct their attention to the music and its structure. It also guides students to learn that there is much to listen for in music. The repeated hearings of the music within a lesson will increase the student's familiarity with the music and its design, thus heightening his aesthetic response to the experience.

Some Teaching Suggestions

General Guidelines

Several general suggestions can be given to help the teacher in planning activities for his particular group. These include:

• Provide for individual differences during the lesson; e.g., have one student play the theme on the piano while another student accompanies him with rhythm sticks; or ask a group of students to move to the rhythm of the piece while several students follow the orchestral score.

• Emphasize involvement with the music rather than verbal knowledge about it.

• Adapt listening sessions to the attention span of the students, and extend a particularly long work over several periods.

• Play the entire selection (or excerpt, if it is an extended work) more than one time in order for students to get an overall impression of the piece before exploring its details.

• Increase familiarity and enjoyment of a piece by repeating it throughout the year, each time increasing the students' awareness of the musical content.

• When preparing for a live music presentation, discuss program materials which explain the music, present background information on the composer or performing groups, and play excerpts from the music to be performed. Following the performance, review what has transpired, replay the music, and use the experience as a frame of reference for new musical experiences.

Beginning the Lesson

The following suggestions should be helpful in introducing a work and motivating the students:

• Create an atmosphere of desire and readiness for listening by setting an example.

• Briefly discuss the background of the music—when it was written, who composed it, and/or its cultural or historical setting.

• Show related pictures, paintings, and real instruments when they are pertinent to the music's design.

• Ask students to listen for some interesting and/or unusual effects in the music.

• Relate an event (a parade, a dance, a move) familiar to students which may have a direct bearing upon the type of music to expect.

• Play the main theme of the music on the piano or melody bells, and ask students to listen for this tune in the selection.

Specific Activities

Many different types of activities which can be used to foster musical understanding in the listening program have been mentioned in Part I of this text. In summary, these activities include:

• Compare two short pieces for similarities and differences in mood, tone color, meter, dynamics, and/or style.

• Direct attention to specific elements to listen for each time the music is played by asking students to move rhythmically or raise hands every time they hear a certain theme, rhythmic pattern, or other structural element.

• Count the number of times a certain theme is heard in the music.

• Place certain key words for mood (happy, sad, dreamy, mysterious), instrumentation (violin, oboe, solo voice, chorus, male singer) and meter (2's, 3's, 4's) on the chalkboard, and ask students to select those words which best fit the music.

• Devise instrumental accompaniments to recorded music to highlight the beat, melodic rhythm, meter, a repeated theme, repetition and contrast of sections, dynamics, and overall mood.

• Distribute pictures of various instruments. Each student holds up the appropriate picture when his instrument is heard in the music.

• Withhold the composer's title until the students have suggested appropriate titles based upon the music's mood.

• Mention the title of a work before playing it. Ask students to listen to the music and decide why the composer chose the title.

• Place several titles on the chalkboard and ask students to select the one which best fits the mood of a work.

• Have students anticipate the mood of a programmatic, descriptive work by discussing what type of melody, rhythm, harmony, dynamics, and tone color might be used to describe a scene or story. Compare students' responses with the actual music.

Using Charts

Charts illustrating the main theme of a work, musical terms and symbols describing the piece's mood, tempo, and dynamics, a dominant rhythmic pattern, the phrase structure, or the use of certain tone colors are a most useful means of developing concepts in the listening lesson. These charts can be made by the teacher. Theme charts are also part of certain record series for the elementary school; e.g., *The Bowmar Orchestral Library*. Some ways of using these various types of charts are:

• Have students point to the theme or rhythmic pattern as it is heard in the music.

• Play the theme on the piano or clap the rhythm as students follow the notation on the chart. Replay the music up to a certain point, asking students to indicate where the music was stopped.

• Have one student point to the notation as others sing or play the melody, or clap the rhythm.

• Play a tonal pattern within the theme, and ask students to identify and frame it on the chart.

• Use the chart in correlation with theme excerpts reproduced in the students' texts.

• Show the students several themes from the work, each one on a different chart. Sing or play one theme, and have students indicate which theme was played by pointing to the appropriate chart.

• List on a chart several terms which could describe a work's tempo, dynamics, or mood, and have students select those terms which best describe the music.

• Place a different series of geometric symbols on individual charts, and ask students to select the series which conforms with the design of a work, such as A B A (□ × □) or A B A C A D A (○ △ ○ □ ○ × ○).

Eight

PERFORMING

Children may make, interpret, and respond to music through *singing, playing instruments,* and *moving rhythmically.* When performance becomes the means through which musical concepts are developed, musical growth and insight into musical structure can take place. This chapter outlines the roles of these performing areas in a conceptually oriented music curriculum, and offers suggestions for implementing them in the classroom.

SINGING

Singing has as its main function the development of each student's aesthetic awareness of music. Through singing, the student can be guided to further his understanding of the musical elements and their interrelationships in a musical work. Every vocal experience should also foster the student's pleasure and enjoyment in making music with his own personal "instrument," both in solo and with other voices. Vocal skills such as singing musically with the head voice, an open throat, good enunciation, and correct posture will help the student learn how to use and control his voice to express himself tonally and rhythmically. By participating in singing the student can learn to appreciate music literature, particularly the vocal repertoire of many peoples, historical periods, and composers. Singing also serves as an outlet for student involvement in leisure-time and recreational activities.

Setting Goals

The teacher needs to set definite *musical* objectives each time he plans a singing experience. Every lesson involving singing should contain at least one specific objective related to the long-range goal of developing musical understanding (see pp. x–xii). Related objectives designed to develop the skill needed to attain this understanding will be included when they are to be emphasized in a particular lesson. An appropriate model for objectives focusing upon the singing experience is:

For understandings

THE STUDENT WILL INDICATE AN UNDERSTANDING THAT (insert specific understanding) *the phrases in a musical work may repeat or contrast*
BY (insert appropriate student behavior which demonstrates attainment of the understanding) *singing only those phrases of "Au Clair de la Lune." which are the same as the first phrase.*

AND

For skills

THE STUDENT WILL INDICATE AN ABILITY TO (insert specific skill) *sing phrasewise*
BY (insert appropriate student behavior which demonstrates the ability) *singing and taking a breath before each of the four phrases of "Au Clair de la Lune."*

The Student's Voice

Listen to children speak, sing, or call from a distance. Observe that their voices are extremely versatile, ranging in quality from light, flutelike tones to harsh, strident sounds. It is the flutelike quality, vital and always expressive, which should be developed in the singing experience. Notice also that the *vocal range*—the tones which a singer can sing—varies from child to child according to his physical maturity and musical experience. Similarly, the *tessitura*—the average or most comfortable range of tones—differs for each student. The approximate vocal ranges and tessituras of elementary school children are shown in Ex. 8–1, p. 152.

Several implications for planning may be derived from the above discussion:

• Choose songs with a limited range for young children and beginning singers.
• Pitch songs within the vocal range of the *student*, not the teacher. Transpose melodies which are too high or low.

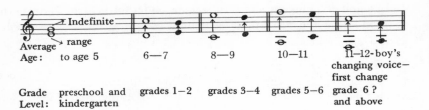

Ex. 8-1. Vocal Ranges (in Whole Notes) and Tessituras (in Small Noteheads)—Grades K-6

• Male teachers, whose voices are an octave lower than those of the students, can reinforce their own voices with instruments so that students can match their voices with another tone of the same pitch.
• The vocal range will increase when attention is given to good posture, correct breathing and breath support, and vocal production. Experience in singing songs that have some relatively high or low tones will help expand the student's vocal range.
• Small group and individual vocal activities are important for every level in order to meet differences in student vocal ranges.
• Successful part-singing experiences are needed for fifth and sixth grade boys whose voices are beginning to change (see discussion on the changing voice, p. 162).

Selecting Songs

The first and most important criteria for the selection of any song is its inherent musical value and quality. This can be determined by asking yourself several questions:

• Does the song have a text which reflects human emotions and is not written to "educate"?
• Does the song have a flowing, vital, and interesting rhythm?
• Does the song's melody give a sense of completeness and beauty?
• Are the uses of repetition and contrast interesting or dull?
• Does the melody have both high and low points of interest, as well as a climax?
• Does the song text fit the rhythm and melodic line?
• Are the text and length of the song appropriate for the student's maturity and musical level?
• Is the melody within a comfortable singing range?

A song should be chosen also to fit the objectives for the lesson. If the aim is to have students develop an awareness of chordwise progression in melody, a song which exhibits this feature must be found. Likewise, if the goal is to help students respond to differences between major and minor tonalities, at least two songs must be chosen which illustrate these differences. Of course, most objectives involving the improvement of vocal technique can be attained through any song.

Several additional suggestions for selecting songs are:

• Use songs from different graded books and other sources, depending on the purpose of the lesson, the suggestions for activities, and the complexity of musical arrangements.

• If the same song appears in many texts and at different grade levels, you can be quite sure that it is a song which will be appropriate to use in your class.

• Vary the songs you select. They should provide examples of different moods, tempi, tonalities, forms, rhythms, and melodies.

• Choose songs representative of different cultures—both Western and non-Western in style. Enhance the repertoire by including folk, art, patriotic, "fun," ethnic, popular, and children's songs.

• Some songs should be of permanent value and sung many times during the year. Others may be of temporary interest, and used only for particular musical purposes.

CHOOSE SONGS ON THE BASIS OF—*MUSICAL QUALITY AND OBJECTIVES*

Planning the Singing Experience

Once the song is chosen, some means of presenting it must be devised. You can sing it to the class, use a recording, have a student or another adult introduce it, or use a combination of these approaches. Whichever means is used, you should *know* the song well before it is taught. Familiarity with the music can be attained by: analyzing the melody for phrases and climaxes; studying its meter, tempo, and rhythm; practicing the correct pronunciation and expressing the meaning of the text; singing the song to yourself at least once, paying particular attention to melodic and rhythmic accuracy; playing the accompaniment for the song; and transposing the song to the children's vocal range, if necessary.

After becoming familiar with the song, you will need to devise strategies for presenting the song to the group. Particular attention should be given to ways in which the song will be introduced, motivation, developmental activities which will help the students learn the song, and the understandings and skills to be stressed.

The best *motivation* in singing a new song is the inherent musical appeal of the song itself. A brief discussion before singing the song can set the stage for the vocal experience and direct attention to:

• the kind of song it is (a carol, a folk or art song)
• its cultural origin
• the story of the text as told in the song

• interesting musical aspects of the song, such as a syncopated rhythm, a modal tonality, or irregular phrasing

Many music series today have accompanying records for songs in each text. The renditions of these songs are generally excellent, since they are musically done, have tasteful accompaniments, and are accurate in their performance. The song recordings are especially helpful to teachers who lack confidence in singing alone, or have limited facility on an accompanying instrument.

Several other suggestions for planning the singing experience may be mentioned. Provide opportunity for the students to hear the song several times before it is sung. Encourage active participation, such as clapping the beat, conducting the meter, counting the number of phrases, listening for scale-line progressions, or noticing the story content, each time the song is sung to the students. Other types of musical experiences, such as listening, playing instruments, or note reading can be interwoven with the singing activity to help accomplish lesson objectives. The general recommendations for lesson planning mentioned on pp. x–xi, should be followed when designing vocal experiences for each lesson.

Teaching the Rote Song

A song may be taught by *rote* or *note*. A rote approach, used predominantly at beginning instructional levels, involves learning the song by ear, without the use of notation. A song taught by note uses a musical score to aid in the presentation. This method is usually used when music reading is becoming an important means of developing musical independence.

If you plan to teach a song by rote, you will use the whole-song method, the phrase method, or a combination of these. In using *the whole-song method*:

• Sing the whole song to the class.
• Discuss the music or story content. Ask students to listen for other musical aspects, or to actively participate by responding to the music during the second rendition of the song; e.g., by moving hands to the phrases or clapping the beat.
• Resing the song. Discuss, and repeat the active listening procedure.
• Continue this process, repeating the song until students are able to join in.
• Review the entire song during this and subsequent lessons.

The key to the success of this method is to have the students listen to the song several times, participating through some musical activity and/or listening for a particular musical element each time the song is heard (see pp. 155–157).

When utilizing *the phrase method:*

• Sing the whole song to the class. Discuss general features about the music and text.

• Sing phrases accumulatively, building each new phrase on those pre-ceding it. Students repeat the phrases until the entire song is learned.

A combination of the whole-song and phrase method is frequently used to introduce a new song. In this method the teacher uses the whole-song approach, but works on difficult phrases when needed. Students are encouraged to join in on certain phrases which are easy to sing as the entire work is repeated by the teacher according to the techniques used in the whole-song method.

Which approach should be used when teaching a song? Use a *com-bination* of the whole-song and phrase method for most songs, since this method permits the students to hear the song several times, yet allows the teacher to stress those phrases which cause difficulty. The *whole-song method* is suitable for songs which are quite short, have "catchy" tunes or rhythmic patterns, and/or have verses which repeat the same words, as in "This Old Man." The *phrase method* is often used for songs which are lengthy and difficult, contain complicated melodic or rhythmic patterns, and have intricate texts.

A *recording* can be a valuable means of introducing a song, and an important adjunct to many singing experiences. In using a recording, teach the song by the whole-song method. Emphasize certain difficult phrases with your own voice after the recording has been played once or twice. Make sure you are familiar with the recording before you use it with the class. If the song is new to the students, encourage them to listen to it several times before joining in. When it is difficult for students to maintain the tempo or follow the words of the recording, write the words on the chalkboard or a chart and review them separately *after* the song has been heard several times. Have the students chant, whisper, and mouth the words, or react rhythmically to the music to help them keep pace with the voice or melody as it is heard. Keep the volume at a moderate level. Ask the students to sing no louder than the recording. Gradually reduce the phonograph volume in order to foster indepen-dence in singing.

REMINDER: *Recordings are not substitutes for teaching. They are but one aid in presenting the song. It is the teacher's responsibility to develop musical under-standings and skills through recordings.*

It is essential that students participate in some meaningful musical response each time the song is heard or sung. Some activities appropriate for all instructional levels include:

• chanting the words of the text in rhythm
• moving rhythmically to the beat, strong beat, or melodic rhythm
• moving hands up and down to the melody's pitch levels
• finding places in the melody which move up, down, or stay the same

- moving hands in arcs to signify phrase patterns
- singing alternate phrases of the song (teacher-pupils, boy-girls, soloist-class)
- counting the number of phrases
- discovering parts of the song which repeat or are in contrast to other parts
- playing certain repeated tonal patterns in the song on a melody instrument
- using rhythm instruments to highlight the phrasing, repeated rhythmic patterns, or the melodic climax
- recognizing and singing with various types of accompaniment
- adding new words, changing the words, or creating additonal stanzas to fit the music's expressive feeling
- dramatizing parts of the song or the entire song, and moving to its rhythmic flow
- deciding upon an appropriate tempo and dynamic level
- discussing the mood as suggested by the melody and text, and working for an expressive rendition of the song
- suggesting ways to improve interpretation and performance
- singing the song with the focus on diction, posture, breathing, and tone production
- humming or whistling sections of the melody
- listening to another pupil or a group sing the song, and evaluating the performance by noticing which part of the song was sung well and which part needed improvement

Certain activities for rote songs are more appropriate for conceptual levels III and above. At these levels students may:

- determine by ear whether the melody is in the major, minor, or another mode
- raise hands every time DO (1, the tonic) is heard
- isolate tonal patterns and write them down in notation
- count the number of times a given tonal or rhythmic pattern is heard
- determine the probable meter of the tune
- conduct the meter of the tune
- listen for syncopation and/or even and uneven rhythms
- listen for a rhythmic pattern which is the same as the beginning of another familiar tune
- recognize repeated and contrasting phrases and periods, label them, and identify the form
- discover whether the form has two distinct sections (binary form—A B) or three (ternary form—A B A)
- raise hands when the melodic cadence or an harmonic change occurs

• improvise harmony on the Autoharp or ukulele
• learn a harmony part which fits well with the tune
• improvise a vocal harmony part to the tune
• recognize and discuss the nature of the homophonic texture of the accompaniment

Many teachers find it particularly difficult to start a song with their classes. How would you begin a song such as "Kookaburra" in Ex. 8–2 if the music were not in front of the students and you were not using a recording? Several steps should be followed, regardless of the maturity of the students:

• Find DO (the keynote, 1, the tonic) by looking at the key signature and noting which tone seems to be the center of tonality (in "Kookaburra" DO is D, and the key is D major).
• Play the key note (D) on the pitch pipe, piano, or resonator bells. Sing or hum it, and ask students to do the same.
• Find the starting tone of the song (in "Kookaburra" this tone is A—SOL); play and hum it. Ask students to hum the starting tone.
• Establish a feeling of tonality and tonal relationships by playing the I (tonic) chord (DO, MI, SOL or D, F♯, A in "Kookaburra") and then singing the chord tones. Have the students repeat this. Playing and singing DO, RE, MI, FA, SOL may be helpful also.
• Sing the first word on the correct pitch and "tune in" the students to make sure they are matching the tone.
• Play an introduction on the piano, Autoharp, ukulele, or guitar, emphasizing the I, IV, V₇ chord progression (D, G, A₇ chords for "Kookaburra") and the tempo; or play the last phrase of the song in the correct tempo; or use the standard conducting pattern (*down-up* in ²⁄₄ for "Kookaburra"), moving the hand noticeably to signify when the song is to begin; or count aloud one full measure of the song

Ex. 8-2. "Kookaburra"

in the desired tempo (say "1, 2, rea-dy be-gin" for "Kookaburra").
• Begin to sing. Emphasize starting the song together, good diction, and a pleasant tone quality.

Increasingly involve the students in gaining independence in starting their own songs by following the above outline. Occasionally a song should be started by giving students only the I (tonic) chord or the starting tone. This will help develop independence in singing many songs by ear with little or no help from the teacher or an accompanying instrument.

Once the song is underway, some means must be devised to keep the students together. This can be done by:

• playing the melody with an accompaniment
• playing an accompaniment without the melody
• playing the melody without an accompaniment
• singing with the students
• choosing a student to lead the singing
• using your hands to show the beat, tempo, rhythmic flow, and dynamics, either with formal conducting patterns or by any patterned hand movement (see p. 34 for illustrations of the basic conducting patterns)
• mouthing the words and having the students follow your lip movements
• clapping the beat or tapping on a drum or other rhythm instrument
• combining some of the above activities; e.g., playing an accompaniment and singing at the same time

Teaching a Song Through Notation

As the student becomes more involved in music and its interpretation he will be introduced gradually to the written language of music. Through the use of crude symbolism and a musical score he will learn that the symbols depict musical meanings previously perceived through aural experience. He will grasp the relationship between musical sound and the printed score. He will become familiar with one aspect of musical structure—the symbols and vocabulary of music—and use this as an aid in listening, performing vocally and instrumentally, and creating music.

Once the student has had broad aural experiences with music and its elements, he is ready to *observe* the notation of a song and become aware of certain aspects of the score, such as the staff, types of notes, tonal movement, rhythm, and symbols for tempo and dynamics. *Observational note reading*, especially important during the latter part of level I and at levels II and III, may consist of the following activities:

• Observe that song books contain both the words and the notes which record the musical tones for future reference.

• Students should follow the notation of familiar songs on charts, the chalkboard, or overhead transparencies as the teacher points to the notes. Guide students in the left-right direction of music reading, and in the ability to follow the rhythmic flow of the tones as symbolized by the various types of notes on the staff.

• Distribute song books when the children are able to hold and handle them, follow printed words and symbols, and understand the reason for using books. Briefly examine the title page, the location of page numbers, the table of contents, and the index. Have students find a familiar song for their first experience in observing notation from their own books.

• Direct attention to the many items on the page, such as the title, composer, tempo marking, various stanzas, and musical symbols.

• Discuss the way several stanzas or verses are written, and note the need to divide certain words into syllables to correspond with individual tones in the melody.

• Students should scan and then mouth the words as the teacher sings. Show students how to point to the notes of the song and follow its melodic line. Notice aspects such as repetition and contrast, note values and rhythmic patterns, passages where the melody rises or falls, phrases and cadences, chord symbols, tonal patterns, dynamics and tempo symbols, the meter signature, and bar lines and measures.

• Begin to develop a sight vocabulary of intervals (see pp. 73–75) and rhythmic and tonal patterns (see pp. 47 and 72). Call attention to them as they appear in much music. Find and utilize these intervals and patterns when undertaking the reading of a new song.

When students have had much experience with observational note reading, they are ready for the *independent reading* of new songs. The following activities are appropriate for students at levels III and above who have had extensive background in observational note reading:

• For initial experiences, choose songs which have many repeated tonal and rhythmic patterns and phrases, use many half and quarter notes, contain a melody which moves primarily by scale or by intervals of thirds, and are similar to familiar tunes. Relate the unfamiliar to previous learnings.

• Ask students to scan the notation for both familiar elements and potential tonal or rhythmic problems. Have them infer how the music may sound by noting its tempo, dynamics, the text and mood, melodic contour, and tonal and rhythmic patterns. Challenge students by asking them to study the score, and then close their books and recall as many aspects of the notation as they can.

• Establish the beat, meter, and tempo of the song. Observe the note values, clap the rhythm, and chant the words in the appropriate rhythm and mood.

• Examine the notation for familiar tonal or rhythmic patterns and other symbols. Call attention to the value of recognizing repetition, variation, and sequence in learning to read music.

• Conduct brief practice-drill sessions for difficult or new rhythmic and tonal patterns found in the song.

• Derive the scale upon which the tune is built (see pp. 78–79). Note the key signature, locate DO (the key note, 1), build the tonic chord (DO, MI, SOL) and find scale-line and chordal passages in the notation.

• Occasionally sing an unfamiliar tune as students observe the score. Make both pitch and rhythmic errors, and ask students to identify mistakes and make corrections. Also sing a phrase or tonal pattern from the song on a neutral syllable, or clap a rhythmic pattern, and have students find the line(s) in which the pattern or phrase appears.

• Emphasize the need to scan several notes at a time when reading music. Relate this to how a story is read.

• Set an even, slow tempo, sing DO, the scale, and the tonic triad (DO, MI, SOL) to develop a feeling for tonality, and attempt to sing the song with numbers or syllables. Occasionally sing with the students when they falter. Encourage a steady beat with no stopping, even when errors are made. Difficult parts of the song may be taught by rote. Initial independent music reading may be limited to only a few tonal patterns or phrases.

• Once the tune is sung accurately by numbers or syllables, have the students repeat the song with words. Review the song during subsequent lessons.

• Practice sight-reading without the crutch of numbers and/or syllables. Students should be encouraged to sing the tune to themselves, using a neutral syllable or a hum.

• An excessive amount of time spent on sight-reading a new song may take the joy out of singing. Regular well-planned short experiences are more rewarding than sporadic, lengthy drill sessions.

• Frequently use melody instruments to assist in reading intervals and tonal patterns, since they help the students to see, hear, and feel the distances between pitches. Also use these instruments to test the accuracy of the vocal pitches.

Problems in Teaching Singing

Probably the most common problem in the singing experience is *poor intonation*, identified by flatting a vocal tone. Singing on pitch, with accurate intonation, is an important skill to be developed at all levels of instruction. Children should be taught to listen carefully as they sing. Various tonal games, singing games that stress tonal awareness, and echo songs (see p. 163) are helpful at beginning instructional levels. Phrases sung alternately by the teacher or soloist and a group give the children a direct aural experience before they sing. Students can cup their ears to listen for pitch discrepancies. Pitching the song within the vocal range and tessituras of the singers may prevent intonation problems (see p. 152). The teacher should work for accuracy in the starting pitch of a song (see p. 157). Techniques for use with untuned singers (see below) are applicable also for beginning singers with intonation problems.

Another problem is that of the *untuned singer*—a student who is unable to match pitches with his voice. Although many children entering kindergarten have problems in matching pitch, they usually learn to sing on pitch by the third grade. Still, about 10% of all students (mostly boys) in the upper elementary school continue to have problems in singing. Unless guided instruction in matching tones is given to all children in grades K-2 and to untuned singers in grades 3-6, many pupils will not learn how to sing. Techniques recommended for *every* student in the lower elementary grades and the untuned singer in the upper grades include having the student:

- pretend he is calling from a distance, and sustain the vowel
- imitate the sound of a bird-call, a siren, a telephone, the wind
- identify the voices of others as they speak, chant, and sing
- use exaggerated vocal inflection as he tells a story, reads aloud, makes a statement, or asks a question
- imagine he is on an elevator, moving and singing up and down on a neutral syllable and stopping at different floors (pitches)
- use up-and-down hand and body movements to indicate pitch and tonal direction as he hears himself and others sing
- sit next to or in front of students who are accurate singers
- attempt to sing tone-calls (short fragments from songs) and nonsense syllables, such as "ding-a-ling-a-ling" and "min-ee-ha-ha"
- chant familiar jingles or rhymes on an indefinite pitch, and then on one, two pitches
- listen to and evaluate the singing of other students who sing on pitch
- engage in musical conversations with the teacher or other students, such as singing "hello," or "how are you?"
- start a tune on any comfortable pitch, accompanied by the teacher singing and/or reinforcing the melody on a melody instrument
- sing and hold the beginning pitch of a tune on a neutral syllable

- listen to the teacher singing softly into the student's ear during group singing
- sing tunes with a limited range (see list, p. 61) or many repeated tones (see list, p. 68)
- sing tunes with "catchy" tonal patterns (examples: S—11, 19, 45, 57, 70, 79, 93, 96, 137)
- work with a friend who will help him match tones
- sing with a small group under the guidance of the teacher, or join a special "singing club" to help him sing on pitch
- listen to and evaluate his own singing voice as recorded on tape
- learn about his vocal instrument and reasons for differences in tone quality and pitch

The teacher who works with children age 11 or 12 may find a few boys whose voices are undergoing initial and subtle changes in vocal range and quality. The *changing voice*, caused by physical maturation and the onset of puberty, evidences itself in the slightly lower and heavier voice of some fifth and sixth grade boys. While only a few boys may begin this voice change before the seventh grade, it is important that both the teacher and students recognize this change and feel comfortable with it. The teacher will find it helpful to:

- anticipate the changing voice by explaining to *all* children at the fifth and sixth grade levels the differences between the child and adult voice
- encourage the students to sing all songs, except when the melody becomes too high
- provide many part-song experiences in which the changing voices often sing the lower part (see also pp. 165–171)
- occasionally have boys with changing voices play suitable accompaniments as the higher, unchanged voices sing
- pitch many songs lower than usual in order to have the boys with changing voices continue to derive satisfaction from unison singing
- note that the voice just before the onset of change and during the change has a quality which is unique and very beautiful, and can never be produced again by the singer

Part-Singing

An essential activity which complements unison singing at levels III and above is singing in harmony, or *part-singing*. This experience provides the student with greater insight into the nature of harmony and texture, and helps to develop both control of his singing voice and accurate intonation. Through part-singing the student will learn how to hear the relationship and balance between two or more harmony parts, attain vocal independence, and improvise harmonically.

Many types of part-songs are found and indexed in grades 3–6 texts of most basal music series, and include:

- *echo songs* and *songs using imitation* as "Ol' Texas" in Ex. 8–3a, in which a second voice echoes a distinctive tonal pattern or the entire melody of the first part
- *rounds* as "Kookaburra" (see p. 157) and "Canoe Song" (see p. 79), in which the same melody is sung in two or more parts, but with each vocal part entering successively
- *canons* as "Dona Nobis Pacem," in which one part or voice is strictly imitated in another part or voice at any pitch or time interval
- *partner (combinable) songs* as "My Bonnie" sung with "Cielito Lindo," in which two songs with identical harmonies, meters, and tempi can be sung together (see especially Frederick Beckman, *Partner Songs* and *More Partner Songs*. Boston: Ginn, 1952, 1958).
- *songs with chants and ostinati* as in Ex. 8–3b, in which a distinctive, simple tonal figure, lower than the melody, is repeated continuously as an harmonic accompaniment for the melody
- *songs with pedal tones* as in Ex. 8–3c, in which one tone in harmony with the melody (usually SOL or scale-step 5) is sung on a neutral syllable throughout the piece
- *songs with chord roots*, as in Ex. 8–3d and "Home on the Range," p. 170, in which the root of the indicated chord is sung as a harmony part to the melody
- *songs with harmonic endings* as in Ex. 8–3e, in which a harmony part, usually in thirds or sixths, is added to the last few tones of a phrase or complete melody to highlight the feeling for cadence
- *descants* and *countermelodies* as in Ex. 8–3f, in which an independent melodic line, often having different words or a simpler rhythm and melody than the principal theme, is added above (descant) or below (countermelody) the main theme
- *two-part songs using a predominance of thirds and sixths* as in Ex. 8–3e, in which a second part, usually moving in intervals of thirds or sixths, is added to the principal melody
- *songs with vocal chording* as in Ex. 8–3g and "Home on the Range," p. 170, in which two or more tones of the accompanying chords indicated in the score are sung in harmony with the melody
- *songs with harmonic improvisation*, in which students hear the melody and then spontaneously sing a vocal line that blends with it
- *songs combining several of the above harmonic techniques*, as in Ex. 8–3h, which uses harmony in thirds and sixths, a vocal chant, chord roots, and an echoing effect
- *three-part songs* as in Exs. 8–3g and 8–3h, in which two additional harmony parts are added to the melody

Ex. 8-3. "Ol' Texas"

The following teaching aids are suggested for part-songs:

• Have students attempt to sing in harmony only after they can sing a single melody accurately. Plan to use many dialogue songs, such as "Old Woman" (see p. 127) and "Reuben and Rachel," at levels II and III. These songs, in which groups sing the dialogue of the characters in the song, help students be responsible for their own part, and learn how to enter at a given point in the music. Ask one group to hold its last tone while the second group "answers." Listen for the resulting harmony.

• Use a variety of materials and techniques which will challenge the students, yet make a musical rendition possible to attain. At level III begin with echo songs, rounds and canons, partner songs, chants and ostinati, and pedal tones. Continue with these types of part-songs at levels IV and V, while gradually introducing the

students to more advanced part-singing experiences. Use both accompanied and unaccompanied part-songs.

• Teach part-songs by rote and through music reading. Observing
the musical score and reinforcing harmony parts through instruments will aid in singing the parts. Have students hear the melody
as the harmony part is added, so that a feeling for the total work
and harmonic blend is developed from the beginning. Frequently
use an harmonic accompaniment to call attention to the harmony
upon which the melody is based.

• Teach a given harmony part to *all* students. Each group should
have experiences singing all the parts. An exception to this is made
for the changing voice (see p. 162), which will normally sing only
the lower part.

• Consider grouping the students for part-singing. Those singing
a given part should frequently, but not always, sit together. Include
some excellent singers on each harmony part. Use fewer voices on
the upper part. Strive for balance by moving students from one group
to another.

• Stress the need for students to listen constantly to each other. Note
the harmonic relationships and tonal movement of each part. Emphasize tonal blend rather than having one group dominate vocally. Ask
several students to evaluate tonal balance and blend as they listen
to their classmates sing. Use the tape recorder as an aid in evaluation.

• Ask students to sustain their parts at a given signal by the teacher
in order for them to hear both their own tones and the tones sung
in harmony. When beginning a song with two or more parts, make
sure that each group can first sing its initial tone alone and then
with the harmonizing parts.

• Relate part-singing experiences to the students' understanding
of harmony, chord structure, harmonic rhythm and change, and
texture (see pp. 92–108). Guide students to improvise and compose
their own harmony parts.

• Encourage students to join in on the harmony part as soon as it
is introduced. Expect more students to master the part each time it
is repeated. Practice those sections of a part-song which may be more
difficult. Isolate each part, then combine both parts, and finally put
the section back into its musical context.

• An harmonic part may be introduced in several ways. The teacher
can sing or play the new part as the group sings or hums the melody.
More advanced students can teach the part-song by singing or playing it for the class, after adequate guided preparation. The teacher
can tape-record the harmony part and play it as the class sings the

melody. Whatever method is used, it is important that the harmony part be introduced *together* with the melody. When the harmonic blend becomes familiar to the students the teacher may then isolate each part for intensive practice before combining the parts again.

• Frequently have one group play the harmonic part on a melody instrument (piano, flutophone, recorder, melody bells) while another group sings the melody. Two groups can also play the melody and the harmony parts together on their instruments. Rhythm instruments may be added to accentuate the rhythmic flow and beat of the music, and thus help to keep the harmony parts together.

• Use excerpts from familiar part-songs, and devise harmonic drills to practice singing in harmony. Also divide the class into two parts and slowly sing each of the following on a neutral syllable:

In addition to the general techniques listed above, there are several which apply specifically to particular types of part-songs, such as the round, chant, descant, and chord root:

Rounds and canons

• Make certain that the melody of the round or canon is very familiar to the students before adding the second part. If necessary, delay teaching the harmonization until a subsequent lesson.

• Have the students listen to the harmony part as a small group begins the melody and the teacher joins in on the second part. Also ask two groups to sing the part-song while the remainder of the class listens.

• Explain voice entrances. Select one student from each part to lead his section and direct the group when to enter. Agree beforehand on the number of times each part will be repeated, and cue in each entrance. Provide a strong conducting pattern for the beat to keep the parts together.

• Encourage balance, blend, and good tone quality. Avoid vocal competition between groups.

• In addition to traditional rounds and canons (examples: S—7, 20, 33, 67, 73, 108, 111, 130, 136, 144) provide experience with pentatonic songs used as rounds or canons (see pp. 87–88). Because of the absence of scale-step 4 (FA) and 7 (TI) pentatonic tunes can be used as part-songs, since the parts combine easily without much dissonance.

Chants and ostinati

• Chants such as the one for "Ol' Texas" in Ex. 8–3b can be devised easily by the teacher and students. The simplest types of chants to create are those based on the root of the indicated chord (see pp. 99 and 169). Other chants should be based on the tones of the harmonizing chord. For measures which are harmonized with the I, IV, and V$_7$ chords, one or more combinations of the following scale-steps may be adopted to the rhythm of the words selected for the chant:

The I Chord	The IV Chord	The V$_7$ Chord
1–1–1, 8–8–8	4–4–4	5–5–5, 5–6–5
1–8, 8–1	4–6–8, 8–6–4	5–4–5, 5–2–5
1–3–5, 5–3–1	4–6–4, 6–4–6	5–4–2–7, 5–7–2–4
5–3–5, 3–5–3	4–6–5–4, 6–6–5–4	5–7–5–7
8–5–8	6–5–4–6	7–7–6–5, 7–6–5–5, 7–6–5–4
8–7–6–5, 8–5–6–5,	4–1–4, 1–4–4	5–4–3–2, 5–6–7–5
8–5–6–7–8		

• Begin with one-tone chants, as 1–1–1 or 5–5–5. Chants using the fifth scale-step (SOL) will sound particularly well with the I and V$_7$ chords, since SOL is a tone in both of these chords. One of the easiest tonal patterns to sing as a chant will be 5–6–5 (SOL-LA-SOL).

• In adding a chant-like tonal pattern to a melody, devise the chant's rhythmic pattern so that it contrasts with the rhythm of the melody. Rhythm instruments may be added to highlight this pattern.

• Early experiences with chants may begin with the melodies of rounds. As a two-part round is sung, a third part, based on the I chord, may be added.

• Chants provide excellent introductions and codas for songs. Sing the chant four times before or after the song to provide an introduction and/or ending.

• Once facility is gained in singing a one-part chant to a melody, two or three parts may be added to extend the chant.

Descants and countermelodies

• Introduce descants before countermelodies, since the former is higher than the melody and, therefore, often easier to sing.

• Establish the starting pitch for both the main tune and the harmony part before beginning the part-song. Ask each group to sing or hum its beginning tone separately, and then together.

• Guide students in devising descants and countermelodies for favorite tunes by selecting tones from the supporting chord structure. For example, when a IV chord (FA-LA-DO) is indicated, the tones of the harmony part in the key of C major might include F, A, and C.

• Apply the general procedures outlined for part-singing (see pp. 165–167) to the singing of descants and countermelodies.

Chord roots

• Introduce the singing of chord roots with other activities related to chord structure, triads, and harmonic change (see pp. 99–100). At first, use rounds, since they normally have only the I chord as harmony. Gradually expand chord root singing to melodies with the IV and V₇ chords, and minor triads as the ii and vi chords.

• Practice singing the root of the indicated chord with note names, scale-step numerals, and syllables on the first beat of each measure. Add words which fit the song text, or sing all the words of the song in rhythm on the chord root tone.

• Reinforce the singing of chord roots with melody instruments and the open strings of the ukulele, guitar, Autoharp, or standard orchestral instruments.

Using thirds and sixths

• Practice adding tones both below and above a melody so that the interval between the principal part and the harmony is either a third or a sixth. Provide much experience in recognizing these intervals by ear (see pp. 95–96) before attempting to sing them in harmony. Achieve success in singing thirds before introducing sixths.

• Use thirds and sixths moving in parallel motion (see "Au Clair de la Lune," p. 95, and "Ol' Texas," p. 164) for endings of phrases, selected sections from a song, and entire pieces. Some songs which can be harmonized almost completely in thirds and sixths include: S—68, 70, 76, 102, 146.

• Experiment with adding vocal harmony parts to familiar songs by using intervals such as the fourth, fifth, second, or seventh (see pp. 95–96). Note tonal effects.

Vocal chording

• Use the tones played for the indicated chord to derive the tones for vocal chording. For example, when the indicated chord is F, a two-part chording could consist of F and A, and a three-part chording might include F, A, and C (see Ex. 8–4 and vocal chording charts on p. 99).

• Introduce vocal chording with experiences in singing chord roots. When the chord root can be sung as a second part, another harmony part consisting of a second tone in the chord can be added. Later, a third tone of the chord can be included. Notice how tones are gradually added in the vocal chording for "Home on the Range" in Ex. 8–4.

Ex. 8-4. "Home on the Range"

• When providing vocal chording experiences, first use songs having only the I and V₇ chords (see list, pp. 102–103) and add only two tones of the chord to the melody part. Continue with two-part chording of songs which are accompanied by the I, IV, and V₇ chords. Expand vocal chording to three tones of the chord at level V, but only after two-part chording has been achieved successfully.

Harmonic improvisation

• Ask students at levels III and above to listen carefully to the accompaniments of familiar tunes and sing one or more of the tones they hear in the harmony. Also practice singing each of the individual tones heard in chords played on the piano, Autoharp, and ukulele (see also discussion on improvisation, pp. 202–203).

• Sing a familiar tune. Resing, having a group of students harmonize on an interval of a third higher or lower than the melody. Practice harmonizing phrases on melodies in parallel thirds without the use of notation.

• Provide students with various choices of tones to add to a melody. Have one group sing the melody as the other students experiment with adding their own harmony part.

• Help students improvise by giving them a chordal tone which fits the melody. Sing or play the melody with accompaniment, and encourage students to add an original harmony part with their voices.

Playing Instruments

Through playing rhythm, melody, harmony, and standard orchestral instruments the student may attain insights into virtually all the musical understandings outlined in Part I of the text. He will use the instruments as a medium for improvising and composing music (see pp. 202–207), and learn how to accompany recorded instrumental and vocal works. He will develop skills in the proper care, use, and technique of playing instruments, both in ensemble and solo. He will achieve some competency in transferring the interpretation of music symbols into an automatic physical response on instruments. Hopefully the student will attain sufficient ability on at least one instrument (the recorder, Autoharp, ukulele, among others) so that he maintains a life-long interest in playing that or another instrument. Finally, participation in instrumental experiences will help the student learn how to evaluate his own instrumental performance and the performances of others.

Teaching Suggestions for All Instruments

Several procedures apply to implementing instrumental performance in the music program:

• All children should be given an opportunity for instrumental performance. Abilities will differ, however, and some students will master the techniques much more quickly than others. Expect these differences despite similarities in levels of conceptual growth.

• Routines should be established for the storage, distribution, and handling of instruments.

• Introduce one instrument at a time. Stress the correct techniques of holding and playing it from the very first experience.

• Note the fingering for melody and harmony instruments by calling the index finger "1," the middle finger "2," the ring finger "3," and the little finger "4" (exception: keyboard instruments, where the thumb is "1").

• Encourage experimentation with the instrument, especially in producing unusual tone colors.

• Use the teachers' editions of the newer basal music texts for many excellent suggestions regarding instrumental performance.

• Some instruments should be displayed in the music corner at all times to permit student experimentation and practice.

• Use familiar music for beginning instruction on any instrument. This permits the student to determine more readily the correctness of his performance.

• Always strive for a quality rendition, regardless of the instrument used. Emphasize the need to listen to one's self and the performances of others. Encourage self-evaluation, and frequently use the tape recorder to allow students to hear the results of their efforts.

• Provide opportunities for students to play many different types of instruments. Rotate the instruments if more than one type is being used in a lesson.

• Instrumental accompaniments for recorded music and songs should support rather than dominate the music. Teach students to play softly enough so that the other instrumental parts can be heard.

• At levels III and above special classes may be organized for more advanced recorder, guitar, banjo, melodica, harp, or piano instruction.

Rhythm Instruments

The use of rhythm instruments should contribute to the development of musical understanding. Rhythm instruments may highlight the beat, strong and weak beats, a repeated rhythmic pattern in the melody or accompaniment, the melodic rhythm, original rhythmic patterns, syncopated rhythms and afterbeats; repeated and contrasting phrases or sections; changes in tone color, tempo, or dynamics; musical climaxes; and the overall mood of the piece. They are also useful in activities involving improvisation, the study of rhythm, and experimentation with sound, sound effects, and tone color.

The various types and specific uses of rhythm instruments in the classroom are summarized in the following chart:

Type of Instrument	*Method of Playing*	*Use*
Rhythm sticks 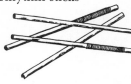	Hold one stick steady and strike it with the other; hit both together in a criss-cross manner; or rub one on the notches of the other.	Beat, melodic rhythm, fast rhythmic patterns
Drums (tom-toms, hand drums, bongos, conga drums)	Use a beater, mallet, the palm, or the finger tips, and strike the drum head's center or rim with a sharp, bouncing motion.	Beat, strong beat, accents, repeated rhythmic patterns
Sand blocks 	Hold one in each hand by the handles, and rub the sandpapered sides together in a vertical direction.	Melodic rhythm, special effects, fast and light music
Tone block 	Hold in one hand and strike it near the opening with a stick or mallet in a sharp, bouncing movement.	Beat, strong beat, accents, rhythmic patterns, "galloping" rhythms
Wood block	Hold in palm and strike it in the same manner as the tone block.	Same as tone block

Type of Instrument	*Method of Playing*	*Use*
Triangle 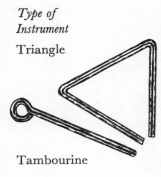	Hold in hand by a string and tap lightly with a bouncing motion, using a metal beater.	Slow, sustained music, strong beat, sounds of bells
Tambourine	Hold in one hand and tap it with finger tips or lower palm of the other hand; shake it, or strike it against the body (knees, elbow, shoulders).	Beat, rhythm, accents, lively and gay music
Wrist bells 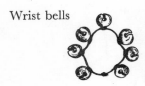	Hold in hand or place on wrists or ankles, and shake vigorously and sharply.	Beat, accents, light, gay music
Jingle clogs (sticks) 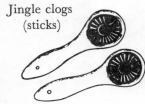	Shake vigorously and sharply; also tap against the palm of the other hand.	Same as wrist bells; also use for accents
Rattle	Shake vigorously with distinct accents.	Beat, accents, special effects
Cymbals	Strike together in a vertical position, with one hand moving up and one down; also tap on edges with a mallet.	Increase in dynamics, strong beat, accents, climaxes, special effects

Type of Instrument	_Method of Playing_	_Use_
Finger cymbals	Same as cymbals; also hold with the first and third fingers of one hand and tap cymbals lightly.	Sustained tones, special effects, calm music
Coconut shells	Hold one in each hand, with the cups facing outward, and knock together in horizontal motion.	Same as tone block
Gong	Suspend freely, and strike with a wool or felt-covered mallet in a bouncing motion.	Climaxes, heavy accents, special effects
Maracas 	Shake vigorously and sharply.	Fast, "busy" music, Latin American music
Clappers (castanets) 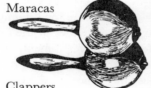	Hold in upright position and jerk harply.	Beat, accents, rhythmic patterns, Latin American music
Hand castanets 	Hold in one hand, using two fingers to click the two edges together.	Same as clappers
Claves	Cup one clave in hand, and strike it briskly with the other clave.	Beat, accents, rhythmic patterns, Latin American rhythms

Type of Instrument		*Method of Playing*	*Use*
Guiro	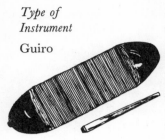	Using a stick or wire, brush the notches with a relaxed, sweeping movement directed away from the body.	Same as claves
Cowbell (cencerro)		Cup it in one hand and strike it with a stick or mallet in a bouncing motion; or shake briskly.	Beats, climax, special effects

The teacher will find the following techniques helpful in providing experiences with rhythm instruments:

• A wide choice of rhythm instruments should be made available to students for experimentation. Guide students in selecting instruments by asking questions such as: "Is the music loud or soft? What instruments would go well with the music? Let's see which of the two types of instruments sounds better with the music. Can you suggest another way to play the instrument?" Consider the tone quality of the instrument, and the mood, tempo, and dynamics of the music when selecting a rhythm instrument for an accompaniment.

• Provide several experiences with one instrument before proceeding to an unfamiliar one. Highlight only one aspect of the music at a time—each with a different rhythm instrument. Gradually combine instruments as students become more skillful in hearing various elements of the music, in performing on their instruments, and in playing their own part while other students play a contrasting part.

• Guide students to classify rhythm instruments according to their tone quality; e.g., metal instruments with a ringing or jingling quality, or wooden instruments which produce a clicking sound.

• Before distributing rhythm instruments have the students clap and move rhythmically to the music and imitate the manner in which the instrument is to be played.

• All students need not use rhythm instruments at the same time. While one group plays on instruments, another group may be clapping, and a third group creating a dance.

• Help students devise rhythm instrument scores to guide them in their playing. Note the many possibilities for rhythm instruments to highlight certain musical elements in "Little 'Liza Jane" in Ex. 8–5.

Ex. 8–5. "Little 'Liza Jane" With Rhythm Instrument Scores

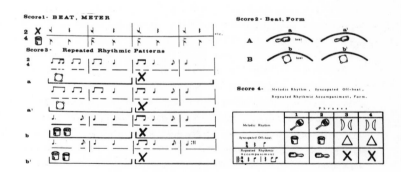

• Use the same or similar sounding instruments to highlight repeated or similar passages, and different instruments to signify contrast (see scores 2, 3, and 4 in Ex. 8–5).

• When some students have trouble following their parts, select a few more capable members from each instrumental group to play for the class. Then ask other students to follow these leaders. Withdraw leaders as the group gains independence in playing.

• Introduce the students to rhythm instruments used by various cultures and ethnic groups; e.g., the Hawaiian *ipu* (gourd), and the Brazilian *reco-recos* (scrapers).

• Encourage and guide students to make their own rhythm instruments outside of class. Relate learnings about acoustics to construction of instruments.

Melody Instruments

Many types of melody instruments are available for use in school music programs. Extremely useful are the *step bells, song* or *melody bells, resonator* or *tone bells, Swiss melodé bells* (hand bells), *marimba* and *xylophone,* and *piano.* In addition, instruments such as the *glockenspiel, tuned glasses, harmonica,* and *ocarina* may be used. At levels III and above students should receive group instruction on at least one of the following melody instruments: the *soprano recorder, flutophone, song flute, tonette, melodica.*

The values of using melody instruments for developing musical concepts are many. They serve as an audio-visual teaching aid and reinforcement for illustrating characteristics of melody such as pitch, scale, range, and interval. Students who have difficulty in singing may find success in playing melody instruments. Many singing activities may be enhanced through the use of these instruments. Students often respond more quickly and with more interest in music reading processes when using a melody instrument. Ear-training experiences using melody instruments are particularly valuable when tonal patterns are sung and then played, or *vice versa.* These instruments also have an important place in many creative experiences (see pp. 206–207) and in the listening program (see pp. 147–148).

Some general suggestions which apply to the use of *all* melody instruments in the instructional program are:

• The first experiences with any melody instrument should be aural. Students should listen to the instrument being played in a musical way, and note some of the skills needed to play it. They should then be allowed to explore the instrument, its parts, and tone quality.

• Direct students in holding, playing, and producing a good tone quality on the instrument. Proper playing habits should be emphasized from the beginning.

• Use the instruments to develop concepts of pitch, tonal direction, contour, range, interval, and scale. For example, ask students to find and play low and high pitches on the instrument; match tones sung or played on a different instrument; show how tones may repeat, move by step, or skip; play the highest and lowest tones of the melody; play the key note and starting pitch of a song, using notation; play a repeated tonal pattern each time it occurs in the melody; create an introduction, interlude, or coda; find and name an enharmonic tone for B♭ (A♯) or F (E♯); find and play an interval of a second or an octave from C; observe the need for accidentals when the key tone is F, G or D; "tune up" before singing by playing and then singing the tones of the I chord (DO, MI, SOL) and the scale upon which the melody is based; and create a melody using only two or three tones.

• At first, have students play short, repeated tonal patterns or scale passages from familiar tunes. Encourage playing many tunes and melodic figures by ear. Introduce line or standard notation when some familiarity with the instrument is established.

• Use the instruments for improvising and composing (see Chapter Nine—Creating—pp. 200–207).

• Try many techniques listed for teaching a new song through music notation (see pp. 158–160) when introducing a new tune to be played.

• Early experiences on melody instruments should involve tunes with a limited range, a slow or moderate tempo, and simple rhythms. Tunes should be transposed to keys with no more than one sharp or flat; i.e., C, F, G major or A, D, E minor—natural form.

• Gradually expand experiences to the tonal range which the students can play. Begin to use the instruments to play unfamiliar tunes, melodies with intervals of a third or more, introductions, interludes, and codas, and themes heard in recorded listening lessons.

• At levels III and above use the instruments for experiences in part-singing and harmony (see pp. 166–167). Play both the melody and harmony parts after they have been sung successfully. Notice the indicated chord symbols for a melody and add two or more simultaneous tones on the melody instruments for an harmonic accompaniment.

• Encourage students at all levels to play their instruments in solo, in small groups, with the entire class, with other types of instruments, and with voices.

Some activities which apply to specific types of melody instruments and voices include:

Step Bells
(*Ludwig Drum Co., Chicago, Ill.*)

• Use the step bells at beginning instructional levels to provide audio-visual reinforcement for pitch. Place them vertically beside a staff to relate tones to the lines and spaces of the staff.

Xylophone
Photo by Curt McClain

• Xylophones or diatonic bells which resemble the white keys of the piano should be introduced first. Chromatic bells, having both the white and black keys of the piano, should be used after facility is obtained with diatonic bells.

Diatonic Bells
Photo by Curt McClain

• Tape numbers, syllables, and/or letter names on the bars of each tone for a visual aid in music reading.
• Relate pitch differences on these instruments to length of the bars.

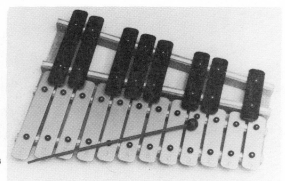

Song or Melody Bells
Photo by Curt McClain

• Inexpensive song or melody bells, with fine tone quality, are available through several manufacturers and can be invaluable aids in developing musical concepts and music reading skills. One set of bells is recommended for *each* student.

• Use only two bars of the instrument for work in dictation. For example, using only C and G, play or sing a pattern with these tones, and have students repeat the pattern by singing and playing it on the instrument. Gradually expand to three or more different tones.

• Use these instruments to introduce basic learnings about the keyboard; i.e., left-right orientation, half and whole steps, black and white keys, accidentals, enharmonic tones.

• Make a number chart to place behind the bell bars. Move it as appropriate so that "1" corresponds with the location of DO in the melody to be played.

[5   6   7   *1*   2   3   4]   5   6   7   8

the tones used in "We Wish
You a Merry Christmas"

Resonator or Tone Bells
Photo by Curt McClain

Swiss Melodé (Hand) Bells
Photo by Curt McClain

• Since the individual metal bars on the resonator or tone bells may be separated and removed from the others, these instruments, as well as the

Swiss melodé bells and other hand bells, are extremely helpful for developing concepts of melody and harmony. The individual tones of a tonal pattern may be isolated and played on these bars as they appear in the music. Each student may play by ear or through notation the particular tone of a melody or pattern when his tone appears; e.g., distribute the three tones used for "e-i-e-i-o" from "Old MacDonald" (A, G, F in F major) and ask each student to hold one bell and play his tone, as appropriate. Three students can also find and play the three tones of any triad. In addition, students can locate the tones used in the chords of a chord progression and play them simultaneously when the chord symbol is indicated, as the following pattern for "On Top of Old Smoky":

Chord pattern:

Play bells simultaneously in $\frac{3}{4}$ meter:

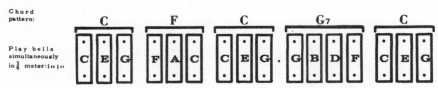

• Use the resonator, tone, and hand bells in the same basic way as for the step and melody bells, and other bell-like instruments.

The *piano* is another valuable melody instrument.

• Use the piano to further understandings about acoustics. Explore and note the vibration of strings, the sound board, the action of the hammers, and the function of the sustaining and damper pedals. Identify its tone color as compared with other instruments (see pp. 25–27).

• Have students make piano keyboard charts out of cardboard or oaktag, or use commercial plastic keyboard charts to point out the arrangement of the black and white keys; the left-right orientation of the keyboard corresponding to low and high pitches; the name of the white key to the left of each set of two black keys (C) and the white key to the left of the three black keys (F); the repetition of C and F over a span of several octaves; the names of all the white keys; the names of the black keys (relate to a study of accidentals); and the meaning of intervals and half and whole-steps as applied to the keyboard.

• Teach the 5-finger position by having students place the right-hand thumb on C and play tonal patterns using C, D, E, F, and G. Extend to the keys of G and F major. Play many tonal patterns and melodies within a range of a fifth (examples: S—45, 56, 64, 78, 145). Repeat patterns, using the left hand (the fifth finger will be placed on the key tone). Expand finger patterns up to include scale-step 1 (LA) and then down to 7 (TI) below scale-step 1. Play tunes in each hand separately and then together. At levels IV and V introduce the fingering and playing of chords and chordal patterns, relating this to a study of chord structure and harmonic progression (see pp. 101–106). Gradually extend tonal range to an octave or more.

• Encourage improvisatory and creative activities on the piano. Create moods and sound effects. Illustrate examples of musical understandings such as pitch, intervals, tonality, harmony, chord structure, and texture.

• Invite students who are taking private lessons to play selections for the class and work with other students in learning basic fundamentals on the piano.

Some simple wind instruments include the:

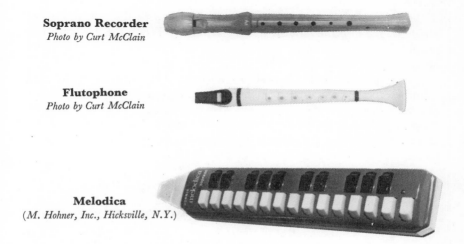

Soprano Recorder
Photo by Curt McClain

Flutophone
Photo by Curt McClain

Melodica
(M. Hohner, Inc., Hicksville, N.Y.)

Activities to use with these instruments are:

• Encourage students to buy their own instruments. All can be purchased for a nominal cost. The recorder is especially recommended since it has an excellent tone quality, is authentic as a musical instrument, and has a vast amount of music literature available for it. Because of simpler fingering patterns, the tonette or flutophone can be introduced at levels II or III and be replaced with the recorder at level IV. The melodica, a relatively expensive instrument, is especially valuable as an introduction to keyboard experiences.

Song Flute
Photo by Curt McClain

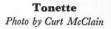

Tonette
Photo by Curt McClain

• It is best not to combine the plastic tonettes, song flutes, and flutophones when playing because of intonation problems. If possible, encourage all students to buy the same type of instrument. Otherwise, supply school instruments.

• Work on intonation problems by having the students check the mouthpieces to see that they are in place; make sure that all the holes which must be closed to produce the tone are covered with the fleshy part of the fingers; place the mouthpiece gently between the lips and about one-half inch into the mouth; sit tall, with both feet on the floor; breathe deeply through the mouth; and use the tongue to say "doo" for each tone as the breath is exhaled slowly.

• Emphasize correct posture, fingering positions, and blowing techniques, especially during the first several lessons. Check the hand and fingering positions of each student before playing. Stress the need for listening to one another and making as beautiful a tone as possible. Occasionally add an harmonic accompaniment to help students keep together and produce an overall musical effect.

• Experiment with various number and fingering systems to foster ease of playing and musical satisfaction. Finger charts and diagrams, as in Ex. 8–6, may be used for the flutophone and similar-type instruments.

• Play many tunes from fingering diagrams (see Ex. 8–7) until some technical facility and control of the instrument are achieved. The teacher should use the system which best fits his objectives. *Only one number system should be used in order to minimize confusion.* Quickly turn to standard music notation once some facility in fingering is obtained.

• If the recorder and flutophone (tonette) are being used together the teacher should guide students to note differences in fingering for certain tones, such as F and third-space C.

• Emphasize the need for students to care for their instruments by periodically cleaning and sterilizing them, and by storing them in bags away from sunlight and heat.

• Use folk tunes and materials from basal music series, instrumental method books, and other sources for students to practice at home.

Harmony Instruments

The two main types of harmony instruments used in the music program are the *Autoharp* (or other automatic chord-harps as the *guitaro*, *harmolin*, and *chromaharp*) and *ukulele*. The *guitar*, although very popular in many musical circles, is probably too difficult for most elementary

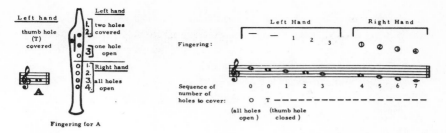

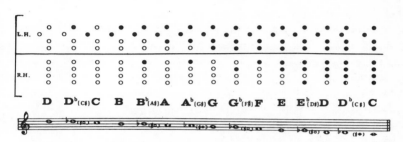

Ex. 8-6. Diagrams and Fingering Charts for the Flutophone and Similar-Type Instruments

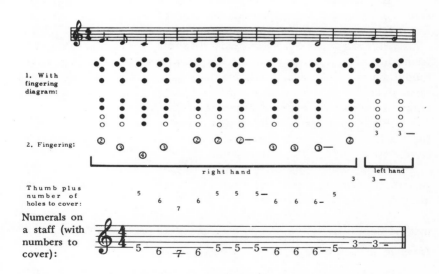

Ex. 8-7. "Mary Had a Little Lamb"—Fingering for Simple Wind Instruments

school students, and should be limited to small-group instruction. In addition to the Autoharp, ukulele, and guitar, melody instruments as the melody and resonator bells, piano, and recorder can be used effectively to produce harmonic effects (see pp. 93 ff).

Harmony instruments are an important means of developing concepts of harmony. These instruments can be used to: play the harmonic accompaniments for songs; illustrate chord structure; provide a support for part-singing; develop recognition of chord qualities, chord change, harmonic texture, and cadence; underscore a rhythmic accompaniment; and provide experiences in harmonic improvisation.

Suggestions for teaching harmony instruments include:

• When only one or two students are involved in playing an harmonic instrument have other students participate in singing, listening, and/or moving to aspects of the music.

• Make sure that the instrument(s) is properly tuned. Use a pitch pipe or resonator bells to obtain accurate pitch.

• Provide many experiences with familiar tunes. In this way the students can readily detect errors in their accompaniments.

• Have students aurally identify chord changes before playing the accompaniment.

• Use techniques listed on pp. 103–104 for development of understandings about harmonic change. Provide experiences in playing harmony both with and without the use of chord symbols.

• Encourage a tonal balance between the melody and the supportive harmony. In any case, the harmony should be more subdued.

• Work on strumming rhythmically to the beat. Steady strumming, with the emphasis on the first beat of each metric grouping, should be practiced with tunes in meters of $\frac{2}{4}$ ($|^2$), $\frac{3}{4}$ ($|^{23}$), $\frac{4}{4}$ ($|^{234}$), and $\frac{6}{8}$ ($|^{23}|^{56}$, if slow; and, $|^2$ if fast).

• Check to see that students understand the meaning of chord symbols such as G, G_7, and gm before playing from a score with these markings. It is often helpful to drill on the fingering patterns of the harmonic progression first, so as to anticipate and prepare for any possible problems which may arise as the harmony is played.

• Before accompanying singing with an harmonic instrument, some feeling for the tonality of the tune should be developed. The process used should be the same as that recommended for beginning any song (see pp. 157–158).

• Students who sing and play the harmony at the same time often concentrate on the instrumental performance and neglect their singing. Ask students to sing first, then play the accompaniment, and finally sing and play together. Emphasize the vocal line rather than the accompaniment.

15-Bar Autoharp
Photo by Curt McClain

In planning activities for the *Autoharp* the teacher should consider the following:

• The 12- or 15-bar Autoharp is most appropriate for school use. Each of these instruments contains the principal chords of C, F, G, and B♭ major, and D, A, and G minor. Songs written in other keys will need to be transposed. In general, select the key on the Autoharp which is closest to the original tonality of the song.

• An Autoharp needs frequent tuning. The easiest way is to use a tuning peg and tune the instrument by octaves (tuning all the F's, G's, etc.) or by chords (strumming various chords and noting which tones sound incorrect).

• Either plastic or felt picks may be used. Encourage experimentation in varying the tone color and volume of the instrument by using picks and other objects (pencils, erasers, sticks, fingers) and by changing the pressure on the strings.

• Students should have experiences with the Autoharp at all instructional levels. At level I the class should listen to the harmony as the teacher strums the instrument. Students can clap the beat as the teacher strums, and then strum the Autoharp as the teacher continues to press the chord bars. Aural discrimination in appropriate chord sequences should be developed at levels I and II, and continued throughout the grades. By the end of level II students should be able to accompany simple rounds and canons using only one chord (examples: S—7, 20, 67, 108, 111, 130, 136). Two students can play the instrument—one strumming and one fingering the chord(s).

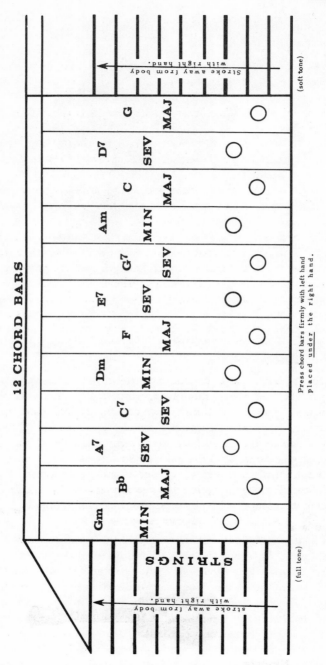

Ex. 8-8. A Diagram of the 12-Bar Autoharp

At levels III and above the students should strum independently and make harmonic changes as they play by ear and read the notation. Work at levels IV and V will consist primarily of learning new fingerings for chordal patterns, experimenting with strumming techniques, and developing a more acute sense of harmonic progression and change.

• Emphasize the various skills needed to play the instrument (see Ex. 8–8).

• Before playing, have the students find the chords needed for the accompaniment, finger the chord bars, and strum in the air in the correct meter and tempo.

• At beginning levels of instruction select students with an acute sense of rhythm to accompany songs. Once skills are developed, provide accompaniment experiences for all students.

• Since there are usually no more than two Autoharps available for any class there is a need to involve musically the other students who are not playing the instrument. Imaginary strumming on Autoharp diagrams will be a valuable experience for all students. Autoharp diagrams or charts are found in the inside covers of texts from many basal music series, or they can be reproduced for distribution to each student (see Ex. 8–8). The children can also sing, or clap a rhythmic element of the music (the beat, meter, melodic rhythm) as the Autoharp is played.

• Once the more basic strumming strokes are mastered, students at levels III and above should experiment with other strumming techniques. Vigorous rhythmic tunes can be accompanied by rapid strumming. Vary the strumming for slower tunes by playing on different sides of the chord bars, or by strumming the thicker strings on the strong beats and the thinner strings on the weaker beats. Use the high-pitched strings to accompany soft music. Produce interesting effects by bouncing wooden mallets on the strings. Teach rhythmic strumming, whereby repeated rhythmic figures as ♩ ♫ ♩♩ or ♩. ♫ ♩ are played to accompany the melody.

Ukulele
Kamaka Hawaii, Inc., Honolulu, Hawaii

The *ukulele* is one of the easiest fretted harmony instruments to play and can be learned by all students at levels III and above. Several ways in which the ukulele can be used are:

• Use the instrument to develop understandings about pitch and string thickness and tightness, the effect on pitch of placing the fingers between different frets, and vibration and reinforcement of sound. Preliminary aural experiences in discriminating between chord changes should take place at levels I and II before attempting to play the instrument.

• Tune the ukulele strings to G, C, E, and A. Develop an understanding of the tablature system of notating chords using either

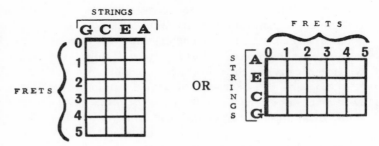

Although the first system above is standard, the second one is acceptable and probably easier for children to use, since it pictures the ukulele in the position to be played. Thus the C and F chords may be shown as

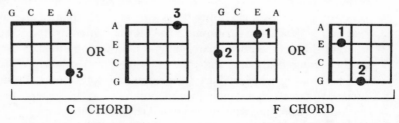

C CHORD   F CHORD

• Make sure that all instruments are tuned before playing. Use the chant "my dog has fleas" for G, C, E, and A, and sing the letter-names to help students remember the tonal sequences.

• Begin with songs which can be harmonized by the C chord, as in most rounds. Then introduce the F and C₇ chords, the G₇ chord, the B♭ chord, the G and D₇ chords, and the D and A minor chords. In each case teach the fingering for the new chord first, then the harmonic progression in which the chord is found in a song, and finally, familiar tunes which are harmonized by that chord. Thus, in teaching the B♭ chord, provide drill on the fingering and strumming, and then use the chord in a common chord progression (F B♭ C₇). Finally, play the chord as it appears in many tunes written in F major.

• Play many songs using the I-V$_7$ and I-IV-V$_7$ chords (see pp. 102–103), as follows:

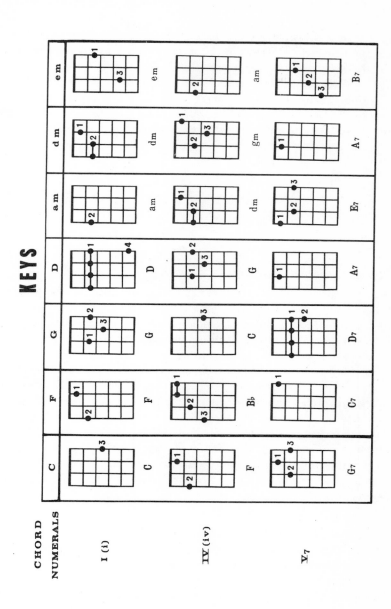

• Relate the distance between each fret to a half-step on the piano. At levels IV and above teach students how to picture chords on the tablature (ukulele fingering chart), using a knowledge of half and whole-steps and chord structure.

• Encourage students to figure out how to play melodies on their ukuleles, using their knowledge of the names of the strings and the half-step arrangement of the frets.

• Work on various strumming techniques. At first, use a steady downward strum to coincide with the beat. Then teach both a downward and upward movement and variations on this. Finally, introduce students to rhythmic strumming and ask them to make up their own rhythmic accompaniments to tunes. Use diagrams to indicate strumming, as:

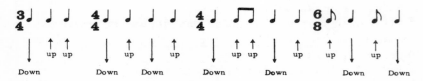

Standard Orchestral Instruments

Standard orchestral instruments may be used in the elementary school music program in several ways. Students who play such instruments may perform for the class. Demonstrations on the instruments can call attention to their parts and distinctive tone colors. Simple instrumental accompaniments for songs and instrumental reinforcement for the vocal lines of a part-song may be arranged. Students should be encouraged to compose tunes for their instruments. The plucked open strings on any string instrument can be used for rhythmic accompaniment if the chord roots are played (see p. 99). Principles of acoustics may be demonstrated on any instrument. The teacher should work with the instrumental music specialist in providing many of these experiences for the students. In this way the potential use of standard orchestral instruments may be expanded to provide unlimited opportunities for music-making and conceptual growth for all students.

MOVING RHYTHMICALLY

Rhythmic movement gives students an opportunity to show their understanding and interpretation of music in an overt manner. It allows them to express their emotions and respond in a physical, non-verbal, but highly significant manner to the various elements in a musical work. The focus of any music lesson involving bodily movement should be the development of each student's aesthetic awareness of these elements and how they interrelate to make musical meaning.

The Nature of Rhythmic Movement

Developing the ability to respond to music through the use of the body is a rather complex process, since it involves:

1) perceiving the music and its expressive qualities
2) moving spontaneously to the music
3) thinking about the design of the music
4) planning the movement
5) blending movement with the music to obtain a musical performance

These processes occur at each instructional level, and take into consideration the three important facets of the experience—the music, the use and control of the body, and the synchronization of music and movement to achieve a musical interpretation.

Rhythmic movement emanates from the listening experience, since the ability to hear and feel the expressiveness of the music must be developed before any meaningful bodily response occurs. Thus, initial activities should focus on listening for various aspects in the music; e.g., beat, phrase, and repetition and contrast, among others (see pp. 147–149), before they are interpreted in physical movement.

Students need guidance in the various ways to move to music. There are three basic types of movement, as outlined in the following chart:

Type of Movement	*Characteristics*	*Examples*
Locomoter (Fundamental)	Movement in which the whole body moves from one place to another	Walking, running, hopping, jumping, sliding, galloping, trotting, whirling
Axial (Body)	Non-locomotor movement, in which the feet remain stationary while other parts of the body move	Swaying, swinging, clapping, bending, turning, twisting, beating, bouncing, pulling, pushing
Combination of Locomotor and/or Axial	Movement in which different locomotor and/or axial movements occur simultaneously or successively	Walking and clapping, rising and falling, pushing and pulling, skipping and galloping, hopping and shaking

Another factor affecting rhythmic movement is the use of space. Guide students to show:

levels—high, medium, and low body positions, as when leaping, bending, lying on the floor, and falling

direction—forward, backward, sideward, and circling

dimension—large or small movements

range—use of a large or small floor area

floor pattern—a design on the floor showing circular, diagonal, or parallel movement

focus—movement, or directed attention with the eyes, toward a specific location on the floor or in the room

Teaching Rhythmic Movement

A sequence of lessons should be organized at every instructional level to help students move rhythmically to aspects of the music as tempo, dynamics, climax, and phrases. Part I of this text presents in detail appropriate rhythmic activities designed to develop specific understandings of musical structure which are summarized here:

Element in the Music	*Appropriate Bodily Response*
Beginning and ending of melody	Move when the music moves; stop when it stops
Beat	Steady, recurring movement using any or all parts of the body
Meter	Stronger movement on the 1's
Melodic rhythm	Fast or sustained movement; even or jerky
Syncopation	Very rhythmical, accented, sharp movements; uneven movement
Changes in tone color, tonality, texture	Changes in bodily movement, as appropriate
Dynamics	Forceful, large movements for loud sections; less intense for soft sections
Tempo	Fast or slow movements; changes in speed of movement
Contour	Rising and falling movements to correspond with shape of melodic contour
Tonality, mood	Overall quality of movement—happy, sad, gay, floating, dream-like, definite movements, as appropriate
Phrases, cadences	Regular flowing patterns, stopping and/ or changing direction or type of movement at the cadence

Element in the Music	Appropriate Bodily Response
Sections, introductions, interludes	A cessation or change of movement to indicate moods of contrasting sections
Repetition, contrast of any element	Repetition or contrast in movement, as appropriate
Stylistic features	Use of movements characteristic of the historical period or ethnic group

Rhythmic movement can be developed in several ways, depending upon the aims of the lesson. The following outline presents examples of approaches to *formal, less-structured,* and *creative* bodily movement:

Movement	Characteristics	Examples	Sample Statements by Teacher
Formal or Structured	Specific movement(s) as indicated by teacher	1. Using locomotor, axial, or combination movements	"Let's see every one walk to this music. Now let's bounce up and down to it." "Can you clap your hands like I do?"
		2. Learning a patterned folk or social dance.	"The first step is to face your partner and bow."
		3. Playing rhythm instruments in a prescribed way	"Play the rhythm sticks to the beat."
Less-structured	Basic movement or type of movement as determined by teacher, but permitting students to respond within the broad limitations	1. Using creative variants of locomotor, axial, or combination movements to the music	"How many different ways can you walk to this music?" "Can you sway to the music like an elephant? a swing? a leaf drifting in the wind?" "This music is called 'March of the Little Lead Soldiers.' Imagine

Movement	Characteristics	Examples	Sample Statements by Teacher
			you're a little lead soldier marching to the music."
		2. Making the specified movements to singing games as "London Bridge," action songs as "This Old Man," and finger plays (songs in which the song's text is acted out by the fingers) as "Eency Weency Spider"	"Let's see how you iron the clothes to the beat of 'Mulberry Bush.'" "Can you show everyone how you turn around to do the 'Hokey Pokey?'"
		3. Dramatizing and impersonating the story and characters of the song's text	"Act out the story of the clock and mouse in 'Hickory Dickory Dock' as you sing the song. See if you can move right along with the music."
		4. Improvising within a given pattern, using either a melody or rhythm instrument	"Try to play something else in the music beside the beat on your tone blocks."
Creative	Freedom to respond to	1. Using creative bodily	"Now that you have listened to the

Movement	Characteristics	Examples	Sample Statements by Teacher
	the music with little or no suggestions by the teacher as to type of movement	movement to recorded music	music, let's see if you can express through your bodies how the music made you feel." "You noticed that the second phrase was different from the first. Can you show this in movement?"
		2. Devising creative movement, with music added later to enhance the movement	"Think of something that moves. Now imitate this movement." "Bill, when you see Alice move, see if you can add a drum accompaniment to her movement."

Recommendations which apply to the use of all types of movement experiences—from the very structured activity to free, creative bodily expression—include:

• Some physical response to music should occur during every lesson. At times it may be a central activity; often it will be used to accompany singing, playing instruments, and reading music.

• Guidance in listening and moving to music is needed before beginning the rhythmic movement. Limit discussion, and try to get right into the music. Teach movement skills in a musical context.

• Although motivation and directions for movement may be given, it is the music itself which must provide the real impetus for movement.

• Emphasize the need to listen to the music at all times in order for the movement to portray the music and its expressive qualities.

• Develop with the students certain routines and rules to follow which will make the activity more successful and enjoyable, as listening intently to the music, allowing room for freedom of movement, and starting and stopping promptly with the music.

• When the problem of space arises, rotate the students so that some will perform as others observe, evaluate, play instruments, or move in a more restricted area with axial movement as tapping or clapping. Whenever possible, arrange for movement activities in a large room or outdoors.

• Expect and provide for differences in the students' abilities to move rhythmically. Some children will show marked creative talent in interpreting the music. Others may move routinely, or imitate the movement of classmates. A few students may lack a sense of rhythm and/or the coordination needed to respond rhythmically.

• At times combine playing instruments with rhythmic movement; e.g., marching with rhythm sticks and drums. Make sure that students can move accurately to the music before adding instruments.

• Props such as scarves, balloons, and ribbons are useful for certain types of movement.

• Frequently encourage students to vary their movements (see p. 194). Briefly provide experiences in exploring movement, as jumping high in the air, growing like a flower, or moving like a hungry tiger.

• Select students to perform for others. Note the positive qualities of their movement, and encourage them to experiment with other types of movement. Refrain from calling attention to a student who has difficulty moving due to lack of coordination.

• Movement activities cannot be confined to one or two weeks. They require a sequential progression of experiences spread out throughout each year of the elementary school.

• Avoid labeling music as "walking" or "galloping" music. Encourage many types of locomotor and axial movement for a particular piece.

• Rhythmic activities involved with fast music should be spaced within the lesson so that the children do not tire. Have one group move as another group observes and evaluates. Reverse roles.

• Accept freedom of choice of movement when it is a genuine musical response to the music.

• Praise students for their efforts with statements such as: "I see many children who are showing exactly how the music makes them feel. Some children are listening very carefully to the tempo (or dynamics, phrasing) of the music. I like the way some children are using their bodies to turn, move high and low, and backward and forward. I'm proud of those children who are thinking only about their own movement, rather than copying others."

• Frequently dramatize music. A story may be suggested as a result of various interpretations of the music. A poem, or a song text, especially that of a ballad, may give clues to rhythmic movement and pantomine. Students should listen for particular musical cues which imply a certain character, event, or mood. Ask students to move creatively by impersonating a character or object, or dramatizing a story or event. Add a musical accompaniment to the movement. Later, have students improvise accompaniments to the movements of their classmates.

• Singing games such as "Looby Loo," "The Mulberry Bush," and "London Bridge" are favorites of children. Begin with singing games requiring no partners. Teach the song first; then encourage students to devise their own actions as they move rhythmically to the music. Students may need to "walk through" the actions at a slow tempo before the game is played. One group may do the motions as another group sings. State directions clearly. Have students evaluate their performance, with particular reference to their singing and movements in relation to the text, rhythm, phrasing, and form of the song.

• Creative movement must be guided by the teacher, since most children need a sequence of activities designed to help them move freely in interpreting music. Some experiences which help to foster creative bodily movement include pantomine, dramatization, and impersonation without music; singing games and finger plays; dramatization of the texts of songs; movement to percussion and piano accompaniment; and work on locomotor and axial movements, both with and without music. The creative experience should include motivation, opportunities to listen and respond to the music; guidance in ways to move to the music; and practice in adjusting to the various qualities and changes in the music.

• A limited number of patterned dances, as square dances, reels, and folk dances, should be used to illustrate how dance movements usually correspond to the rhythm, form, and overall mood of the music. Teaching the formal dance steps, the circle, line, and square formations, and the movement skills required of these dances should occur at other times of the day rather than during the regularly scheduled music period.

Nine

CREATING

All of us have created music. We have hummed an original tune, improvised a rhythmic pattern when dancing, tried to write the "number one" tune on the Hit Parade, or composed a pep song for our school or club. While we may not have been too successful with our final products, we undoubtedly had fun in the process!

THE NATURE AND VALUE OF CREATING

Think about the times you have created a picture or painting, a clay figure, a song, a tune on the piano, a poem, a story, a dance step, or a play. What were some of the characteristics of that creative process? You could say that:

- it was a personal expression
- it involved periods of intense preoccupation with the materials (crayons, paints, clay, tones, or words)
- discovery was a constant factor in the process
- it included the use of imagination and intelligence in reordering and reconstructing the material into something new and unique to you
- self-evaluation took place as you worked
- the product was a work which probably satisfied you, and belonged to you in a personal way

Both the adult composer and the elementary school child deal with the same processes as they create a musical work. The student at all levels should have regularly planned lessons which help him recognize, appreciate, and develop his creative potential to reorganize known elements of music into new musical works which are satisfying to him. Through these lessons aesthetic insight into music and its structure will be fostered. The student will also develop an understanding and appreciation of the creative process and artistic works of others. In addition, the student's need for self-expression will be fulfilled.

Examples of objectives which indicate how the creative experience may be used as a means of obtaining conceptual goals are:

- *The student will indicate an understanding that* a melody has tones of varying pitch *by* improvising a tune using one, two, three, and finally, five different tones on the Swiss melodé or resonator bells.
- *The student will indicate an understanding that* phrases may repeat or contrast *by* creating a four-phrase tune having similar first and third phrases, and contrasting second and fourth phrases.
- *The student will indicate an understanding* of the relationship of a song's text to meter, melodic rhythm, and rhythmic patterns *by* composing a tune which expresses the mood of a given poem.
- *The student will indicate an understanding* of the pentatonic mode and its construction *by* creating a pentatonic melody using C, D, E, G, and A of the resonator bells.

A SYNTHESIZING EXPERIENCE

A class engages in composing a tune for the resonator bells. The probable mood, tempo, and dynamics are discussed, with implications for melodic construction. The students clap interesting rhythms and decide upon a meter and rhythmic patterns. They improvise on the resonator bells to find out the melody's tonal potential. A phrase is composed, and contrasting or repeated phrases are added. When the melody is completed, it is sung with "LA," evaluated, altered as necessary, and notated. Later students may add an harmonic or rhythm instrument accompaniment. This creative experience involves a use of the basic elements of music and the processes of singing, rhythmic movement, playing instruments, critical listening, and music reading and writing. Thus, the creative experience encompasses a synthesis and utilization of many musical understandings and skills. The teacher can guide the students in this experience by asking questions such as:

- What will be the overall feeling and mood of the music? Will it be lilting, sad, heroic? How, then, will the tones move? What about the tune's dynamics, tempo, meter, rhythm, and tonality?
- Should the melody start high and descend, or start low and

ascend? Where might the melody move scalewise, skipwise? What word in the poem suggests a leap in the melody? How can the melody be made more interesting?

• Will the rhythm be even and flowing, uneven, or syncopated? Which tones could be accented? Are there places where the interesting rhythmic pattern in phrase one can be repeated? Does the melodic rhythm fit the rhythm of the words?

• What instrument(s) could be used for an accompaniment? Where would some dissonance be appropriate? Where might an harmonic change occur? Where could a broken chord accompaniment be used?

• How many phrases does the melody have? Where is the end of each phrase? How do you know? How many sections will the tune have? Should some parts repeat? Could some phrases or sections be made similar and some contrasting? How can we change section two so that it contrasts with section one?

• Should the notation be in the treble or bass clef? How can tempo and dynamics be indicated? Which tone is DO? What about the key signature and the meter signature? Which measure in the notation has too many beat-notes? Who can find an error in the rhythm of the last measure?

BASIC TYPES OF CREATIVE EXPERIENCES

The creative act in music is one in which tonal and rhythmic elements are reshaped to produce a new, meaningful, and satisfying musical work for the composer. Students at any level are composers when they are involved in this process. In contrast, creative experiences not directly concerned with restructuring the elements of music; e.g., creative bodily movement and dramatization to music, writing stories and painting to music, and making up titles and sentences to describe the mood of instrumental works, are all *interpretive responses to music*. These responses have an important place in the music program and are discussed elsewhere in the text (for example, see p. 148). In this chapter our main concern is to develop ways in which students can create *music* through the processes of improvisation and composition.

Improvising Music

Improvisation involves extemporaneous music-making. It occurs on the spur of the moment, rather than with previous thought and planning. Some activities which are suitable for elementary school students include improvising:

    • question-and-answer rhythms by clapping or playing rhythm instruments

    • question-and-answer tonal patterns using the voice

- a chant-like tune to accompany various games and classroom activities as doing exercises or passing out books
- a rhythm instrument accompaniment to a melody using several different instruments to achieve variety and effect
- rhythmic patterns within the framework of various meters
- variations in phrases and endings of familiar tunes
- a tune on a melody instrument, utilizing a given set of tones
- a melody to a given set of words
- a harmony part to a given melody, using the voice and/or melody instrument (see vocal improvisation, p. 171)
- a tune over a given chordal accompaniment
- repeated tonal figures (ostinati) which fit well with the melody

Some improvisation experiences can occur during every lesson. Students should be encouraged to add a rhythmic accompaniment to a piece they are listening to or performing. Improvising a harmony part to a tune is both fun and challenging for older students. Adding an introduction or coda to a song is well within the capability of even the youngest student. Regardless of the improvisation experience used, the teacher should:

- set some guidelines and provide clear directions for what is to be accomplished
- provide a beginning pattern for students too hesitant to improvise on their own
- offer one or more examples of possibilities for improvising a rhythmic or tonal pattern, or a harmony part
- encourage improvisation to a song or instrumental work only after students have had an opportunity to develop some familiarity with the music
- provide a broad selection of instruments with which to improvise instrumental arrangements
- limit the tones used to improvise a melody on an instrument to two or three until the student has gained confidence in the procedure and on his instrument
- make sure that the experience is well within the cognitive and skill development of the students
- choose a few arrangements by the more creative students to illustrate some of the results which can be attained
- praise students who originate their own musical ideas
- make the students aware of their unique and original efforts as they improvise

Composing Music

Composition involves the process of planning and relating various elements of music into a musical design through the voice, instruments, tape and electronic processes, or a combination of these. The resulting work may be as simple as several rhythmic patterns created by a five-year-old on his rhythm sticks, or as complex as an opera or symphony written by a noted composer.

Activities in singing provide an excellent means for initiating creative experiences. Each student can use his own "instrument" spontaneously and without concern for technical skills required for certain instruments. Even kindergarten children can engage in musical conversations and song-making activities. In composing tonal patterns, phrases, and songs the words and music can be composed at the same time, or a tune may be added to words written by the group, an individual, or a poet. In addition, the relationship between text and melody can be developed by adding words to a folk tune or a melody written by the group, one student, or a composer. The creative experience described below provides a background for guiding students in the composition of a song.

One cool, rainy, and windy morning the students in a second and third grade class were asked to make up a poem about the weather. A melody was added, and within thirty minutes a song had been composed!

Ex. 9-1. "A Miserable Day"

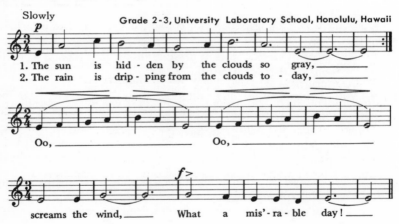

[Note the use of irregular phrase patterns, the $\frac{2}{4}$ and $\frac{3}{4}$ meters, and the modal tonality]

How was this song composed? What are some useful techniques for guiding the composition of songs?

1) For beginning levels of instruction, a short verse or poem, or the words of an unfamiliar song may be selected. The song text may also be devised in class, as was done for "A Miserable Day."

2) Write the text in word-syllables on the chalkboard under a music staff (at level I just recite the words). Place one phrase of the text under each line of the staff.

3) Students study the text and read it expressively to obtain its meaning, phrase structure, and rhythm. Discuss the mood and have students state ideas regarding the possible type of melody, rhythm, form, tempo, and dynamics. Call attention to important words in the text, and elements of repetition and contrast.

4) Set a beat according to the desired tempo and have the students chant the words to the beat. Experiment with several rhythmic patterns which fit the rhythmic flow of the words.

5) Agree upon a rhythm. Have students clap this rhythm and then clap only on the accented words or word-syllables. Underline these accented syllables and, if notating on the staff, put a bar line before each accented word or syllable.

6) Guide the students to figure out the notation for the meter and rhythm. Place the notated rhythmic patterns below the words. Use "line" notation for levels I and II, as:

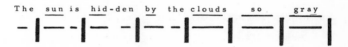

7) Discuss places in the text where the melody might ascend, descend, leap up or down, or have repeated tones. Determine whether the melody will start on a relatively low or high tone.

8) Play a starting tone. Have students "think" a melody and then sing a phrase. Encourage everyone's participation. Call upon individuals to sing their phrases. The teacher might help by singing a few tones to get the students started. Have students select phrases they prefer. Constantly encourage constructive criticism and evaluation. Notate pitches of the melody using "line" notation, as:

The sun is hid - den by the clouds so gray

Have students help fill in the notes on the staff. Use a tape recorder to record results if the process of notation is difficult and tedious for both the teacher and students.

9) Have all students sing the selected first phrase and add other phrases progressively. Continually repeat from the beginning, evaluating each part in relation to the whole.

10) Once the song is completed, have another evaluation of the entire melody as to its range, mood, rhythm, and the use of repetition and contrast for unity and variety.

11) Students may wish to keep their song. If so, copy it (or have the students do so), duplicate it, and have the students sing or transcribe it for playing on instruments during subsequent lessons.

Procedures described above are generally applicable for both group and individual compositions. Teacher guidance should focus on the musical aspects of the tune, with leading questions asked to help the student learn self-evaluation of his creative efforts. Standards should be self-imposed by the student, with frequent advice and encouragement given by the teacher. A class songbook of students' original songs can be compiled, sung, played on instruments, and serve as one motivating force for making up songs and learning notation. Once an original song is completed and notated, the student may be asked to add harmony or an instrumental accompaniment to it, depending upon his musical background and maturity.

Elementary school students enjoy composing music for various rhythm, melody, and harmony instruments. Activities will vary, depending upon past experiences and musical ability. Using *rhythm instruments*, students can:

• devise rhythmic accompaniments for songs and recordings
• utilize the instruments for sound-effects to highlight the mood of a particular piece or story
• create interesting rhythmic patterns or a composition for these instruments
• compose a rhythmic pattern to accompany the dramatization of galloping horses or marching soldiers
• achieve various tonal effects by playing the rhythm instruments in different ways
• make up a composition designed to illustrate a musical understanding as $\frac{3}{4}$ meter, "question" and "answer" phrasing, a rhythmic round or canon (p. 43), a rondo, and syncopation

Using *melody instruments*, students can:

• complete an unfinished phrase or tune
• create sound effects and a given mood for a story or poem
• compose a melody using only two or three prescribed tones, or in a given tonality, key, or meter
• create introductions, interludes, and codas to familiar and original songs
• compose a tune to accompany dramatization of a story
• make up a bugle call, a march, a lullaby, or a piece using phrase repetition or a certain rhythmic pattern

- achieve various effects on instruments by playing them in different ways and in novel combinations
- write a melody depicting a certain mood
- experiment with adding harmony to familiar or original tunes
- supply the middle section to a tune in A B A form
- create a melody to indicate an understanding of a certain musical idea; e.g., phrasing, dynamics, minor tonality, syncopation, climax, cadence, range, a specified form (A B or rondo)

Students can use *harmony instruments* to:

- create sound effects to enhance the intended mood of a story, poem, song, or dance
- make up a chordal introduction, interlude, or coda to a tune
- devise original harmonic progressions which can serve as the starting point for a composition
- add an accompaniment to a familiar or original tune
- create interesting-sounding harmonies
- create a composition illustrating harmonic change, triads, chordal texture, tone clusters, or homophony

The use of unusual sounds in original compositions provides much challenge for both teachers and students. Sources for these sounds are limitless. Combining sounds such as a clock ticking, a shout, fingers snapping, a pencil being rubbed on wood, and water being poured into a bucket suggests many possibilities for experimentation in original musical works. Some of these sounds may be combined with traditional vocal and instrumental effects to produce a composition. Tape recorders can be used to record and alter sounds for more interesting effects. Guided experience with the tape and electronic works by certain contemporary composers (see pp. 28–29) can offer additional motivation and stimulus for the students' own compositions.

Recommended techniques for helping students compose on instruments are similar to those listed for improvising and composing songs (see pp. 203 and 204–206). Students should be encouraged to think about how their music will be organized before playing. Experimentation and improvisation should precede the compositional process. The teacher can guide the student to plan the tune's length, dynamics, tempo, phrasing, contour, meter, rhythmic and tonal patterns, and, at upper levels, its harmony. Students should be asked to compose on instruments they can play with ease. A review of certain finger patterns or playing techniques may be necessary before the students perform. As in vocal composition, the teacher should aid the students in notating the piece they have composed.

Appendix A

SCOPE AND
SEQUENCE CHART

This chart outlines the generalizations and understandings for Tone, Rhythm, Melody, Harmony, Form, Style, and the Associative Concepts developed in Part I of the text. Topics are arranged sequentially in five conceptual levels (see p. 2) to provide for a growing awareness of the structure of music.

To use this chart in overall planning:

1) Estimate the levels of conceptual growth of your students by trial sampling of activities accompanying each understanding in Part I of this text. Refer to this chart and note the appropriate pages in Part I where the understandings for these levels are outlined.

2) Turn to the indicated pages and list the understandings which are to be developed for the particular conceptual levels. Skim through the related activities and find sources for pertinent repertoire and needed materials (see Appendices B and C).

3) Note the predominant approaches used in the activities listed below the understandings, refer to these approaches in Part II of the text, and outline various listening, performing, creating, and music reading skills appropriate for developing the understandings.

213

L
E
V
E
L

III

(3-4)

215

Appendix B

SOURCES FOR MUSICAL

EXAMPLES CITED IN THE TEXT

Songs

This section consists of an alphabetical listing of songs referred to in the text. A numeral in parenthesis following the song title indicates the page on which the notation of the song is located.

Most songs can be found in one or more basal music texts commonly used in the elementary school. Abbreviations for these texts are coded as follows:

BMS—*Birchard Music Series* (Summy-Birchard)
DMT—*Discovering Music Together* (Follett)
EM—*Exploring Music* (Holt, Rinehart, and Winston)
GWM—*Growing with Music* (Prentice-Hall)
MFL—*Music for Living* (Silver Burdett)
MMYO—*Making Music Your Own* (Silver Burdett)
MOM—*The Magic of Music* (Ginn)
MYA—*Music for Young Americans*, 2nd ed. (American Book Co.)
OSW—*Our Singing World* (Ginn)
TIM—*This Is Music* (Allyn and Bacon)
TWS—*Together We Sing* (Follett)

The numeral(s) following these keyed abbreviations refers to the book level number (as Grade 4 or Book Two).

1. *Ach Ja*—BMS 4; EM 2; MFL 4; MYA 5; TIM 2
2. *Ahrirang*—BMS 6; DMT 6; EM 6; GWM 6; MMYO 6; MYA 6; TIM 4; TWS 6
3. *All Through the Night*—DMT 4, 6; GWM 5; MFL 6; MMYO 6; MOM 3, 4; MYA K, 4, 6; OSW 6; TIM 6; TWS 4
4. *Aloha Oe*—BMS 6; DMT 4, 6; GWM 6; MFL 5; MMYO 6; MOM 3; MYA 6; TIM 5; TWS 6
5. *America*—BMS 4, 5; DMT K–6; EM 1, 2, 4; GWM 1, 4; MFL 1–3, 5; MMYO K–6; MOM K–6; MYA 2–4; OSW K–5; TIM 1–6; TWS 1, 3–5
6. *America the Beautiful*—BMS 2, 3, 5; DMT 1–6; EM 3; GWM 2, 5; MFL 3–6; MMYO 2–6; MOM K, 2–6; MYA 2–4, 6; OSW K–3, 6; TIM 2, 3, 5, 6; TWS 1, 2, 4, 5
7. *Are You Sleeping?* or *Frère Jacques*—BMS 1, 2; DMT 1–3; EM 3; GWM 3, 4; MFL 3; MMYO 3; MOM K, 4; MYA 1, 2; OSW 2, 6; TIM 1–4; TWS 1, 3
8. *Au Clair de la Lune* (95)— DMT 3; EM 4; MMYO 3
9. *Auld Lang Syne*—MFL 6; MYA 6; TIM 4, 6; TWS 3, 5
10. *Battle Hymn of the Republic* (97)—BMS K, 5; DMT 4, 6; EM 5; GWM 6; MFL 1, 5; MMYO K–2, 5, 6; MOM K, 1, 5; MYA 5; OSW K–2, 4, 6; TIM 5; TWS 3

11. *B-I-N-G-O*—DMT 3; EM 1; MFL 3; MMYO 2, 3; TIM 5
12. *Black Is the Color of My True Love's Hair*—MYA 5; MOM 6
13. *Blow the Man Down*—BMS 5; DMT 4, 5; GWM 5; MFL 6; MMYO 5; OSW 6; TIM 5, 6; TWS 4
14. *Blowin' in the Wind* by Bob Dylan—ⓒ 1962 by M. Witmark and Sons, New York City, N. Y.
15. *The Blue-Bells of Scotland* (78)—DMT 4; GWM 3; MOM 4; TIM 5
16. *Blue-Tail Fly*—BMS 4; MFL 6; MMYO 3; TIM 5
17. *Bridge of Avignon, The*—DMT 2; EM 3; GWM 3; MMYO 2; MOM 1, 2; OSW 4; TIM 2, 3; TWS 2
18. *Brother Come and Dance with Me*—BMS 3; EM 3; MFL 4; OSW 4, 5; TWS 3
19. *Camptown Races* (46)—DMT 4, 6; MMYA 6; TIM 5; TWS 6
20. *Canoe Song* (79)—DMT 5; EM 3; GWM 3; MFL 4; MMYO 5; MOM 4; TWS 3, 5
21. *Children's Prayer*—DMT 4, 6; MOM 3; MYA 6; TWS 5
22. *Christmas Caroling Song*— DMT 5; TWS 5
23. *Cielito Lindo*—BMS 6; DMT 6; GWM 5; MFL 6; OSW 6; TWS 6
24. *Cindy*—DMT 5; EM 6; MFL 6; MMYO 4; MYA 4; OSW 5; TIM 6; TWS 5

25. *Clementine* (60)—MFL 5; MMYO 4; OSW 6; TIM 5; TWS 5

26. *Cockles and Mussells*—BMS 6; DMT 6; EM 6; MFL 6; MYA 6; TIM 6; TWS 6

27. *Cruel War, The*, by Paul Stocky and Peter Yarrow— ©1962 by Pepamar Music Corp., New York City, N. Y.

28. *Deck the Halls*—BMS 4; DMT 4; EM 3, 4; GWM 6; MFL 4; MMYO 5, 6; MOM 4; MYA 3; OSW 4; TIM 2; TWS 4

29. *Did You Ever See a Lassie?*— DMT 2; OSW 1; TWS 2

30. *Dixie* (51)—BMS 5; DMT 4, 6; GWM 5; MFL 5; MMYO 5; MOM 6; MYA 5; TIM 5; TWS 4

31. *Do, Re, Mi* from "The Sound of Music"—©1962 by Wilkinson Music Co, New York City, N. Y. Recorded in *New Dimensions in Music—Listening Album*—K

32. *Dogie Song*—DMT 5; EM 5; GWM 6; MFL 4; MMYO 5; MOM 4; MYA 5; TIM 5; TWS 5

33. *Dona Nobis Pacem*—EM 6; GWM 6; MOM 5; MYA 6

34. *Down by the Riverside* (17)— Alan Lomax, *Penguin Book of American Folk Songs.* Baltimore: Penguin Books, 1964. p. 85

35. *Down in the Valley* (40)— BMS 2; DMT 4, 5; EM 5; GWM 3; MFL 4, 5; MMYO 3; MOM 4, 5; MYA 6; TIM 2, 6; TWS 5

36. *Drill Ye Tarriers*—BMS 5; DMT 4; MFL 5; MMYO 5; MYA 6; OSW 5, 6; TIM 4

37. *Eency Weency Spider* (111)— BMS K; EM 1; GWM K; MYA K; OSW 1, 2

38. *Erie Canal*—BMS 5; DMT 5; EM 5; GWM 5; MFL 5; MMYO 5; MOM 6; MYA 6; OSW 5; TIM 5

39. *Farmer in the Dell, The*—BMS K; DMT 1; OSW K; TIM 2, 3; TWS 1

40. *Feng Yang Song*—DMT 6; MFL 6; MMYA 6; TWS 6

41. *First Noel, The* (84)—BMS 6; DMT 4; EM 6; MFL 4; MMYO 5, 6; MOM 5; MYA 6; OSW 1, 3, 6; TIM 5

42. *Friendly Beasts, The*—DMT 2; EM 2; GWM 4; MFL 2; MMYO 1, 2; MOM 3; OSW 4; TIM 6; TWS 2

43. *Fum, Fum, Fum*—BMS 5; MFL 6; MMYA 6; TWS 6

44. *Go Down Moses*—GWM 6; MFL 6; MOM 6; MYA 6

45. *Go Tell Aunt Rhodie*—DMT K; EM 2; GWM 1; MFL 2; MMYO K, 1, 5; MYA 6; OSW 2; TIM 3; TWS 4

46. *Go Tell It On the Mountain*— BMS 1, 4; DMT K, 6; EM 6; GWM 4; MFL 4; MOM 5; MYA 5; TIM 6

47. *Greensleeves*—BMS 6; EM 6; MFL 6; MMYO 6; MOM 5, 6; TIM 6

48. *Hava Nagila* (91)—MOM 5; MYA 6

49. *Here We Come A-Wassailing*—EM 5; MMYO 3, 4, 6; MOM 5; MYA 6
50. *He's Got the Whole World in His Hands* (77)—EM 6; MMYO 6; TIM 4, 6
51. *Hey Betty Martin* (60)—BMS K; DMT K, 2; EM 1; GWM 1; MMYO 1; OSW 3, 4; TIM 1; TWS 4
52. *Hickory Dickory Dock*—BMS K; GWM K; MFL 1; MMYO K, 1; MOM K; OSW 1, 3; TIM 1, 2
53. *Hole in the Bucket, A* (104)—DMT 4; MFL 4; MMYO 4; MYA 4; TIM 4; TWS 3
54. *Home on the Range* (170)—BMS 6; DMT 3, 6; EM 3; GWM 5; MFL 4, 5; MMYO 5; MOM 4; MYA 3, 6; OSW 3, 4, 6; TIM 3, 6; TWS 2, 3
55. *Hop Up, My Ladies*—DMT 3; EM 5; GWM 3; MFL 3; MYA 4; TIM 1
56. *Hot Cross Buns*—BMS 1, 2; DMT 1; EM 1; GWM K; MYA 1; OSW 2; TIM 2, 3
57. *Hush Little Baby* (31)—BMS 2; DMT K, 2, 4; EM 1, 2; GWM 1; MFL 2; MMYO 1; MYA K; OSW 4; TIM K
58. *I Wonder as I Wander*—EM 6
59. *If I Had a Hammer*—a popular folk-type song made famous by Peter, Paul, and Mary
60. *If You're Happy* (36)—DMT K, 2; EM 2; GWM K; MMYO K; MOM 3; TIM 1–3
61. *I'm a Little Teapot*—EM 1; GWM K; OSW 1
62. *Jacob's Ladder*—EM 6; GWM 4; MMYO 6; MOM 6; MYA 6; OSW 5; TIM 4
63. *Jeannie With the Light Brown Hair*—EM 5
64. *Jingle Bells* (64)—BMS K, 2, 3; DMT 2; EM 1; GWM 1; MFL 1, 3; MMYO K, 1; OSW K, 1, 4; TIM 2, 4; TWS 1
65. *Joshua Fit the Battle of Jericho* (86)—GWM 6; MYA 5
66. *Joy to the World* (75)— BMS 3, 5; DMT 3, 5; EM 5; GWM 6; MFL 6; MMYO 6; OSW 6; TIM 5; TWS 5
67. *Kookaburra* (157)—BMS 4; DMT 6; GWM 4; MFL 4; MMYO 3, 4; MYA 6; OSW 5, 6; TIM 2; TWS 6
68. *Lightly Row*—OSW 3, 5
69. *Little 'Liza Jane* (177)—MFL 4; OSW 4, 5
70. *London Bridge* (82)—BMS 1; DMT K, 1, 3; GWM K; MYA 6; OSW 2; TIM 2; TWS 1, 3
71. *Londonderry Air*—MYA 6
72. *Looby Loo*—BMS K; DMT 2; EM 1; MYA K, 2; OSW 1, 2; TWS 2
73. *Lovely Evening*—DMT 5; EM 4; MFL 4; MOM 3; OSW 4; TIM 5; TWS 5
74. *Lullaby* (67)—DMT 3; EM 4; GWM 5; MFL 5; MOM 3, 5; OSW 3, 5; TIM 3, 4; TWS 3
75. *Maori Stick Game*—BMS 6
76. *Marching to Pretoria* (40)—

BMS 6; EM 4; GWM 4; MMYO 2, 3, 6; MYA 4; TIM 2, 6

77. *Marine's Hymn, The* (121)— BMS 1, 4; DMT 5; GWM 5; MFL 5; MOM 4; MYA 6; OSW 5; TIM 5, 6; TWS 5

78. *Mary Had a Little Lamb*— DMT K; EM 1; GWM K; MFL 1; MOM K; MYA 6; OSW K, 2; TIM 1

79. *Michael Row Your Boat* (92)— DMT K; EM 3; MMYO 3; MYA 4

80. *More We Get Together*—BMS 2; GWM 4; MFL 3; MOM 4; OSW 6

81. *Muffin Man, The* (64)— BMS K; DMT 2; GWM 1; MMYO 1; TWS 2

82. *Mulberry Bush, The*—BMS K, 1

83. *My Bonnie*—BMS 1; MFL 2 MYA 1; OSW 6

84. *My Hat Has Three Corners* (87)—BMS 2; EM 1; GWM 2; MFL 4; MMYO 6; MYA 3; TIM 1, 3

85. *Night Herding Song* (34)— BMS 5; DMT 6; EM 3; GWM 4; MFL 5; MMYO 3; MOM 3; MYA 4; OSW 4; TWS 6

86. *Nobody Knows the Trouble I've Seen* (87)—MYA 1

87. *Now Thank We All Our God*— BMS 6; DMT 2; EM 5; MFL 5; MOM K, 4; MYA 5; OSW 5; TIM 6; TWS 2, 4

88. *O Come All Ye Faithful*— DMT 3; EM 4; MFL 3, 4;

MMYO 3, 4; MOM 2, 4, 5; MYA 6; OSW 4, 6; TWS 3

89. *O Come Emmanuel*—DMT 6; EM 6; GWM 5; OSW 2; TWS 3

90. *Oh Susanna* (105)—BMS 3; DMT 4, 5; EM 2; GWM 5; MFL 5; MMYO 2–4, 6; MYA K; OSW 4, 5; TIM 3, 5; TWS 4, 5

91. *Oh What a Beautiful Morning* from "Oklahoma"—ⓒ 1943 by Marlo Music Corp., New York City, N. Y.

92. *Ol' Texas* (164–165)—DMT 4; EM 4; GWM 4; MFL 5; TIM 3, 5; TWS 4

93. *Old Brass Wagon*—BMS K; DMT 4; EM 2; GWM 1; MFL 3; MYA 2; TIM 3; TWS 4

94. *Old Folks at Home*—BMS 3; EM 4; MYA 4; OSW 3, 5

95. *Old Joe Clark*—EM 5; MFL 5; MMYO 5; MOM 1; TIM 1, 5

96. *Old MacDonald*—DMT 3; EM 1; MYA K; OSW 3, 4; TIM 3; TWS 3

97. *Old Woman* or *The Deaf Woman's Courtship* (127)— BMS 3; EM 3; MOM 4; TIM 5; TWS 5

98. *On Top of Old Smoky* (102)— EM 5; MFL 6; MMYO 4, 5; MYA 5; TIM 6

99. *One More River*—DMT 4; GWM 5; TIM 4

100. *Over the River and Through the Wood*—BMS 1; DMT 3; EM 2; GWM 2; MFL 1, 2; MMYO K–2; MYA 3;

OSW 1, 2; TIM 2; TWS 3

101. *Paw Paw Patch*—BMS 2; DMT K, 3; EM 2; GWM 4; MFL 1; MMYO 1; OSW 4; TIM 2; TWS 3

102. *Polly Wolly Doodle*—BMS 3; DMT 4; EM 4; GWM 3; MMYO 3, 4; OSW 3, 4; TIM 5; TWS 5

103. *Poor Wayfaring Stranger*— DMT 6; MFL 6; MMYO 6; MOM 5; MYA 6; TIM 5; TWS 6

104. *Pop Goes the Weasel*—BMS 1, 2, 5; DMT 4; EM 2; GWM 3; MFL 3, 4; MOM K; MYA 3; OSW 1, 4; TWS 4

105. *Praise God From Whom All Blessings Flow—the Old Hundredth* (104)—BMS 6; EM 5; GWM 2; MFL 5; OSW 1, 4; TWS 4;

106. *Prayer of Thanksgiving*— BMS 4; DMT 4, 6; EM 6; GWM 6; MFL 4, 6; MMYO 4–6; MOM 5; MYA 5; OSW 5; TIM 5; TWS 4, 6

107. *Red River Valley*—DMT 5; EM 5; GWM 5; MFL 6; MMYO 4, 5; MYA 6; OSW 6; TIM 5, 6

108. *Reuben and Rachel*—BMS 4; DMT 5; MFL 5; OSW 6; TWS 5

109. *Riddle Song, The*—EM 4; GWM 6; MFL 3; MYA 6; TWS 3

110. *Rock-a-bye Baby* (73)—GWM K; OSW 1

111. *Row, Row, Row Your Boat*— BMS 1; DMT 3; EM 2; GWM 1, 3; MFL 1; MMYO

3; OSW 1, 2; TIM 3; TWS 4

112. *Sakura*—BMS 3; EM 3; MMYO 4; MOM 4; TWS 6

113. *Sandy Land*—DMT K, 3; EM 3; MFL 3, 4; MMYO 2–4; TWS 4

114. *Santa Lucia*—DMT 5; EM 5; MFL 5; MYA 6; OSW 6; TWS 6

115. *Scarborough Fair* (77)—MOM 6

116. *Shenandoah* (39)—BMS 4; DMT 4, 5; EM 5; GWM 6; MFL 5, 6; MMYO 5; MOM 5; MYA 5; OSW 6; TIM 4; TWS 4, 5

117. *Shortnin' Bread*—MMYO 6; OSW 6

118. *Sidewalks of New York, The* (100)—GWM 4; MFL 5; TIM 4; TWS 4

119. *Silent Night*—BMS K, 1; DMT 2, 4, 6; EM 2; GWM 4; MFL 5, 6; MMYO 3–6; MOM K–2, 4, 5; MYA 6; OSW K–2, 5, 6; TIM 4, 5; TWS 2

120. *Sing a Song of Sixpence* (112)— GWM 2; MFL 2; MYA K; OSW 1, 2; TIM 1

121. *Skip to My Lou*—BMS 2, 3; DMT K, 2, 3; EM 2, 5; MFL 1, 2; MMYO 1, 4; MOM 2, 4; MYA K; OSW 3, 5; TWS 4

122. *Skye Boat Song*—DMT 6; EM 5; MOM 4; MYA 5; TIM 1; TWS 6

123. *Star-Spangled Banner, The*— BMS K–3, 5; DMT 3–6; EM 3, 5; GWM 4; MFL

4–6; MMYO 4–6; MOM K–6; MYA 4–6; OSW K–6; TIM 4–6; TWS 3, 5, 6

124. *Steal Away* (9)—MYA 6

125. *Stodola Pumpa*—EM 4; GWM 5; MFL 5; OSW 5; TIM 6

126. *Streets of Laredo*—EM 6; MFL 6; MMYO 6; MYA 6; TIM 6

127. *Suliram*—EM 6; MFL 6; MMYO 6

128. *Susie Little Susie* (114)—BMS 3; DMT 4; EM 3; MOM 3; OSW 3–5; TWS 3

129. *Sweet and Low*—BMS 3; EM 4; GWM 6; MOM 1; MYA 5; OSW 4

130. *Sweetly Sings the Donkey* (119)—GWM 5; MMYO 3; OSW 5; TIM 3, 5

131. *Swing Low, Sweet Chariot* (51)—DMT 4; EM 5; GWM 1; MFL 6; MMYO 6; MOM 5; OSW 3, 6; TIM 5

132. *Tailor and the Mouse, The*—BMS 4; DMT 3; EM 3; MFL 4; OSW 3; TWS 3

133. *Ten Little Indians* (44)—BMS 1; DMT 1; GWM 1; MFL 3; OSW 1, 2

134. *This Land is Your Land*—DMT 4; EM 5; GWM 4; MMYO 3, 5; TIM 2

135. *This Old Man*—BMS 1; DMT 2; EM 1; GWM 1; MFL 2; MMYO 1; MYA 1; OSW 1, 2; TIM 1, 4; TWS 2

136. *Three Blind Mice*—DMT 1, 3; EM 3; MYA K; OSW 3, 6; TIM 4

137. *Tinga Layo* (103)—BMS 5;

DMT 4; EM 3; MFL 3, 4; MMYO 3; TIM 2, 3; TWS 4

138. *Twelve Days of Christmas, The*—BMS 5; DMT 4; MFL 6; MMYO 5, 6; MOM 4; MYA 4; OSW 5; TIM 4; TWS 3

139. *Twinkle, Twinkle* (63)—BMS K; DMT 1, 2; EM 2; GWM K; MFL 1; MOM 1, 2; OSW 2; TIM 1, 2, 4; TWS 1

140. *Vive L'Amour*—MFL 6; MYA 4; TIM 6

141. *We Three Kings* (77)—DMT 4; MFL 5; MOM K, 1, 3; OSW 3, 4

142. *We Wish You a Merry Christmas* (32)—DMT K, 3; EM 4; GWM 2; MFL 2; MMYO K–2, 4; MOM 1, 2; MYA K; OSW 2, 4; TIM 3; TWS 1, 3

143. *When Johnny Comes Marching Home*—DMT 4, 5; EM 5; GWM 6; MFL 5; MMYO 2; MOM 4; MYA 5; OSW 6; TIM 4

144. *White Choral Bells*—DMT 2, 4; EM 4; MFL 4, 5; MMYO 3; TWS 2, 4

145. *Who's That Tapping at My Window?*—DMT K; EM 1; TIM K

146. *Yankee Doodle*—BMS K, 2, 3; DMT 2, 3, 6; EM 2; GWM 3; MFL 1–3, 5; MMYO K, 3, 4, 6; MOM K, 2, 3; MYA K, 2, 4, 5; OSW K–3; TIM K, 5; TWS 2

RECORDINGS

This section consists of a list of recordings referred to in the text. A numeral in parentheses following the title indicates the page on which the notation of a theme from the work is located.

Most recordings listed are found in one or more of the standard record libraries for schools. Abbreviations for these record series are coded as follows:

AM—*Adventures in Music* (RCA Victor)

BOL—*Bowmar Orchestral Library* (Bowmar Records)

DMT—*Discovering Music Together*—Music for Listening (Follett)

EM—*Exploring Music*—Listening Lessons (Holt, Rinehart, and Winston)

MMYO—*Making Music Your Own*—Integrated Listening Selections (Silver Burdett)

MRL—*Music Resource Library*—Keyboard Junior Boxed Units (Keyboard Junior Publications)

MSBL—*Musical Sound Book Libraries* (Sound Book Press Society)

NDM—*New Dimensions in Music* (American Book Co.)

RCA—*RCA Basic Record Library for the Elementary School*, Listening (**L**), Rhythms (**R**), Singing (**S**), American Indian (**AI**)—(RCA Victor)

The numeral(s) following these keyed abbreviations refers to the record number (as Volume 3, Number 7, 64203-2, or Grade 5).

1. Alford—*Col. Bogey March*— BOL 54

2. *All Day and All of the Night*— Teen Beat Discoteque, RCA Camden CAS–884

3. Anderson—*The Girl I Left Behind Me* from *Irish Suite*— AM 5–2

4. Arel—*Stereo Electronic Music No. 1*—EM 6

5. Babbit—*Composition for Synthesizer*—EM 6

6. Babbit—*Imitations for Two Instruments*—EM 3

7. Bach—*Badinerie* from *Suite No. 2 in B Minor*—AM 3–1; MMYO 5

8. Bach—*Chorale: Awake, Thou Wintry Earth*—BOL 83

9. Bach—*Gigue* from *Suite No. 3* —AM 1–1; MSBL 78041

10. Bach—*Jesu, Joy of Man's Desiring* from *Cantata No. 147* —AM 5–1; BOL 62; MSBL 78316; NDM K

11. Bach—*Little Fugue in G Minor* —AM 6–1; BOL 86

12. Bartok—*Bear Dance* from *Hungarian Sketches*—AM 3–2

13. Bartok—*Evening in the Village* from *Hungarian Sketches*— AM 5–2

14. Bartok — *Mikrokosmos* — Vox SBVX 5420–5425

15. Bartok—*My Daughter Lidi*— BOL 68

16. Bartok—*Teasing*—BOL 68

17. Beatles—*A Day in the Life*

from *Sgt. Pepper's Lonely Hearts Club Band*—Capitol MAS–2653

18. Beethoven—*Scherzo* from *Seventh Symphony*—BOL 62; DMT 5; RCA L–1 (excerpt)

19. Benjamin—*Jamaican Rhumba*—BOL 56; NDM 3

20. Berlioz—*Ballet of the Sylphs* from *The Damnation of Faust*—AM 1–1

21. Bernstein—*Symphonic Dances* (excerpts) from *West Side Story*—BOL 74

22. Bizet—*The Ball* from *Children's Games*—AM 1–1; MSBL 78009

23. Bizet—*Carillon*—BOL 78; EM 4

24. Bizet—*Changing of the Guard* from *Carmen*—AM 3–2; DMT K, 5; MSBL 78136

25. Bizet—*Cradle Song*—AM 1–1; MSBL 78008

26. Bizet—*Farandole* from *L'Arlésienne Suite No. 2*—AM 6–1; BOL 78; EM 6

27. Bizet—*Leap Frog* from *Children's Games*—AM 1–1; DMT 2; MSBL 78210

28. Bizet—*March—The Trumpet and Drum* from *Petite Suite*—BOL 53; MSBL 78008; RCA L–1

29. Bizet—*Minuetto* from *L'Arlésienne Suite No. 1*—AM 4–2; BOL 78

30. Bizet—*The Top* from *Petite Suite* (117)—BOL 53; RCA L–1

31. Borodin—*In the Steppes of Central Asia*—AM 6–1; BOL 78

32. Brahms—*Hungarian Dance No. 5*—BOL 55; MMYO 5; MSBL 78110; RCA L–6

33. Brahms—*Hungarian Dance No. 6*—BOL 62; MMYO 5; MSBL 78110

34. Brahms—*Little Sandman*—MSBL 78314; RCA L–1

35. Brahms — *Lullaby* (67) — DMT 1; MSBL 78312; NDM K; RCA L–1

36. Britten—*Young Person's Guide to the Orchestra*—BOL 83; EM 6; MRL 2; NDM 3

37. Cage—*Dance*—EM 2; NDM 6

38. Cailliet—*Variations on "Pop Goes The Weasel"*—AM 4–1; BOL 65; MSBL 78114

39. Canning, arranger—*Rock-a-bye Baby*—RCA L–1

40. Castelnuovo-Tedesco—*Guitar Concerto, Second Movement*—BOL 84

41. Chabrier—*Marche Joyeuse*—AM 4–1

42. *Chant of the Eagle Dance*—Hopi Indians—RCA AI

43. Charpentier—*On Muleback* from *Impressions of Italy*—AM 5–1

44. Chopin—*Waltz in D♭* ("Minute")—EM 3; RCA L–1

45. *Chopsticks*, a traditional piece for piano (94)—see basal music texts: GWM 5; MYA 6; OSW 4

46. Coates—*Knightsbridge March* from *London Suite*—AM 5–2; BOL 60; MSBL 78150

47. Copland—*Circus Music* from *The Red Pony Suite*—AM 3–1; DMT 6; EM 1

48. Copland—*El Salón Mexico*—
    BOL 74; MRL 18
49. Copland—*Hoe Down* from
    Rodeo—AM 5–2; BOL 55;
    DMT 3; EM 5
50. Copland—*A Lincoln Portrait*
    —BOL 75
51. Copland—*Simple Gifts* from
    Appalachian Spring—BOL 65;
    MRL 29; MSBL 78152;
    NDM 3
52. Corelli-Pinelli — *Sarabande*
    from *Suite for` Strings*—AM
    6–2; see also no. 53
53. Corelli-Pinelli — *Suite for
    Strings*—BOL 63; MSBL
    78101, 78207
54. Couperin—*Little Windmills*—
    BOL 64; MSBL 26
55. Cowell — *Banshee* — EM 3;
    MMYO 3; NDM 2
56. Debussy — *Children's Corner
    Suite* — BOL 63; MSBL
    78036–78037
57. Debussy—*Clair de Lune*—
    BOL 52; MRL 40; MSBL
    78153; RCA L–5 (excerpt)
58. Debussy—*Dialogue of the
    Wind and Sea* from *La Mer*—
    BOL 70
59. Debussy—*Doctor Gradus ad
    Parnassum* from *Children's Cor-
    ner Suite*—see no. 56
60. Debussy—*En Bateau*—BOL
    53; EM 1
61. Debussy—*Festivals (Fêtes)*—
    BOL 70
62. Debussy — *Golliwog's Cake
    Walk* from *Children's Corner
    Suite*—MRL 40; RCA L–2
    (piano); see also no. 56
63. Debussy—*Jumbo's Lullaby*

from *Children's Corner Suite*—
see no. 56
64. Debussy—*The Little Shepherd*
    from *Children's Corner Suite*—
    RCA L–2; see also no. 56
65. Debussy—*Play of the Waves*
    from *La Mer*—AM 6–2
66. Debussy—*Serenade of the Doll*
    from *Children's Corner Suite*—
    see no. 56
67. Debussy—*The Snow is Danc-
    ing* from *Children's Corner
    Suite*—AM 3–1; see also no.
    56
68. Debussy—*Voiles* from *Pre-
    ludes, Book I*—EM 6; MRL
    57; MMYO 5
69. Donaldson—*Camels* from *Un-
    der the Big Top*—BOL 51
70. Donaldson—*The Emperor's
    Nightingale*—BOL 66
71. Dowland—*My Lady Huns-
    don's Puffe*—EM 6
72. Druckman—*Animus 1 (1966)
    for Trombone and Tape*—
    Turnabout TV 34177
73. Dukas—*Sorcerer's Apprentice*—
    BOL 59; MRL 15
74. Dvorak—*Humoresque*—RCA
    L–1
75. Dvorak—*Slavonic Dance No. 7*
    —AM 4–2
76. El-Dabh—*Leilya and the Poet*
    —EM 6
77. Elgar—*Fairies and Giants* from
    Wand of Youth Suite No. 1—
    AM 3–1
78. Elgar—*Fountain Dance* from
    Wand of Youth Suite No. 2—
    AM 2–1; MSBL 78149
79. Elgar—*Pomp and Circumstance*

No. 1—BOL 54; MSBL 78120

80. Elgar—*Tame Bears* from *Wand of Youth Suite No. 2*— MSBL 78148; RCA L–2

81. Enciña—*Hoy comamos*—EM 2

82. Falla—*Spanish Dance No. 1* from *La Vida Breve*—AM 6–1

83. Gabrieli—*Canzona in C Major for Brass Ensemble and Organ*— BOL 83; EM 3

84. Gershwin—*American in Paris* —BOL 74; DMT 1 (excerpt); MRL 29; NDM 2

85. Gershwin—*Prelude for Piano No. 2*—EM 5; MMYO 2; MRL 41

86. Giannini—*Symphony No. 3 for Band, Fourth Movement*— EM 5

87. Ginastera—*Wheat Dance* from *Estancia*—AM 4–1

88. Glière—*Russian Sailors' Dance* from *The Red Poppy*—AM 6–2; BOL 78

89. Gluck—*March* from *Iphigenia in Aulis*—RCA R–5

90. Goldman—*Children's March* —EM 1

91. Gottschalk-Kay — *Grand Walkaround* from *Cakewalk Ballet Suite*—AM 5–1

92. Gould—*American Salute*—AM 5–1; BOL 65; NDM 3

93. Gounod—*Lovely Appear* from *The Redemption*—see basal music texts: MOM 3, 5; MYA 6

94. Grainger, arranger—*Londonderry Air*—AM 4–2; BOL 60; DMT 6; MSBL 78023, 78025

95. Grétry—*Gavotte in D Minor*— RCA R–5

96. Grieg—*Anitra's Dance* from *Peer Gynt Suite No. 1*—AM 1–2; see also no. 101

97. Grieg—*Ase's Death* from *Peer Gynt Suite No. 1*—MSBL 78203; see also no. 101

98. Grieg—*In the Hall of the Mountain King* from *Peer Gynt Suite No. 1*—AM 3–2; MMYO 4; see also no. 101

99. Grieg—*Morning* from *Peer Gynt Suite No. 1*—see also no. 101

100. Grieg — *Norwegian Rustic March* from *Lyric Suite*—AM 4–1

101. Grieg—*Peer Gynt Suite No. 1* —BOL 59; DMT 4; MSBL 78029–78031

102. Grieg—*Piano Concerto, First Movement*—BOL 84; MRL 5

103. Grieg—*To Spring*—RCA L–6

104. Griffes—*The White Peacock*— AM 6–1

105. Grofé—*Cloudburst* from *Grand Canyon Suite*—BOL 61; DMT 2; MRL 28

106. Grofé—*Desert Water Hole* from *Death Valley Suite*—AM 4–1

107. Grofé—*Huckleberry Finn* from *Mississippi Suite*—BOL 61; EM 5

108. Grofé—*On the Trail* from *Grand Canyon Suite*—BOL 61; DMT 4

109. Guarnieri—*Brazilian Dance* —AM 6–2; BOL 55

110. Handel—*Bourrée* from *Royal Fireworks Music*—BOL 62;

MMYO 4; EM 1; MRL 7; MSBL 78003

111. Handel—*A Ground*—BOL 53

112. Handel—*Hallelujah Chorus* from *Messiah*—DMT 6; EM 5; MRL 7

113. Handel—*He Shall Feed His Flock* from *Messiah*—see basal music texts: EM 5; GWM 6; MFL 4; MMYO 6; MOM 5; OSW 5; recorded on RCA S–6

114. Handel—*Messiah*—EM 5 (excerpts)

115. Handel—*Minuet* from *Royal Fireworks Music*—AM 3–2; DMT K; EM 1; MMYO 4; MSBL 78003

116. Hanson—*Children's Dance* from *Merry Mount Suite*—AM 3–1

117. Haydn—*Andante* from *Surprise Symphony*—BOL 62; EM 2; MRL 8; MSBL 78042; RCA L–4

118. Haydn—*Gypsy Rondo*—BOL 64

119. Haydn—*Minuet* from *Surprise Symphony*—BOL 63; EM 3; MRL 45

120. Herbert—*Babes in Toyland*— see basal music text MOM 5

121. Herbert—*Dagger Dance* from *Natoma*—AM 3–1

122. Herbert—*March of the Toys* from *Babes in Toyland*—AM 2–1; MSBL 78153; NDM K

123. Holst—*Mercury* from *The Planets*—BOL 70

124. Holst—*Spirits of the Earth* from *The Perfect Fool*—AM 6–2

125. Humperdinck—*Hansel and Gretel*— Capitol SGBO— 7256; EM 3

126. Humperdinck—*Prelude* to *Hansel and Gretel*—AM 5–2; BOL 58; MSBL 78051

127. *Hunter's Horn, The*—Young People's Records 726

128. Ibert—*Parade* from *Divertissement*—AM 1–1

129. Ippolitoff-Ivanoff—*Cortege of the Sardar* from *Caucasian Sketches*—BOL 54; RCA R–6

130. Ippolitoff–Ivanoff—*In the Village* from *Caucasian Sketches*—BOL 78

131. Isaac—*Music for Instruments* —EM 4

132. Ives—*Putnam's Camp* from *Three Places in New England*— BOL 75; EM 5

133. Järnefelt—*Praeludium*—RCA R–2

134. *Jerk, The*—Camden CAS– 884

135. Kabalevsky—*March* from *The Comedians*—AM 3–1; EM 1

136. Kabalevsky—*Pantomine* from *The Comedians*—AM 1–1; MMYO K

137. Kern—*Show Boat*—MSBL 78163–78169

138. Khatchaturian — *Russian Dance* from *Gayne Suite No. 2* —BOL 56

139. *King's Trumpet, The*—Children's Record Guild 5040K

140. Kleinsinger—*Tubby, The Tuba*—Columbia CL 671

141. Kodaly—*Entrance of the Emperor and His Court* from *Háry*

János Suite—AM 4–2; BOL 81

142. Kodaly—*Intermezzo* from *Hary János Suite*—BOL 81

143. Kodaly—*Viennese Musical Clock* from *Háry János Suite*—AM 2–1; BOL 81; EM 3; NDM 4

144. Koyama—*Kobiki-Uta, The Woodcutter's Song*—BOL 66; MRL 21, 36

145. Kraft—*Theme and Variations for Percussion Quartet*—BOL 83

146. Lecocq—*Polka* from *Mlle. Angot Suite*—BOL 53

147. Lecuona—*Andalucia* from *Suite Andalucia*—AM 4–1

148. Liadov—*Dance of the Mosquito*—BOL 52; DMT 1; MSBL 78106

149. Liadov—*Music Box* from *The Musical Snuff Box*—BOL 64; MSBL 78016; RCA L–5

150. *Licorice Stick*—Young People's Records YPR 420

151. Loesser—*Music* from *Hans Christian Anderson*—see basal music texts: *Wonderful Copenhagen* in GWM 4; EM 6; and *Thumbelina* in EM 6; MOM 5

152. Lully—*March* from *Thésée Ballet Suite*—AM 3–2

153. MacDowell—*In Wartime* from *Second Indian Suite*—AM 5–1

154. MacDowell—*Of a Tailor and a Bear*—MSBL 1; RCA L–2

155. MacDowell—*To a Water Lily* from *Woodland Sketches*—MSBL H3; RCA L–3

156. Mahler—*Symphony No. 1, Third Movement*—BOL 62; DMT K

157. Massanet—*Aragonaise* from *Le Cid* (45)—AM 1–1; EM 6

158. McDonald—*Children's Symphony, Third Movement*—AM 2–1

159. Mendelssohn—*How Lovely Are the Messengers* from *St. Paul*—RCA S–6; also see basal music texts: MYA 6; OSW 2

160. Mendelssohn—*Nocturne* from *Midsummer Night's Dream*—MSBL 78027; NDM K; RCA L–4

161. Mendelssohn—*Scherzo* from *Midsummer Night's Dream*—BOL 57; MSBL 78026

162. Menotti—*Amahl and the Night Visitors*—RCA Victor LM 2762

163. Menotti—*Shepherd's Dance* from *Amahl and the Night Visitors*—AM 4–2; BOL 58

164. Menotti—*Suite* from *Amahl and the Night Visitors*—BOL 58

165. Milhaud—*Copacabana* from *Saudades Do Brazil*—AM 4–2

166. Milhaud—*Creation of the World*—EM 6

167. Milhaud—*Laranjeiras* from *Saudades Do Brazil*—AM 2–1

168. Mompou—*Young Girls in the Garden*—RCA L–6

169. Moore—*The Emperor's New Clothes*—Young People's Records YPR 1007/B, BA

170. Moszkowski — *Sparks* — RCA R–1

171. Moussorgsky—*Ballet of the Unhatched Chicks* from *Pictures at an Exhibition*—AM 1–1; MMYO K; see also no. 177

172. Moussorgsky—*Bydlo* from *Pictures at an Exhibition*—AM 2–1; see also no. 177

173. Moussorgsky — *Catacombs* from *Pictures at an Exhibition* —see no. 177

174. Moussorgsky—*Gnomes* from *Pictures at an Exhibition*—see also no. 177

175. Moussorgsky—*Great Gates of Kiev* from *Pictures at an Exhibition*—DMT K; see also no. 177

176. Moussorgsky — *Old Castle* from *Pictures at an Exhibition* —see also no. 177

177. Moussorgsky—*Pictures at an Exhibition*—BOL 82; EM 4; MRL 50

178. Moussorgsky — *Promenade* from *Pictures at an Exhibition* —AM 1–2; see also no. 177

179. Moussorgsky—*Samuel Goldenberg and Schmuyle* from *Pictures at an Exhibition* (19)— DMT K; see also no. 177

180. Moussorgsky—*Tuileries* from *Pictures at an Exhibition*—see also no. 177

181. Mozart—*Gavotte* from *Les Petits Riens*—RCA R–5

182. Mozart—*March of the Priests* from *Magic Flute*—RCA R–5

183. Mozart—*Minuet* from *Don Giovanni*—EM 5; MSBL 78004; RCA R–5

184. Mozart—*Romanze* from *Eine Kleine Nachtmusik*—AM 4–1; BOL 86; MSBL 78004; NDM 2

185. Mozart—*Theme and Variations* from *Serenade for Wind Instruments, K. 301*—BOL 83

186. Offenbach—*Barcarolle* from *The Tales of Hoffman*—AM 3–1; DMT 5; NDM 1

187. Paderewski — *Minuet* — RCA R–1

188. *Pan, the Piper* — Columbia CL–671

189. Pierné—*Entrance of the Little Fauns* (88)—AM 2–2; BOL 54; MSBL 78015; RCA L–4

190. Pierné—*March of the Little Lead Soldiers* — BOL 54; DMT 1; MSBL 78015; RCA L–1

191. Pinto—*Memories of Childhood* BOL 68; RCA L–1

192. Pinto—*Run, Run* from *Memories of Childhood*—DMT K; see also no. 191

193. Poldini — *Valse Serenade* — RCA R–1

194. Poldini — *Waltzing Doll* — RCA R–2

195. Porter—*Kiss Me Kate*— MSBL 78163–78169

196. Prokofiev—*Birth of Kije* from *Lieutenant Kije*—BOL 81; MMYO 3

197. Prokofiev—*March* from *Summer Day Suite*—AM 1–1

198. Prokofiev—*Midnight Waltz* from *Cinderella*—BOL 67

199. Prokofiev—*Peter and the Wolf* —Columbia CL 671; EM 1

200. Prokofiev—*The Summer Fairy* from *Cinderella*—BOL 67

201. Prokofiev—*Troika* from *Lieutenant Kije*—AM 2–2; BOL 81
202. Ravel—*The Conversations of Beauty and the Beast* from *Mother Goose Suite*—AM 5–1; BOL 57; MRL 11; MSBL 78014
203. Ravel—*Fairy Garden* from *Mother Goose Suite*—BOL 57; MRL 11; MSBL 78014
204. Ravel—*Hop o' My Thumb* from *Mother Goose Suite*—BOL 57; MRL 11; MMYO K; MSBL 78013
205. Ravel—*Laideronette, Empress of the Pagodas* from *Mother Goose Suite*—AM 4–2; BOL 57; MRL 11; MMYO K; MSBL 78013
206. Ravel—*Pavanne of the Sleeping Beauty* from *Mother Goose Suite*—BOL 57; MRL 11; MSBL 78013; RCA L–5
207. Resphigi—*Pines Near a Catacomb* from *Pines of Rome*—BOL 85
208. Resphigi—*Pines of the Appian Way* from *Pines of Rome*—BOL 85
209. Resphigi—*Pines of the Villa Borghese* from *Pines of Rome*—AM 4–1; BOL 85; DMT 1 (excerpt)
210. Resphigi—*Prelude* to *The Birds*—AM 2–2; BOL 85
211. Rimsky-Korsakoff — *Bridal Procession* from *Le Coq D'Or Suite*—AM 4–1; MRL 57
212. Rimsky-Korsakoff—*The Festival at Bagdad* from *Scheherezade*—BOL 77
213. Rimsky-Korsakoff—*Flight* of

the *Bumble Bee*—BOL 52; DMT 6; MSBL 78050
214. Rimsky-Korsakoff — *Scheherezade* (52)—BOL 77
215. Rimsky-Korsakoff—*Tale of the Princess Kalendar* from *Scheherezade*—BOL 77
216. Rogers—*March of the Siamese Children* from *The King and I*—BOL 54; NDM 1
217. Rogers and Hammerstein—*Oklahoma*—EM 5; MSBL 78163–78169; NDM 3
218. Rogers and Hammerstein—*South Pacific*—MSBL 78163–78169
219. Rossini—*Calm* from *William Tell Overture*—see no. 223
220. Rossini—*Dawn* from *William Tell Overture*—see no. 223
221. Rossini—*Finale* from *William Tell Overture*—AM 3–1; see also no. 223
222. Rossini—*Storm* from *William Tell Overture*—see no. 223
223. Rossini—*William Tell Overture*—BOL 76; EM 6; MSBL 78047–78048
224. Rossini-Resphigi — *Can-Can* from *The Fantastic Toyshop*—AM 2–1
225. Rossini-Resphigi — *Pizzicato* from *The Fantastic Toyshop*—BOL 53
226. Rossini-Resphigi — *Tarantella* from *The Fantastic Toyshop*—AM 3–2; BOL 56; MRL 23
227. Rubinstein — *Barcarolle* — RCA R–1
228. Rubinstein—*Melody in F*—RCA R–2

229. Saint-Saëns—*Aquarium* from *Carnival of the Animals*—see no. 230

230. Saint-Saëns—*Carnival of the Animals*—BOL 51; EM 2; MSBL 78010–78012

231. Saint-Saëns—*Danse Macabre* —BOL 59; MRL 15; MSBL 78124

232. Saint-Saëns— *The Elephant* from *Carnival of the Animals*— AM 1–2; MRL 53; see also no. 230

233. Saint-Saëns—*Hens and Cocks* from *Carnival of the Animals*— DMT 2; see also no. 230

234. Saint-Saëns—*Kangaroos* from *Carnival of the Animals*—see no. 230

235. Saint-Saëns— *The Swan* from *Carnival of the Animals*—AM 3–2; MSBL 78314; see also no. 230

236. Saint-Saëns—*Symphony No. 3, Fourth Movement*—BOL 71

237. Saint-Saëns — *Tarantella* — RCA R–2

238. Saint-Saëns — *Turtles* from *Carnival of the Animals*—see no. 230

239. *Sakura*—BOL 66; EM 4

240. Scarlatti—*Sonata in A Minor, K. 175*—EM 4

241. Schoenberg—*Fourth String Quartet, Op. 37, Third Movement*—EM 6

242. Schoenberg—*Peripetia* from *Five Pieces for Orchestra* (90) —BOL 86

243. Schubert, Francois—*The Bee* —BOL 64; RCA L–3

244. Schubert—*Symphony No. 5, First Movement*—AM 6–1

245. Schubert—*Trout Quintet, Fourth Movement*—BOL 83; EM 6; MMYO 6; MRL 43

246. Schubert—*Waltz op. 33, no. 2*—RCA R–4

247. Schubert—*Waltz op. 33, no. 6*—RCA R–4

248. Schubert—*Waltz op. 33, no. 7*—RCA R–4

249. Schuller—*Concertino for Jazz Quartet and Orchestra, Third Movement*—MMYO 6

250. Schumann — *Jaglied* — RCA R–1

251. Schumann—*Traumerei* from *Scenes from Childhood* (70)— AM 4–2; BOL 63; MSBL 78006

252. Schumann—*Wild Horsemen* from *Album for the Young*— BOL 64; MMYO K, 1; MSBL 78303; RCA L–2

253. Schumann-Glazounov—*Chopin*—BOL 53

254. Shostakovich—*Petite Ballerina* from *Ballet Suite No. 1*— AM 2–1

255. Shostakovich—*Pizzicato Polka* from *Ballet Suite No. 1*— AM 1–1

256. Sibelius — *Finlandia* — BOL 60; DMT 6; MRL 27; NDM 3

257. Skilton—*Deer Dance*—*Rogue River Indian* from *Suite Primeval*—MSBL 78202; RCA L–4

258. Skilton—*War Dance of the Cheyenne* from *Suite Primeval*— MRL 17; MSBL 78024; RCA AI

259. Smetana—*Dance of the Come-*

dians from *The Bartered Bride*
—AM 6–2; BOL 56; DMT
6; EM 3; MSBL 78109

260. Smetana—*The Moldau*—
BOL 60; DMT 5; EM 6

261. Sousa—*El Capitán*—DMT 4

262. Sousa—*Semper Fidelis*—AM
3–2; DMT 5; EM 1; MRL
6; NDM K, 2

263. Sousa—*Stars and Stripes For-
ever*—AM 4–2; BOL 54;
DMT 3; EM 5; MRL 6;
MSBL 78120; NDM 5

264. Sousa—*Washington Post March*
—EM 3

265. Strauss, R.—*Suite* from *Der
Rosenkavalier*—AM 6–1

266. Strauss, R.—*Til Eulenspie-
gel's Merry Pranks*—BOL 81;
EM 5; MRL 14

267. Stravinsky—*Berceuse* from
Firebird Suite—AM 1–1;
DMT 4; MRL 24; NDM 5

268. Stravinsky—*Circus Polka*—
BOL 51

269. Stravinsky—*Dance of the Prin-
cesses* from *Firebird Suite*—
BOL 69

270. Stravinsky — *Devil's Dance*
from *A Soldier's Tale*—BOL
68; EM 3; MMYO K

271. Stravinsky—*Firebird Suite*—
BOL 69

272. Stravinsky—*Infernal Dance of
King Kastchei* from *Firebird
Suite*—AM 5–2; BOL 69

273. Stravinsky—*Magic Sleep of
the Princess Tzarvena* from
Firebird Suite—BOL 69

274. Stravinsky—*Palace of the
Chinese Emperor* from *Le
Rossignol*—BOL 69; NDM 3

275. Stravinsky — *Petrouchka* —
BOL 80

276. Stravinsky—*Ragtime* from
The Soldier's Tale—BOL 69

277. Stravinsky—*Sacrificial Dance*
from *The Rite of Spring*—
BOL 69

278. Stravinsky — *Tango* from
The Soldier's Tale—BOL 69

279. Stravinsky—*Waltz* from *The
Soldier's Tale*—BOL 69

280. Taylor—*Garden of Live Flowers* from *Through the Looking
Glass*—AM 3–2

281. Tchaikowsky—*Album for the
Young*—BOL 68

282. Tchaikowsky—*Arabian Dance*
from *The Nutcracker Suite*—
see no. 290

283. Tchaikowsky—*Chinese Dance*
from *The Nutcracker Suite*—
see no. 290

284. Tchaikowsky—*Dance of the
Little Swans* from *Swan Lake*
(107)—AM 1–1; DMT 5

285. Tchaikowsky—*Dance of the
Sugar-Plum Fairy* from *The
Nutcracker Suite*—AM 1–2;
MMYO K; see also no. 290

286. Tchaikowsky—*Dance of the
Toy Flutes* from *The Nutcracker Suite*—AM 1–2; see
also no. 290

287. Tchaikowsky—*Doll's Burial*
from *Album for the Young*—
BOL 68; RCA R–3

288. Tchaikowsky—*The Lark Song*
from *Scenes of Youth*—BOL 52

289. Tchaikowsky—*March of the
Tin Soldiers* from *Album for
the Young*—BOL 58; RCA
R–3

290. Tchaikowsky—*The Nutcrack-er Suite*—BOL 58; DMT 3; EM 2; MSBL 78033–78035; NDM 1 (excerpts)

291. Tchaikowsky—*Overture Min-iature* from *The Nutcracker Suite*—see no. 290

292. Tchaikowsky—*Peasant Plays the Accordion* from *Album for the Young*—BOL 68

293. Tchaikowsky — *Puss-in-Boots and the White Cat* from *The Sleeping Beauty*—AM 3–1

294. Tchaikowsky—*Symphony No. 4, Third Movement*—BOL 71; MRL 3

295. Tchaikowsky—*Symphony No. 4, Fourth Movement*—AM 6–2; DMT 6; MRL 56

296. Tchaikowsky—*Trepak* from *The Nutcracker Suite*—see no. 290

297. Tchaikowsky—*Waltz* from *The Sleeping Beauty*—AM 4–1; BOL 67; MSBL 78108

298. Tchaikowsky—*Waltz of the Flowers* from *The Nutcracker Suite*—see no. 290

299. Thomas — *Andantino* — RCA L–2

300. Thomson—*The Alligator and the 'Coon* from *Acadian Songs and Dances*—AM 3–2; EM 5

301. Thomson—*Blues* from *Plow That Broke the Plains*—BOL 65

302. Thomson—*Cattle* from *Plow That Broke the Plains*—BOL 65

303. Thomson—*Sea Piece with Birds*—BOL 70

304. Thomson—*Walking Song* from *Acadian Songs and Dances*—AM 1–1

305. Torjussen—*Folk Song* from *Fjord and Mountain, Norwe-gian Suite No. 2*—BOL 60

306. Torjussen—*Lapland Idyll* from *Fjord and Mountain, Norwegian Suite No. 2*—BOL 60

307. *Two Spanish Songs for Recorder* —EM 2

308. Ussachevsky—*Sonic Contours* —EM 1

309. Varese—*Ionisation*—EM 4; NDM 5

310. Vaughan Williams—*Fantasia on "Greensleeves"*—AM 6–2; DMT 5; MSBL 78151

311. Vaughan Williams—*March Past of the Kitchen Utensils* from *The Wasps*—AM 3–1

312. Verdi—*Dance of the Moorish Slaves* from *Aïda*—RCA R–3

313. Verdi—*Triumphal March* from *Aïda*—BOL 62; MSBL 78048; RCA R–4

314. Villa-Lobos—*Let Us Run A-cross the Hill*—BOL 68

315. Villa-Lobos—*The Little Train of the Caipira* from *Bachianas Brasileiras No. 2*—AM 3–1; BOL 64; DMT 3; NDM 3

316. Vivaldi—*Concerto in C for Two Trumpets*—BOL 84

317. Wagner—*Festival March* from *Tannhäuser*—DMT 5; MSBL 78117; RCA L–5

318. Wagner—*Prelude to Act III* from *Lohengrin*—AM 6–1; BOL 79; MMYO 5; MSBL 78133

319. Wagner—*Ride of the Valkyries*

from *Die Walküre*—BOL 62; MSBL 78049

320. Waldteufel—*Skater's Waltzes*—BOL 55; DMT 3; RCA R–4

321. Walton—*Popular Song* from *Façade Suite*—BOL 55

322. Walton—*Valse* from *Façade Suite*—AM 6–2

323. Webern—*Six Pieces for Orchestra Op. 6, First and Third Pieces*—EM 4, 6

324. *Wonderful Violin, The*—Young People's Records YPR 311

325. Zador—*Children's Symphony, First Movement*—BOL 64

Appendix C

SOURCES OF INFORMATION

FOR

INSTRUCTIONAL MATERIALS

American Music Conference, 3505 East Kilgore, Kalamazoo, Michigan 49002.

Bessom, Malcolm E., *Supervising the Successful School Music Program*. New York: Parker, 1969. pp. 169–187, 195–208.

Cheyette, Irving and Herbert, *Teaching Music Creatively in the Elementary School*. New York: McGraw-Hill, 1969. pp. 362–402.

Collins, Thomas C., ed., *Music Education Materials*. Washington, D. C.: Music Educators National Conference, 1968.

Gary, Charles L., ed. *The Study of Music in the Elementary School—A Conceptual Approach*. Washington, D. C.: Music Educators National Conference, 1967. pp. 178–181.

Lehman, Paul R., *Tests and Measurements in Music*. Englewood Cliffs, New Jersey: Prentice-Hall, 1968.

Marvel, Lorene M., *Music Resource Guide: Primary Grades*. Minneapolis: Schmidt, Hall and McCreary, 1961.

Music Educators National Conference, 1201 16th Street N.W., Washington, D. C. 20036.

Music Industry Council, *Music Educators Business Handbook*. Washington, D. C.: The Council, 1969.

Nye, Robert E. and Vernice T., *Music in the Elementary School*, 3rd ed., Englewood Cliffs, New Jersey: Prentice-Hall, 1970.

Raebeck, Lois, and Lawrence Wheeler, *New Approaches to Music in the Elementary School*, 2nd ed. Dubuque, Iowa: William C. Brown, 1969. pp. 271–373.

Runkle, Aleta, and Mary LeBow Eriksen, *Music for Today's Boys and Girls*. Rockleigh, New Jersey: Allyn and Bacon, 1966. pp. 241–268.

Schwann Long Playing Record Catalog, W. Schwann Inc., 137 Newbury St., Boston, Massachusetts 02116.

Shetler, Donald J., *Film Guide for Music Educators*. Washington, D. C.: Music Educators National Conference, 1968.

Swanson, Bessie, R., *Music in the Education of Children*, 3rd ed. Belmont, Calif.: Wadsworth, 1969. pp. 338–351.

INDEX

INDEX

(With italicized page references for definition of terms)